Algorithmic High-Dimensional Robust Statistics

Robust statistics is the study of designing estimators that perform well even when the dataset significantly deviates from the idealized modeling assumptions, such as in the presence of model misspecification or adversarial outliers in the dataset. The classical statistical theory, dating back to pioneering works by Tukey and Huber, characterizes the information-theoretic limits of robust estimation for most common problems. A recent line of work in computer science gave the first computationally efficient robust estimators in high dimensions for a range of learning tasks.

This reference text for graduate students, researchers, and professionals in machine learning theory provides an overview of recent developments in algorithmic high-dimensional robust statistics, presenting the underlying ideas in a clear and unified manner while leveraging new perspectives on the developed techniques to provide streamlined proofs of these results. The most basic and illustrative results are analyzed in each chapter, while more tangential developments are explored in the exercises.

ILIAS DIAKONIKOLAS is an associate professor of computer science at the University of Wisconsin–Madison. His current research focuses on the algorithmic foundations of machine learning. Diakonikolas is a recipient of a number of research awards, including the best paper award at NeurIPS 2019.

DANIEL M. KANE is an associate professor at the University of California, San Diego, in the departments of Computer Science and Mathematics. He is a four-time Putnam Fellow and two-time IMO gold medalist. Kane's research interests include number theory, combinatorics, computational complexity, and computational statistics.

Algorithmic High-Dimensional Robust Statistics

ILIAS DIAKONIKOLAS
University of Wisconsin–Madison

DANIEL M. KANE
University of California, San Diego

Shaftesbury Road, Cambridge CB2 8EA, United Kingdom

One Liberty Plaza, 20th Floor, New York, NY 10006, USA

477 Williamstown Road, Port Melbourne, VIC 3207, Australia

314–321, 3rd Floor, Plot 3, Splendor Forum, Jasola District Centre,
New Delhi – 110025, India

103 Penang Road, #05–06/07, Visioncrest Commercial, Singapore 238467

Cambridge University Press is part of Cambridge University Press & Assessment,
a department of the University of Cambridge.

We share the University's mission to contribute to society through the pursuit of
education, learning and research at the highest international levels of excellence.

www.cambridge.org
Information on this title: www.cambridge.org/9781108837811
DOI: 10.1017/9781108943161

First published 2023

A catalogue record for this publication is available from the British Library

*A Cataloging-in-Publication data record for this book is available from the Library of
Congress*

ISBN 978-1-108-83781-1 Hardback

To our wives, Jelena Diakonikolas and Xinjie Yang.

Contents

Preface

In recent years, the amount of available data in science and technology has exploded and is currently expanding at an unprecedented rate. Such massive high-dimensional datasets are typically too complex to precisely fit a pre-specified model. This state of affairs poses significant challenges to our ability to understand and extract useful information from such complex datasets, as it requires the design of efficient estimators that are stable with respect to model misspecification or the existence of arbitrary outliers.

The field of robust statistics studies the general problem of designing estimators that perform well even when the data significantly deviate from the idealized modeling assumptions. The systematic study of robust statistical procedures dates back to the pioneering works by Tukey and Huber in the 1960s. The classical statistical theory essentially characterizes the information-theoretic limits of robust estimation for a number of statistical tasks. On the other hand, until fairly recently, the computational aspects of this field were poorly understood. Specifically, no scalable methods for robust estimation were known in high dimensions, even for the most basic task of mean estimation. Consequently, the practical successes of robust statistical procedures were restricted to the low-dimensional setting.

A recent line of work in computer science gave the first computationally efficient robust estimators in high dimensions for a range of learning tasks. Specifically, two independent and concurrent works in 2016 developed the first efficient algorithms for basic high-dimensional robust statistics tasks, including mean and covariance estimation. Since the dissemination of these works, there has been a flurry of research activity on algorithmic high-dimensional robust estimation in a variety of settings.

This book provides an overview of the recent developments in algorithmic high-dimensional robust statistics. Our goal is to present the underlying ideas in a clear and unified manner while leveraging new ways of thinking about the

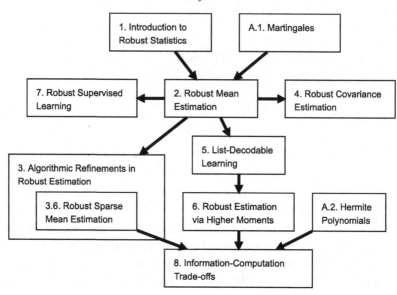

Figure 1 Dependency structure of book chapters.

developed techniques to provide the "correct" proofs of these results. As such, we do not always follow the historical development of these ideas, although the "Related Work" section in each chapter provides references and puts the material into historical context. We also attempt to focus on the most basic and most illustrative results in each chapter, relegating some of the more tangential developments to the exercise sections.

The book is intended as an introduction to the field of algorithmic robust statistics, and is suitable as a graduate text for a one-semester course. The reader is assumed to have an understanding of algorithms at the undergraduate level, including basic knowledge of convex programming techniques, as well as a solid background in linear algebra and probability theory. Beyond these topics, the book is intended to be largely self-contained, with background on a few mathematical topics included in the Appendix.

In terms of content, Chapter 1 contains a succinct overview of "classical" robust statistics. Chapter 2 provides an introduction to the modern algorithmic theory of high-dimensional robust statistics, including the key ideas behind the developments of 2016. These ideas will be heavily relied upon throughout the rest of the book. Chapters 1 and 2 are the most critical chapters in the book; after covering them, the reader has some freedom to select what to study next (though not complete impunity; see Figure 1 for the chapter dependencies).

Chapter 3 presents several refinements over the basic algorithms of Chapter 2. Chapter 4 gives an algorithm for robustly estimating the covariance of Gaussian-like distributions. Chapter 5 develops techniques for list-decodable learning, corresponding to the regime that the outliers comprise a majority of the dataset. Chapter 6 covers algorithmic techniques that leverage higher-moment information for robust estimation, including techniques using the Sum-of-Squares method. Chapter 7 develops robust algorithms for supervised learning problems. Finally, Chapter 8 presents a number of techniques for establishing information-computation trade-offs for robust statistical tasks.

Acknowledgments This book would not have been possible without the hard work of many colleagues and researchers over the past several years in developing the theory of algorithmic robust statistics. Special thanks are due to Alistair Stewart, who was there with us at the whiteboard in Edinburgh where this whole journey began. We would also like to thank Ainesh Bakshi, Yu Cheng, Rong Ge, Shivam Gupta, Samuel Hopkins, He Jia, Gautam Kamath, Sushrut Karmalkar, Daniel Kongsgaard, Pravesh Kothari, Jerry Li, Ankur Moitra, Ankit Pensia, Thanasis Pittas, Eric Price, Mahdi Soltanolkotabi, Jacob Steinhardt, Yuxin Sun, Kevin Tian, Santosh Vempala, and Nikos Zarifis for their contributions to our understanding of the subject.

We are grateful to those who helped us by providing feedback on early drafts of this book, including Yu Cheng, Vitaly Feldman, Sam Hopkins, Jonathan Kane, Ravi Kannan, Sushrut Karmalkar, Jasper Lee, Jerry Li, Shuyao Li, Sihan Liu, Anthony Ostuni, Ankit Pensia, Thanasis Pittas, and Aaron Potechin. In addition, we would like to thank the many graduate students who took our courses on computational statistics and machine learning, as these gave us the opportunity to rehearse the explanation of these ideas. Finally, special thanks are due to Tim Roughgarden, whose invitation for us to write a chapter on these topics for his book *Beyond the Worst-Case Analysis of Algorithms* provided the impetus to write what became an early draft of Chapter 2 of this book.

Finally, we would like to thank those at Cambridge University Press, and especially our editor Lauren Cowles, for their patience and encouragement along this journey and for providing the technical infrastructure to bring the physical instantiation of this book into being.

Ilias Diakonikolas and Daniel Kane

Notation

$\mathbf{E}[X]$ the expectation of the random variable X.

$\mathbf{E}_{X\sim\mathcal{D}}[f(X)]$ the expectation of $f(X)$, where X is a random variable distributed according to $\mathcal{D}$.

μ_S the (empirical) mean of the set S, i.e., $\mu_S = \mathbf{E}_{x\sim_u S}[x]$.

μ_X the mean of the distribution X, i.e., $\mu_X = \mathbf{E}_{x\sim X}[x]$.

$\mathbf{Var}[X]$ the variance of the random variable X.

$\mathbf{Cov}[X]$ the covariance matrix of the (multidimensional) random variable X.

$\mathbf{Cov}[S]$ the covariance of the set S, i.e., $\mathbf{Cov}[S] = \mathbf{E}_{x\sim_u S}[(x-\mu_S)(x-\mu_S)^\top]$.

Σ_S the covariance of the set S.

Σ_X the covariance of the distribution X, i.e., $\Sigma_X = \mathbf{E}_{x\sim X}[(x-\mu_X)(x-\mu_X)^\top]$.

$\|X\|_p$ the L^p norm of the random variable X, given by $\mathbf{E}[|X|^p]^{1/p}$.

$d_{\mathrm{TV}}(X, Y)$ the total variation distance between distributions X and Y.

$\mathcal{N}(\mu, \Sigma)$ the Gaussian distribution with mean μ and covariance matrix Σ.

$aX + bY$ this will usually refer to the corresponding *mixture* of the probability distributions X and Y. In particular, this represents a distribution that with probability a returns a random sample from X and with probability b returns a random sample from Y. Occasionally, when the context is clear, this will instead have the more standard meaning of the distribution obtained by sampling $x \sim X$ and $y \sim Y$ and returning $ax + by$.

Linear Algebra

$\|v\|_p$ the ℓ_p norm of the vector $v \in \mathbf{R}^d$, given by $\left(\sum_{i=1}^d |v_i|^p\right)^{1/p}$.

$\|M\|_2$ the operator norm of a matrix M, given by $\sup_{v\neq 0}\|Mv\|_2/\|v\|_2$.

$\|M\|_F$ the Frobenius norm of the matrix M, given by $\mathrm{tr}(M^\top M)^{1/2}$, or as the square root of the sum of the squares of the entries of M.

$A \succeq B$ the symmetric matrix A is greater than the symmetric matrix B in the Loewner ordering, namely: $A-B$ is a positive semidefinite symmetric matrix.

$A^\top$ the transpose of the matrix A.

Other

$\mathbf{Z}_+$ the set of nonnegative integers.

$\mathbf{R}_+$ the set of nonnegative reals.

$\mathbb{S}^{d-1}$ the unit ℓ_2-ball in $\mathbf{R}^d$.

1

Introduction to Robust Statistics

1.1 Introduction

Consider the following basic statistical task: Given n independent samples from a Gaussian, $\mathcal{N}(\mu, I)$, in $\mathbf{R}^d$ with identity covariance and unknown mean, estimate its mean vector μ to within small error in the ℓ_2-norm. It is not hard to see that the empirical mean has ℓ_2-error at most $O(\sqrt{d/n})$ with high probability. Moreover, this error upper bound is best possible among all n-sample estimators.

The Achilles heel of the empirical estimator is that it crucially relies on the assumption that the observations were generated by an identity covariance Gaussian. The existence of even a *single* outlier can arbitrarily compromise this estimator's performance. However, the Gaussian assumption is only ever approximately valid, as real datasets are typically exposed to some source of contamination. Hence, any estimator that is to be used in practice must be *robust* in the presence of outliers or model misspecification.

Learning in the presence of outliers is an important goal in statistics and has been studied within the robust statistics community since the 1960s. In recent years, the problem of designing robust and computationally efficient estimators for high-dimensional statistical tasks has become a rather pressing challenge in a number of data analysis applications. These include the analysis of biological datasets, where natural outliers are common and can contaminate the downstream statistical analysis, and data poisoning attacks in machine learning, where even a small fraction of fake data (outliers) can substantially degrade the quality of the learned model.

While classical work in robust statistics managed to determine most of the information-theoretic limits of robust estimation, the computational aspects were left wide open in high dimensions. In particular, a number of known robust estimators for basic high-dimensional statistical problems have been

1

shown to be computationally intractable to compute. In fact, the conventional wisdom within the statistics community was that some of these problems were not solvable in a computationally efficient manner. In the Conclusions chapter of his book *Robust Statistical Procedures*, Peter J. Huber writes:

The bad news is that with all currently known algorithms the effort of computing those estimates increases exponentially in d. We might say they break down by failing to give a timely answer! ...

The current trend toward ever-larger computer-collected and computer-managed data bases poses interesting challenges to statistics and data-analysis in general. [...] Only simple algorithms (i.e., with a low degree of computational complexity) will survive the onslaught of huge data sets. This runs counter to recent developments in computational robust statistics.

It appears to me that none of the above problems will be amenable to a treatment through theorems and proofs. They will have to be attacked by heuristics and judgement, and by alternative "what if" analyses.

In the subsequent decades, there was a striking tension between robustness and computational efficiency in high dimensions. Specifically, even for the most basic task of high-dimensional mean estimation, all known estimators were either hard to compute or were very sensitive to outliers. This state of affairs changed fairly recently with the development of the first computationally efficient estimators for high-dimensional robust statistics problems. This book is dedicated to describing these developments and the techniques that have built upon them in the intervening years.

Before getting into the core of these recent developments, it is prudent to first describe the state of affairs before these algorithms were discovered. In this chapter, we will cover this basic background by describing the underlying models that we will be considering, analyzing basic robust estimators in one dimension, and discussing some of the difficulties involved with generalizing these estimators to higher dimensions.

1.2 Contamination Model

In order to specify a robust statistics problem, one needs to know three things:

1. What does the clean (uncorrupted) data look like?
2. What statistics of this data is the algorithm trying to estimate?
3. What kinds of contamination is the algorithm expected to deal with?

As we will see, most robust estimation tasks are provably impossible without imposing some sort of niceness assumptions on the clean data (inliers). At a high level, this is because without assuming anything about the inlier data, one would have no way of determining whether an extreme outlier is a corruption or simply an uncorrupted datapoint that happens to be far from most of the rest of the data. Thus, for most problems, we will need to make some assumptions on the distribution that the uncorrupted data is drawn from. One of the strongest niceness assumptions is that the inliers are distributed according to a Gaussian distribution. More generally, one might also consider what can be accomplished with weaker assumptions, such as log-concavity or simply some bounds on the higher moments of the inlier distribution. In fact, a lot of the progress in algorithmic robust statistics has involved investigating what kinds of assumptions about the inlier data can be relaxed without sacrificing computational efficiency.

In terms of what our algorithm is trying to estimate, we will usually focus on fairly simple statistics like the mean or covariance of the uncorrupted data. However, sometimes we will have more sophisticated goals, such as trying to learn the entire distribution up to small error, or learn some other more complicated underlying parameter.

Finally, the choice of contamination model bears a deeper discussion. We will elaborate on various natural assumptions over the course of the next few sections.

1.2.1 Contamination Model Basics

There are many ways that datasets might be corrupted, and many models to describe such corruptions. If one is optimistic, one might assume that the corruptions are *random*; that is, some datapoints are randomly replaced by samples from a known error distribution or are otherwise corrupted by some known random process. Given such an understanding of the underlying errors, robust estimation tasks typically become much easier, as one can try to find efficient ways to cancel out the effects of these *predictable* errors.

One might also assume that one is merely dealing with *small* measurement errors. That is, perhaps every datapoint is corrupted in some unpredictable way, but no datapoint is corrupted by very much. In this case, one might hope that these small corruptions will not be enough to substantially change the outcome of the estimator being used. In other words, robustness against these kinds of errors amounts to a question about the numerical stability of the estimators.

Unfortunately, these kinds of assumptions are too optimistic in a number of applications. Random corruption models assume that the source of errors is understood sufficiently well that they can essentially be incorporated as just another parameter in the model. Meanwhile, algorithms robust to small errors may be unable to cope with the presence of a small number of outliers.

The error models that we focus on in this book generally allow for worst-case corruptions that affect only a small constant fraction (usually denoted by ϵ) of our data. This means that, for example, 1% of our data is not coming from the inlier distribution, but instead from some source of errors that we have no control over. These errors might produce very extreme outliers, and they will not necessarily come from any model that we could predict ahead of time. In the worst case, one might even consider an adversary designing these errors in such a way to best thwart our algorithm. The latter kind of error model might be slightly more pessimistic than necessary about how bad our errors are; but if we can design algorithms that work under these pessimistic models, the results will apply very broadly. Such algorithms will work against *any* kind of corruptions, as long as these corruptions do not affect too large a fraction of our inputs.

That said, there are still a few things that we need to specify about these corruption models, having to do with whether they add or remove points and whether they are adaptive or not.

1.2.2 Additive and Subtractive Nonadaptive Corruptions

Among the types of contamination models that we will consider in this book, one important defining feature is what the errors are allowed to do to the clean (inlier) data. At a high level, this will leave us with three basic types of error models:

- **Additive Contamination:** In additive contamination models, the errors consist of new, incorrect, datapoints being inserted into our dataset.
- **Subtractive Contamination:** In subtractive contamination models, the errors consist of clean datapoints being selectively removed from our dataset.
- **General Contamination:** In general contamination models, both kinds of errors can occur. Erroneous datapoints can be inserted and clean ones can be removed. Equivalently, we can think of these corruptions as *replacing* our clean datapoints with outliers.

We formally define the corresponding contamination models below.

Definition 1.1 (Additive, Nonadaptive Contamination (Huber Model))   Given a parameter $0 < \epsilon < 1$ and a distribution D on inliers, we say that one can sample from D with ϵ-additive contamination if one can obtain independent samples from a distribution X of the following form: A sample from X returns

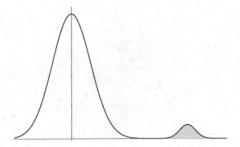

Figure 1.1 Example of a Gaussian with additive contamination. The error distribution corresponds to the gray bump on the right.

a sample from D with probability $(1 - \epsilon)$, and otherwise returns a sample from some (unconstrained and unknown) error distribution E.

See Figure 1.1 for an example of additive contamination.

The parameter ϵ is the proportion of contamination and quantifies the power of the adversary. Among the samples, an unknown $(1-\epsilon)$-fraction are generated from a distribution of interest; we will call these samples *inliers*. The remaining samples are drawn from an arbitrary distribution; we will call these samples *outliers*.

Note that the distribution X being sampled in Definition 1.1 is a mixture of the distribution D over inliers (clean/good samples) and the distribution E over outliers (errors or corruptions). As we will often want to talk about these kinds of mixtures, we introduce the relevant notation.

Notation We will use linear combinations of probability distributions to denote the mixtures defined by the corresponding linear combination of the associated density functions. For example, if X_i are probability distributions and $p_i \geq 0$ are real numbers summing to 1, we will use $p_1 X_1 + p_2 X_2 + \cdots + p_k X_k$ or $\sum_{i=1}^{k} p_i X_i$ to denote the mixture X, where one can obtain a sample from X by first picking a number $1 \leq i \leq k$ so that a given i is picked with probability p_i, and then returning a sample from the corresponding X_i.

For example, the distribution X sampled from in the additive contamination model can be written as $X = (1 - \epsilon)D + \epsilon E$.

We note that if the distributions X_i are random variables, this is also the standard notation for taking a linear combination of the random variables X_i. In this text, we will typically use this notation to denote mixtures, and will make it clear from the context in the rare cases where we want it to denote a linear combination instead.

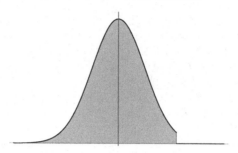

Figure 1.2 Example of a Gaussian with subtractive contamination. In particular, the right tail of the distribution has been removed.

For subtractive contamination, instead of inserting new samples (outliers), there is a probability of at most ϵ that samples are censored from the data that the algorithm observes. One way to define this is as follows.

Definition 1.2 (Subtractive, Nonadaptive Contamination)   Given a parameter $0 < \epsilon < 1$ and a distribution D on inliers, we say that one can sample from D with ϵ-subtractive contamination if the following holds: For some event R with probability $1 - \epsilon$, one can obtain independent samples from the distribution of D conditioned on R.

See Figure 1.2 for an example of subtractive contamination.

In other words, with probability ϵ, the event R^c occurs and these samples are removed from the data stream. This allows an adversary to remove an ϵ-fraction of inlier samples. It is tempting to write that the observed distribution is proportional to $D - \epsilon E$, where E is the distribution over samples of D conditioned on R^c (i.e., the distribution over samples that are removed). We can make this rigorous with a slight extension of our above notation.

Notation   We define a *pseudo-distribution* to be a real-valued measure. This means that a probability distribution is simply a nonnegative pseudo-distribution normalized to have total mass equal to 1. More generally, for any pseudo-distributions $X_1, \ldots, X_k$ and real numbers $p_1, \ldots, p_k$, we use $p_1 X_1 + p_2 X_2 + \cdots + p_k X_k$ or $\sum_{i=1}^{k} p_i X_i$ to denote the pseudo-distribution X whose density is given by the corresponding linear combination of densities of the pseudo-distributions X_i. In particular, for any set S, $X(S) = \sum_{i=1}^{k} p_i X_i(S)$.

We will often want to think of pseudo-distributions as some kind of non-normalized or nonpositive probability distributions, and think of these linear combinations as "mixtures" of these "distributions" even when neither term really applies. For example, one can write the distribution X on the observed samples from subtractive contamination as

$$X = \left(\frac{1}{1-\epsilon}\right)D - \left(\frac{\epsilon}{1-\epsilon}\right)E.$$

While this is not technically a mixture, it is useful to think of X as being obtained from D by first "subtracting" an ϵ-fraction of the distribution E and then renormalizing. Of course, this only makes sense if this ϵE was already contained in the distribution D. To convey this type of information, we introduce one further piece of notation.

Notation Given two pseudo-distributions X and Y, we use $X \leq Y$ to denote that the density of X is pointwise at most the density of Y. Equivalently, for every set S we have $X(S) \leq Y(S)$.

This means, for example, that the distribution E in the subtractive contamination model of Definition 1.2 must satisfy $\epsilon E \leq D$. Equivalently, the final distribution X must satisfy $(1 - \epsilon)X \leq D$. Similarly, the additive contamination model of Definition 1.1 is defined by $X \geq (1 - \epsilon)D$.

Finally, for the general contamination model, there are a few essentially equivalent reasonable definitions depending on the relative amounts of additive and subtractive contamination allowed. Perhaps the easiest way to deal with things is to allow the adversary to remove an ϵ-fraction of the probability mass of the inlier distribution and replace it with equal mass from some other distribution.

Definition 1.3 (General, Nonadaptive Contamination) Given a parameter $0 < \epsilon < 1$ and an inlier distribution D, we say that one can sample from D with ϵ-general contamination if one can obtain independent samples from a distribution of the form $X = D - \epsilon L + \epsilon E$, for distributions L and E with $\epsilon L \leq D$.

See Figure 1.3 for an example of general contamination.

This leads to a natural question as to which distributions X one can obtain in the general contamination model. It turns out that it is those that are close to D in *total variation distance*.

Definition 1.4 (Total Variation Distance) Given distributions X and Y, the *total variation distance* between them, denoted $d_{\mathrm{TV}}(X, Y)$, is defined to be half the L_1-norm of their difference, namely: $d_{\mathrm{TV}}(X, Y) := \frac{1}{2}\|X - Y\|_1$. If X and Y have probability density functions $p(x)$ and $q(x)$, we have $d_{\mathrm{TV}}(X, Y) = \frac{1}{2}\int |p(x) - q(x)|dx$. We also have the following equivalent definitions:

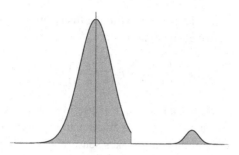

Figure 1.3 Example of a Gaussian with general contamination. The right tail of the distribution has been removed and replaced by the outlying bump on the right.

- The total variation distance is the biggest discrepancy between the probabilities of X and Y on any set, that is, $d_{\text{TV}}(X, Y) = \sup_S (|X(S) - Y(S)|)$.
- If Y is thought of as being a copy of the distribution X with some small probability of error, the total variation distance characterizes how small that error can be. In particular, we can write $d_{\text{TV}}(X, Y) = \inf_{A \sim X, B \sim Y} \mathbf{Pr}[A \neq B]$.

It is not hard to see that the general contamination model is equivalent to saying that one can sample from a distribution X with $d_{\text{TV}}(X, D) \leq \epsilon$. This is particularly informative given the last of the above formulations of total variation distance, as it essentially says that the algorithm is receiving samples from D with probability $1 - \epsilon$ and with probability ϵ is getting some kind of error.

Remark 1.5   In many settings, the subtractive contamination model is much easier to deal with than the additive contamination model. For example, if the goal is to estimate the mean of the inlier distribution D, even a single additive error can corrupt the sample mean by an arbitrary amount. Subtractive errors on the other hand are limited in how much damage they can do, since they are only allowed to remove existing samples. For a single removed sample to have a large effect on the sample mean, it would need to be the case that the initial sample set already had some extreme outliers which could be removed. Because of this, most of this book will focus on the more challenging models of additive or general contamination.

1.2.3 Adaptive Corruptions

There is one aspect in which even the general contamination model is not as strong as it could be. All of the contamination models from the last section are what might be called *nonadaptive*. That is, they replace the distribution D

over inlier samples by a distribution X by introducing some errors. But after doing this, the algorithm is then given honest, independent samples from the distribution X. A more insidious adversary might be able to choose what errors to introduce and which samples to corrupt, based on a knowledge of what the uncorrupted samples are. This idea leads us to our strongest contamination model.

Definition 1.6 (Strong Contamination Model) Given a parameter $0 < \epsilon < 1$ and an inlier distribution D, an algorithm receives samples from D with ϵ-contamination as follows: The algorithm specifies an integer number of samples n, and n samples are drawn independently from the distribution D. An adversary is then allowed to inspect these samples, remove up to $\lceil \epsilon n \rceil$ of them, and replace them with arbitrary points. The modified set of n points are then given to the algorithm.

In analogy with this adaptive version of the general noise model, we can devise an adaptive version of the additive noise model (that inserts $\lceil \epsilon n/(1-\epsilon) \rceil$ new samples into the dataset) and the adaptive subtractive noise model (that selects and removes $\lceil \epsilon n \rceil$ clean samples).

Although there are a few cases where it is useful to know that the errors that an algorithm is observing are i.i.d. samples from some distribution, most of the algorithms developed in this book can be shown to work in the strong contamination model. As this is the most powerful of the corruption models, we will state most of our results in this model.

1.3 Information-Theoretic Limits

Before we get into describing basic algorithms for robust estimation, we provide a succinct outline of the information-theoretic limits of such algorithms. The most basic of these limits is the following: If the samples are ϵ-contaminated (even by a nonadaptive adversary), then one cannot hope to learn the underlying distribution to total variation distance better than (approximately) ϵ. To state this formally, we present the following proposition.

Proposition 1.7 *Let X and Y be distributions with $d_{\mathrm{TV}}(X, Y) \le 2\epsilon$ for some $0 < \epsilon < 1$. A distribution D is taken to be either X or Y. Then an algorithm, given any number of samples from D with ϵ-general contamination, cannot reliably distinguish between the cases $D = X$ and $D = Y$. Furthermore, the same holds if (i) $d_{\mathrm{TV}}(X, Y) \le \epsilon/(1 - \epsilon)$ and the samples have ϵ-additive contamination or if (ii) $d_{\mathrm{TV}}(X, Y) \le \epsilon$ and the samples have ϵ-subtractive contamination.*

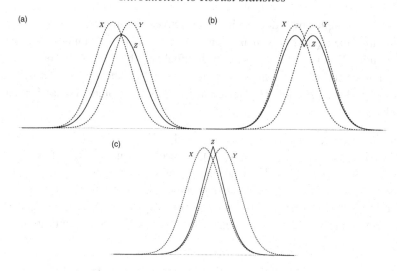

Figure 1.4 Illustration of construction of Z from X and Y: general contamination (a), additive contamination (b), subtractive contamination (c).

Proof In all three cases, the basic idea is that the adversary can find a single distribution Z such that Z is both an ϵ-contaminated version of X and an ϵ-contaminated version of Y. If the algorithm is then presented with independent samples from Z, there is no way to distinguish when these are contaminated samples from $D = X$ or contaminated samples from $D = Y$.

The constructions needed for our three types of contamination will be slightly different. See Figure 1.4 for an example of the construction of Z in each of the three cases.

In the case of general contamination, one can simply take $Z = (X + Y)/2$. In this case, we have

$$d_{\mathrm{TV}}(X, Z) = \frac{1}{2}\|X - Z\|_1 = \frac{1}{2}\|X - (X + Y)/2\|_1 = \frac{1}{2}\|(X - Y)/2\|_1 = \frac{1}{4}\|X - Y\|_1$$
$$= d_{\mathrm{TV}}(X, Y)/2 \le \epsilon.$$

A similar bound on $d_{\mathrm{TV}}(Y, Z)$ completes the argument.

For additive and subtractive contamination, the argument is slightly more complicated. If X and Y have total variation distance δ, then writing $X - Y$ as a positive part and a negative part, we obtain $X = Y - \delta L + \delta A$, for some distributions L and A with $\delta L \le Y$. Writing this slightly more symmetrically, we can take $W = (Y - \delta L)/(1 - \delta)$, and we have $X = (1 - \delta)W + \delta A$ and $Y = (1 - \delta)W + \delta L$.

For the case of subtractive contamination, we can take $Z = W$ as above.

Then Z can be obtained from either X or Y by subtracting a δ-fraction of the mass and renormalizing.

For additive contamination, we can take $Z = ((1 - \delta)W + \delta A + \delta L)/(1 + \delta)$. We note that this can be obtained by adding $\delta/(1 + \delta)$ additive contamination to either X and Y (adding L to X or A to Y). As long as $\delta \leq \epsilon/(1 - \epsilon)$, we have $\delta/(1 + \delta) \leq \epsilon$, which completes our proof. □

Remark 1.8 The distances at which X and Y are indistinguishable given corruptions, presented in Proposition 1.7, are essentially tight. See Exercise 1.3 for more details.

One interesting takeaway from Proposition 1.7 is that if $\epsilon \geq 1/2$, then one cannot reliably distinguish between *any* pair of distributions X and Y in the presence of ϵ additive or general contamination. This is because the total variation distance of any two distributions is at most 1. This means that for essentially every problem that we consider in this book (with the exception of topics covered in Chapter 5), we will need to assume that the proportion of contamination ϵ is less than $1/2$ in order for any guarantees to be possible.

Another implication of Proposition 1.7 is that it puts limits on our ability to robustly estimate basic statistics of the underlying distribution. For example, if one makes no assumptions on the underlying distribution D, it will be impossible (even with an unlimited number of samples) to learn the mean of D to within *any* bounded error. This is simply because one can find pairs of distributions X, Y with $d_{\mathrm{TV}}(X, Y) < \epsilon$ but with $\|\mathbf{E}[X] - \mathbf{E}[Y]\|$ unbounded.

Consequently, in order for meaningful results to be possible, we will need to consider settings where the inlier distribution is restricted to some well-behaved family. Broadly speaking, the best we can hope to achieve is to learn the underlying distribution within error $O(\epsilon)$ in total variation distance. If our distribution family is one where no ϵ-fraction of the probability mass can contribute too much to the mean (which is a measure of the concentration of the distribution), then this may suffice to obtain relatively good estimates of the mean. On the other hand, for families without this kind of concentration, we will be limited in how well we can expect to do.

The information-theoretic limitations for some basic distribution families are summarized below.

Lemma 1.9 *Let $\mathcal{D}$ be the family of one-dimensional Gaussian distributions with standard deviation 1. An algorithm with access to ϵ-corrupted samples (additive, subtractive, or general contamination) from an unknown distribution $D \in \mathcal{D}$ cannot reliably estimate $\mathbf{E}[D]$ to additive error $o(\epsilon)$.*

Proof Let δ be a sufficiently small constant multiple of ϵ. It is not hard to see that $d_{\text{TV}}(\mathcal{N}(0,1), \mathcal{N}(\delta,1)) < \epsilon$. Therefore, by Proposition 1.7, no algorithm can reliably distinguish between $G = \mathcal{N}(0,1)$ and $G = \mathcal{N}(\delta,1)$. However, these distributions have means that differ by δ. If an algorithm could estimate the mean to error better than $\delta/2$, it could use this estimate to distinguish between these distributions, yielding a contradiction. □

Using similar logic, we can obtain analogous results for some other natural distribution families.

Lemma 1.10 *Let $\mathcal{D}$ be the family of one-dimensional log-concave distributions with standard deviation 1. An algorithm with access to ϵ-corrupted samples from an unknown distribution $D \in \mathcal{D}$ cannot reliably estimate $\mathbf{E}[D]$ to additive error $o(\epsilon \log(1/\epsilon))$.*

Lemma 1.11 *Let $\mathcal{D}$ be the family of all one-dimensional distributions with standard deviation at most 1. An algorithm with access to ϵ-corrupted samples from an unknown distribution $D \in \mathcal{D}$ cannot reliably estimate $\mathbf{E}[D]$ to within additive error $o(\sqrt{\epsilon})$.*

Lemma 1.12 *Let $\mathcal{D}$ be the family of one-dimensional distributions D satisfying $\mathbf{E}[|D - \mu_D|^k] < 1$, for some $k \geq 2$, and $\mu_D = \mathbf{E}[D]$ (i.e., distributions with kth central moment bounded above by 1). An algorithm with access to ϵ-corrupted samples from an unknown distribution $D \in \mathcal{D}$ cannot reliably estimate $\mathbf{E}[D]$ to additive error $o(\epsilon^{1-1/k})$.*

1.4 One-Dimensional Robust Estimation

We begin our analysis of computationally efficient robust statistics by solving some of the most fundamental estimation tasks for natural families of one-dimensional distributions. This will allow us to gain a basic understanding of some useful techniques and principles without having to deal with many of the difficulties introduced by high-dimensional versions of these problems. In particular, we focus on robust estimators of the mean and standard deviation. For these problems, we will assume that the distribution D over inlier samples comes from some known family $\mathcal{D}$, and we will give algorithms that robustly estimate the mean and variance of D, given access to ϵ-corrupted samples from D.

1.4.1 Estimators Based on Order Statistics

One of the difficulties of robust mean estimation is that the empirical mean itself is very far from being robust. In particular, a single extreme outlier can corrupt the mean of a finite sample set by an arbitrarily large error. This is not an issue for the median and other order statistics, thus making them good candidates for designing robust estimators. To set things up, we define the quantiles of a distribution or a set.

Definition 1.13 (Quantiles)   Let X be a distribution on $\mathbf{R}$ and $q \in [0, 1]$. We define the q-quantile of X to be the infimum over all $t \in \mathbf{R}$ such that $\Pr[X \le t] \ge q$. If S is a multiset of real numbers, then the q-quantile of S is the q-quantile of the uniform distribution over S.

The basic result about quantiles is that the empirical q-quantile of a distribution is a fairly good empirical estimator of the true q-quantile.

Proposition 1.14   *Let X be a distribution on $\mathbf{R}$ and let $0 < \epsilon, \delta < 1/2$. Let S be a set of n samples from X that are ϵ-corrupted under the strong contamination model. Then with probability at least $1 - \delta$, the q-quantile of S is between the $(q - \epsilon + O(\sqrt{\log(1/\delta)/n}))$-quantile of X and the $(q + \epsilon + O(\sqrt{\log(1/\delta)/n}))$-quantile of X.*

Proof   We will show that with probability at least $1 - \delta/2$, the q-quantile of S is at least the $(q - \epsilon + O(\sqrt{\log(1/\delta)/n}))$-quantile of X. The upper bound will follow similarly. By definition, the q-quantile of S is the minimum value that is bigger than at least qn elements of S. In other words, we need to show that if we take t to be the $(q - \epsilon - C(\sqrt{\log(1/\delta)/n}))$-quantile of X for $C > 0$ some sufficiently large constant, then with probability at least $1 - \delta/2$, there are at most qn elements of S less than t.

The proof is quite simple. The set S was generated by first sampling n independent elements from X. Each of these elements independently and with probability at most $(q - \epsilon - C(\sqrt{\log(1/\delta)/n}))$ are less than t. Therefore, by the Chernoff bound, with probability at least $1 - \delta/2$, the number of original samples with value less than t was no more than $(q - \epsilon)n$. Upon corrupting ϵn of these samples, we still have at most qn samples less than t. This completes the proof of the lower bound. The upper bound follows analogously.   □

Proposition 1.14 is useful for estimating the mean of distributions for which the mean can be related to an order statistic. Perhaps the most common such case is that of distributions symmetric about their mean, as for such distributions the mean and median will be the same. This result can be applied in particular for the case of Gaussian distributions.

Corollary 1.15   *Let $D = \mathcal{N}(\mu, \sigma^2)$ be a one-dimensional Gaussian distribution. Let S be an ϵ-corrupted set of n samples from D, for some $\epsilon < 1/3$, and* *let m be its median. Then, if δ is at least e^{-an} for some sufficiently small a, with probability 1 − δ we have*

$$|m − μ| = O(ε + \sqrt{\log(1/δ)/n})σ.$$

Proof By Proposition 1.14, with probability 1 − δ we have that m is between the $(1/2 − ε + O(\sqrt{\log(1/δ)/n}))$-quantile and the $(1/2 + ε + O(\sqrt{\log(1/δ)/n}))$-quantile of D. Since the $(1/2 + η)$-quantile of D is $μ + O(ησ)$ for $η < 2/5$, the result follows.   □

In order to robustly estimate the standard deviation for certain distribution families, one can express the standard deviation in terms of a difference between order statistics. For example, the Inter-Quartile-Range (IQR) is the difference between the 1/4-quantile and the 3/4-quantile. Specifically, it is not hard to see that for Gaussian distributions, $D = \mathcal{N}(μ, σ^2)$, the IQR of D is equal to $c_{iqr}\, σ$, for some universal constant c_{iqr}. Using this fact, we can obtain a robust estimator for the standard deviation of a Gaussian distribution.

Corollary 1.16 *Let $D = \mathcal{N}(μ, σ^2)$ be a one-dimensional Gaussian distribution. Let S be an ε-corrupted set of n samples from D, for some $ε < 1/8$, and let r be the IQR of S. Let c_{iqr} be the aforementioned universal constant. Then, if δ is at least e^{-an} for some sufficiently small a, with probability 1 − δ we have*

$$σ = c_{iqr}\, r\, (1 + O(ε + \sqrt{\log(1/δ)/n})).$$

Proof By Proposition 1.14, with probability at least 1 − δ, each of the empirical quartiles correspond to the $(1/4 ± ε + O(\sqrt{\log(1/δ)/n}))$-quantile and the $(3/4 ± ε + O(\sqrt{\log(1/δ)/n}))$-quantile of D. This means that they are each within $O(ε+O(\sqrt{\log(1/δ)/n}))σ$ of the 1/4- and 3/4-quantiles. Thus, r is within $O(ε + O(\sqrt{\log(1/δ)/n}))σ$ of the IQR of D (and also at least a constant multiple of) $σ$, and the result follows.   □

One point worth making about Corollaries 1.15 and 1.16 is that both have error proportional to $σ$. This means that while the mean can be estimated to an additive error of $O(εσ)$, the standard deviation can only be estimated up to multiplicative error. This is a fairly common phenomenon.

Unfortunately, while the above-described estimators work quite well for Gaussian distributions, they are fairly specific and not generalizable. The median estimator essentially requires that the mean and median be the same; this works for symmetric distributions, but for skewed ones it does not work in general. The IQR, as an estimator of the standard deviation, is even more fragile. While it is not hard to show, using Chebyshev's inequality, that the IQR is never more than a constant factor larger than the standard deviation (and not much smaller for "nice" distributions), getting a precise relationship between the two essentially only worked here because the family of Gaussians has only one distribution up to affine transformation.

In order to obtain estimators for more complicated families, we will need to do something more similar to computing an actual mean. However, we will need to do this in such a way that an ϵ-fraction of samples being very extreme errors will not significantly affect the estimate. One fairly straightforward way to achieve this is by simply throwing away the few most extreme datapoints on each side and computing a *truncated mean*.

1.4.2 Estimators Based on Truncation

In general, we need an estimator that is not too much affected by an ϵ-fraction of the points being either very large or very small. A natural way to correct this is to take any points in the top or bottom ϵ-fraction and either throw them away or reduce them to something more manageable. There are a few ways to define the relevant truncation operation; the following is perhaps the most efficient version.

Definition 1.17 (Truncation) Given a distribution X on **R** and $0 < \epsilon < 1/2$, we define the *ϵ-truncation* of X to be the distribution obtained by taking X conditioned on the values lying between the ϵ-quantile and the $(1 - \epsilon)$-quantile.

See Figure 1.5 for an illustration of this definition.

The following proposition shows that, under reasonable assumptions, the mean of the truncated empirical distribution can provide a good robust estimate of the true mean.

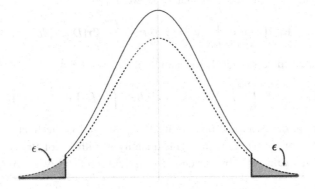

Figure 1.5 A Gaussian (dotted line) and its ϵ-truncation (solid line) for $\epsilon = 0.1$. The ϵ-tails of the distribution on both sides are removed and the remaining distribution rescaled.

Proposition 1.18 *Let $0 < \epsilon < \epsilon' < 1/2$. Let D be a distribution on $\mathbf{R}$ with mean μ such that removing any $2\epsilon'$-fraction of the mass of D changes the mean by at most $\eta > 0$ in absolute value. Let n be an integer at least a sufficiently large constant multiple of $\log(1/\delta)/(\epsilon' - \epsilon)^2$, for some $0 < \delta < 1/2$. Let S_0 be a set of n independent samples from D and let S be obtained from S_0 by adversarially corrupting an ϵ-fraction of its elements. Then, with probability at least $1 - \delta$, the mean $\widehat{\mu}$ of the ϵ'-truncated empirical distribution of S satisfies $|\widehat{\mu} - \mu| \leq \eta$.*

Remark 1.19 Some version of the assumption made in Proposition 1.18 – that removing a $2\epsilon'$-fraction of the mass of D does not change the mean by much – is essentially necessary for robust mean estimation to be possible. For example, suppose that D' can be obtained from D by removing a 2ϵ-fraction of its mass and that $|\mathbf{E}[D] - \mathbf{E}[D']| > \eta$. Then, $d_{\mathrm{TV}}(D, D') \leq 2\epsilon$, so by Proposition 1.7 one cannot distinguish between D and D' with any number of samples. Therefore, one cannot hope to estimate the mean to error better than $\eta/2$.

Proof First, we note that for any distribution X and any $m \in \mathbf{R}$, we have

$$\mathbf{E}[X] - m = \int_m^\infty \mathbf{Pr}[X > t]dt - \int_{-\infty}^m \mathbf{Pr}[X < t]dt.$$

If X_ϵ is the ϵ-truncation of X, then we can write $\mathbf{Pr}[X_\epsilon > t]$ as

$$f_\epsilon(\mathbf{Pr}[X > t]) \stackrel{\mathrm{def}}{=} \begin{cases} 0 & \text{if } \mathbf{Pr}[X > t] < \epsilon, \\ (\mathbf{Pr}[X > t] - \epsilon)/(1 - 2\epsilon) & \text{if } 1 - \epsilon > \mathbf{Pr}[X > t] > \epsilon, \\ 1 & \text{if } \mathbf{Pr}[X > t] > 1 - \epsilon. \end{cases}$$

In particular, letting m be the median of D, we have

$$\mathbf{E}[D] - m = \int_m^\infty \mathbf{Pr}[D > t]dt - \int_{-\infty}^m \mathbf{Pr}[D < t]dt.$$

For the truncated version of S, we can write

$$\mathbf{E}[S_{\epsilon'}] - m = \int_m^\infty f_{\epsilon'}(\mathbf{Pr}_{x \sim_u S}[x > t])dt - \int_{-\infty}^m f_{\epsilon'}(\mathbf{Pr}_{x \sim_u S}[x < t])dt.$$

By definition, the empirical probability $\mathbf{Pr}_{x \sim_u S}[x > t]$ is the fraction of elements of S that are bigger than t. This quantity is within ϵ of $\mathbf{Pr}_{x \sim_u S_0}[x > t]$. For any given value of t, by our choice of n, with probability $1 - \delta/2$, it will hold that

$$\left|\mathbf{Pr}_{x \sim_u S_0}[x > t] - \mathbf{Pr}[D > t]\right| < (\epsilon' - \epsilon).$$

In fact, by the VC inequality (Theorem A.12), with probability $1 - \delta$, this holds simultaneously for all t. If this is the case, we have

$$\mathbf{E}[S_{\epsilon'}] - m = \int_m^\infty f_{\epsilon'}(\mathbf{Pr}[D > t] \pm \epsilon')dt - \int_{-\infty}^m f_{\epsilon'}(\mathbf{Pr}[D < t] \pm \epsilon')dt.$$

This is at most

$$\mathbf{E}[S_{\epsilon'}] - m \leq \int_m^\infty f_{\epsilon'}(\mathbf{Pr}[D > t] + \epsilon')dt - \int_{-\infty}^m f_{\epsilon'}(\mathbf{Pr}[D < t] - \epsilon')dt$$

$$\leq \int_m^\infty \mathbf{Pr}[D > t]/(1 - 2\epsilon')dt - \int_{-\infty}^m \max(0, \mathbf{Pr}[D < t] - 2\epsilon')/(1 - 2\epsilon')dt.$$

Letting $D_{2\epsilon'}^+$ be the distribution obtained by conditioning D on x being larger than the $2\epsilon'$-quantile, then the above can be seen to equal $\mathbf{E}[D_{2\epsilon'}^+] - m$. Since $D_{2\epsilon'}^+$ is obtained from D by removing a $2\epsilon'$-fraction of the mass, we have

$$\widehat{\mu} - \mu = (\mathbf{E}[S_{\epsilon'}] - m) - (\mathbf{E}[D] - m)$$

$$\leq (\mathbf{E}[D_{2\epsilon'}^+] - m) - (\mathbf{E}[D] - m)$$

$$\leq \eta.$$

The lower bound follows similarly. □

Proposition 1.18 applies to a much broader family of distributions than just Gaussians. Specifically, it is not hard to see that if $D = \mathcal{N}(\mu, \sigma^2)$ is a Gaussian and ϵ' is $O(\epsilon)$ and at most $1/3$, the error η can be taken to be $O(\epsilon \sqrt{\log(1/\epsilon)}\sigma)$. The exact same guarantee holds if D is any sub-Gaussian distribution with standard deviation σ, that is, a distribution whose tails decay at least as fast as the tails of the Gaussian with the same standard deviation.

On the other hand, if D is a general log-concave distribution with standard deviation σ, η is at most $O(\epsilon \log(1/\epsilon)\sigma)$. More generally, if D has kth central moment at most 1, we have that $\eta = O(\epsilon^{1-1/k})$.

Finally, we note that if one wants to robustly compute the variance of D for these more general families, the simplest technique is to first use a truncated mean to obtain an estimate $\widehat{\mu}$ for the mean of D, and then use another truncated mean to estimate the average value of $(D - \widehat{\mu})^2$.

1.5 Higher-Dimensional Robust Mean Estimation

While the techniques in the previous section do a fairly good job of estimating the mean of a one-dimensional random variable, generalizing these techniques to higher dimensional problems is somewhat tricky. For concreteness, we will work with perhaps the simplest problem in this family. Let $D = \mathcal{N}(\mu, I_d)$ be a

d-dimensional Gaussian with identity covariance matrix and unknown mean μ. Given access to ϵ-corrupted samples from D, the goal is to estimate its mean μ up to a small error in ℓ_2-norm.

We start by discussing the difficulties involved with robustly estimating μ in higher dimensions. First, we would like to understand the information-theoretic limits for this problem. By Proposition 1.7, we know that we cannot hope to distinguish between a pair of Gaussians with total variation distance at most ϵ. For the family of spherical Gaussians, it is not hard to show that $d_{\text{TV}}(\mathcal{N}(\mu, I_d), \mathcal{N}(\mu', I_d)) = \Theta(\min(1, \|\mu - \mu'\|_2))$. Therefore, we cannot hope to learn the mean to ℓ_2-error $o(\epsilon)$ in the presence of ϵ-corruptions.

Switching our attention to algorithms, perhaps the most natural approach is to try to generalize the one-dimensional median-based estimator; alas, it is unclear how to achieve this, as there are various ways to define a notion of "median" in high dimensions. One natural idea is to use the coordinate-wise median: That is, take a number of samples x_i and for each coordinate j take the median of the jth coordinates of the x_i. Since the jth-coordinates are distributed as $\mathcal{N}(\mu_j, 1)$, this gives an $O(\epsilon)$-approximation for each coordinate of μ by Corollary 1.15. Unfortunately, an estimator that guarantees error $O(\epsilon)$ in each coordinate might still have ℓ_2 error as large as $\Omega(\epsilon \sqrt{d})$, which is significantly worse than our desired error.

Interestingly, it turns out that a generalization of this idea does work – leading to a sample-efficient (but computationally inefficient) multivariate robust mean estimator. Note that if v is a unit vector in $\mathbf{R}^d$, then $v \cdot D$ is distributed as $\mathcal{N}(v \cdot \mu, 1)$. Using a one-dimensional robust mean estimator for this Gaussian random variable (such as the empirical median), we can obtain an estimate m_v such that with high probability $|m_v - v \cdot \mu| = O(\epsilon)$. The idea of our high-dimensional robust mean estimator is the following: If we can compute these approximations for *every* unit vector v, this will suffice to estimate μ. In particular, if we can find *any* $\widehat{\mu} \in \mathbf{R}^d$ such that $|m_v - v \cdot \widehat{\mu}| = O(\epsilon)$ for all unit vectors v (note that such vectors $\widehat{\mu}$ exist, since μ satisfies this requirement), then we have

$$\|\mu - \widehat{\mu}\|_2 = \sup_{\|v\|_2 = 1} |v \cdot (\mu - \widehat{\mu})| \leq \sup_{\|v\|_2 = 1} (|v \cdot \mu - m_v| + |v \cdot \widehat{\mu} - m_v|) = O(\epsilon). \quad (1.1)$$

In order to be able to actually find such a $\widehat{\mu}$, we will need that the median be a good estimator of the mean in every linear projection. Looking at the proof of Proposition 1.14, it can be seen that this will hold if for our set S of uncorrupted samples and every unit vector v and $t \in \mathbf{R}$, we have

$$\left| \mathbf{Pr}_{x \sim_u S}[v \cdot x > t] - \mathbf{Pr}[v \cdot G > t] \right| < \epsilon.$$

By the VC inequality (Theorem A.12), this holds with high probability, as long as the number of samples is at least a sufficiently large constant multiple of d/ϵ^2.

This argument shows that multivariate robust mean estimation of a spherical Gaussian with ℓ_2-error of $O(\epsilon)$ – independent of the dimension! – is in fact possible information-theoretically; alas, the implied estimator is highly nontrivial to compute. Taken literally, one would first need to compute m_v for every unit vector v (i.e., for infinitely many directions), and then find some appropriate $\widehat{\mu}$. Via a slight relaxation of the aforementioned argument, the situation is not this bad. If we modify Equation (1.1), we note that it is actually sufficient to have $|v \cdot \widehat{\mu} - m_v| = O(\epsilon)$ for all unit vectors v in some finite cover C of the unit sphere. In particular, we will need to know that

$$\|\mu - \widehat{\mu}\|_2 = O(\sup_{v \in C} |v \cdot (\mu - \widehat{\mu})|).$$

Fortunately, there exist finite covers C of the unit sphere such that for any $x \in \mathbf{R}^d$,

$$\|x\|_2 = O(\sup_{v \in C} |v \cdot x|). \tag{1.2}$$

See Theorem A.10. On the other hand, it is not hard to see that for Equation (1.2) to hold for even a random x, we need to have $|C|$ scale exponentially in d.

In summary, this relaxation *does* give us the following exponential-time algorithm for robust mean estimation: Given such a set C of size $2^{O(d)}$, we first compute m_v for each $v \in C$, and then solve a linear program (of exponential size) to find a $\widehat{\mu}$ satisfying $|v \cdot \widehat{\mu} - m_v| = O(\epsilon)$ for all $v \in C$. This yields an algorithm with runtime $\text{poly}(2^d/\epsilon)$.

This discussion is summarized in the following proposition.

Proposition 1.20 *There exists an algorithm that, on input of an ϵ-corrupted set of samples from $D = \mathcal{N}(\mu, I_d)$ of size $n = \Omega((d + \log(1/\tau))/\epsilon^2)$, runs in $\text{poly}(n, 2^d)$ time, and outputs $\widehat{\mu} \in \mathbf{R}^d$ such that with probability at least $1 - \tau$, it holds that $\|\widehat{\mu} - \mu\|_2 = O(\epsilon)$.*

For distributions other than Gaussians, one can provide a similar analysis. As long as there exists a one-dimensional robust mean estimator that can approximate $v \cdot \mu$ to error δ for every unit vector v (and assuming that we can make this hold in all directions simultaneously with a limited number of samples), then one can use this to construct an estimator of μ with ℓ_2 error $O(\delta)$ in exponential time (see Exercise 1.12).

Connection with Tukey Median There is a classical method to robustly estimate the mean of symmetric distributions known as the *Tukey median*, which can be thought of as a variation on the estimator from Proposition 1.20 by using median-based estimators. In particular, given a distribution D, we define the *Tukey depth* of a point y with respect to D as the minimum over unit vectors v of $\mathbf{Pr}_{x \sim D}[v \cdot x > v \cdot y]$. The Tukey median of a distribution D is then any point with maximum Tukey depth.

If $D = \mathcal{N}(\mu, I_d)$ is a Gaussian distribution, then the Tukey depth of the mean μ will be $1/2$. Similarly, for the sample case, the Tukey depth of μ with respect to the uniform distribution over a sufficiently large number of samples from D will be arbitrarily close to $1/2$ with high probability. If D is replaced by an ϵ-corruption of D (or if an ϵ-fraction of the samples are corrupted), then the Tukey depth of μ_D will still be $1/2 - O(\epsilon)$. Moreover, it is not hard to show that *any* point y with Tukey depth $1/2 - O(\epsilon)$ with respect to the ϵ-corruption of D (or its samples) will satisfy $\|x - y\|_2 = O(\epsilon)$ with high probability.

In summary, for Gaussians and other symmetric distributions, the Tukey median provides another method of robustly estimating the mean to near-optimal error. Unfortunately, computing the Tukey median also leads to computational issues. In particular, it has been shown that computing a Tukey median of an arbitrary point set is NP-Hard.

The kind of results described in this section were the state of the art for several decades. High-dimensional robust mean estimation, even for the simple case of spherical Gaussians, had three kinds of algorithms: Those that were of an entirely heuristic nature (i.e., without provable error guarantees); those that had error guarantees which scaled polynomially in the dimension; and those that had runtimes which scaled exponentially in the dimension. This held until a new class of algorithms arose to circumvent both of these problems; we will discuss these developments in the next chapter.

1.6 Connection with Breakdown Point

The focus of this book is on developing robust estimators to approximate a desired parameter of a distribution given an ϵ-corrupted dataset. Specifically, we want robust estimators that approximate a target parameter as accurately as possible, and in particular with no dependence on the underlying dimensionality of the data. Until recently, such dimension-independent error guarantees could not be achieved in high dimensions with computationally efficient algorithms.

Classical work in robust statistics largely focused on designing robust estimators with large *breakdown point*. The breakdown point of an estimator is a natural notion that quantifies the effect (or influence) of the outliers on its performance. Here we define a population variant of the breakdown point, specifically for the problem of robust mean estimation. Similar definitions exist for various other parameter estimation tasks.

While estimators typically act on finite sample sets, for simplicity we think about estimators as acting on distributions (by treating samples as the uniform distribution over the samples and considering the infinite sample regime). That is, we view an estimator T as a function mapping a distribution to the desired parameter (mean vector). For a distribution p and an estimator T, we will denote by $T(p)$ the mean vector estimate that T outputs given p.

Given this notation, we start by defining the notion of maximum bias.

Definition 1.21 (Maximum Bias) For a fixed distribution p and a contamination parameter $0 < \epsilon < 1/2$, the maximum ϵ-bias $b_T(p, \epsilon)$ of the estimator T is defined to be the supremum ℓ_2-distance between $T(p)$ and $T(\widetilde{p})$, where $\widetilde{p}$ is an ϵ-corruption of p (under additive, subtractive, or general contamination). For general contamination, we can write

$$b_T(p, \epsilon) = \sup \{\|T(p) - T(\widetilde{p})\|_2 \mid d_{\text{TV}}(\widetilde{p}, p) \le \epsilon\}.$$

The breakdown point $\epsilon^*(p)$ is defined as the minimum fraction of corruptions that can drive the maximum bias to infinity.

Definition 1.22 (Breakdown Point) For a fixed distribution p, the breakdown point $\epsilon^*(T, p)$ of the estimator T on p is defined to be the infimum value of ϵ such that the maximum ϵ-bias of T on p is unbounded. For general contamination, we can write $\epsilon^*(T, p) = \inf\{\epsilon \mid b_T(p, \epsilon) = \infty\}$. For a family of distributions $\mathcal{D}$, the breakdown point of an estimator T on $\mathcal{D}$ is the worst breakdown point for any distribution $p \in \mathcal{D}$, that is, $\epsilon^*(T, \mathcal{D}) = \inf\{\epsilon^*(T, p), p \in \mathcal{D}\}$.

While the notion of breakdown point can be quite informative in certain settings, it is generally not sufficiently precise to quantify the robustness of an estimator in high dimensions. We provide a few illustrative examples for the problem of robust mean estimation when the inlier distribution is an identity covariance Gaussian, that is, when the family $\mathcal{D}$ is $\{\mathcal{N}(\mu, I), \mu \in \mathbf{R}^d\}$. A first observation is that the empirical mean has a breakdown point of 0. In particular, arbitrarily small corruptions (in total variation distance) to the underlying distribution can produce arbitrarily large errors in the mean. This agrees with the intuition that the empirical mean is highly nonrobust in the presence of outliers. A second example is that of the coordinate-wise median. It turns out that the coordinate-wise median has breakdown point of $1/2$ (which is the maximum possible) in any dimension d. This may suggest that the coordinate-wise median is *the most robust* mean estimator in high dimensions. On the other hand, it is not difficult to construct examples where the coordinate-wise median will have ℓ_2-distance of $\Omega(\epsilon\sqrt{d})$ from the true mean. A third example is that of the Tukey median. Recall that the Tukey median is known to have ℓ_2-error of $O(\epsilon)$ from the true mean (which is information-theoretically best possible). On the other hand, for Gaussians in $d \geq 2$ dimensions and additive contamination, its breakdown point can be shown to be equal to $1/3$ (see Exercise 1.8). In particular, it would be considered inferior to the coordinate-wise median with respect to this criterion. In essence, the breakdown point is a measure of how many corruptions an estimator can deal with before it becomes totally useless. However, if one cares about the size of the errors that one incurs (more precisely than simply knowing whether or not they are finite), the breakdown point will be an insufficient measure of robustness.

1.7 Exercises

1.1 (Definitions of Total Variation Distance) Prove that the different formulations of total variation distance given in Definition 1.4 are equivalent.

1.2 (Contamination Models) In this exercise, we will compare three contamination models – the strong contamination model, the total variation distance model, and the Huber contamination model – in terms of the difficulty they impose on a learner. In particular, we say that error model A can *simulate* error model B for sample size N if for every strategy the adversary for error model B can employ to corrupt a set of N samples, an adversary for error model A can employ a corresponding strategy, so that the distributions over sets of samples received by the algorithm are close in total variation distance.

(a) Show that if error model A can simulate error model B for sample size N, then any learning algorithm that works against corruptions of type A will also work against corruptions of type B. In particular, this shows that corruptions of type B are weaker than corruptions of type A.

(b) Show that for any $\epsilon' > \epsilon > 0$, the strong contamination model with the ability to corrupt an ϵ'-fraction of samples can simulate the ϵ-total variation distance error model over N samples, for any N a sufficiently large function of ϵ, ϵ'.

(c) Show that the ϵ-error total variation distance contamination model can simulate the ϵ-error Huber contamination model for any number of samples.

1.3 (Precise Limits of Robust Learning) Here we will show that Proposition 1.7 is tight in the following sense: Let X and Y be two given probability distributions with $d_{\mathrm{TV}}(X, Y) = \delta$, for some $\delta > 0$. Let D be a distribution known to be either X or Y. An algorithm is given corrupted samples from D and is asked to determine whether $D = X$ or $D = Y$. Show that it can reliably make this determination with a bounded number of samples if:

(a) The algorithm is given samples with ϵ-additive contamination and $\delta > \epsilon/(1 - \epsilon)$.

(b) The algorithm is given samples with ϵ-subtractive contamination and $\delta > \epsilon$.

(c) The algorithm is given samples with ϵ-general contamination and $\delta > 2\epsilon$.

(Hint: Note that there is a set S so that $|X(S) - Y(S)| = \delta$. Consider the fraction of samples that lie in S.)

1.4 (Robustness of the Median)

(a) We showed in this chapter that the median is a robust mean estimator for $\mathcal{N}(\mu, 1)$ with error $O(\epsilon)$. What is the optimal constant factor in the $O(\cdot)$ for small ϵ?

(b) A distribution D on $\mathbf{R}$ with mean $\mu \in \mathbf{R}$ is called (s, ϵ)-smooth, where $\epsilon > 0$ and $s = s(\epsilon)$, if it satisfies $\mathrm{Pr}_{X \sim D}[X \geq \mu + s] \leq 1/2 - \epsilon$ and $\mathrm{Pr}_{X \sim D}[X \leq \mu - s] \leq 1/2 - \epsilon$. Show that given a sufficiently large ϵ'-corrupted set T of samples from D (for some $\epsilon > \epsilon' > 0$), the median of T is a robust estimator of the mean μ with error at most s.

(c) Construct a one-dimensional distribution D with sub-Gaussian tails such that the median of D does not perform well as a robust mean estimator. What about a symmetric distribution D?

1.5 (Robust Mean Estimation Under Bounded kth Moment) Let D be a distribution on $\mathbf{R}$ with bounded kth moment, for some $k \geq 2$. That is, D satisfies $\mathbf{E}_{X \sim D}[|X - \mu|^k] \leq \sigma^k$, for some known parameter $\sigma > 0$ and positive integer k, where μ is the mean of D.

(a) Show that the truncated mean of D is a robust mean estimator of the mean μ with error $O(\sigma \epsilon^{1-1/k})$.

(b) Show that the bound from part (a) is minimax optimal by proving Lemma 1.12. In particular, show that if an algorithm is given an ϵ-corrupted set of samples (in the Huber model) from a distribution D guaranteed to have bounded kth moments in the above sense (and for which nothing else is known), it is information-theoretically impossible to learn the mean of D within error better than $\Omega(\sigma\epsilon^{1-1/k})$ with more than $2/3$ probability of success.

1.6   (Robust Mean Estimation for Log-Concave Distributions) Let D be a log-concave distribution on $\mathbf{R}$ with standard deviation at most 1. A standard result about such distributions tells us that D has sub-exponential tails, in the sense that the probability that a sample from D is at distance more than t from its mean is $O(\exp(-\Omega(t)))$.

(a) Show that the truncated mean of D is a robust mean estimator of the mean μ with error $O(\epsilon \log(1/\epsilon))$.

(b) Show that the bound from part (a) is minimax optimal by proving Lemma 1.10. In particular, show that if an algorithm is given an ϵ-corrupted set of samples (even in the Huber model) from a distribution D guaranteed to be log-concave with variance at most 1 (and for which nothing else is known), it is information-theoretically impossible to learn the mean of D within error better than $\Omega(\epsilon \log(1/\epsilon))$ with more than $2/3$ success probability.

1.7   (Obliviousness to Contamination Parameter) Note that, in contrast to the median, the truncated mean requires a priori knowledge of the contamination parameter $\epsilon > 0$. In this problem, we will explore to what extent this can be avoided.

(a) Let D be a distribution on $\mathbf{R}$ with variance at most $\sigma > 0$, where σ is a known parameter. Consider the following estimator for the mean μ of D: Draw n ϵ-corrupted points from D, where $n \gg 1/\epsilon^2$. Let $X_1 \le X_2 \le \cdots \le X_n$ be an ordering of these points. Find the minimum $1 \le a \le n/2$ such that the subsequence $X_a \le X_{a+1} \le \cdots \le X_{n+1-a}$ has empirical variance at most 3σ. Output the empirical mean of $\{X_a, X_{a+1}, \ldots, X_{n+1-a}\}$. Show that this gives a robust estimator of μ with error $O(\sigma \sqrt{\epsilon})$.

(b) Let D be a distribution on $\mathbf{R}$ with variance at most $\sigma > 0$, where σ is *unknown*. Show that it is information-theoretically impossible to robustly estimate the mean of D without a priori knowledge of the contamination parameter $\epsilon > 0$. In particular, show that even given an unlimited number of samples, no algorithm that does not know either ϵ or σ can learn the mean of D to error $O(\sigma \sqrt{\epsilon})$ with probability $2/3$.

(c) Let D be a distribution on $\mathbf{R}$ with bounded kth moment, for some $k \ge 2$ in the sense of Problem 1.5. Design an algorithm that learns the mean of D to error $O(\sigma\epsilon^{1-1/k})$ in the presence of an ϵ-fraction of outliers without knowing ϵ.

1.8 (Breakdown Point Computations)

   (a) Show that the breakdown point of the median of a continuous, one-dimensional distribution is $1/2$.

   (b) Show that the breakdown point of the Tukey median of a two-dimensional Gaussian with additive contamination is at most $1/3$.

   (c) Show that the breakdown point of the Tukey median of any symmetric, continuous distribution with respect to additive contamination is at least $1/3$.

   (d) Show that the breakdown point of the Tukey median of any symmetric, continuous distribution with respect to total variation contamination is at most $1/4$.

1.9 (Estimation Accuracy with Corruption Rate Close to $1/2$) In this exercise, we examine what happens to the error rates for robust mean estimation problems when the fraction of outliers ϵ is close to $1/2$ (note that when *equals* $1/2$, mean estimation is usually impossible, by Proposition 1.7).

   (a) Let $X = \mathcal{N}(\mu, 1) \in \mathbf{R}$ be a Gaussian with unknown mean μ. Show that if one is given sufficiently many samples from X with ϵ-general contamination for some $\epsilon < 1/2$, the empirical median estimates μ to error $O(\sqrt{\log(1/(1/2 - \epsilon))})$ with high probability.

   (b) Show that the bound in part (a) is best possible in the sense that no algorithm given such ϵ-corrupted samples can reliably learn μ to error $o(\sqrt{\log(1/(1/2 - \epsilon))})$ as ϵ approaches $1/2$.

   (c) Let $X \in \mathbf{R}$ be a distribution with variance at most 1 and unknown mean μ. Show that if one is given sufficiently many samples from X with ϵ-general contamination for some $\epsilon < 1/2$, an appropriate truncated mean can approximate μ to error $O(1/\sqrt{1/2 - \epsilon})$ with high probability.

   (d) Show that the bound in part (c) is best possible in the sense that no algorithm given such ϵ-corrupted samples can reliably learn μ to error $o(1/\sqrt{1/2 - \epsilon})$, as ϵ approaches $1/2$.

1.10 (High Probability Mean Estimation) Estimation problems for heavy-tailed distributions exhibit many of the same difficulties that problems of estimating with adversarial noise do. These issues become particularly clear when we want to construct estimators with very small probability of error. In this exercise, we explore some of these connections.

(a) Consider the sample mean as an estimator of the mean of a one-dimensional Gaussian $\mathcal{N}(\mu, \sigma^2)$. Show that for any $\delta \in (0, 1)$, given n i.i.d. samples from $\mathcal{N}(\mu, \sigma^2)$, with probability $1 - \delta$, the sample mean has distance $O(\sigma \sqrt{\log(1/\delta)/n})$ from the true mean.

(b) Show that the sample mean does not work well for general distributions with bounded variance. In particular, for $n \in \mathbf{Z}_+$, $\delta \in (0, 1)$, show that there is a one-dimensional distribution X with standard deviation at most σ such that with probability at least δ the empirical mean of X computed from n i.i.d. samples differs from the true mean by at least $\Omega(\sigma \sqrt{1/(n\delta)})$.

(c) Show that the rate from part (b) can be improved by taking an appropriate truncated mean. In particular, given n a positive integer and $\delta \in (0, 1)$, design an estimator that given n i.i.d. samples from a distribution X with standard deviation at most σ produces an estimator that is within distance $O(\sigma \sqrt{\log(1/\delta)/n})$ of the true mean of X with probability at least $1 - \delta$.

Hint: You may need to make use of Bernstein's Inequality (Theorem A.7) in order to prove this.

(d) Show that the estimator from part (c) can be made robust to contamination. In particular, in the presence of an ϵ-fraction of adversarial errors, this estimator can be modified to achieve error $O(\sigma \sqrt{\log(1/\delta)/n} + \sigma \sqrt{\epsilon})$ with probability at least $1 - \delta$.

1.11 (Robustness of Geometric Median) For a finite set $S \subset \mathbf{R}^d$, define its *geometric median* to be the point $x \in \mathbf{R}^d$ minimizing $\sum_{y \in S} \|x - y\|_2$. Let S be an ϵ-corrupted set of samples from $\mathcal{N}(\mu, I) \in \mathbf{R}^d$ of sufficiently large size.

(a) Show that the geometric median of S has ℓ_2-distance $O(\epsilon \sqrt{d})$ from μ with high probability.

(b) Show that this upper bound is tight for a worst-case adversary.

1.12 (Sample-Efficient Robust Estimation) Use the methodology we introduced to establish Proposition 1.20 to obtain robust (and computationally inefficient) estimators for the following tasks:

(a) Estimating the mean of a distribution $X \in \mathbf{R}^d$ with bounded kth moments. In particular, show that if the kth moment of X is at most σ^k in any direction, there is an estimator that approximates the mean of X to error $O(\epsilon^{1-1/k}\sigma)$ from ϵ-corrupted samples with high probability.

(b) Sparse mean estimation of $\mathcal{N}(\mu, I)$. Here the goal is to estimate the mean μ under the assumption that it is k-sparse, that is, if μ is supported on an unknown subset of k coordinates. The sample complexity should depend polynomially on k, but only logarithmically on the underlying dimension.

(c) Estimating the covariance of $\mathcal{N}(0, \Sigma)$ under the assumption that $\Sigma \preceq I$. Specifically, find a $\widehat{\Sigma}$ that is close to Σ in spectral norm. What about Frobenius norm?

1.8 Discussion and Related Work

The traditional approach in statistics is to design estimators that perform well under the assumption that the underlying observations are i.i.d. samples from a model of interest. Robust statistics aims to design estimators that are insensitive or stable against small deviations from this classical assumption. That is, a small change in the underlying distribution should result in a small change in the performance of the estimator. Two closely related approaches of quantifying the deviation from the standard i.i.d. assumption involve outlying observations or model misspecification.

As a subfield of Statistics, Robust Statistics was initiated in the pioneering works of [140], [3], and [95]. The latter work introduced the contamination model of Definition 1.1. More general contamination models, with respect to other metrics, were studied in [83]. The reader is referred to some early introductory textbooks from the statistics community [85, 97]. The quote by Peter Huber given in the introduction of this chapter is from Chapter 8 of [96].

Early work in the robust statistics community focused on the sample complexity of robust estimation and on the notion of the breakdown point [72, 73, 84]. Interestingly, recent work in robust statistics [26] advocates that achieving robustness under Huber contamination is more general than achieving large breakdown point, and provides a unified way of studying robustness.

The Tukey median was defined by [141]. It is known that in the presence of ϵ-contamination, when the inlier data is drawn from an unknown mean and identity covariance Gaussian, the Tukey median achieves the optimal robustness of $O(\epsilon)$. The same guarantee holds for other symmetric distributions as well; see, for example, [26]. Several other depth functions have been studied in the relevant statistics literature [26, 133, 135]. Unfortunately, the Tukey median is NP-hard to compute in general [103] and the many heuristics proposed to approximate it degrade in the quality of their approximation as the dimension scales. Similar hardness results have been shown [15, 86] for essentially all known classical estimators in robust statistics.

In recent years, learning in the presence of outliers has become a pressing challenge in a number of high-dimensional data analysis applications. These include the analysis of biological datasets, where natural outliers are common [116, 124, 132] and can contaminate the downstream statistical analysis, and *data poisoning attacks* in machine learning [14], where even a small fraction of fake data (outliers) can substantially degrade the quality of the learned model [19, 137]. In the following chapters of this book, we develop a general algorithmic theory that leads to computationally efficient estimators for a wide range of high-dimensional estimation tasks, including the mean estimation task considered in this chapter. These efficient estimators have led to practical improvements in the analysis of genetic data [46] and in adversarial machine learning [44, 88, 139].

2

Efficient High-Dimensional Robust Mean Estimation

2.1 Introduction

In Chapter 1, we analyzed some standard efficient robust estimators for the one-dimensional setting and discussed the information-theoretic aspects of basic robust statistics problems in any dimension. Unfortunately, in high dimensions, the methods discussed in that chapter are inherently unsatisfactory. In particular, these approaches either incur runtime exponential in the dimension or lead to error that scales polynomially in the dimension. In fact, over several decades, this dichotomy persisted in all known algorithms for even the most basic high-dimensional unsupervised problems in the presence of adversarial outliers. The first algorithmic progress in this direction was made in the context of high-dimensional robust mean estimation for Gaussians and other well-behaved distributions. These developments form the basis for essentially all algorithms in this book. Thus, it is natural for our discussion on algorithmic high-dimensional robust statistics to begin there.

Recall that in order for robust mean estimation to be at all possible, one needs to make some assumptions on the behavior of the inlier distribution X. As we will see, these assumptions usually amount to certain concentration properties. While many of the algorithms we present work for distributions with only weak assumptions of this form (e.g., bounded covariance), the basic case of Gaussians with identity covariance (i.e., distributions of the form $X \sim \mathcal{N}(\mu, I)$, for some unknown mean μ) is particularly illuminating. As such, many of our motivating examples will be specific to this case.

2.1.1 Key Difficulties and High-Level Intuition

Arguably, the most natural attempt at robustly estimating the mean of a distribution would be to identify the outliers and output the empirical mean of the remaining points. The key difficulty in high dimensions is the fact that the outliers cannot be identified at an individual level, even when they move the mean significantly. In a number of cases, we can easily identify the "extreme outliers" via a pruning procedure exploiting the concentration properties of the inliers. Alas, such naive approaches typically do not suffice to obtain nontrivial error guarantees.

The simplest example illustrating this difficulty is that of a high-dimensional spherical Gaussian. Typical samples will be at ℓ_2-distance approximately $\Theta(\sqrt{d})$ from the true mean, where d is the dimension. Given this, we can apply a kind of basic, "naive filtering" by removing all points at Euclidean distance more than $10\sqrt{d}$ from the coordinate-wise median. It is not hard to see that only a tiny fraction of inliers will be removed by this procedure, while all of the sufficiently extreme outliers will be. Unfortunately, it is difficult to remove much else by this kind of procedure. In particular, since any point at distance approximately $\sqrt{d}$ from the mean is just as likely to appear as any other, none of them can safely be eliminated without risking the removal of inliers as well. However, if an ϵ-fraction of outliers are placed at distance $\sqrt{d}$ *in roughly the same direction* from the unknown mean (see Figure 2.1), an adversary can corrupt the sample mean by as much as $\Omega(\epsilon\sqrt{d})$.

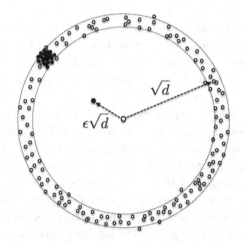

Figure 2.1 A hard instance for naive filtering. Note that the inlier samples (white) for a high-dimensional spherical Gaussian are concentrated in a spherical shell of distance approximately $\sqrt{d}$ from the mean. If the outliers (black) are placed within this shell, they will be difficult to detect. Moreover, if the outliers are all placed in roughly the same location in the shell, they can corrupt the mean by as much as $\epsilon\sqrt{d}$.

This leaves the algorithm designer with a dilemma of sorts. On the one hand, potential outliers at distance $\Theta(\sqrt{d})$ from the unknown mean could lead to large ℓ_2-error, scaling polynomially with d. On the other hand, if the adversary places outliers at distance approximately $\Theta(\sqrt{d})$ from the true mean in *random directions*, it may be information-theoretically impossible to distinguish them from the inliers. The way out is the realization that, in order to obtain a robust estimate of the mean, *it is in fact not necessary to detect and remove all outliers*. It is only required that the algorithm can detect the "consequential outliers," that is, the ones that can significantly impact our estimates of the mean.

So how can we make progress? To begin with, let us assume that there are no extreme outliers (as these can be removed via naive filtering). Then we claim that *the only way that the empirical mean can be far from the true mean is if there is a "conspiracy" of many outliers, all producing errors in approximately the same direction*. Intuitively, if our corrupted points are at distance $O(\sqrt{d})$ from the true mean in random directions, their contributions will on average cancel out, leading to a small error in the sample mean. In conclusion, it suffices to be able to detect these kinds of conspiracies of outliers.

The next key insight is simple and powerful. Let T be an ϵ-corrupted set of points drawn from $\mathcal{N}(\mu, I)$. If such a conspiracy of outliers substantially moves the empirical mean μ_T of T, it must move μ_T in some direction. That is, there is a unit vector v such that these outliers cause $v \cdot (\mu_T - \mu)$ to be large. For this to happen, it must be the case that these outliers are on average far from μ in the v-direction. In particular, if an ϵ-fraction of corrupted points in T move the sample average of $v \cdot (U_T - \mu)$, where U_T is the uniform distribution on T, by more than δ (δ should be thought of as small, but substantially larger than ϵ), then on average these corrupted points x must have $v \cdot (x - \mu)$ at least δ/ϵ, as shown in Figure 2.2. This in turn means that these corrupted points will have a contribution of at least $\epsilon \cdot (\delta/\epsilon)^2 = \delta^2/\epsilon$ to the variance of $v \cdot U_T$. Fortunately, this condition can actually be algorithmically detected! In particular, by computing the top eigenvector of the sample covariance matrix, we can efficiently determine whether or not there is any direction v for which the variance of $v \cdot U_T$ is abnormally large.

The aforementioned discussion leads us to the overall structure of the algorithms we will describe in this chapter. Starting with an ϵ-corrupted set of points T (perhaps weighted in some way), we compute the sample covariance matrix and find the eigenvector v^* with largest eigenvalue λ^*. If λ^* is not much larger than it should be (in the absence of outliers), by the above discussion, the empirical mean is close to the true mean, and we can return that as an answer. Otherwise, we have obtained a particular direction v^* for which we know

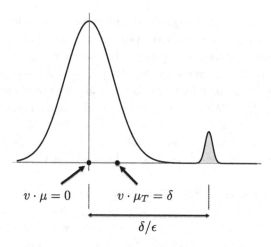

$$v \cdot \mu = 0 \qquad v \cdot \mu_T = \delta$$

$$\delta/\epsilon$$

Figure 2.2 An example of an ϵ-fraction of outliers changing the empirical mean of T by δ in the v-direction. The graph represents the projections of the samples onto the v-direction. Notice that the errors must on average have $v \cdot x$ at least δ/ϵ-far from $v \cdot \mu$. This means that they must contribute at least δ^2/ϵ to the variance of $v \cdot T$.

that the outliers play an unusual role, that is, the outliers behave significantly differently than the inliers. The distribution of the points projected in the v^*-direction can then be used to perform some sort of outlier removal. As to how exactly to perform this outlier removal step, there are several different techniques that we will discuss, some of which depend on particular features of the inliers.

2.2 Stability and Robust Mean Estimation

In the strong contamination model, we begin by drawing a set S of n independent samples from the true distribution. We will typically call these uncorrupted sample points *inliers*. The adversary can then select up to an ϵ-fraction of these points, changing them arbitrarily and giving our algorithm a new dataset T to work with.

For our algorithm to succeed, we want it to satisfy the fairly strong requirement that with high probability over the set S of inliers, no matter what corruptions the adversary decides to make, our algorithm when run on T will output a good approximation to the target parameter. To prove such a statement, we typically want to define a deterministic condition on S under which our algorithm is guaranteed to succeed. In particular, we will require a condition on the set of uncorrupted samples such that:

1. A sufficiently large collection S of independent samples from our inlier distribution satisfies this condition with high probability.
2. If the set S of inliers satisfies this condition, our algorithm will succeed when run on T no matter what corruptions the adversary chooses to apply.

Toward this goal, we introduce a condition called *stability* (Definition 2.1), which will form the core of our conditions on the uncorrupted samples. In particular, we will show that if the uncorrupted samples are assumed to be stable, then there is an efficiently checkable condition on the ϵ-corrupted dataset that will imply that the true mean is close to the sample mean of the corrupted (i.e., including the outliers) dataset (see Lemma 2.6). Although some algorithms presented later in this chapter (and in this book) may require stronger conditions on their inliers in order to be effective, some version of this stability condition will almost always be involved.

The robust mean estimation algorithms in this chapter will depend heavily on computing means and covariances of various sets of samples. Although additive corruptions will always have the power to induce large changes in the sample mean and covariance, we will at least want to know that any large set of inliers has close to the right value. It is this requirement that makes up the core of the stability condition.

Definition 2.1 (Stability Condition)   Fix $0 < \epsilon < 1/2$ and $\delta \geq \epsilon$. A finite set $S \subset \mathbf{R}^d$ is (ϵ, δ)-*stable* (with respect to a vector μ or a distribution X with $\mu_X := \mathbf{E}[X] = \mu$) if for every unit vector $v \in \mathbf{R}^d$ and every $S' \subseteq S$ with $|S'| \geq (1 - \epsilon)|S|$, the following conditions hold:

1. $\left| \frac{1}{|S'|} \sum_{x \in S'} v \cdot (x - \mu) \right| \leq \delta$, and
2. $\left| \frac{1}{|S'|} \sum_{x \in S'} (v \cdot (x - \mu))^2 - 1 \right| \leq \delta^2/\epsilon.$

Similarly, we say that a *distribution* X on $\mathbf{R}^d$ is (ϵ, δ)-stable with respect to a vector μ if for every unit vector $v \in \mathbf{R}^d$ and distribution X' obtained from X by ϵ-subtractive contamination, the following conditions hold:

1. $|\mathbf{E}[v \cdot (X' - \mu)]| \leq \delta$, and
2. $\left| \mathbf{E}[(v \cdot (X' - \mu))^2] - 1 \right| \leq \delta^2/\epsilon.$

Some comments are in order. The first condition (for the finite set stability condition) is equivalent to $\|\mu_{S'} - \mu\|_2 \leq \delta$, where $\mu_{S'}$ is the empirical mean of S'. The second condition is equivalent to $\|\bar{\Sigma}_{S'} - I\|_2 \leq \delta^2/\epsilon$, where $\bar{\Sigma}_{S'} = (1/|S'|) \sum_{x \in S'} (x - \mu)(x - \mu)^{\mathsf{T}}$ is the empirical second moment matrix of S' with respect to μ. Since μ is close to $\mu_{S'}$ by the first condition, this is equivalent (up to changing δ by a constant factor) to saying that $\|\mathbf{Cov}[S'] - I\|_2 = O(\delta^2/\epsilon)$.

In other words, *removing any ϵ-fraction of the points will not change the mean by more than δ nor the variance in any direction by more than δ^2/ϵ.*

It is also worth nothing that Definition 2.1 is intended for distributions X with covariance $\Sigma_X \preceq I$. If one wants to perform robust mean estimation for distributions X with other covariance matrices, one can usually reduce to this case by applying the linear transformation $x \to \Sigma_X^{-1/2} x$ to the data.

Finally, it is worth comparing the notions of stability for finite sets and distributions. While these definitions are fairly similar, we believe it is important to include both, as it is sometimes more convenient to work with one or the other. The close relationship between these two definitions will also be important to us, and can be made rigorous via the following simple lemma.

Lemma 2.2 *If S is a set of points in $\mathbf{R}^d$ and $\delta > \epsilon > 0$ with $\epsilon|S|$ an integer, then S is (ϵ, δ)-stable with respect to some vector μ if and only if the uniform distribution over S is (ϵ, δ)-stable with respect to μ.*

Proof The "only if" part here is immediate, since if S' is a subset $S' \subseteq S$ with $|S'| \geq (1 - \epsilon)|S|$, then the uniform distribution over S' can be obtained from the uniform distribution over S by ϵ-subtractive contamination. To show the reverse, we note that for a specific choice of unit vector v, if one wants to find a distribution X' for which one of conditions 1 or 2 above does not hold, one will want to remove the ϵ-fraction of the distribution on which $v \cdot (X - \mu)$ or $(v \cdot (X' - \mu))^2 - 1$ takes its most extreme values. This is equivalent to throwing away some $\epsilon|S|$ points from the support, but if S is stable, this will be insufficient to change the mean or variance by enough.   □

Although Lemma 2.2 only applies when $\epsilon|S|$ is an integer, by combining it with the results of Exercise 2.1, we find that, so long as $|S| \geq 1/\epsilon$, S is (ϵ, δ)-stable if and only if the uniform distribution over S is $(\epsilon, \Theta(\delta))$-stable.

The fact that the conditions of Definition 2.1 must hold *for every* large subset S' of S might make it unclear if they can hold with high probability. It can in fact be shown that these conditions are satisfied for various distribution classes with appropriate concentration properties. Morally speaking, if a distribution X is stable, then we would expect a large enough set S of i.i.d. samples from X to be stable (with comparable parameters) with high probability.

2.2.1 Sample Complexity Bounds for the Stability Condition

Before we explain how to leverage stability for the design of computationally efficient algorithms, we show that for some natural distributions the stability of the set of inliers can be achieved with high probability given a reasonable number of i.i.d. samples. The sample complexity bounds presented in this section are intentionally rough; the reader interested in more precise bounds is referred to Section 3.2.

We start with the class of sub-Gaussian distributions. Recall that a distribution on $\mathbf{R}^d$ is sub-Gaussian if any univariate projection has sub-Gaussian tails. For this distribution class, we can show:

Proposition 2.3 *If N is at least a sufficiently large degree polynomial in d/ϵ, then a set of N i.i.d. samples from an identity covariance sub-Gaussian distribution in $\mathbf{R}^d$ is $(\epsilon, O(\epsilon \sqrt{\log(1/\epsilon)}))$-stable with high probability.*

In order to see why this is the correct value of δ, we note that the Gaussian distribution, $X = \mathcal{N}(\mu, I)$, is $(\epsilon, O(\epsilon \sqrt{\log(1/\epsilon)}))$-stable with respect to μ. This is because removing an ϵ-fraction of the mass will have the greatest impact on $\mathbf{E}[v \cdot X]$ or $\mathbf{Var}[v \cdot X]$ if we remove the ϵ-tails of $v \cdot X$. A simple calculation shows that this affects the mean by $O(\epsilon \sqrt{\log(1/\epsilon)})$ and the variance by $O(\epsilon \log(1/\epsilon))$. This is because the ϵ-tails of the distribution are $O(\sqrt{\log(1/\epsilon)})$ far from the mean.

To help formalize this intuition, we provide a proof sketch of Proposition 2.3 here. It turns out that the optimal sample complexity in Proposition 2.3 is $\tilde{\Theta}(d/\epsilon^2)$. The reader is referred to Section 3.2 for the proof of this optimal bound.

Proof Sketch. An easy way to prove this result is by noting that it suffices for our dataset S to have the empirical distribution of $v \cdot S := \{v \cdot x, x \in S\}$ mimic the real distribution $v \cdot X$ for all unit vectors v. To formalize this, we consider thresholds. In particular, we would like it to hold for every vector v and every threshold $t \in \mathbf{R}$ that

$$|\mathbf{Pr}_{x \sim_u S}[v \cdot x > t] - \mathbf{Pr}_{x \sim X}[v \cdot x > t]| \tag{2.1}$$

should be small. By the VC Inequality (Theorem A.12), the error in Equation (2.1) is never more than η with high probability, as long as N is at least a sufficiently large constant multiple of d/η^2.

Note that the average value of $v \cdot (x - \mu)$ or $(v \cdot (x - \mu))^2$ can be computed from these tail probabilities as

$$\frac{1}{|S|} \sum_{x \in S} v \cdot (x - \mu) = \int_{v \cdot \mu}^{\infty} \mathbf{Pr}_{x \sim_u S}[v \cdot x > t] dt - \int_{-\infty}^{v \cdot \mu} \mathbf{Pr}_{x \sim_u S}[v \cdot x < t] dt,$$

and

$$\frac{1}{|S|} \sum_{x \in S} (v \cdot (x - \mu))^2 = \int_0^{\infty} 2t \, \mathbf{Pr}_{x \sim_u S}[|v \cdot x - v \cdot \mu| < t] dt.$$

Knowing that each probability above is within $O(\eta)$ of the corresponding probability for $x \sim X$ is *almost* sufficient to show that the mean and covariance of S are close to μ and $\mathbf{Cov}[X] = I$, respectively. A slight technical difficulty, however, comes from the fact that these integrals have infinite range of t, and thus an $O(\eta)$ error for each given t produces an infinite error overall. We can fix this slight glitch by noting that with high probability each $x \in S$ satisfies $\|x - \mu\|_2 < O(\sqrt{d \log(dN)})$ (for example, because each coordinate of $x - \mu$ is at most $O(\sqrt{\log(dN)})$). This observation allows us to truncate these integrals to ones of finite length and show that $\|\mu_S - \mu\|_2 = O(\eta \sqrt{d \log(dN)})$ and $\|\mathbf{Cov}[S] - I\|_2 = O(\eta d \log(dN))$.

Having established good bounds on the mean and covariance of the full set S, we next need to prove a stronger statement. We actually need to bound these quantities for S', where S' is *any* $(1 - \epsilon)$-dense subset of S. To that end, we note that

$$\left| \mathbf{Pr}_{x \sim_u S}[v \cdot x > t] - \mathbf{Pr}_{x \sim_u S'}[v \cdot x > t] \right| \le \min\{\mathbf{Pr}_{x \sim_u S}[v \cdot x > t], O(\epsilon)\}.$$

This inequality holds because removing elements can decrease a tail probability by ϵ, but cannot decrease it to less than 0. This allows us to bound the differences between the averages over S and S'. For example, we have that

$$\left| \frac{1}{|S|} \sum_{x \in S} v \cdot (x - \mu) - \frac{1}{|S'|} \sum_{x \in S'} v \cdot (x - \mu) \right|$$

$$\le \int_0^{O(\sqrt{d \log(dN)})} \min\{\mathbf{Pr}_{x \sim_u S}[v \cdot (x - \mu) > t], O(\epsilon)\} dt$$

$$+ \int_{-O(\sqrt{d \log(dN)})}^0 \min\{\mathbf{Pr}_{x \sim_u S}[v \cdot (x - \mu) < t], O(\epsilon)\} dt$$

$$\le \int_{-O(\sqrt{d \log(dN)})}^{O(\sqrt{d \log(dN)})} \min\{\exp(-\Omega(t^2)) + O(\eta), O(\epsilon)\} dt$$

$$\le O(\eta \sqrt{d \log(dN)}) + \int_{-O(\sqrt{\log(1/\epsilon)})}^{O(\sqrt{\log(1/\epsilon)})} O(\epsilon) dt + \int_{|t| \gg \sqrt{\log(1/\epsilon)}} \exp(-\Omega(t^2)) dt$$

$$\le O(\eta \sqrt{d \log(dN)}) + O(\epsilon \sqrt{\log(1/\epsilon)}).$$

This is $O(\epsilon \sqrt{\log(1/\epsilon)})$, assuming that η is sufficiently small. A similar argument can be used to bound the covariance term, and this completes our proof.   □

Note that the proof of Proposition 2.3 essentially boiled down to an argument about the tail bounds of the distribution X. Morally speaking, if X is an identity covariance distribution where the ϵ-tails in any direction contribute no more than δ to the mean and δ^2/ϵ to the variance in that direction, sufficiently many samples from X will be (ϵ, δ)-stable with high probability (see Exercise 2.4).

A more general setting considers inlier distributions with bounded and unknown covariance matrix. For this more general class of bounded covariance distributions, one can show the following.

Proposition 2.4 *Let S be a multiset of N i.i.d. samples from a distribution with covariance $\Sigma \preceq I$, where N is at least a sufficiently large degree polynomial in d/ϵ. With high probability, there exists a subset $S' \subseteq S$ of cardinality $|S'| \geq (1 - \epsilon)|S|$ such that S' is $(\epsilon, O(\sqrt{\epsilon}))$-stable.*

It is worth pointing out a qualitative difference between Proposition 2.4 and its analogue Proposition 2.3 (for identity covariance sub-Gaussian distributions). For the bounded covariance case, a sufficiently large set of i.i.d. samples S from the inlier distribution is *not* guaranteed to be stable. On the other hand, Proposition 2.4 shows that there exists a $(1 - \epsilon)$ density, stable subset S' (this still suffices for our purposes, as T, the set of corrupted samples, will be an $O(\epsilon)$-corruption of S'). This relaxation is necessary as there are simple examples where the proposition fails if we do not consider such subsets (see Exercise 2.3).

To see why Proposition 2.4 holds, we note that in order for a set S to be $(\epsilon, O(\sqrt{\epsilon}))$-stable with respect to μ, it suffices to check that $\|\mu_S - \mu\|_2 = O(\sqrt{\epsilon})$ and $\mathbf{Cov}[S] = O(I)$. We note that all but an ϵ-fraction of the mass of a bounded covariance distribution is within distance $O(\sqrt{d/\epsilon})$ of its mean μ. Moreover, if we throw away the points further away, this does not affect the mean by much. Letting S' be the set of samples not too far from the mean μ will have roughly the correct mean and covariance matrix with high probability.

The reader is referred to Section 3.2 for a proof of this result with the optimal sample complexity, which turns out to be $\tilde{\Theta}(d/\epsilon)$.

Remark 2.5 Analogous bounds can be shown for identity covariance distributions with bounded higher central moments. For example, if our distribution has identity covariance and its kth central moment, where $k \geq 4$, is bounded from above by a constant, it can be shown that a set of $\Omega(d \log(d)/\epsilon^{2-2/k})$ samples contains a large subset that is $(\epsilon, O(\epsilon^{1-1/k}))$-stable with high probability.

2.2.2 Stability and Algorithm Design

We now return to the use of the stability condition in algorithm design. In particular, we show how one can certify – under certain conditions – that the sample mean of an ϵ-corrupted version of a stable set is a good approximation to the true mean. This is perhaps the most important property of stability for us and can be quantified in the following lemma.

Lemma 2.6 (Certificate for Empirical Mean) *Let S be an (ϵ, δ)-stable set with respect to a vector μ, for some $\delta \geq \epsilon > 0$ and $\epsilon \leq 1/3$. Let T be an ϵ-corrupted version of S. Let μ_T and Σ_T be the empirical mean and covariance of T. If the largest eigenvalue of Σ_T is at most $1 + \lambda$, for some $\lambda \geq 0$, then $\|\mu_T - \mu\|_2 \leq O(\delta + \sqrt{\epsilon\lambda})$.*

This lemma states that if our set of inliers S is stable and our set of corrupted samples T has bounded covariance, then the empirical mean of T is certifiably close to the true mean.

Lemma 2.6 follows by applying the following slightly more general statement to the uniform distribution over S.

Lemma 2.7 (Certificate for Empirical Mean, Strong Version) *Let X be an (ϵ, δ)-stable distribution with respect to a vector μ, for some $\delta \geq \epsilon > 0$ and $\epsilon \leq 1/3$. Let Y be a distribution with $d_{\mathrm{TV}}(X, Y) \leq \epsilon$ (i.e., Y is an ϵ-corrupted version of X). Denote by μ_Y and Σ_Y the mean and covariance of Y. If the largest eigenvalue of Σ_Y is at most $1 + \lambda$, for some $\lambda \geq 0$, then $\|\mu_Y - \mu\|_2 \leq O(\delta + \sqrt{\epsilon\lambda})$.*

Proof of Lemma 2.7 Let $Y = (1 - \epsilon)X' + \epsilon E$ for some distribution X' obtained from X by ϵ-subtractive contamination. Let $\mu_X, \mu_{X'}, \mu_E$ and $\Sigma_X, \Sigma_{X'}, \Sigma_E$ denote the means and covariances of X, X', and E, respectively. A simple calculation gives

$$\Sigma_Y = (1 - \epsilon)\Sigma_{X'} + \epsilon\Sigma_E + \epsilon(1 - \epsilon)(\mu_{X'} - \mu_E)(\mu_{X'} - \mu_E)^\mathsf{T}.$$

Let v be the unit vector in the direction of $\mu_{X'} - \mu_E$. We have

$$1 + \lambda \geq v^\mathsf{T}\Sigma_Y v = (1 - \epsilon)v^\mathsf{T}\Sigma_{X'}v + \epsilon v^\mathsf{T}\Sigma_E v + \epsilon(1 - \epsilon)v^\mathsf{T}(\mu_{X'} - \mu_E)(\mu_{X'} - \mu_E)^\mathsf{T}v$$
$$\geq (1 - \epsilon)(1 - \delta^2/\epsilon) + \epsilon(1 - \epsilon)\|\mu_{X'} - \mu_E\|_2^2$$
$$\geq 1 - O(\delta^2/\epsilon) + (\epsilon/2)\|\mu_{X'} - \mu_E\|_2^2,$$

where we used the variational characterization of eigenvalues, the fact that Σ_E is positive semidefinite, and the second stability condition for X. By rearranging, we obtain $\|\mu_{X'} - \mu_E\|_2 = O(\delta/\epsilon + \sqrt{\lambda/\epsilon})$. Therefore, we can write

$$\|\mu_Y - \mu\|_2 = \|(1 - \epsilon)\mu_{X'} + \epsilon\mu_E - \mu\|_2 = \|\mu_{X'} - \mu + \epsilon(\mu_E - \mu_{X'})\|_2$$
$$\leq \|\mu_{X'} - \mu\|_2 + \epsilon\|\mu_{X'} - \mu_E\|_2 = O(\delta) + \epsilon \cdot O(\delta/\epsilon + \sqrt{\lambda/\epsilon})$$
$$= O(\delta + \sqrt{\lambda\epsilon}),$$

where we used the first stability condition for X and our obtained upper bound on $\|\mu_{X'} - \mu_E\|_2$. □

Remark 2.8 It is worth noting that the proof of Lemma 2.7 only used the lower bound part in the second condition of Definition 2.1, namely, that the variance of X' in each direction is *at least* $1 - \delta^2/\epsilon$. Although this is sufficient for certifying that our mean is close, the corresponding upper bound will be crucially used in the design and analysis of our robust mean estimation algorithms in the following sections.

Lemma 2.6 says that if our input set of points T is an ϵ-corrupted version of any stable set S and has bounded covariance, the sample mean of T closely approximates the true mean of the original distribution. This lemma, or a variant thereof, is a key result in all known robust mean estimation algorithms.

Unfortunately, we are not always guaranteed that the set T we are given has this property. In particular, if the corrupted set T includes some large outliers, or many outliers in the same direction, there may well be directions of large variance. In order to deal with this, we will want to compute a subset, T', of T such that T' has bounded covariance and large intersection with S. If we can achieve this, then since T' will be a corrupted version of S with bounded covariance, we can apply Lemma 2.6 to show that $\|\mu_{T'} - \mu\|_2$ is small.

For some of the algorithms presented, it will be convenient to find a probability distribution over T rather than a subset. For these cases, we can use Lemma 2.7 applied to the appropriate distribution on T.

For the more general outlier removal procedure, we are given our initial ϵ-corrupted set T, and we will attempt to find a distribution W supported on T such that the "weighted" covariance matrix Σ_W has no large eigenvalues. For such a solution, the weight $W(x)$ of an $x \in T$ can be thought of as quantifying our belief about whether point x is an inlier or an outlier. It will also be important for us to ensure that W is close to the uniform distribution over S in total variation distance. This is complicated by the fact that we must be able to guarantee this closeness without knowing exactly what the set S is. Intuitively, we can do this by ensuring that W is obtained by removing at most ϵ mass from the uniform distribution over T.

More concretely, the following general framework can be used for robust mean estimation.

Definition 2.9 For a finite set T and $\epsilon \in (0, 1)$, we will denote by Δ^T the set of all probability distributions W supported on T, whose probability mass function $W(x)$ satisfies $W(x) \leq \frac{1}{|T|(1-\epsilon)}$, for all $x \in T$.

Lemma 2.10 *Let S be a $(3\epsilon, \delta)$-stable set with respect to μ and let T be an ϵ-corrupted version of S for some $\epsilon < 1/6$. Given any $W \in \Delta^T$ such that $\|\Sigma_W\|_2 \leq 1 + \lambda$, for some $\lambda \geq 0$, we have $\|\mu - \mu_W\|_2 = O(\delta + \sqrt{\epsilon \lambda})$.*

Proof We note that *any* distribution in Δ^T differs from U_S, the uniform distribution on S, by at most 3ϵ. Indeed, for $\epsilon \leq 1/3$, we have

$$
\begin{aligned}
d_{\mathrm{TV}}(U_S, W) &= \sum_{x \in T} \max\{W(x) - U_S(x), 0\} \\
&= \sum_{x \in S \cap T} \max\{W(x) - 1/|T|, 0\} + \sum_{x \in T \setminus S} W(x) \\
&\leq \sum_{x \in S \cap T} \frac{\epsilon}{|T|(1 - \epsilon)} + \sum_{x \in T \setminus S} \frac{1}{|T|(1 - \epsilon)} \\
&\leq |T| \left(\frac{\epsilon}{|T|(1 - \epsilon)} \right) + \epsilon |T| \left(\frac{1}{|T|(1 - \epsilon)} \right) \\
&= \frac{2\epsilon}{1 - \epsilon} \leq 3\epsilon.
\end{aligned}
$$

Therefore, by Lemma 2.7 we have $\|\mu - \mu_W\|_2 = O(\delta + \sqrt{\epsilon \lambda})$. $\qquad\square$

Lemma 2.10 provides us with a clear plan for how to perform robust mean estimation. Given a set T (promised to be an ϵ-corruption of a $(3\epsilon, \delta)$-stable set), we merely need to find a $W \in \Delta^T$ with bounded covariance matrix.

A natural first question is whether such a distribution W exists. Fortunately, this can be easily guaranteed. In particular, if we take W to be W^*, the uniform distribution over $S \cap T$, the largest eigenvalue is at most $1 + \delta^2/\epsilon$ by the stability of S. Thus, for this choice of W, we can take $\lambda = \delta^2/\epsilon$, and we have $\|\mu - \mu_{W^*}\|_2 = O(\delta)$.

At this point, we have an *inefficient* algorithm for approximating μ: Find any $W \in \Delta^T$ with Σ_W bounded above by $(1 + \delta^2/\epsilon)I$ and return its mean. The remaining question is *how we can efficiently find* such a W. There are two basic algorithmic techniques to achieve this, which we present in the subsequent sections.

The first algorithmic technique we will describe is based on convex programming. We will call this *the unknown convex programming method*. Note that Δ^T is a convex set and that finding a point in Δ^T that has bounded covariance is *almost* a convex program. It is not quite a convex program because the variance of $v \cdot W$, for fixed v, is not a convex function of W. However, one can show that given a W with variance in some direction significantly larger than $1 + \delta^2/\epsilon$, we can efficiently construct a hyperplane separating W from W^* (the uniform distribution over $S \cap T$). This method works naturally under only the stability condition. On the other hand, as it relies on the ellipsoid algorithm, it is quite slow (although polynomial time). See Section 2.3 for more details.

Our second technique, which we will call *(iterative) filtering*, is an iterative outlier removal method that is typically faster, as it relies only on spectral techniques. The main idea of the method is the following: If Σ_W does not have large eigenvalues, then the empirical mean is close to the true mean. Otherwise, there is some unit vector v such that $\mathbf{Var}[v \cdot W]$ is substantially larger than it should be. This can only be the case if W assigns substantial mass to elements of $T \setminus S$ that have values of $v \cdot x$ very far from the true mean of $v \cdot \mu$. This observation allows us to perform some kind of outlier removal, in particular by removing (or down-weighting) the points x that have $v \cdot x$ inappropriately large.

An important conceptual point here is that one cannot afford to remove only outliers. However, it is possible to ensure that more outliers are removed than inliers. Given a W where Σ_W has a large eigenvalue, one filtering step gives a new distribution $W' \in \Delta^T$ that is closer to W^* than W was. Repeating the process eventually gives a W with no large eigenvalues. The filtering method and its variations are discussed in Section 2.4.

2.3 The Unknown Convex Programming Method

Given an ϵ-corruption T of a stable set S, we would like to estimate the mean of the corresponding distribution X. To achieve this, by Lemma 2.10, it suffices to find a distribution $W \in \Delta^T$ such that Σ_W has no large eigenvalues. We note that this condition *almost* defines a convex program. This is because Δ^T is a convex set of probability distributions and the bounded covariance condition says that $\mathbf{Var}[v \cdot W] \leq 1 + \lambda$ for all unit vectors v. Unfortunately, the variance $\mathbf{Var}[v \cdot W] = \mathbf{E}[|v \cdot (W - \mu_W)|^2]$ is not quite linear in W. (If we instead had $\mathbf{E}[|v \cdot (W - \mu_0)|^2]$, for some fixed vector μ_0, this *would* be linear in W.) However, we will show that a unit vector v for which $\mathbf{Var}[v \cdot W]$ is too large can still be used to obtain a separation oracle, that is, a linear function L for which $L(W) > L(W^*)$, where W^* is the uniform distribution over $S \cap T$.

In particular, suppose that we identify a unit vector v such that $\mathbf{Var}[v \cdot W] = 1 + \lambda$, where $\lambda > C(\delta^2/\epsilon)$ for a sufficiently large universal constant $C > 0$. Applying Lemma 2.10 to the one-dimensional projection $v \cdot W$ gives

$$|v \cdot (\mu_W - \mu_X)| \leq O(\delta + \sqrt{\epsilon\lambda}) = O(\sqrt{\epsilon\lambda}).$$

For a probability distribution Y, let $L(Y) := \mathbf{E}[|v \cdot (Y - \mu_W)|^2]$. Note that L is a linear function of the probability distribution Y with $L(W) = 1 + \lambda$. We can write

$$L(W^*) = \mathbf{E}_{W^*}[|v \cdot (W^* - \mu_W)|^2] = \mathbf{Var}[v \cdot W^*] + |v \cdot (\mu_W - \mu_{W^*})|^2$$
$$\leq 1 + \delta^2/\epsilon + 2|v \cdot (\mu_W - \mu_X)|^2 + 2|v \cdot (\mu_{W^*} - \mu_X)|^2$$
$$\leq 1 + O(\delta^2/\epsilon + \epsilon\lambda) < 1 + \lambda = L(W).$$

In summary, we have an explicit convex set Δ^T of probability distributions from which we want to find one with eigenvalues bounded by $1 + O(\delta^2/\epsilon)$. Given any $W \in \Delta^T$ which does not satisfy this condition, we can produce a linear function L that separates W from W^*. In fact, it is not hard to see that L also separates W from some small neighborhood R of W^*. Using the ellipsoid algorithm, we obtain the following general theorem.

Theorem 2.11 *Let S be a $(3\epsilon, \delta)$-stable set with respect to a distribution X for some $\epsilon > 0$ sufficiently small. Let T be an ϵ-corrupted version of S. There exists a polynomial time algorithm which given ϵ, δ, and T returns $\widehat{\mu}$ such that $\|\widehat{\mu} - \mu_X\|_2 = O(\delta)$.*

Proof Sketch. Simply run the ellipsoid algorithm with the above separation oracle. At each stage one of two things happens. On the one hand, we may have found a $W \in \Delta^T$ with $\mathbf{Cov}[W] \preceq (1 + O(\delta^2/\epsilon)) I$. In this case, $\mathbf{E}[W]$ is an appropriate approximation of μ_X by Lemma 2.10. Otherwise, we find a separation oracle L, separating W from R. This lets us find a smaller ellipsoid containing R. As the volume of this ellipsoid decreases by a $(1 - \text{poly}(1/d))$-factor at every iteration, after at most a polynomial number of rounds the ellipsoid will be smaller than R. This shows that we must reach the first case after at most a polynomial number of iterations, and thus our algorithm will run in polynomial time. □

Implications for Concrete Distribution Families Combining Theorem 2.11 with corresponding stability bounds, we obtain concrete applications for various distribution families of interest. Using Proposition 2.3, we obtain:

Corollary 2.12 (Identity Covariance Sub-Gaussian Distributions) *Let T be a set of N ϵ-corrupted samples from an identity covariance sub-Gaussian distribution X on $\mathbf{R}^d$, where N is at least a sufficiently large polynomial in d/ϵ. There exists a polynomial time algorithm which given ϵ and T returns $\widehat{\mu}$ such that with high probability $\|\widehat{\mu} - \mu_X\|_2 = O(\epsilon \sqrt{\log(1/\epsilon)})$.*

We note that Corollary 2.12 can be immediately adapted for identity covariance distributions satisfying weaker concentration assumptions. For example, if X satisfies subexponential concentration in each direction, we obtain an efficient robust mean estimation algorithm with ℓ_2-error of $O(\epsilon \log(1/\epsilon))$. If X has identity covariance and bounded kth central moments, $k \geq 2$, we obtain error $O(\epsilon^{1-1/k})$. As shown in Chapter 1, these error bounds are information-theoretically optimal up to constant factors.

For distributions with unknown and bounded covariance, using Proposition 2.4 we obtain:

Corollary 2.13 (Unknown Bounded Covariance Distributions) *Let T be a set of N ϵ-corrupted samples from a distribution X on $\mathbf{R}^d$ with unknown covariance $\Sigma_X \preceq \sigma^2 I$, for some known $\sigma > 0$, where N is at least a sufficiently large polynomial in d/ϵ. There exists a polynomial time algorithm which given ϵ, σ, and T returns $\widehat{\mu}$ such that with high probability $\|\widehat{\mu} - \mu_X\|_2 = O(\sigma \sqrt{\epsilon})$.*

Similarly, as shown in Chapter 1, this error bound is information-theoretically optimal up to constant factors.

2.4 The Filtering Method

As in the unknown convex programming method, the goal of the filtering method is to find a distribution $W \in \Delta^T$ such that Σ_W has bounded eigenvalues. Given a $W \in \Delta^T$, Σ_W either has bounded eigenvalues (in which case the weighted empirical mean works) or there is a direction v in which $\mathbf{Var}[v \cdot W]$ is too large. In the latter case, the projections $v \cdot W$ must behave very differently from the projections $v \cdot S$ or $v \cdot X$. In particular, since an ϵ-fraction of outliers are causing a much larger increase in the standard deviation, this means that the distribution of $v \cdot W$ will have many "extreme points" – more than one would expect to find in $v \cdot S$. This fact allows us to identify a nonempty subset of extreme points, the majority of which are outliers. These points can then be removed (or down-weighted) in order to "clean up" our sample. Formally, given a $W \in \Delta^T$ without bounded eigenvalues, we can efficiently find a $W' \in \Delta^T$ such that W' is closer to W^* than W was. Iterating this procedure eventually terminates giving a W with bounded eigenvalues.

While it may be conceptually useful to consider the above scheme for general distributions W over points, in most cases it suffices to consider only W given as the uniform distribution over some set of points. The filtering step in this case consists of replacing the set T by some subset $T' = T \setminus R$, where $R \subset T$. To guarantee progress toward W^* (the uniform distribution over $S \cap T$), it suffices to ensure that at most a third of the elements of R are also in S, or equivalently that at least two-thirds of the removed points are outliers (perhaps in expectation). The algorithm will terminate when the current set of points T' has bounded empirical covariance, and the output will be the empirical mean of T'.

Before we proceed with a more detailed technical discussion, we note that there are several possible ways to implement the filtering step, and that the method used has a significant impact on the analysis. In general, a filtering step removes all points that are "far" from the sample mean in a large variance direction. However, the precise way that this is quantified can vary in important ways.

2.4.1 Tail-Bound-Based Filtering

In this section, we present a filtering method that yields efficient robust mean estimators with optimal error bounds for identity covariance (or, more generally, known covariance) distributions whose univariate projections satisfy appropriate tail bounds. For the purposes of this section, we will restrict ourselves to the Gaussian setting. We note however that this method immediately extends to distributions with weaker concentration properties, for example, subexponential or even inverse polynomial concentration, with appropriate modifications.

We note that the filtering method presented here requires an additional condition on our set of inlier samples, on top of the stability condition. This is quantified in the following definition.

Definition 2.14   A set $S \subset \mathbf{R}^d$ is *tail-bound-good (with respect to $X = \mathcal{N}(\mu_X, I)$)* if for every unit vector v and every $t > 0$, we have

$$\mathbf{Pr}_{x \sim_u S} \left[|v \cdot (x - \mu_X)| > 2t + 2 \right] \leq e^{-t^2/2}. \tag{2.2}$$

Since any univariate projection of X is distributed like a standard Gaussian, Condition (2.2) should hold if the uniform distribution over S were replaced by X. It can be shown that this condition holds with high probability if S is a set of i.i.d. samples from X of a sufficiently large size. Unfortunately, the sample size required for this condition to hold can be exponential in the dimension. In the rest of this section, to avoid cluttering in the relevant expressions, we develop and analyze our filtering algorithm under this condition. We will then explain (see Remark 2.16) how a simple modification to Definition 2.14 suffices for our algorithm to work and will be satisfied with a polynomial sample size.

Intuitively, the additional tail condition of Definition 2.14 means that the univariate projections of our inlier set satisfy strong tail bounds. If we can find a direction in which one of these tails bounds are substantially violated, we will know that most of the extreme points in this direction must be outliers. Formally, we have the following:

Lemma 2.15 *Let $\epsilon > 0$ be a sufficiently small constant. Let $S \subset \mathbf{R}^d$ be both $(2\epsilon, \delta)$-stable and tail-bound-good with respect to $X = \mathcal{N}(\mu_X, I)$, with $\delta = C\epsilon\sqrt{\log(1/\epsilon)}$, for $C > 0$ a sufficiently large constant. Let $T \subset \mathbf{R}^d$ be such that $|T \cap S| \geq (1 - 2\epsilon)\max(|T|, |S|)$ and assume we are given a unit vector $v \in \mathbf{R}^d$ for which $\mathbf{Var}[v \cdot T] > 1 + 2\delta^2/\epsilon$ and $\mathbf{Var}[v \cdot T] > \|\mathbf{Cov}[T]\|_2 - \epsilon$. There exists a polynomial-time algorithm that returns a subset $R \subset T$ satisfying $|R \cap S| < |R|/3$.*

To see why Lemma 2.15 suffices for our purposes, note that by replacing T by $T' = T \setminus R$, we obtain a less noisy version of S than T was. In particular, it is easy to see that the size of the symmetric difference between S and T' is strictly smaller than the size of the symmetric difference between S and T. From this it follows that the hypothesis $|T \cap S| \geq (1 - 2\epsilon)\max(|T|, |S|)$ still holds when T is replaced by T', allowing us to iterate this process until we are left with a set with small variance.

Proof Let $\mathbf{Var}[v \cdot T] = 1 + \lambda$. Our goal will be to compute some threshold L such that the substantial majority of the samples x with $|v \cdot (x - \mu_T)| > L$ are outliers, as is shown in Figure 2.3. This ought to be possible since by assumption

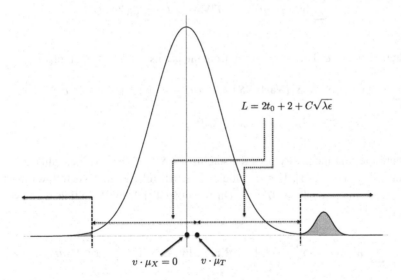

Figure 2.3 Illustration of tail-bound-based filtering. The figure shows the graph of $v \cdot x$ for samples x, with the bump on the right representing the error distribution. The grayed out portions represent the points with $|v \cdot (x - \mu_T)| > L$ that are removed by the filtering algorithm. Notice that the majority of these points are outliers.

the inliers are well-concentrated about the mean. On the other hand, we must have many faraway outliers in order to cause $\mathbf{Var}[v \cdot T]$ so large.

We know that since the set S is tail-bound-good, the univariate projection $v \cdot S$ is well-concentrated about $v \cdot \mu_X$. Unfortunately, the algorithm only knows μ_T. However, applying Lemma 2.6 to the set T (and noting that $\|\mathbf{Cov}[T]\|_2 \leq 1 + O(\lambda)$), we get that $|v \cdot \mu_X - v \cdot \mu_T| \leq C\sqrt{\lambda\epsilon}$. Thus, by Condition (2.2),

$$\mathbf{Pr}_{x \sim_u S}\left[|v \cdot (x - \mu_T)| > 2t + 2 + C\sqrt{\lambda\epsilon}\right] \leq e^{-t^2/2}.$$

We claim that there exists a threshold t_0 such that

$$\mathbf{Pr}_{x \sim_u T}\left[|v \cdot (x - \mu_T)| > 2t_0 + 2 + C\sqrt{\lambda\epsilon}\right] > 4e^{-t_0^2/2}. \qquad (2.3)$$

Given this claim, the set $R = \{x \in T : |v \cdot (x - \mu_T)| > 2t_0 + 2 + C\sqrt{\lambda\epsilon}\}$ will satisfy the conditions of the lemma.

To prove our claim, we analyze the variance of $v \cdot T$ and note that much of the excess must be due to points in $T \setminus S$. In particular, by our assumption on the variance in the v-direction, we have that

$$\sum_{x \in T} |v \cdot (x - \mu_T)|^2 = |T|\mathbf{Var}[v \cdot T] = |T|(1 + \lambda),$$

where $\lambda > 2\delta^2/\epsilon$. The contribution from the points $x \in S \cap T$ is at most

$$\sum_{x \in S} |v \cdot (x - \mu_T)|^2 = |S|\left(\mathbf{Var}[v \cdot S] + |v \cdot (\mu_T - \mu_S)|^2\right) \leq |S|(1 + \delta^2/\epsilon + 2C^2\lambda\epsilon)$$

$$\leq |T|(1 + 2C^2\lambda\epsilon + 3\lambda/5),$$

where the first inequality uses the stability of S, and the last inequality uses that $|T| \geq (1 - 2\epsilon)|S|$. If ϵ is sufficiently small relative to C, it follows that $\sum_{x \in T \setminus S} |v \cdot (x - \mu_T)|^2 \geq |T|\lambda/3$. On the other hand, by definition we have that

$$\sum_{x \in T \setminus S} |v \cdot (x - \mu_T)|^2 = |T| \int_0^\infty 2t\mathbf{Pr}_{x \sim_u T}\left[|v \cdot (x - \mu_T)| > t, x \notin S\right] dt. \qquad (2.4)$$

Assume for the sake of contradiction that there is no t_0 for which Condition (2.3) is satisfied. Then the RHS of (2.4) is at most

$$|T| \left(\int_0^{2+C\sqrt{\lambda\epsilon}+10\sqrt{\log(1/\epsilon)}} 2t \mathbf{Pr}_{x \sim_u T} [x \notin S] dt \right.$$

$$\left. + \int_{2+C\sqrt{\lambda\epsilon}+10\sqrt{\log(1/\epsilon)}}^{\infty} 2t \mathbf{Pr}_{x \sim_u T} [|v \cdot (x - \mu_T)| > t] dt \right)$$

$$\leq |T| \left(\epsilon(2 + C\sqrt{\lambda\epsilon} + 10\sqrt{\log(1/\epsilon)})^2 + \int_{5\sqrt{\log(1/\epsilon)}}^{\infty} 16(2t + 2 + C\sqrt{\lambda\epsilon}) e^{-t^2/2} dt \right)$$

$$\leq |T| \left(O(C^2\lambda\epsilon^2 + \epsilon\log(1/\epsilon)) + O(\epsilon^2(\sqrt{\log(1/\epsilon)} + C\sqrt{\lambda\epsilon})) \right)$$

$$\leq |T| O(C^2\lambda\epsilon^2 + (\delta^2/\epsilon)/C) < |T|\lambda/3,$$

which is a contradiction. Therefore, the tail bounds and the concentration violation together imply the existence of such a t_0 (which can be efficiently computed by simple enumeration). □

Remark 2.16 We note that although exponentially many samples are required to ensure that Condition (2.2) holds with high probability, one can carefully weaken this condition so that it can be achieved with polynomially many samples without breaking the aforementioned analysis. Specifically, it suffices to add an inverse polynomially small slack term in the right-hand side to account for the difference between the empirical and population values of the corresponding probability. Using the VC Inequality (Theorem A.12), one can show that this weaker condition holds for the uniform distribution over S with high probability, where S is a set of i.i.d. samples from X of a sufficiently large polynomial size. This slightly alters the analysis, as one needs to add this slack term to all of the relevant probability integrals. However, these integrals can still be truncated to cover only a polynomial range (using the fact that likely no inliers will be too far from the true mean), and thus the total integral of this additional error will remain small.

2.4.2 Randomized and Weighted Filtering

The filtering method described in Section 2.4.1 works by guaranteeing that (assuming the set of inliers is stable and tail-bound-good) each filtering step removes more outliers than inliers. For some of the more general settings one instead requires a randomized filtering method that merely removes more outliers *in expectation*. In this section, we will develop the general theory of such randomized filters. This will then be applied in Section 2.4.3, where we produce a specific randomized filter that works assuming only the stability of the set of inliers.

Randomized Filtering The tail-bound-based filtering method of the previous section is deterministic, relying on the violation of a concentration inequality satisfied by the inliers. In some settings (such as robust estimation of the mean of a bounded covariance distribution), deterministic filtering seems to fail to give optimal results, and we require the filtering procedure to be randomized.

The main idea of randomized filtering is simple: Suppose we can identify a nonnegative function $f(x)$, defined on the samples x, for which (under some high probability condition on the inliers) it holds that $\sum_T f(x) \geq 2 \sum_S f(x)$, where T is an ϵ-corrupted set of samples and S is the corresponding set of inliers. Then we can create a randomized filter by removing each sample point $x \in T$ with probability proportional to $f(x)$. This ensures that the *expected* number of outliers removed is at least the *expected* number of inliers removed. The analysis of such a randomized filter is slightly more subtle, so we will discuss it in the following paragraphs.

The key property the above randomized filter ensures is that the sequence of random variables

(# Inliers removed) − (# Outliers removed)

(where "inliers" are points in S and "outliers" points in $T \setminus S$) across iterations is a supermartingale. Since the total number of outliers removed across all iterations accounts for at most an ϵ-fraction of the total samples, this means that with probability at least $2/3$, at no point does the algorithm remove more than a 2ϵ-fraction of the inliers. A formal statement follows.

Theorem 2.17 (Randomized Filtering) *Let $S \subset \mathbf{R}^d$ be a $(4\epsilon, \delta)$-stable set with respect to some distribution X, for $\epsilon < 1/12$, and let T be an ϵ-corrupted version of S. Suppose that given any $T' \subseteq T$ with $|T' \cap S| \geq (1 - 4\epsilon)|S|$ for which $\mathbf{Cov}[T']$ has an eigenvalue bigger than $1 + \lambda$, for some $\lambda \geq 0$, there is a polynomial-time algorithm that computes a nonzero function $f : T' \to \mathbf{R}_+$ such that $\sum_{x \in T'} f(x) \geq 2 \sum_{x \in T' \cap S} f(x)$. Then there exists a polynomial-time randomized algorithm that given T computes a vector $\widehat{\mu}$ that with probability at least $2/3$ satisfies $\|\widehat{\mu} - \mu_X\|_2 = O(\delta + \sqrt{\epsilon\lambda})$.*

The algorithm is described in pseudocode below:

Algorithm Randomized-Filtering

1. Compute $\mathbf{Cov}[T]$ and its largest eigenvalue ν.
2. If $\nu \leq 1 + \lambda$, return $\mu_T = (1/|T|) \sum_{x \in T} x$.
3. Else

   - Compute f as guaranteed in the theorem statement.
   - Remove each $x \in T$ with probability $f(x)/\max_{x \in T} f(x)$ and return to Step 1 with the new set T.

Proof of Theorem 2.17 First, it is easy to see that this algorithm runs in polynomial time. Indeed, as the point $x \in T$ attaining the maximum value of $f(x)$ is definitely removed in each filtering iteration, each iteration reduces $|T|$ by at least one. To establish correctness, we will show that, with probability at least $2/3$, it holds throughout the algorithm that $|S \cap T| \geq (1 - 4\epsilon)|S|$. Assuming this claim, Lemma 2.6 implies that our final error will be as desired.

To prove the desired claim, we consider the sequence of random variables

$$d(T_i) := |(S \cap T) \setminus T_i| + |T_i \setminus S|,$$

where T_i denotes the version of T after the ith iteration of our algorithm. Note that $d(T_i)$ is essentially the number of remaining outliers plus the number of inliers that our algorithm has removed so far. We note that, initially, $d(T_0) \leq \epsilon|S|$ and that $d(T_i)$ cannot drop below 0. Finally, we note that at each stage of the algorithm $d(T_i)$ increases by (# Inliers removed) − (# Outliers removed), and that the expectation of this quantity is

$$\sum_{x \in S \cap T_i} f(x) - \sum_{x \in T_i \setminus S} f(x) = 2 \sum_{x \in S \cap T_i} f(x) - \sum_{x \in T_i} f(x) \leq 0.$$

This means that the sequence of random variables $d(T_i)$ is a supermartingale (at least until we reach a point where $|S \cap T| \leq (1 - 4\epsilon)|S|$). However, if we set a stopping time at the first occasion where this condition fails, we note that the expectation of $d(T_i)$ is at most $\epsilon|S|$. Since it is always at least 0, Proposition A.5 implies that with probability at least $2/3$ it is never more than $3\epsilon|S|$, which in turn implies that $|S \cap T| \geq (1 - 4\epsilon)|S|$ throughout the algorithm. If this is the case, the inequality $|T' \cap S| \geq (1 - 4\epsilon)|S|$ will continue to hold throughout our algorithm, thus eventually yielding such a set with the variance of T' bounded. By Lemma 2.6, the mean of this subset T' will be a suitable estimate for the true mean, completing the proof of Theorem 2.17. □

Methods of Point Removal The randomized filtering method described above only requires that each point x is removed with probability $f(x)/ \max_{x \in T} f(x)$, without any assumption of independence. Therefore, given an f, there are several ways to implement this scheme. A few natural ones are given here:

- *Randomized Thresholding:* Perhaps the easiest method for implementing our randomized filter is generating a uniform random number y in the interval $[0, \max_{x \in T} f(x)]$ and removing all points $x \in T$ for which $f(x) \geq y$. This method is practically useful in many applications. Finding the set of such points is often fairly easy, as this condition may well correspond to a simple threshold.

- *Independent Removal:* Each $x \in T$ is removed independently with probability $f(x)/\max_{x \in T} f(x)$. This scheme has the advantage of leading to less variance in $d(T)$. A careful analysis of the random walk involved allows one to reduce the failure probability to $\exp(-\Omega(\epsilon|S|))$ (see Exercise 2.11).

- *Deterministic Reweighting:* Instead of removing points, this scheme allows for weighted sets of points. In particular, each point will be assigned a weight in $[0, 1]$, and we will consider weighted means and covariances. Instead of removing a point x with probability proportional to $f(x)$, we can multiplicatively reduce the weight assigned to x by a quantity proportional to $f(x)$. This ensures that the appropriate weighted version of $d(T)$ is definitely nonincreasing, implying deterministic correctness of the algorithm.

Weighted Filtering The last of the aforementioned methods being deterministic is useful in some settings, and so the algorithm is worth explicitly stating. To begin, for a weight function $w: T \to \mathbf{R}_+$, we define the weighted mean and covariance of T by

$$\mu_w[T] := \frac{1}{\|w\|_1} \sum_{x \in T} w_x x,$$

$$\mathbf{Cov}_w[T] := \frac{1}{\|w\|_1} \sum_{x \in T} w_x (x - \mu_w)(x - \mu_w)^\top.$$

One can observe that these quantities are simply the mean and covariance of the probability distribution on T that assigns each point $x \in T$ probability of $w_x / \|w\|_1$.

With this setup, we have the following theorem, a direct analogue of Theorem 2.17.

Theorem 2.18 (Weighted Filtering) *Let $S \subset \mathbf{R}^d$ be a $(4\epsilon, \delta)$-stable set with respect to some distribution X, for $\epsilon < 1/12$, and let T be an ϵ-corrupted version of S. Suppose that for any weight vector $w: T \to \mathbf{R}_+$ for which the corresponding probability distribution is (3ϵ)-close to the uniform distribution on S in total variation distance and for which $\mathbf{Cov}_w[T]$ has an eigenvalue larger than $1 + \lambda$, for some $\lambda \geq 0$, there is a polynomial-time algorithm that computes a nonzero function $f: T \to \mathbf{R}_+$ such that $\sum_{x \in S \cap T} w_x f(x) \leq (1/2) \sum_{x \in T} w_x f(x)$. Then there exists a polynomial-time algorithm that outputs a vector $\widehat{\mu}$ which with probability at least $2/3$ satisfies $\|\widehat{\mu} - \mu_X\|_2 = O(\delta + \sqrt{\epsilon\lambda})$.*

Proof The algorithm is described in pseudocode below.

Algorithm Weighted-Filtering

1. Set $t = 1$ and $w_x^{(1)} = 1/|T|$ for all $x \in T$.
2. While $\mathbf{Cov}_{w^{(t)}}[T]$ has an eigenvalue larger than $1 + \lambda$:
   1. Compute a weight function $f(x)$ as described above.
   2. Let $f_{\max}$ be the maximum value of $f(x)$ over $x \in T$ with $w_x^{(t)} \neq 0$.
   3. Let $w_x^{(t+1)} = w_x^{(t)}(1 - f(x)/f_{\max})$. Set t to $t + 1$.
3. Return $\mu_{w^{(t)}}$.

To analyze this algorithm we make the following observations. First, at each iteration, the support of w decreases by at least 1, as $w_x^{(t+1)} = 0$ for x with $f(x) = f_{\max}$. This implies that the algorithm will terminate after polynomially many iterations.

To prove correctness, as long as the distribution defined by $w^{(t)}$ is close to the uniform distribution on S, we have that

$$\sum_{x \in S \cap T} w_x^{(t+1)} = \sum_{x \in S \cap T} [w_x^{(t)} - w_x^{(t)} f(x)/f_{\max}] = \sum_{x \in S \cap T} w_x^{(t)} - (1/f_{\max}) \sum_{x \in S \cap T} w_x^{(t)} f(x)$$

$$\geq \sum_{x \in S \cap T} w_x^{(t)} - \frac{1}{2}(1/f_{\max}) \sum_{x \in T} w_x^{(t)} f(x),$$

where the first equality follows from the definition of $w_x^{(t+1)}$ and the inequality follows from the definition of f. On the other hand, we can write

$$\sum_{x \in T} w_x^{(t+1)} = \sum_{x \in T} [w_x^{(t)} - w_x^{(t)} f(x)/f_{\max}] = \sum_{x \in T} w_x^{(t)} - (1/f_{\max}) \sum_{x \in T} w_x^{(t)} f(x).$$

This means that in each iteration the weight function $w_x^{(t)}$ decreases half as much over S as it does over T as a whole. Thus, the amount that $w_x^{(t)}$ decreases on $S \cap T$ is at most the amount it decreases on $T \setminus S$. Since initially we have that $\sum_{x \in T \setminus S} w_x^{(1)} = |T \setminus S|/|T| \leq \epsilon$, this means that at every stage t of the algorithm the following holds

$$\sum_{x \in S \cap T} w_x^{(t)} \geq 1 - 2\epsilon.$$

This implies that the distribution defined by $w^{(t)}$ remains (3ϵ)-close to the uniform distribution on S, even at the end of the algorithm when $\mathbf{Cov}_{w^{(t)}}[T] \leq (1 + \lambda)I$. Thus, by Lemma 2.7, we have that $\|\mu_{w^{(t)}} - \mu_S\|_2 = O(\delta + \sqrt{\epsilon}\lambda)$, completing our proof. □

Practical Considerations While the aforementioned point removal methods have similar theoretical guarantees, recent implementations suggest that they have different practical performance on real datasets. The deterministic reweighting method is somewhat slower in practice as its worst-case runtime and its typical runtime are comparable. In more detail, one can guarantee termination by setting the constant of proportionality so that at each step at least one of the nonzero weights is set to zero. However, in practical circumstances, we will not be able to do better. That is, the algorithm may well be forced to undergo $\epsilon|S|$ iterations. On the other hand, the randomized versions of the algorithm are likely to remove several points of T at each filtering step.

Another reason why the randomized versions may be preferable has to do with the quality of the results. The randomized algorithms only produce bad results when there is a chance that $d(T_i)$ ends up being very large. However, since $d(T_i)$ is a supermartingale, this will only ever be the case if there is a corresponding possibility that $d(T_i)$ will be exceptionally small. Thus, although the randomized algorithms may have a probability of giving worse results some of the time, this will only happen if a corresponding fraction of the time they also give *better* results than the theory guarantees. This consideration suggests that the randomized thresholding procedure might have advantages over the independent removal procedure, precisely because it has a higher probability of failure. This has been observed experimentally: In real datasets poisoned with a constant fraction of adversarial outliers, the number of iterations of randomized filtering is typically bounded by a small constant.

2.4.3 Universal Filtering

In this section, we show how to use randomized filtering to construct a universal filter that works under only the stability condition (Definition 2.1) – not requiring the tail-bound condition of the tail-bound filter (Lemma 2.15). To do this, we construct an appropriate score function f, as in the statement of Theorem 2.17. Formally, we show the following.

Proposition 2.19 Let $S \subset \mathbf{R}^d$ be a $(2\epsilon, \delta)$-stable set for $\epsilon, \delta > 0$ sufficiently small constants with δ at least a sufficiently large multiple of ϵ. Let T be an ϵ-corrupted version of S. Suppose that $\mathbf{Cov}[T]$ has largest eigenvalue $1 + \lambda > 1 + 8\delta^2/\epsilon$. Then there exists a polynomial time algorithm that, on input ϵ, δ, T, computes a nonzero function $f \colon T \to \mathbf{R}_+$ satisfying $\sum_{x \in T} f(x) \geq 2 \sum_{x \in T \cap S} f(x)$.

By combining Theorem 2.17 and Proposition 2.19, we obtain a randomized filtering algorithm establishing Theorem 2.11.

Proof of Proposition 2.19. The algorithm to construct f is the following. We start by computing the sample mean of T, μ_T, and the top (unit) eigenvector v of $\mathbf{Cov}[T]$. For $x \in T$, we define the function

$$g(x) = (v \cdot (x - \mu_T))^2.$$

Let L be the set of $\epsilon \cdot |T|$ elements of T on which $g(x)$ is largest. We define f to be

$$f(x) = \begin{cases} 0 & x \notin L, \\ g(x) & x \in L. \end{cases} \tag{2.5}$$

Our basic plan of attack is as follows: First, we note that the sum of $g(x)$ over $x \in T$ is the variance of $v \cdot T$, which is substantially larger than the sum of $g(x)$ over $x \in S$, which is approximately the variance of $v \cdot S$. Therefore, the sum of $g(x)$ over the $\epsilon|S|$ elements of $T \setminus S$ must be quite large. In fact, using the stability condition, we can show that the latter quantity must be larger than the sum of the largest $\epsilon|S|$ values of $g(x)$ over $x \in S$. However, since $|T \setminus S| \leq |L|$, we have that $\sum_{x \in T} f(x) = \sum_{x \in L} g(x) \geq \sum_{x \in T \setminus S} g(x) \geq 2 \sum_{x \in S} f(x)$.

We now proceed with the detailed analysis. First, note that

$$\sum_{x \in T} g(x) = |T|\mathbf{Var}[v \cdot T] = |T|(1 + \lambda).$$

Moreover, for any $S' \subseteq S$ with $|S'| \geq (1 - 2\epsilon)|S|$, we have that

$$\sum_{x \in S'} g(x) = |S'|(\mathbf{Var}[v \cdot S'] + (v \cdot (\mu_T - \mu_{S'}))^2). \tag{2.6}$$

By the second stability condition, we have that $|\mathbf{Var}[v \cdot S'] - 1| \leq \delta^2/\epsilon$. Furthermore, the stability condition and Lemma 2.6 give

$$\|\mu_T - \mu_{S'}\|_2 \leq \|\mu_T - \mu_X\|_2 + \|\mu_X - \mu_{S'}\|_2 = O(\delta + \sqrt{\epsilon\lambda}).$$

Since $\lambda \geq 8\delta^2/\epsilon$, combining the above gives

$$\sum_{x \in T \setminus S} g(x) \geq \sum_{x \in T} g(x) - \sum_{x \in S} g(x) \geq (2/3)|S|\lambda.$$

Moreover, since $|L| \geq |T \setminus S|$ and g takes its largest values on points $x \in L$, we have

$$\sum_{x \in T} f(x) = \sum_{x \in L} g(x) \geq \sum_{x \in T \setminus S} g(x) \geq (16/3)|S|\delta^2/\epsilon.$$

Comparing the results of Equation (2.6) for $S' = S$ and $S' = S \setminus L$, we find that

$$\sum_{x \in S \cap T} f(x) = \sum_{x \in S \cap L} g(x) = \sum_{x \in S} g(x) - \sum_{x \in S \setminus L} g(x)$$

$$= |S|(1 \pm \delta^2/\epsilon + O(\delta^2 + \epsilon\lambda)) - |S \setminus L|(1 \pm \delta^2/\epsilon + O(\delta^2 + \epsilon\lambda))$$

$$\leq 2|S|\delta^2/\epsilon + |S|O(\delta^2 + \epsilon\lambda).$$

The latter quantity is at most $(1/2) \sum_{x \in T} f(x)$ when δ and ϵ/δ are at most sufficiently small constants. This completes the proof of Proposition 2.19.   □

Remark 2.20   One can straightforwardly obtain a weighted version of Proposition 2.19 (essentially by replacing subsets by "weighted subsets"), which provides the function f required in the statement of Theorem 2.18. By doing so, we obtain a weighted filtering algorithm establishing Theorem 2.11.

2.5 Exercises

2.1   (Scaling Stability) Show that if the set $S \subset \mathbf{R}^d$ is (ϵ, δ)-stable with respect to μ, and if $\epsilon' > \epsilon$ is less than a sufficiently small constant, then S is $(\epsilon', O(\delta\epsilon'/\epsilon))$-stable with respect to μ.

2.2   (Resilience) Suppose that S is a set of points in $\mathbf{R}^d$ such that for every $S' \subseteq S$ with $|S'| \geq (1 - 2\epsilon)|S|$ we have $\|\mu_{S'} - \mu_S\|_2 \leq \delta$. (Note that this is the first condition in the definition of $(2\epsilon, \delta)$-stability, but not the second.) Show that if one is given a set T obtained by adversarially corrupting an ϵ-fraction of the points in S, it is information-theoretically possible to find a 2δ-approximation of the mean of S.

Remark 2.21   This condition was referred to as *resilience* by [136]. That work showed that it is information-theoretically sufficient to robustly learn to error $O(\delta)$, and computationally sufficient to learn to error $O(\delta/\sqrt{\epsilon})$. Although robust learning is possible with this weaker condition information-theoretically, it is believed that obtaining error $O(\delta)$ is computationally intractable without additional assumptions.

2.3   (Stability for Bounded Covariance) Recall that in Proposition 2.4 we needed to restrict to a subset of the sample points to ensure that the resulting subset is stable with high probability. Show that this assumption is necessary. In particular, show that for any positive integers N, d and real $\epsilon > 0$ sufficiently small, there is a distribution X on $\mathbf{R}^d$ with $\mathbf{Cov}[X] \preceq I_d$ such that, with probability at least $1/2$, the empirical distribution of N samples from X is *not* $(\epsilon, \sqrt{d\epsilon/2})$-stable with respect to X.
(Hint: Produce a distribution that has a $1/N$ probability of returning a very large vector.)

2.4   (Generic Stability Bound) Suppose that X is a probability distribution in $\mathbf{R}^d$ with mean μ with $\|X - \mu\|_2 \leq R$ almost surely, and such that no ϵ-fraction of the mass of X contributes more than δ^2/ϵ to the expectation of $(v \cdot (X - \mu))^2$ for any unit vector v. Prove that, for some $N = \text{poly}(Rd/\epsilon)$, a set of N i.i.d. samples from X is $(\epsilon, O(\delta))$-stable with respect to μ with high probability.

(Hint: Use the VC Inequality, Theorem A.12, to show that with high probability the empirical distribution satisfies tail bounds similar to those that X does.)

2.5 (Other Tail-Bound-Based Filters) Devise filtering algorithms along the lines of the tail-bound-based filter for Gaussians that work for the following inlier distributions X:

(a) X is isotropic and logconcave. [Here you should be able to achieve error $O(\epsilon \log(1/\epsilon))$.]

(b) X is isotropic and has $\mathbf{E}[|v \cdot (X - \mu_X)|^k] \le M$ (for some constants M and $k > 2$). [Here you should be able to achieve error $O_k(M^{1/k}\epsilon^{1-1/k})$.]

(c) X is an arbitrary distribution with $\mathbf{Cov}[X] \le I$. [Although one can get sample sets that are $(\epsilon, O(\sqrt{\epsilon}))$-stable here, it seems impossible to achieve error $O(\sqrt{\epsilon})$ with a filter of this type. Show that it is possible to get error $O(\sqrt{\epsilon} \log(d/\epsilon))$.]

2.6 (Dimension Halving) Another approach for robust mean estimation of spherical Gaussians uses a dimension-halving technique. This method proceeds as follows:

(a) Use a naive filter to remove all points at distance more than roughly $\sqrt{d}$ from the mean.

(b) Compute the sample covariance matrix. Let V be the subspace spanned by eigenvalues larger than $1 + \Omega(\epsilon)$.

(c) Use the sample mean as an estimate for the projection of the true mean onto $V^{\perp}$, and recursively approximate the projection of the mean onto V.

Show that an algorithm along these lines can be used to obtain error $O(\epsilon \sqrt{\log(d)})$ with polynomial time and sample complexity.

(Hint: Show that $\dim(V) \le d/2$.)

Remark 2.22 The dimension-halving technique was developed in [114].

2.7 (Robust Estimation in Other ℓ_p-Norms) Let $1 \le p < 2$ and let $1/p+1/q = 1$. Suppose that S is a set of points such that $\mathbf{Var}[v \cdot S] \le 1$ for all v with $\|v\|_q \le 1$. Show that there is an algorithm that given p, ϵ, and T, an ϵ-corrupted version of S, computes in polynomial time an estimate $\widehat{\mu}$ such that with high probability $\|\widehat{\mu} - \mu_S\|_p = O(\sqrt{\epsilon})$.

(Hint: Show that it suffices to find a large (weighted) subset T' of T for which the variance of $v \cdot T'$ is $O(1)$ for any v with $\|v\|_q \le 1$. In order to

find such a subset, you may need the following result of [123]:
For any positive-definite matrix A, the following holds

$$\sup_{\|v\|_q=1} v^T A v = \Theta\left(\sup_{Y\succeq 0, \|\text{Diag}(Y)\|_{q/2}\leq 1} \text{tr}(AY)\right).$$

This is particularly convenient, as the right-hand side can be efficiently computed using convex programming.)

2.8 (Learning from Untrusted Batches) In the *learning from untrusted batches* problem, one is attempting to learn a distribution p over a finite domain $[n] := \{1, 2, \ldots, n\}$, in a distributed setting where many samples are partitioned across a few servers, but a constant fraction of the servers may be corrupted. More precisely, we are given m i.i.d. samples from p divided into *batches* of k samples each. However, an ϵ-fraction of these batches are allowed to be adversarially corrupted (usually in the Huber sense). The goal is to learn a distribution $\widehat{p}$ that is close to p in total variation distance.

(a) Show that for $k = 1$ one cannot learn p to error better than ϵ, no matter how large m is.

(b) Show that for any subset $S \subseteq [n]$, there is a polynomial-time algorithm to estimate the probability $p(S)$ that p assigns to S within error of $O(\epsilon/\sqrt{k})$. Use this to devise an inefficient algorithm to estimate p to error $O(\epsilon/\sqrt{k})$ in total variation distance.

(c) Show that the learning from untrusted batches problem is equivalent to estimating the mean of a multinomial distribution to small ℓ_1 error, given access to ϵ-corrupted samples. Show that the algorithm from Exercise 2.7 can be used to efficiently learn p to ℓ_1-error $O(\sqrt{\epsilon/k})$.

(d) One can actually do somewhat better than the above. The idea is to find sets $S \subset [n]$ such that the empirical variance of the number of samples in a batch from S is substantially larger than the variance over just the good batches, and using this set to filter. This can be done by comparing the sample covariance matrix to an approximation of the true covariance, and using a known result that gives a polynomial-time algorithm for the following task: Given a matrix M, compute a vector v with $\|v\|_\infty \leq 1$ and $v^T M v \gg \sup_{\|w\|_\infty \leq 1} w^T M w$. Give a polynomial-time algorithm that estimates p to error $O(\epsilon \sqrt{\log(1/\epsilon)/k})$ in total variation distance.

Remark 2.23 The learning from untrusted batches problem was introduced by [128] and subsequently studied in a sequence of works [27, 28, 99, 100, 101].

2.9 (Robust Mean Estimation for Balanced Product Distributions) Let X be a balanced product distribution on $\{0, 1\}^d$. Namely, X_i is 1 with probability p_i and 0 otherwise, for some $1/3 \le p_i \le 2/3$, and the coordinates X_i are independent of one another. Note that $\Sigma := \mathbf{Cov}[X]$ is a diagonal matrix with entries $p_i(1 - p_i)$. Give an efficient algorithm to estimate the mean of X to ℓ_2-error $O(\epsilon \sqrt{\log(1/\epsilon)})$ from a polynomial number of ϵ-corrupted samples.

(Hint: Compute an approximation to Σ and find a way to adjust for the fact that Σ is not close to I.)

2.10 (Achieving Breakdown Point of 1/2) The algorithms presented in this chapter all require that the fraction of corruptions ϵ is at most a sufficiently small positive constant. Adaptations of these algorithms can be made to work for ϵ approaching $1/2$. (For the more challenging setting when $\epsilon > 1/2$, see Chapter 5). Show that for all $0 < \epsilon < 1/2$ there is an algorithm that takes poly$(d/(1/2 - \epsilon))$ samples from $X = \mathcal{N}(\mu, I)$ in $\mathbf{R}^d$, runs in polynomial time, and with high probability computes an estimate $\widehat{\mu}$ with $\|\widehat{\mu} - \mu\|_2 \le f(\epsilon)$, for some function f.

(Hint: Some version of a filter should work, though you may need to be more careful either about the ratio of inliers versus outliers removed or about the properties that you can assume for $S \cap T$.)

2.11 (High-Probability Guarantees in Randomized Filtering) Consider the version of the randomized filter where each sample is removed independently with probability $f(x)/f_{\max}$. Show that if this algorithm is given a set T, which is an ϵ-corruption of a set S, the probability that the algorithm ever reaches a state where more than $3\epsilon|S|$ samples have been removed from S is at most $\exp(-\Omega(\epsilon|S|))$.

(Hint: Consider the expectation $\mathbf{E}\left[\exp(\eta(2|T_i \backslash S| + |(S \cap T)\backslash T_i|))\right]$ for $\eta > 0$ some sufficiently small constant.)

2.12 (Different Scores for the Universal Filter) Recall that for our universal filter we let $g(x) = |v \cdot (x - \mu_T)|^2$ and defined our scores to be $g(x)$ if x was in the top ϵ-fraction of values and 0 otherwise.

(a) Show that if instead $g(x)$ is used directly as the score function, this may throw away more good samples than bad ones, unless $\delta \gg \sqrt{\epsilon}$.

(b) Let m be an $O(1)$-additive approximation to $v \cdot \mu_S$ (for example, the median of $v \cdot T$ often works). Let $g(x) = |v \cdot x - m|^2$ and

$$f(x) := \begin{cases} g(x) & \text{if } g(x) > C(\delta/\epsilon)^2, \\ 0 & \text{otherwise} \end{cases}$$

for $C > 0$ some suitably large constant. Show that this score function works. Namely, show that if T is an ϵ-corruption of S, S is (ϵ, δ)-stable and if $\mathbf{Var}[v \cdot T] > 1 + C'\delta^2/\epsilon$, for some sufficiently large C', then $\sum_{x \in S \cap T} f(x) < \frac{1}{2} \sum_{x \in T} f(x)$.

2.6 Discussion and Related Work

The first computationally efficient algorithms for high-dimensional robust mean estimation with dimension-independent error guarantees were obtained in [45]. The same work introduced both the unknown convex programming and filtering techniques described in this chapter. The filtering technique was further refined in [46], specifically for the class of bounded covariance distributions. In this chapter, we gave a simplified and unified presentation of these techniques. In more detail, the stability condition of Definition 2.1 first appeared in [50], although a special case was implicitly used in [45]. Similarly, the universal filtering method that succeeds under the stability condition first appeared in [50].

The idea of removing outliers by projecting on the top eigenvector of the empirical covariance goes back to [110], who used it in the context of learning linear separators with malicious noise. That work [110] used a "hard" filtering step which only removes outliers, and consequently leads to errors that scale logarithmically with the dimension. Subsequently, the work of [5] employed a soft-outlier removal step in the same supervised setting as [110], to obtain improved bounds for that problem. It should be noted that the soft-outlier method of [5] is similarly insufficient to obtain dimension-independent error bounds for the unsupervised setting.

Contemporaneously with [45], [114] developed a recursive dimension-halving technique for high-dimensional robust mean estimation. Their technique leads to error $O(\epsilon \sqrt{\log d})$ for Gaussian robust mean estimation in Huber's contamination model. The algorithm of [114] begins by removing extreme outliers from the input set of ϵ-corrupted samples. This ensures that, after this basic outlier removal step, the empirical covariance matrix has trace $d(1 + \tilde{O}(\epsilon))$, which in turn implies that the $d/2$ smallest eigenvalues are all at most $1 + \tilde{O}(\epsilon)$. This allows [114] to show, using techniques akin to Lemma 2.6, that the projections of the true mean and the empirical mean onto the subspace spanned by the corresponding (small) eigenvectors are close. The [114] algorithm then uses this approximation for this projection of the mean, projects the remaining points onto the orthogonal subspace, and recursively finds the mean of the other projection. See Exercise 2.6 for more details.

In addition to robust mean estimation, [45, 114] developed efficient robust learning algorithms for a number of more complex statistical tasks, including robust covariance estimation, robust density estimation for mixtures of spherical Gaussians and binary product distributions (see Exercise 2.9), robust independent component analysis (ICA), and robust singular value decomposition (SVD). Building on the techniques of [45], a line of works [34, 35, 66] gave robust parameter estimation algorithms for Bayesian networks (with known graph structure) and Ising models. Another extension of these results was given in [136], who obtained an efficient algorithm for robust mean estimation with respect to all ℓ_p-norms (see Exercise 2.7 for more details).

The algorithmic approaches described in this chapter robustly estimate the mean of a spherical Gaussian within ℓ_2 error $O(\epsilon \sqrt{\log(1/\epsilon)})$ in the strong contamination model. A more sophisticated filtering technique that achieves the optimal error of $O(\epsilon)$ in the *additive* (adaptive) contamination model was developed in [47]. This method will be described and analyzed in Chapter 3. Very roughly, this algorithm proceeds, by using a novel filtering method, to remove corrupted points if the empirical covariance matrix has *many* eigenvalues of size $1 + \Omega(\epsilon)$. Otherwise, the algorithm uses the empirical mean to estimate the mean on the space spanned by small eigenvectors, and then uses brute-force to estimate the projection onto the few principal eigenvectors. For the total variation contamination model (and, therefore, the strong contamination model), [63] gave evidence (in the form of Statistical Query lower bounds) that any improvement on the $O(\epsilon \sqrt{\log(1/\epsilon)})$ error requires super-polynomial time. These developments will be described in Chapter 8.

The focus of this chapter was on developing efficient robust mean estimation algorithms in high dimensions that succeed if the fraction of outliers is $\epsilon < \epsilon_0$, where $\epsilon_0 > 0$ is a sufficiently small universal constant. In principle, it is possible to do better than this, in particular to, obtain efficient robust mean estimators with breakdown point of $1/2$. This goal can be achieved by conceptually simple adaptations of the filtering method. The reader is referred to [39, 94, 144] and Exercise 2.10.

A related problem is that of *high probability mean estimation*. If one is given independent samples from a Gaussian (with no corruptions), the empirical mean gives a good estimate of the true mean, and furthermore one can show that this estimate is accurate with high probability. However, if the underlying distribution is replaced by a heavy-tailed distribution (such as, one with merely bounded covariance), these high probability bounds may no longer hold without a more sophisticated estimator. A sequence of works in the mathematical statistics community determined the optimal sample complexity of heavy-tailed mean estimation both without outliers [120] and in the strong contamination model [121]. (See also [119] for a related survey.)

Interestingly, there is a connection between high probability mean estimation and robust mean estimation, obtained by treating the extreme points from the heavy-tailed distribution (which make the high-probability estimation task challenging) as outliers; see, for example, [126]. In particular, [59] showed that robust mean estimation techniques could be used to obtain essentially optimal high probability mean estimation algorithms.

The first sample-optimal and polynomial-time algorithm for heavy-tail mean estimation (without outliers) was developed in [90]. Subsequent works [37, 42] developed simpler algorithms with significantly improved asymptotic runtime that also succeed with additive contamination. More recently, the work of [59] showed that any robust mean estimation algorithm that succeeds under the stability condition when combined with a simple preprocessing step achieves optimal rates for finite covariance distributions and works even in the strong contamination model. The latter work also establishes the sample complexity bounds stated in Remark 2.5 for identity covariance distributions with bounded kth central moments.

3

Algorithmic Refinements in Robust Mean Estimation

3.1 Introduction

The goal of Chapter 2 was to lay down the basic algorithmic techniques that lead to the first computationally efficient algorithms for high-dimensional robust mean estimation. Given this groundwork, in this chapter we present a number of improvements and refinements. Although the algorithms in the previous chapter have sample complexities and runtimes polynomial in d and $1/\epsilon$, they can be further optimized in a number of ways. The goal of this chapter will be to describe some of these improvements.

The first direction concerns obtaining robust mean estimation algorithms with near-optimal sample complexity and runtime. In Section 3.2, we establish (near-)optimal sample complexity bounds for stability-based algorithms, that is, robust mean estimation algorithms that rely only on the stability condition. To achieve this, we give a tighter analysis that leads to near-optimal bounds on the number of samples required to obtain stable sets for various classes of distributions. In Section 3.3, we describe a robust mean estimation algorithm with near-optimal computational complexity. This algorithm builds on the filtering technique of the previous chapter.

Another direction of improvement comes from being able to leverage stronger assumptions on the contamination model. For example, all the algorithms in Chapter 2 worked in the strong contamination model and obtained error of $O(\epsilon \sqrt{\log(1/\epsilon)})$ for Gaussian mean estimation. There is reason to believe (see Chapter 8) that this is the best error that can be obtained computationally efficiently in the strong contamination model, despite the fact that $O(\epsilon)$ error is possible information-theoretically. On the other hand, if one weakens the contamination model to allow only additive noise or only subtractive noise, then it is possible to efficiently obtain $O(\epsilon)$ error. We will give an efficient algorithm achieving this error guarantee in Section 3.4.

Along similar lines, the algorithms developed thus far rely only on some stability-related assumptions on the underlying distribution. In a number of settings, we may have additional prior information about the target mean that we would like to take advantage of. Of substantial interest are sparsity-related assumptions, in particular that the mean has relatively few nonzero coordinates. In Section 3.6, we discuss how to adapt our previously developed algorithmic techniques for leveraging this kind of sparsity structure.

A final direction of improvement concerns algorithmic simplicity. The filtering and unknown convex programming techniques are somewhat conceptually complicated, involving some kind of iterative noise reduction and require carefully tuned parameters. It turns out that one can perform robust mean estimation more directly using standard first-order optimization methods. We discuss these ideas in Section 3.5.

3.2 Near-Optimal Sample Complexity of Stability

In Chapter 2, we described various polynomial-time robust mean estimation algorithms. Each of these algorithms succeeds assuming that the uncorrupted samples satisfy an appropriate condition (usually the stability condition given in Definition 2.1). While showing that a polynomial (in the dimension d and $1/\epsilon$, where ϵ is the fraction of outliers) number of independent samples from the distribution of interest satisfies the stability condition (with high probability) is typically relatively easy (as was done in Section 2.2.1), obtaining a tight sample complexity analysis often requires more careful arguments.

In this section, we establish nearly tight sample complexity bounds for two prototypical families of distributions:

1. Identity covariance Gaussian distributions, and
2. Distributions with unknown bounded covariance.

It should be noted that in order to learn the mean of such a distribution to ℓ_2 error δ (even without corruptions) requires $\Omega(d/\delta^2)$ samples. With a careful analysis, one can show that even in the presence of corruptions, $O(d/\delta^2)$ samples suffice in the Gaussian setting (assuming the noise rate is not too high), and that $\tilde{O}(d/\delta^2)$ samples suffice for general bounded covariance distributions.

The techniques required to obtain these near-optimal bounds are classical in probability theory. The purpose of this section is to obtain a direct and self-contained analysis in tandem with introducing the necessary probabilistic tools.

A first useful lemma we will require for our analysis is the following simplified characterization of stability.

Lemma 3.1 (Alternate Characterization of Stability)   *Let $0 < \epsilon \le \delta < 1/2$. A finite set $S \subset \mathbf{R}^d$ is $(\epsilon, O(\delta))$-stable with respect to a distribution X with mean μ if the following conditions hold:*

1. $\left\| \frac{1}{|S|} \sum_{x \in S} x - \mu \right\|_2 \le \delta$.

2. *For every unit vector $v \in \mathbf{R}^d$, we have $\left| \frac{1}{|S|} \sum_{x \in S} |v \cdot (x - \mu)|^2 - 1 \right| \le \delta^2/\epsilon$.*

3. *For every unit vector $v \in \mathbf{R}^d$ and every subset $T \subset S$ with $|T| \le \epsilon|S|$, we have $\left| \frac{1}{|S|} \sum_{x \in T} |v \cdot (x - \mu)|^2 \right| \le \delta^2/\epsilon$.*

Remark 3.2   It is easy to see that a set S satisfying the original definition of stability (Definition 2.1) also satisfies the conditions of Lemma 3.1. Therefore, Lemma 3.1 can be seen as an alternative characterization of stability.

Proof   We will show that a set S satisfying the above conditions also satisfies the definition of stability. Specifically, we will need to show that after replacing S by any $S' \subseteq S$ with $|S'| \ge (1 - \epsilon)|S|$, the sample mean and sample covariance of S' in any direction $v \in \mathbf{R}^d$ are approximately correct. To do this, we relate these sums over S' by taking the difference between the sum over S and the sum over $T := S \setminus S'$, noting that T is a subset of S with $|T| \le \epsilon|S|$. Proving the covariance stability condition boils down to a direct computation. To prove the mean condition, we need to use the bounds on the second moments of $v \cdot (x - \mu)$ over T and the Cauchy–Schwarz inequality to get appropriate bounds on the error.

For the mean estimation error, we let $v \in \mathbf{R}^d$ be a unit vector and let $T = S \setminus S'$ with $|S'| \ge (1 - \epsilon)|S|$. We have that

$$
\begin{aligned}
\left| \frac{1}{|S'|} \sum_{x \in S'} v \cdot (x - \mu) \right| &= \left(\frac{|S|}{|S'|} \right) \left(\frac{1}{|S|} \right) \left| \sum_{x \in S} v \cdot (x - \mu) - \sum_{x \in T} v \cdot (x - \mu) \right| \\
&\le (1 + O(\epsilon)) \left(\left| \frac{1}{|S|} \sum_{x \in S} v \cdot (x - \mu) \right| + \left| \frac{1}{|S|} \sum_{x \in T} v \cdot (x - \mu) \right| \right) \\
&\le (1 + O(\epsilon)) \left(\delta + \frac{1}{|S|} \sqrt{\sum_{x \in T} |v \cdot (x - \mu)|^2} \sqrt{\sum_{x \in T} 1} \right) \\
&\le (1 + O(\epsilon))(\delta + \sqrt{|S|\delta^2/\epsilon} \sqrt{|T|/|S|}) \\
&= O(\delta),
\end{aligned}
$$

where the third line above used the Cauchy–Schwarz inequality. Since this equation holds for any unit vector v, the first stability condition holds.

For the covariance condition, we again let $v \in \mathbf{R}^d$ be a unit vector and let $T = S \setminus S'$ with $|S'| \geq (1 - \epsilon)|S|$. We have

$$\left| \frac{1}{|S'|} \sum_{x \in S'} |v \cdot (x - \mu)|^2 - 1 \right|$$

$$= \left(\frac{|S|}{|S'|} \right) \left(\frac{1}{|S|} \left| \sum_{x \in S} (|v \cdot (x - \mu)|^2 - 1) - \sum_{x \in T} (|v \cdot (x - \mu)|^2 - 1) \right| \right)$$

$$\leq (1 + O(\epsilon)) \left(\left| \frac{1}{|S|} \sum_{x \in S} |v \cdot (x - \mu)|^2 - 1 \right| + \left| \frac{1}{|S|} \sum_{x \in T} |v \cdot (x - \mu)|^2 - 1 \right| \right)$$

$$\leq (1 + O(\epsilon)) \left(\delta^2/\epsilon + \left| \frac{1}{|S|} \sum_{x \in T} |v \cdot (x - \mu)|^2 \right| + \left| \frac{1}{|S|} \sum_{x \in T} 1 \right| \right)$$

$$\leq (1 + O(\epsilon)) \left(\delta^2/\epsilon + \delta^2/\epsilon + |T|/|S| \right)$$

$$\leq O(\delta^2/\epsilon),$$

recalling that $\epsilon \leq \delta$. This completes the proof. $\qquad\qquad\qquad\square$

We can now proceed with the proofs of the sample complexity bounds in our two contexts. In both cases, we want to show that given an appropriately large number of samples, the conditions of Lemma 3.1 are satisfied with high probability. This will amount to proving some sort of concentration bounds.

3.2.1 Sample Complexity for Spherical Gaussians

In this section, we will prove a sample complexity bound for the setting that the inliers are drawn from an unknown mean and identity covariance Gaussian.

Proposition 3.3 *Let $\mu \in \mathbf{R}^d$ and $0 < \epsilon < 1/2$. Let N be an integer, with N at least a sufficiently large constant multiple of $d/(\log(1/\epsilon)\epsilon^2)$, and let S be a set of N i.i.d. samples from $X = \mathcal{N}(\mu, I)$. Then, with probability at least $1 - \exp(-\Omega(N\epsilon^2 \log(1/\epsilon)))$, we have that S is $(\epsilon, O(\epsilon \sqrt{\log(1/\epsilon)}))$-stable with respect to X.*

We will show that with high probability S satisfies the conditions of Lemma 3.1, for some $\delta = O(\epsilon \sqrt{\log(1/\epsilon)})$. The first condition will be relatively easy to show, while the latter two will be somewhat more challenging. At a high level, the proof proceeds by a cover argument. In particular, we will show that for any fixed unit vector v, these conditions hold, except with exponentially small probability. Once we establish this, we will use a union bound to show that these conditions hold for all vectors v in a relatively dense subset of the unit sphere. Finally, with some additional work, we can show that the conditions hold for every unit vector v.

First Condition: The first condition of Lemma 3.1 says that the empirical mean of S is close to μ. We note that

$$\widehat{\mu} := \frac{1}{|S|} \sum_{x \in S} (x - \mu) \sim \mathcal{N}\left(0, (1/\sqrt{N})\, I\right).$$

While it is not hard to show directly that this has ℓ_2 norm $O(\sqrt{d/N})$ with high probability, it will be instructive for us to show it by demonstrating that with high probability $|v \cdot \widehat{\mu}| \leq \delta$ for all unit vectors v. In particular, for any given unit vector v, by Gaussian concentration, we have $|v \cdot \widehat{\mu}| \leq \delta$, except with probability $\exp(-\Omega(N\delta^2))$. It turns out that it suffices that this holds for every unit vector v in a cover of the unit sphere. We will use the following standard fact (see Theorem A.10):

Fact 3.4 *There exists a set C of $2^{O(d)}$ unit vectors in $\mathbf{R}^d$ such that for any vector $w \in \mathbf{R}^d$ there exists a $v \in C$ with $v \cdot w \geq (9/10)\|w\|_2$.*

Note that if we considered all unit vectors v, we could always find a v so that $v \cdot w = \|w\|_2$. The cover C needs to have a vector v that is sufficiently close to every possible unit vector.

By a union bound over all points in C, we have that except with probability $\exp(O(d) - \Omega(N\delta^2))$, for every $v \in C$ it holds that $|v \cdot \widehat{\mu}| \leq \delta$. Since by definition there must be a $v \in C$ with $v \cdot \widehat{\mu} \geq (9/10)\,\|\widehat{\mu}\|_2$, this implies that $\|\widehat{\mu}\|_2 \leq (10/9)\delta$. Choosing δ to be an appropriately large constant multiple of $\epsilon \sqrt{\log(1/\epsilon)}$ and noting that $N\delta^2 \gg d$, we have that the first condition holds with high probability.

Second and Third Conditions: We begin by showing that for any given v these conditions hold with high probability.

For the second condition, we note that $v \cdot (x - \mu)$ is distributed as a standard Gaussian, and thus the individual terms $|v \cdot (x - \mu)|^2 - 1$ are independent mean zero random variables. Showing that their average is close to zero amounts to some kind of concentration bound. A natural attempt to prove a high probability bound on this event would involve an application of Bernstein's inequality.

Theorem 3.5 (Bernstein's Inequality) *Let $X_1, \ldots, X_n$ be independent, mean 0 random variables with $|X_i| \leq M$ almost surely. Then*

$$\mathbf{Pr}\left(\left|\sum_{i=1}^n X_i\right| \geq t\right) \leq 2\exp\left(-\frac{t^2/2}{\sum_{i=1}^n \mathbf{E}[X_i^2] + Mt/3}\right).$$

Unfortunately, we cannot apply this inequality directly in our setting, because the $|v \cdot (x - \mu)|^2$ terms are not bounded. To fix this technical issue, we apply a standard probabilistic technique known as *truncation*. We pick r to be a sufficiently large constant multiple of $\sqrt{\log(1/\epsilon)}$ and define:

$$g_r^v(x) := \begin{cases} |v \cdot (x - \mu)|^2 - 1, & \text{if } |v \cdot (x - \mu)| \le r, \\ 0, & \text{otherwise}, \end{cases}$$

$$h_r^v(x) := \begin{cases} 0, & \text{if } |v \cdot (x - \mu)| \le r, \\ |v \cdot (x - \mu)|^2 - 1, & \text{otherwise}. \end{cases}$$

By construction, we have $g_r^v(x) + h_r^v(x) = |v \cdot (x - \mu)|^2 - 1$ and $g_r^v(x)$ is bounded, allowing us to apply Theorem 3.5. On the other hand, while $h_r^v(x)$ is unbounded, it returns zero except with small probability, and we can analyze it using first principles. We now commence with this analysis.

Lemma 3.6 *For any fixed unit vector v in $\mathbf{R}^d$, except with probability $\exp(-\Omega(N\delta^2))$ over the choice of S, we have $\frac{1}{|S|} \left| \sum_{x \in S} g_r^v(x) \right| \le \delta$.*

Proof The proof essentially amounts to an application of Bernstein's inequality. A small technical complication arises from the fact that $\mathbf{E}[g_r^v(x)]$ is not zero. Recall that without the truncation this would be the case, but the truncation process might slightly alter the expectation.

An elementary calculation gives that the expected value $m = \mathbf{E}_{x \sim N(\mu, I)}[g_r^v(x)]$ satisfies $|m| < \epsilon$. For $S = \{x_1, x_2, \ldots, x_N\}$, we note that $g_r^v(x_i) - m$ are i.i.d. zero mean random variables that satisfy $|g_r^v(x_i) - m| < 2r^2$ almost surely and $\mathbf{E}[|g_r^v(x_i) - m|^2] = O(1)$. Thus, applying Theorem 3.5 with $t = N\delta/2$, we have

$$\mathbf{Pr}\left(\left| \sum_{x \in S} (g_r^v(x) - m) \right| > N\delta/2 \right) < 2\exp\left(-\frac{N^2\delta^2/8}{O(N + N\delta r^2)} \right) = \exp(-\Omega(N\delta^2)).$$

Noting that $m < \delta/2$, the lemma follows. □

We next bound the sum $\sum_{x \in S} h_r^v(x)$. This step requires a less black box argument. The fact that $h_r^v(x)$ is not bounded means that we cannot readily use out-of-the-box concentration bounds. However, most of these concentration bounds for sums of independent random variables $X_1, \ldots, X_n$ are proved by bounding the expectation of $\exp(\sum X_i)$. It turns out that this technique works in our setting.

Lemma 3.7 *For any fixed unit vector v in $\mathbf{R}^d$, except with probability $\exp(-\Omega(N\delta))$ over the choice of S, we have that $\frac{1}{|S|} \sum_{x \in S} h_r^v(x) \le \delta$.*

Proof We begin by estimating the quantity $\mathbf{E}_{x \sim N(\mu, I)}[\exp(h_r^v(x)/4)]$. This is easily seen to be

$$\mathbf{Pr}(|v \cdot (x - \mu)| < r) + \frac{2}{\sqrt{2\pi}} \int_r^\infty \exp(-x^2/2) \exp((x^2 - 1)/4) dx$$

$$\leq 1 + r^2 \exp(-\Omega(r^2)),$$

which is at most e^ϵ since r is a sufficiently large constant multiple of $\sqrt{\log(1/\epsilon)}$. Letting $S = \{x_1, \ldots, x_N\}$ with the x_i's independent, we have

$$\mathbf{E}\left[\exp\left(\sum_{x \in S} h_r^v(x)\right)/4\right] = \prod_{i=1}^N \mathbf{E}[\exp(h_r^v(x_i)/4)]$$

$$\leq \exp(N\epsilon).$$

Thus, by Markov's inequality, we have $\sum_{x \in S} h_r^v(x) > N\delta$ with probability at most $\exp(N(\epsilon - \delta/4)) = \exp(-\Omega(N\delta))$. This completes the proof. $\quad\square$

Using Lemmas 3.6 and 3.7, it can be easily deduced that Conditions 2 and 3 of Lemma 3.1 hold for any given v with probability $1 - \exp(-\Omega(N\delta^2))$. Condition 2 follows by noting that

$$\left|\frac{1}{|S|} \sum_{x \in S} |v \cdot (x - \mu)|^2 - 1\right| = \left|\frac{1}{|S|} \sum_{x \in S} g_r^v(x) + \frac{1}{|S|} \sum_{x \in S} h_r^v(x)\right|$$

$$\leq \left|\frac{1}{|S|} \sum_{x \in S} g_r^v(x)\right| + \left|\frac{1}{|S|} \sum_{x \in S} h_r^v(x)\right|.$$

Lemmas 3.6 and 3.7 immediately imply that this is at most 2δ except with probability $\exp(-\Omega(N\delta^2))$.

To prove Condition 3, we note that $|v \cdot (x - \mu)|^2 \leq r^2 + h_r^v(x)$ for all x, where we used $r \geq 1$. Therefore, we have

$$\frac{1}{|S|} \sum_{x \in T} |v \cdot (x - \mu)|^2 \leq \frac{1}{|S|} \sum_{x \in T} r^2 + \frac{1}{|S|} \sum_{x \in S} h_r^v(x)$$

$$\leq \frac{r^2|T|}{|S|} + \frac{1}{|S|} \sum_{x \in S} h_r^v(x).$$

Noting that $r^2|T|/|S| = O(\epsilon \log(1/\epsilon))$ and applying Lemma 3.7, we have that the above is $O(\epsilon \log(1/\epsilon))$ except with probability at most $\exp(-\Omega(N\delta))$.

Letting C be a cover of the kind guaranteed in Fact 3.4, and applying a union bound over $v \in C$, we have that except with probability $\exp(-\Omega(N\delta^2))$, Conditions 2 and 3 of Lemma 3.1 hold for all $v \in C$ and some $\delta = O(\epsilon \sqrt{\log(1/\epsilon)})$. We claim that this actually suffices to show that the conditions hold (with slightly worse value δ) for all unit vectors v.

To show this, we note that after fixing the set T, the conditions in question say that for some specific symmetric matrix M it holds that $|v^\top M v| \leq \delta^2/\epsilon$, for all unit vectors v. We claim that if such a statement holds for all $v \in C$, then it will hold that $|v^\top M v| \leq O(\delta^2/\epsilon)$ for *all* unit vectors v. This will finish our proof of Proposition 3.3.

Specifically, we have the following lemma.

Lemma 3.8   *Let M be a real symmetric matrix with $|v^\top M v| \leq B$ for all $v \in C$ and some $B \geq 0$. Then, it holds that $v^\top M v = O(B)$ for all unit vectors $v \in \mathbf{R}^d$.*

Proof   Diagonalizing M, we can write $M = \sum_i \lambda_i w_i w_i^\top$ for some real numbers λ_i and orthonormal vectors w_i. We sort the indices so that $|\lambda_1| \geq |\lambda_2| \geq \dots$. It is clear that for any unit vector v, it holds $|v^\top M v| \leq |\lambda_1|$. It remains to show that $|\lambda_1| = O(B)$. To show this, we note that by the defining property of C there exists a $v \in C$ with $v \cdot w_1 \geq 9/10$. We can write this v as $\sum_i a_i w_i$ with $1 = \|v\|_2^2 = \sum_i a_i^2$ and $a_1 \geq 9/10$. It is easy to see that

$$|v^\top M v| = \left| \sum_i \lambda_i a_i^2 \right| \geq |\lambda_1| a_1^2 - \sum_{i>1} |\lambda_i| a_i^2 \geq |\lambda_1|((9/10)^2 - (1-(9/10)^2)) \geq |\lambda_1|/2.$$

Therefore, $B \geq |\lambda_1|/2$, which completes the proof.   □

This completes the proof of Proposition 3.3. We note that a similar proof holds for samples drawn from any sub-Gaussian distribution with identity covariance.

3.2.2 Sample Complexity for Bounded Covariance Distributions

In this section, we analyze the next most important case: that of a random variable X with bounded covariance matrix $\mathbf{Cov}[X] \preceq I$.

One might reasonably expect that a sufficiently large sample of i.i.d. points from X is $(\epsilon, O(\sqrt{\epsilon}))$-stable with reasonable probability. As we will see, this statement turns out to hold only after a slight – but necessary – modification (to see why this is necessary, see Exercise 2.3).

In this section, we establish the following proposition.

Proposition 3.9   *Let $0 < \epsilon < 1/2$ be a real number, and N be an integer, with N at least a sufficiently large constant multiple of $d \log(d)/\epsilon$. Let S be a set of N i.i.d. samples from a distribution X with bounded covariance $\mathbf{Cov}[X] \preceq I$. Then, with probability at least $9/10$, there exists a set S' obtained by changing an ϵ-fraction of the points of S such that S' is $(\epsilon, O(\sqrt{\epsilon}))$-stable with respect to X.*

Remark 3.10 Note that if the set T is an ϵ-corruption of S, then T is also a 2ϵ-corruption of S'. Since S' is stable with respect to X, running a standard robust mean estimation algorithm on T will still give an $O(\sqrt{\epsilon})$ error estimate of the mean of X.

We start with the following simple reformulation of stability for our setting:

Lemma 3.11 *A set S is $(\epsilon, O(\sqrt{\epsilon}))$-stable with respect to a distribution X if and only if the following conditions hold:*

1. $\|\mu_S - \mu_X\|_2 = O(\sqrt{\epsilon})$.
2. $\mathbf{Cov}[S] \le O(I)$.

Proof The "only if" part is easy to see. For the "if" part, we use Lemma 3.1 to show that S is $(\epsilon, O(\sqrt{\epsilon}))$-stable if

1. $\|\mu_S - \mu_X\|_2 = O(\sqrt{\epsilon})$.
2. For every unit vector v, it holds that $\frac{1}{|S|}\sum_{x \in S}(|v \cdot (x - \mu_X)|^2 - 1) = O(1)$.
3. For every unit vector v, and $T \subset S$ with $|T| \le \epsilon|S|$, we have

$$\frac{1}{|S|}\sum_{x \in T}|v \cdot (x - \mu_X)|^2 = O(1).$$

Observe that the second condition here is equivalent to $\frac{1}{|S|}\sum_{x \in S}|v \cdot (x - \mu_X)|^2 = O(1)$, which subsumes the third. We note that the left-hand side is

$$v^\top\left(\frac{1}{|S|}\sum_{x \in S}(x - \mu_X)(x - \mu_X)^\top\right)v = v^\top(\mathbf{Cov}[S] + (\mu_X - \mu_S)(\mu_X - \mu_S)^\top)v$$

$$= v^\top\mathbf{Cov}[S]v + O(\epsilon),$$

assuming that the first condition holds. This is $O(1)$ for all unit vectors v if and only if $\mathbf{Cov}[S] \le O(I)$, which completes the proof. $\square$

The first of these new conditions is relatively easy to verify. If S is a set of N i.i.d. samples drawn from X – a distribution with mean μ_X and covariance at most I – then $\mu_S - \mu_X$ is a random vector with mean 0 and covariance at most $(1/N)I$. Thus, the expected squared ℓ_2-norm of this random vector is at most d/N. Hence, for $N \gg d/\epsilon$, the Markov inequality implies that $\|\mu_S - \mu_X\|_2 = O(\sqrt{\epsilon})$ with large constant probability.

Unfortunately, the second condition need not be true even for arbitrarily large sets of samples. In particular, consider the probability distribution on $\mathbf{R}^d$ that (a) with probability $1/N$ returns a random vector of length $\sqrt{Nd}$, and (b) otherwise returns the zero vector. It is not hard to see that this distribution has mean 0 and identity covariance. However, a sample of size N will have constant probability of containing exactly one vector v of norm $\sqrt{Nd}$, and the empirical covariance matrix will be $(1/N)(1 - 1/N)vv^\top$, which has spectral norm $d(1 - 1/N)$.

The aforementioned problem can arise only when some reasonable fraction of the covariance of X comes from points very far from the mean. However, the fact that X has bounded covariance implies that such points cannot have a large impact on the mean, and if we ignore them we will be able to get a better analysis of the stability. In particular, since $\mathbf{Cov}[X] \leq I$, we have $\mathbf{E}[\|X - \mu_X\|_2^2] \leq d$. By the Markov inequality, it follows that $\|X - \mu_X\|_2 \leq 2\sqrt{d/\epsilon}$ except with probability $\epsilon/2$. We can therefore think of these additional points as "outliers." In particular, we can define a new distribution X', which is equal to X when $\|X - \mu_X\|_2 \leq 2\sqrt{d/\epsilon}$ and equal to μ_X otherwise. Note that

$$\mathbf{Cov}[X'] \leq \mathbf{E}[(X' - \mu_X)(X' - \mu_X)^\top] \leq \mathbf{E}[(X - \mu_X)(X - \mu_X)^\top] = \mathbf{Cov}[X] \leq I.$$

That is, X and X' both have bounded covariance and differ with only ϵ probability. The bound on the covariance along with the Cauchy–Schwarz inequality implies that the ϵ-probability event on which X and X' differ can only contribute $O(\sqrt{\epsilon})$ to their respective means, and thus $\|\mathbf{E}[X] - \mathbf{E}[X']\|_2 = O(\sqrt{\epsilon})$.

Since a collection of N i.i.d. samples from X' will with high probability contain at most ϵN points that were truncated, and since the means of X and X' differ by $O(\sqrt{\epsilon})$, it suffices to show that N samples from X' are stable with respect to X' with high probability. We can show this by demonstrating that a sufficiently large sample of i.i.d. points drawn from X' has bounded covariance with high probability.

While this goal might seem itself challenging, there is a well-known inequality that suffices for this purpose. In particular, we will make use of the Matrix-Chernoff bound.

Theorem 3.12 (Matrix Chernoff Inequality) *For $d \in \mathbf{Z}_+$ and $R > 0$, let $\{X_k\}$ be a sequence of independent random $d \times d$ symmetric matrices with $0 \leq X_k \leq R \cdot I$ almost surely. Let $\mu_{\max} = \left\|\mathbf{E}\left[\sum_k X_k\right]\right\|_2$. Then, for any $\delta > 0$, we have*

$$\mathbf{Pr}\left(\left\|\sum_k X_k\right\|_2 > (1 + \delta)\mu_{\max}\right) \leq d\left[\frac{e^\delta}{(1 + \delta)^{1+\delta}}\right]^{\mu_{\max}/R}.$$

We apply Theorem 3.12 as follows: Letting $S = \{x_1, x_2, \ldots, x_N\}$ be a set of i.i.d. samples from the distribution X', we define the matrices

$$X_k = (x_k - \mu_{X'})(x_k - \mu_{X'})^\top/N.$$

We can take R to be the maximum possible value of $\|x - \mu_{X'}\|_2^2/N$, that is, $R = O(d/(\epsilon N))$. We note that

$$\mathbf{E}\left[\sum_k X_k\right] = \mathbf{Cov}[X'] \leq I,$$

and therefore $\mu_{\max} \leq 1$. Setting $\delta = 2/\mu_{\max} \geq 2$, Theorem 3.12 gives

$$\mathbf{Pr}\left[\left\|\frac{1}{|S|}\sum_{x \in S}(x - \mu_{X'})(x - \mu_{X'})^\top\right\|_2 \geq 2 + \mu_{\max}\right] \leq d(e/(1+\delta))^{\delta\mu_{\max}/R}$$

$$\leq d\exp(-\Omega(N\epsilon/d)).$$

Therefore, so long as N is at least a sufficiently large constant multiple of $d\log(d)/\epsilon$, with probability at least $1 - 1/d$, we have

$$\mathbf{Cov}[S] \leq \frac{1}{|S|}\sum_{x \in S}(x - \mu_{X'})(x - \mu_{X'})^\top \leq (2 + \mu_{\max})I \leq 3I.$$

This completes the proof of Proposition 3.9.

Discussion The above sample complexity upper bound is nearly optimal. In particular, learning the mean of X to error $\sqrt{\epsilon}$, even from uncorrupted samples, will require $N \geq d/\epsilon$. Removing the extra logarithmic factor turns out to be somewhat subtle, as explained below.

On the one hand, consider the distribution X that with probability ϵ returns $+$ or $-\sqrt{d/\epsilon}$ times a random basis vector e_i. This distribution has zero mean and identity covariance, and cannot be readily simplified by throwing away its largest samples. Unfortunately, if $N = o(d\log(d)/\epsilon)$ samples are taken from X, it will usually be the case that there is some coordinate i such that more than an ϵ/d-fraction of the samples taken are $\pm \sqrt{d/\epsilon}\, e_i$. This will cause the variance of X in the e_i-direction to be too large.

On the other hand, the above example is not necessarily enough to prevent the existence of robust mean estimation algorithms with optimal sample complexity. In particular, in [59] it is shown that for ϵ a small constant, for any distribution X with bounded covariance, a set S of $\Omega(d)$ i.i.d. samples from X will contain a *subset* $S' \subset S$ with $|S'| \geq (1 - \epsilon)|S|$ such that S' is $(\epsilon, O(1))$-stable. This suffices to robustly learn the mean of X to error $O(1)$, even after introducing an ϵ-fraction of corruptions. That is, $O(d/\epsilon)$ samples are sufficient for ϵ a constant. Whether or not this still holds for smaller ϵ remains an open question. Interestingly, using a slightly different algorithm, we can still efficiently and robustly learn the mean to error $O(\sqrt{\epsilon})$ with $O(d/\epsilon)$ samples (see Exercise 3.2).

3.3 Robust Mean Estimation in Near-Linear Time

Thus far, we have developed polynomial-time robust mean estimation algorithms without focusing on their precise runtimes. While the unknown convex programming approach leads to polynomial-time algorithms, the inherent use of the ellipsoid method renders such algorithms impractical. The iterative filtering technique on the other hand relies on spectral methods that are somewhat more practical. However, we did not provide a detailed analysis of its runtime.

We start this section by analyzing the runtime of the vanilla filtering-based algorithm, given as input ϵ, δ, and a set T of n points in $\mathbf{R}^d$. Roughly speaking, each iteration of the algorithm requires the following steps:

---

1. Compute v, an approximate largest eigenvector of $\Sigma := \mathbf{Cov}[T]$ and the corresponding eigenvalue λ.
2. If $\lambda > 1 + C\delta^2/\epsilon$, for a sufficiently large constant $C > 0$:

   (a) Compute $v \cdot x$ for all $x \in T$.
   (b) Sort the projected points.
   (c) Determine which elements to filter.
   (d) Apply filter and go back to Step 1 on the filtered set T.
3. Else

   Return the sample mean of the final dataset T.

Runtime per Iteration With careful implementation, each iteration of the filtering algorithm can be made to run in near-linear, i.e., $\tilde{O}(dn)$, time. For most of the steps of the algorithm, it is straightforward to establish this runtime upper bound. Note that the initial eigenvector computation in Step 1 requires some care, as naively it would take time $\Omega(d^2n)$ to even compute Σ. Fortunately, an approximate largest eigenvector can be computed using the power iteration method. In particular, taking $v = \Sigma^t w / \|\Sigma^t w\|_2$, for w a random unit vector, and $t = O(\log(d/\tau))$, it is not hard to show that with probability $1 - \tau$ we have $v^\top \Sigma v \geq (0.99) \|\Sigma\|_2$. Applying this procedure to the matrix $\Sigma - (1 - C\delta^2/\epsilon)I$ (which will be positive definite for sufficiently large C) gives a suitably good approximate largest eigenvector.

It remains to show how to multiply a vector by Σ efficiently. This can be done by noting that $\Sigma = \frac{1}{|T|} \sum_{x \in T} (x - \mu_T)(x - \mu_T)^\top$, and thus,

$$\Sigma w = \frac{1}{|T|} \sum_{x \in T} (w \cdot (x - \mu_T))(x - \mu_T),$$

which can be computed in $O(dn)$ time.

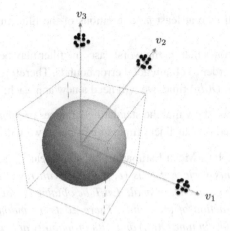

Figure 3.1 Illustration of hard instance for the standard filtering algorithms. The sphere represents the projection of the inliers into the space spanned by the top three eigenvectors v_1, v_2, v_3. Outliers are then placed at distance about $\sqrt{d}$ from the mean along each of these axes. The standard filtering algorithms will only remove one batch of outliers per iteration.

Number of Iterations The thornier issue with the runtime analysis of a filtering algorithm has to do with the *number* of iterations. A naive analysis can only show that at each iteration the number of remaining points decreases by at least 1. This bounds from above the number of iterations somewhat suboptimally at ϵn for a final runtime of $\tilde{O}(dn^2)$. While this worst-case number of iterations may not appear in practice, it is not hard to construct examples where the standard implementation of the filtering method will be required to undergo many iterations.

For example, consider the following instance in the additive contamination model, where the true mean μ is 0. Suppose that the top m eigenvectors of the sample covariance matrix of the inliers are $v_1, v_2, \ldots, v_m$, respectively. An adversary then adds $\epsilon n/m$ outliers at the points $\sqrt{d}v_i$, for each $1 \le i \le m$, as shown in Figure 3.1. (We note that the outliers should be at distance at most $\sqrt{d}$ from the origin, so that they cannot be discovered by naive filtering.) It is not hard to see that after adding these outliers the vectors $v_1, v_2, \ldots, v_m$ will remain the top m eigenvectors of the empirical covariance matrix. Unfortunately, when filtering in direction v_i, the algorithm will pick up only one of the batches of outliers. Thus, the filtering method will take m filter iterations to remove all of these outliers; and even after only $m/2$ iterations the remaining outliers will still contribute to the mean an error of $\sum_{i=m/2}^{m} v_i \epsilon \sqrt{d}/m$, which has ℓ_2-norm $\Omega(\epsilon \sqrt{d/m})$. If we are in the Gaussian case, and if m is much less than

$d/\log(1/\epsilon)$, it will take at least $m/2$ iterations of the filter in order to obtain optimal error.

This example shows that, in the worst case, the filter may be forced to apply $\Omega(d)$ iterations in order to obtain good error bounds. Therefore, if we want our algorithm to run in $\tilde{O}(dn)$ time, we will need a new approach.

In this section, we show that the standard guarantees of robust mean estimation can be achieved in near-linear time. In particular, we will show:

Theorem 3.13 (Robust Mean Estimation in Near-linear Time)   *Let $S \subset \mathbf{R}^d$ be a set of n points such that S is (ϵ, δ)-stable with respect to μ for some $1 \geq \delta \geq \epsilon > 0$ with ϵ sufficiently small. Let T be obtained from S by arbitrarily corrupting an ϵ-fraction of the points. There exists a randomized algorithm that given T, ϵ, δ runs in time $\tilde{O}(dn)$ and with probability at least $3/5$ computes a $\widehat{\mu}$ such that $\|\widehat{\mu} - \mu\|_2 = O(\delta)$.*

High-level Intuition   To get some intuition for how such an algorithm might work, it is instructive to consider the hard example described above. Essentially, this example works by carefully constructing the set of outliers with foreknowledge of the filtering directions that the algorithm is going to use. This allows the adversary to arrange things in such a way that each filtering step will only remove a small number of outliers. A natural approach toward counteracting the adversary's power is via slightly randomizing the filter directions. In the setting of the example defined above, it is natural to define the subspace $V = \mathrm{span}(\{v_1, v_2, \ldots, v_m\})$ (which can be approximated as the span of the top eigenvectors of the sample covariance matrix), and filtering in a direction v given by a *random* unit vector in V. It is not hard to see that for such a v, the projection of an outlier onto v will have size $|v \cdot (\sqrt{d}v_i)|$, which will typically be on the order of $\sqrt{d/m}$. On the other hand, a typical inlier will have $|v \cdot x|$ typically on the order of 1. Recalling that we need $d/m \gg \log(1/\epsilon)$ in order for the outliers to substantially corrupt the sample mean, a typical outlier has a good chance of being far enough from the mean in the v-direction to be detectable. Thus, at least in this simple hard example – where the sample covariance matrix has m large, approximately equal, eigenvalues and many small eigenvalues – this sort of "filtering in a random direction (in the appropriate subspace)" approach suffices to detect a constant fraction of outliers in each iteration.

Unfortunately, while it is relatively easy to pick a good choice of random filter direction in the above simple setting, the choice of an appropriate filtering direction v in more complicated situations is far from obvious. Specifically, one needs to find a way to balance different directions with eigenvalues of different sizes against each other. It turns out that taking v proportional to $\Sigma^{\log(d)}w$, for a random vector w, works reasonably well. Intuitively, this is because the matrix $\Sigma^{\log(d)}$ can be thought of as an approximation to the projection matrix onto the set of eigenvectors of Σ whose eigenvalues are within a factor of 2 of the largest one. This is because taking the $\log(d)$-power means that even d eigenvectors with half the eigenvalue will contribute less to the final trace than the single largest eigenvector. Actually, we will want to consider instead a random vector v proportional to $B^{\log(d)}w$, where B is Σ minus an appropriate multiple of the identity. This is necessary so that when $\|\Sigma\|_2$ is close to 1 our algorithm will be able to distinguish between the eigenvalues of magnitude $1 + \delta^2/\epsilon$ (which correspond to directions where we want to filter) and eigenvalues of 1 (which correspond to directions in which we do not).

Once we have the direction v, we will filter in the v-direction. This should be achieved via a variation of our randomized, universal filter. However, it is not sufficient to filter only a single time. This is because if there is one very extreme outlier in the v-direction, there may be a reasonable probability that a filter will remove only that one outlier. Instead, in order to ensure that our algorithm makes significant progress, we will need to repeatedly filter in the v-direction until enough of the outliers have been removed. However, the standard randomized filtering guarantee will still hold at each step. The expected number of inliers removed will be less than the expected number of outliers removed, and thus with constant probability, the algorithm will never remove more than $O(\epsilon)$ fraction of elements of S.

This discussion explains what happens to the inliers, but it remains to understand what happens to the outliers. In particular, suppose that v is chosen to be Mw, for some symmetric matrix M and w a standard Gaussian vector. We note that $\mathbf{E}[\|v\|_2^2] = \mathbf{E}[w^\top M^\top M w] = \text{tr}(M^2)$. Our filter will tend to remove points x where $|v \cdot (x - \mu_S)|^2$ is substantially larger than $\|v\|_2^2 \approx \text{tr}(M^2)$. On the other hand, we have:

$$\mathbf{E}[|v \cdot (x - \mu_S)|^2] = \mathbf{E}[w^\top M(x - \mu_S)(x - \mu_S)^\top M w] = \text{tr}(M(x - \mu_S)(x - \mu_S)^\top M).$$

Thus, roughly speaking, our filter will remove some reasonable fraction of the points x for which $\text{tr}(M(x - \mu_S)(x - \mu_S)^\top M)$ is substantially larger than $\text{tr}(M^2)$. Morally, this means that after the filtering step the average value of $(x-\mu_S)(x-\mu_S)^\top$ (a stand-in for the new covariance matrix) will approximate the identity matrix, at least in the directions that M cares about. Specifically, this means that $\text{tr}(M\Sigma'M)$ will be substantially less than $\text{tr}(M\Sigma M) = \text{tr}(\Sigma^{2\log(d)+1})$, unless the eigenvalues of Σ are already small. From this, we conclude (using Fact 3.15) that $\text{tr}(\Sigma^{2\log(d)+1})$ decreases by a constant factor at every iteration. By performing some basic naive filtering at the start, we can ensure that the initial value of $\text{tr}(\Sigma^{2\log(d)+1})$ is only quasi-polynomial, and therefore, after only polylogarithmically many iterations, it will become manageable, leading to a case where $\textbf{Cov}[T]$ is bounded; so by the stability condition we will have that $\|\mu_T - \mu_S\|_2$ is small.

The pseudocode of the algorithm is given below.

Algorithm `Near-Linear-Time Randomized-Filtering`

1. Let $C > 0$ be a sufficiently large constant.
2. Let x be a random element of T and $R = 4n$, where $n = |T|$ is the size of the original dataset T. Remove from T all points at distance more than $R/2$ from x.
   /*We will henceforth use T to denote the remaining dataset.*/
3. Repeat the following $r = C\log(R/\epsilon)\log(d)$ times:
   (a) Let $\Sigma = \textbf{Cov}[T]$, $B = (|T|/n)\Sigma - (1 - C\delta^2/\epsilon)I$, and $M = B^{\log(d)}$.
       /*We do not actually compute these matrices.*/
   (b) Let $w \sim \mathcal{N}(0, I)$ be a Gaussian random vector.
   (c) Let $v = Mw$.
       /* Compute v efficiently using iterated multiplication by Σ.*/
   (d) Let m be an $O(\delta\|v\|_2)$-approximation of $v \cdot \mu_S$ (computed, e.g., via a trimmed mean of $v \cdot x$ for x in the original set T).
   (e) For $x \in T$, let $f(x) = |v \cdot x - m|^2$. Let

   $$\tau(x) := \begin{cases} f(x) & \text{if } f(x) > 10(\delta/\epsilon)^2\|v\|_2^2, \\ 0 & \text{otherwise.} \end{cases}$$

   (f) If $\sum_{x \in T} \tau(x) > C(n\delta^2/\epsilon)\|v\|_2^2$, pick t uniformly at random from $[0, \max_{x \in T} \tau(x)]$; remove from T all elements $x \in T$ with $\tau(x) > t$, and repeat this step.
4. Return μ_T, the sample mean of T.

Runtime Analysis To begin with, we provide the runtime analysis of this algorithm. We note that the main loop has only $r = \text{polylog}(nd/\epsilon)$ iterations. In each iteration, we compute v, which requires logarithmically many matrix multiplications by Σ (each of which can be done in $\tilde{O}(dn)$ time, as described previously). We note that the filter in Step 3(f) may need to be performed several times. However, at each iteration the largest value of $\tau(x)$ is at most the value of t selected in the previous iteration. This means that in expectation t decreases by a factor of 2 in each iteration. Since $\tau(x)$ is never larger than $(R\|v\|_2)^2$ nor smaller than $\|v\|_2^2$ (unless it is 0), this step will terminate in an expected $O(\log(R))$-iterations. All other steps can be straightforwardly implemented in $\tilde{O}(dn)$ time.

Correctness Analysis Next we need to show that if T is (ϵ, δ)-stable with respect to μ, the output of this algorithm with 2/3 probability returns an $O(\delta)$-approximation of μ. For this analysis, we begin with Step 2. This is a naive filtering step designed to ensure that all points of T are contained in a ball of radius R about μ_S. We note that if the chosen x was in S, then all other points in S must be within distance $R/2$ of x. Otherwise, we would have that $\mathbf{Cov}[S] = \frac{1}{n^2} \sum_{x,y \in S} (x - y)(x - y)^\top$ would have a direction in which the norm was at least 4 (coming from a single term in the sum), violating the stability condition, given that $\delta \leq 1$.

The next few steps compute an appropriate random direction v to consider, and the loop in Step 2 is just a particular instantiation of a randomized filter along the lines of our universal filter from Chapter 2. The correctness of the trimmed mean for approximating $v \cdot \mu$ follows from Proposition 1.18 and the first condition in the definition of stability (Definition 2.1).

To establish correctness, we need to verify that our randomized filter has the property that in expectation it removes fewer good points (i.e., elements of $T \cap S$) than bad ones. Recall, that this condition amounts to showing that $\sum_{x \in S \cap T} \tau(x) < (1/2) \sum_{x \in T} \tau(x)$ whenever the filter is being applied. To show this, we note that S has at most ϵn elements with positive $\tau(x)$ (as otherwise removing them would alter the variance of S in the v-direction by $10\delta^2/\epsilon$, violating stability). If $\sum_{x \in S} \tau(x)$ were more than $(C/2)n\delta^2/(2\epsilon)$, removing the (at most ϵn) elements with positive $\tau(x)$ would again change the variance in the v-direction by too much and violate stability. Thus, when the initial condition in Step 3(f) holds, at most half of the total sum of $\tau(x)$ comes from good elements, and, in particular, $\sum_{x \in S \cap T} \tau(x) \leq (1/2) \sum_{x \in T} \tau(x)$. Since the probability of removing x is proportional to $\tau(x)$, the expected number of good elements removed is at most half the total.

Remark 3.14 Note that the filter we used here is essentially the alternative universal filter discussed in Exercise 2.12. This has the advantage over the universal filter discussed in Section 2.4.3 that the scores do not change as we remove samples.

The above discussion along with the martingale argument used in the proof of Theorem 2.17 implies that with probability at least 2/3, $|T \cap S|$ never drops below $n(1 - 4\epsilon)$ throughout the course of our algorithm. We assume in the following that this holds.

Next, we need to analyze what happens to the bad points. Our goal is to show that after filtering, the value of $\mathrm{tr}(B^{2\log(d)+1})$ will decrease in expectation unless it was already small. Although the intuition behind this is relatively straightforward, the mechanics of proving it require some work.

We note that x is likely to be filtered out when $|v \cdot (x - \mu_S)|$ is substantially larger than $(\delta/\epsilon)\|v\|_2$. On the one hand, note that

$$\mathbf{E}[\|v\|_2^2] = \mathbf{E}[w^\top M M^\top w] = \mathbf{E}[\mathrm{tr}(M w w^\top M)] = \mathrm{tr}(M^2).$$

On the other hand, we have

$$v \cdot (x - \mu_S) = (Mw) \cdot (x - \mu_S) = w \cdot (M(x - \mu_S)).$$

This latter term is a Gaussian random variable with mean zero and variance $\|M(x - \mu_S)\|_2^2 = \mathrm{tr}(M(x - \mu_S)(x - \mu_S)^\top M)$. Notice that with probability at least $1/2$, we have

$$|v \cdot (x - \mu_S)|^2 > \mathrm{tr}(M(x - \mu_S)(x - \mu_S)^\top M)/10.$$

Therefore, for every x, with probability at least $1/2$ over the choice of w, we have

$$\tau(x) \geq \Omega(\mathrm{tr}(M(x - \mu_S)(x - \mu_S)^\top M)) - O(\delta/\epsilon)^2 \|v\|_2^2. \qquad (3.1)$$

Call x satisfying Condition (3.1) *full* and other x *empty*.

The other condition we have to use is that after applying our filters if we end up with a new set T', we have $\sum_{x \in T'} \tau(x) = O(n(\delta^2/\epsilon)\|v\|_2^2)$. In particular, this holds if we just sum over $x \in T' \setminus S$ with x full. Thus, we have

$$\sum_{\substack{x \in T' \setminus S \\ x \text{ full}}} \left(\Omega(\mathrm{tr}(M(x - \mu_S)(x - \mu_S)^\top M)) - O(\delta/\epsilon)^2 \|v\|_2^2 \right)$$

$$\leq \sum_{\substack{x \in T' \setminus S \\ x \text{ full}}} \tau(x) \leq O(n(\delta^2/\epsilon)\|v\|_2^2).$$

Noting that $|T' \setminus S| = O(n\epsilon)$, this gives

$$\sum_{\substack{x \in T' \setminus S \\ x \text{ full}}} \mathrm{tr}(M(x - \mu_S)(x - \mu_S)^\top M) \leq O(n(\delta^2/\epsilon)\|v\|_2^2). \qquad (3.2)$$

Taking the expectation over w of the right-hand side of Condition (3.2) gives $O(n(\delta^2/\epsilon))\mathrm{tr}(M^2)$. On the other hand, we have

$$\sum_{x \in T' \setminus S} \mathrm{tr}(M(x - \mu_S)(x - \mu_S)^\top M)$$

$$= \sum_{\substack{x \in T' \setminus S \\ x \text{ full}}} \mathrm{tr}(M(x - \mu_S)(x - \mu_S)^\top M) + \sum_{\substack{x \in T' \setminus S \\ x \text{ empty}}} \mathrm{tr}(M(x - \mu_S)(x - \mu_S)^\top M).$$

Employing Condition (3.2) and the fact that any given x has at most a $1/2$ probability of being empty, we have

$$\mathbf{E}\left[\sum_{x \in T' \backslash S} \operatorname{tr}(M(x - \mu_S)(x - \mu_S)^\top M)\right]$$

$$\le \frac{1}{2} \sum_{x \in T \backslash S} \operatorname{tr}(M(x - \mu_S)(x - \mu_S)^\top M) + O(n(\delta^2/\epsilon))\operatorname{tr}(M^2).$$

On the other hand, we can write

$$\sum_{x \in T' \cap S} \operatorname{tr}(M(x - \mu_S)(x - \mu_S)^\top M) = \operatorname{tr}\left(M\left(\sum_{x \in T' \cap S}(x - \mu_S)(x - \mu_S)^\top\right)M\right)$$

$$= n \operatorname{tr}(M^2)(1 + O(\delta^2/\epsilon)),$$

where the last equality is because the stability of S implies that the matrix $\sum_{x \in T' \cap S}(x - \mu_S)(x - \mu_S)^\top$ has eigenvalues $n(1 + O(\delta^2/\epsilon))$. Therefore, we obtain

$$\mathbf{E}\left[\operatorname{tr}\left(M\left(\frac{1}{n}\sum_{x \in T'}(x - \mu_S)(x - \mu_S)^\top - (1 - C\delta^2/\epsilon)I\right)M\right)\right]$$

$$\le O(\delta^2/\epsilon)\operatorname{tr}(M^2) + \operatorname{tr}\left(M\left(\frac{1}{n}\sum_{x \in T}(x - \mu_S)(x - \mu_S)^\top - (1 - C\delta^2/\epsilon)I\right)M\right)/2$$

$$= O(\delta^2/\epsilon)\operatorname{tr}(M^2) + \operatorname{tr}(MBM)/2.$$

We note that the term $((1/n)\sum_{x \in T'}(x - \mu_S)(x - \mu_S)^\top - (1 - C\delta^2/\epsilon)I)$ is very close to the value of B computed from T' (call it B'). In fact, the two differ only by an additive $(|T'|/n)(\mu_{T'} - \mu_S)(\mu_{T'} - \mu_S)^\top$. On the other hand, it is not hard to see that this is less than $O(\delta^2)I + O(\epsilon)B'$ in the Loewner ordering. Combining this with the above, we obtain the critical result

$$\mathbf{E}\left[\operatorname{tr}(MB'M)\right] \le O(\delta^2/\epsilon)\operatorname{tr}(M^2) + \operatorname{tr}(MBM)/2.$$

At this point, we would like to relate this quantity to $\operatorname{tr}((B')^{2\log(d)+1})$. For that, we will require the following simple linear-algebraic fact.

Fact 3.15 *Let A, B be symmetric PSD matrices such that $A \succeq B$. For all $k \in \mathbf{Z}_+$, we have that $\operatorname{tr}(B^k) \le \operatorname{tr}(A^{k-1}B)$.*

To verify the hypotheses of Fact 3.15, we need two things: First, it is not hard to see that because of the stability of S and because $|S \setminus T'| = O(\epsilon n)$, we have B' is positive definite. Next, we note that

$$(|T'|/n)\mathbf{Cov}[T'] = \frac{1}{n}\sum_{x\in T'}(x-\mu_T')(x-\mu_T')^\top \le \frac{1}{n}\sum_{x\in T'}(x-\mu_T)(x-\mu_T)^\top$$

$$\le \frac{1}{n}\sum_{x\in T}(x-\mu_T)(x-\mu_T)^\top = (|T|/n)\mathbf{Cov}[T].$$

Thus, $B' \le B$. This allows us to conclude that

$$\mathbf{E}[\mathrm{tr}((B')^{2\log(d)+1})] \le \mathbf{E}[\mathrm{tr}(MB'M)] \le O(\delta^2/\epsilon)\mathrm{tr}(B^{2\log(d)}) + \mathrm{tr}(B^{2\log(d)+1})/2. \tag{3.3}$$

Finally, we claim that $\mathrm{tr}(B^{2\log(d)+1}) = \Theta(\|B\|_2)\mathrm{tr}(B^{2\log(d)})$. Morally, this holds because $B^{2\log(d)}$ already approximates a projection onto the largest eigenvalues (within a factor of 2 of the biggest) of B. Formally, we have that if B has eigenvalues $\lambda_1 \ge \lambda_2 \ge \cdots \ge \lambda_d \ge 0$, then

$$\mathrm{tr}(B^{2\log(d)+1}) = \sum_{i=1}^{d}\lambda_i^{2\log(d)+1} \le \lambda_1\sum_{i=1}^{d}\lambda_i^{2\log(d)} = \lambda_1\mathrm{tr}(B^{2\log(d)}).$$

On the other hand, we have the following chain of inequalities:

$$\mathrm{tr}(B^{2\log(d)+1}) = \sum_{i=1}^{d}\lambda_i^{2\log(d)+1} \ge (\lambda_1/2)\sum_{i=1}^{d}\lambda_i^{2\log(d)} - (\lambda_1/2)\sum_{i:\lambda_i<\lambda_1/2}\lambda_i^{2\log(d)}$$

$$\ge (\lambda_1/2)\mathrm{tr}(B^{2\log(d)}) - d\lambda_1^{2\log(d)+1}/d^2 \ge (\lambda_1/3)\mathrm{tr}(B^{2\log(d)}).$$

Thus, $\mathrm{tr}(B^{2\log(d)+1}) = \Theta(\|B\|_2)\,\mathrm{tr}(B^{2\log(d)})$ for any positive semidefinite B.

Combining this with Condition (3.3), we have that unless $\|B\|_2 = O(\delta^2/\epsilon)$, each iteration of our main loop will decrease $\mathrm{tr}(B^{2\log(d)+1})$ (in expectation) by a constant factor. In particular, this means that the expectation of $\mathrm{tr}(B^{2\log(d)+1})$ times the indicator function of the event that $\|B\|_2$ is bigger than a sufficiently large multiple of δ^2/ϵ decreases by a constant factor in every iteration. Note that this quantity initially takes a value of at most $dR^{2\log(d)+1}$, and at the end is either zero or at least $d\epsilon^{2\log(d)+1}$. Therefore, after $r \gg \log(R/\epsilon)(2\log(d) + 1)$ rounds, the Markov inequality implies that the probability that $\|B\|_2$ is larger than a constant multiple of δ^2/ϵ is small.

Thus, with probability at least $3/5$, by the end of our algorithm we have a set T that differs from S on at most $O(\epsilon n)$ points and has $\mathbf{Cov}[T] = I + O(\delta^2/\epsilon)$. This property and the stability of S implies that $\|\mu_T - \mu\|_2 = O(\delta)$.

This completes the proof of Theorem 3.13.

3.4 Robust Mean Estimation with Additive or Subtractive Corruptions

The robust mean estimation algorithms presented thus far can approximate the mean of an ϵ-corrupted Gaussian to ℓ_2-error $\Theta(\epsilon \sqrt{\log(1/\epsilon)})$. On the other hand, it is information-theoretically possible to achieve ℓ_2-error of $O(\epsilon)$ (e.g., via Proposition 1.20 or the Tukey median). Unfortunately, there is a good reason for this gap. Consider an adversary that removes the ϵ-tails of a Gaussian along some random direction. It is easy to see that this operation moves the mean by $\Theta(\epsilon \sqrt{\log(1/\epsilon)})$ and decreases the variance in this direction by $\Theta(\epsilon \log(1/\epsilon))$. By changing the values of the removed points and adding them back at distance $\Theta(\sqrt{\log(1/\epsilon)})$ from the mean in the opposite direction, the adversary can restore the variance of the corrupted distribution (in the direction under consideration) to what it was originally, while leaving the mean off by $\Theta(\epsilon \sqrt{\log(1/\epsilon)})$.

Recall that the robust mean estimation algorithms we have studied look for discrepancies in the sample covariance matrix in order to find directions to filter along. Therefore, such algorithms will be unable to correct for these errors, and thus cannot achieve a final error rate better than $\Omega(\epsilon \sqrt{\log(1/\epsilon)})$. In fact, as we shall see in Chapter 8, there is reason to believe that achieving error $o(\epsilon \sqrt{\log(1/\epsilon)})$ may not be possible in polynomial time.

Crucially, this example makes essential use of the strong contamination model and the ability of the adversary to both add outliers and remove inliers. The former increases the variance by $\Theta(\epsilon \log(1/\epsilon))$ in the critical direction and the latter decreases it by the same amount to render the net change undetectable. It turns out that if only one kind of corruption is allowed (either additive or subtractive contamination), more accurate computationally efficient robust mean estimation algorithms are possible. In this section, we will prove the following theorem.

Theorem 3.16 *Given a set of $N = \text{poly}(d/\epsilon)$ ϵ-corrupted samples from $X = \mathcal{N}(\mu, I)$ on $\mathbf{R}^d$, where the corruptions are either only additive or only subtractive, there exists a $\text{poly}(N, d)$ time algorithm that with high probability returns an estimate $\widehat{\mu}$ such that $\|\widehat{\mu} - \mu\|_2 = O(\epsilon)$.*

Our first lemma shows that if purely additive or purely subtractive errors alter the sample mean by more than a sufficiently large constant multiple of ϵ in some direction, they must also change the variance in this direction by $\Omega(\epsilon)$ – an effect that is algorithmically detectable.

Lemma 3.17 *Let $S \subseteq \mathbf{R}^d$ be such that $\text{Cov}[S] \leq O(I)$. Let $0 < \epsilon < 1/3$ and $T \subseteq \mathbf{R}^d$ be such that either:*

1. $S \subseteq T$ and $|T| \leq (1 + \epsilon)|S|$ *(additive contamination)*, or
2. $S \supseteq T$ and $|T| \geq (1 - \epsilon)|S|$ *(subtractive contamination)*.

Suppose that for some unit vector $v \in \mathbf{R}^d$ it holds that $|v \cdot (\mu_S - \mu_T)| \gg \epsilon$. Then, we have

$$|v^\top (\mathbf{Cov}[T] - \mathbf{Cov}[S])v| = \Omega(\epsilon),$$

with $v^\top (\mathbf{Cov}[T] - \mathbf{Cov}[S])v$ being positive in Case 1 and negative in Case 2.

Note that there exists such a unit vector v if and only if $\|\mu_S - \mu_T\|_2 \gg \epsilon$.

Proof As in the proof of Lemma 2.7, we leverage the fact that if a small fraction of corruptions has a large influence on the mean, it must also have a correspondingly large influence on the covariance.

For Case 1, let $T = S \cup E$ with $|E| = \delta|T|$ for some $\delta \leq \epsilon/(1 + \epsilon)$. A simple calculation gives that

$$\mu_T = (1 - \delta)\mu_S + \delta\mu_E = \mu_S + \delta(\mu_E - \mu_S)$$

and

$$\begin{aligned}
\mathbf{Cov}[T] &= (1 - \delta)\mathbf{Cov}[S] + \delta\mathbf{Cov}[E] + \delta(1 - \delta)(\mu_S - \mu_E)(\mu_S - \mu_E)^\top \\
&= \mathbf{Cov}[S] + \delta(\mathbf{Cov}[E] - \mathbf{Cov}[S]) + \delta(1 - \delta)((\mu_T - \mu_S)/\delta)((\mu_T - \mu_S)/\delta)^\top \\
&\geq \mathbf{Cov}[S] - O(\epsilon I) + ((1 - \epsilon)/\epsilon)(\mu_S - \mu_T)(\mu_S - \mu_T)^\top.
\end{aligned}$$

Thus, if $|v \cdot (\mu_S - \mu_T)|$ is at least a sufficiently large constant multiple of ϵ, we have

$$v^\top (\mathbf{Cov}[T] - \mathbf{Cov}[S])v \geq -O(\epsilon) + \Omega(|v \cdot (\mu_S - \mu_T)|^2/\epsilon) = \Omega(\epsilon),$$

as desired.

For Case 2, we note that $\mathbf{Cov}[T] \leq \mathbf{Cov}[S]/(1 - \epsilon)$, and so interchanging the roles of S and T, and appealing to Case 1, we have that if $|v \cdot (\mu_T - \mu_S)|$ is at least a sufficiently large constant multiple of ϵ, then $v^\top (\mathbf{Cov}[S] - \mathbf{Cov}[T])v$ will be $\Omega(\epsilon)$. This completes the proof. □

Lemma 3.17 allows us to either (1) detect when additive or subtractive errors may have been sufficient to move the sample mean by at least $\Omega(\epsilon)$, or (2) certify that the mean has not been corrupted by this much. Unfortunately, if we do detect some direction v in which the mean might be far off, we do not have any obvious way to make progress. In particular, the filtering techniques we developed so far will not work in this setting. For the case of subtractive contamination, the reason is quite simple: There is no real way to build a filter to add back removed points.

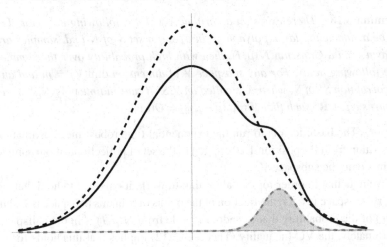

Figure 3.2 Illustration of univariate instance where the additive contamination is at distance $\Theta(1)$ from the true mean and it is information-theoretically impossible to separate from the inliers. Notice that the density of outliers (gray curve) at any point is substantially less than the density of inliers at that point (dotted black curve). Thus, if one removes any collection of points based on their x-coordinates, one will remove substantially more inliers than outliers.

For additive contamination, an error of ϵ can be introduced by adding an ϵ-fraction of outliers at distance $\Theta(1)$ from the true mean, as shown in Figure 3.2. Unfortunately, a constant fraction of the inliers will also be located in this range, and it may be information-theoretically impossible to separate the two. In particular, there may be no way to construct a filter that is guaranteed to remove more outliers than inliers.

To circumvent the obstacle just mentioned, we introduce two new ingredients. The first ingredient allows us to efficiently and robustly learn the mean when restricted to any low-dimensional subspace. In particular, for any given subspace V, our inefficient algorithm from Proposition 1.20 allows us to robustly estimate $\text{Proj}_V(\mu)$, the projection of μ onto V, within ℓ_2-error $O(\epsilon)$ in time $2^{O(\dim(V))}\text{poly}(d/\epsilon)$, simply by robustly estimating the mean of $\text{Proj}_V(X)$. We would like to apply this algorithm where V is the subspace defined by the large eigenvalues of the empirical covariance matrix. Unfortunately, this leads to a problem where the subspace V we are using is no longer independent of the samples we have received (and in fact might even depend on the adversarial corruptions). To deal with this issue, we will need a subtly stronger version of the algorithm from Proposition 1.20. Specifically, we want to know that with high probability over the samples from X for any subspace V and any set of corruptions our algorithm will still work. In particular we prove.

Lemma 3.18 *There exists an algorithm A with the following behavior: Let N be a sufficiently large polynomial in d/ϵ. If a set S of N i.i.d. samples are drawn from a Gaussian $N(\mu, I)$, then with high probability over the samples the following holds: For any subspace V of dimension $\dim(V) = m$ and any ϵ-corruption S' of S, when A is called on V, S' it runs in time $\text{poly}(N, 2^m)$ and returns a $\widehat{\mu} \in \mathbf{R}^d$ such that $\|\text{Proj}_V(\widehat{\mu} - \mu)\|_2 = O(\epsilon)$.*

Proof The basic idea is to run the exponential-time robust mean estimation algorithm from Proposition 1.20 applied to the set of projections of our sample points onto the subspace V.

We note that in order for that algorithm to work, it only had to hold that for every halfspace $v \cdot x \geq t$, the fraction of the points of S in this halfspace is within $O(\epsilon)$ of the probability that a random sample from $N(\mu, I)$ is in the halfspace. Fortunately, the VC-Inequality (Theorem A.12) implies that this holds for all halfspaces with high probability, as long as N is a sufficiently large constant multiple of d/ϵ^2. □

As a corollary of Lemma 3.18, we can efficiently approximate the projection of μ onto any low-dimensional subspace. In particular, if we take $m = \dim(V) = O(\log(1/\epsilon))$, the algorithm from Lemma 3.18 runs in $\text{poly}(d/\epsilon)$ time.

Suppose that our initial set of clean samples (inliers) S was sufficiently large ($\text{poly}(d/\epsilon)$ size suffices). Then we know that with high probability we have that $\text{Cov}[S] = I + O(\epsilon I)$ and $\|\mu_S - \mu\|_2 = O(\epsilon)$. Given access to an (additive or subtractive) ϵ-corrupted set of samples T, Lemma 3.17 implies that $|v \cdot (\mu - \mu_T)| = O(\epsilon)$, so long as the unit direction v is orthogonal to every eigenvector corresponding to an $\Omega(\epsilon)$-sized eigenvalue of $\text{Cov}[T] - \text{Cov}[S]$, or equivalently an eigenvalue of $\text{Cov}[T] - I$ with absolute value $\Omega(\epsilon)$. In particular, if we let V be the span of the eigenvectors of $\text{Cov}[T] - I$ with eigenvalue whose absolute value is at least a sufficiently large constant multiple of ϵ, we have that $\|\text{Proj}_{V^\perp}(\mu - \mu_T)\|_2 = O(\epsilon)$. If $\dim(V) = O(\log(1/\epsilon))$, we can use Lemma 3.18 to compute a $\widehat{\mu}$ with $\|\text{Proj}_V(\mu - \widehat{\mu})\|_2 = O(\epsilon)$. Piecing these two components together, we get an $O(\epsilon)$ ℓ_2-approximation to μ, as desired. In summary, we have described an efficient robust mean estimation algorithm with optimal error $O(\epsilon)$, as long as there are not too many large eigenvalues of $\text{Cov}[T] - I$.

It remains to handle the case that $\text{Cov}[T] - \text{Cov}[S]$ has many large eigenvalues. For this to happen, we must have not only added or removed many points far from the mean in a single direction, but in fact must have added or removed points that were far from the mean in many of these directions. It turns out that while looking at any given direction is insufficient to distinguish these outliers from the inliers, considering many directions simultaneously suffices.

In particular, for a point $x \in \mathbf{R}^d$ the sum of its contributions to the eigenvectors in a subspace W will be $\|\text{Proj}_W(x - \mu)\|_2^2$. For good samples (inliers), this quantity will be approximately $m = \dim(W)$ with high probability. However, for an ϵ-fraction of outliers to corrupt all these m eigenvalues by $\Omega(\epsilon)$ in the same direction, the average outlier will need to have $\left|\|\text{Proj}_W(x - \mu)\|_2^2 - m\right| = \Omega(m)$. It is not hard to show that only an $\exp(-\Omega(m))$-fraction of inliers will satisfy

$$\left|\|\text{Proj}_W(x - \mu)\|_2^2 - m\right| > m/10.$$

This suggests that we should be able to reliably distinguish outliers from inliers, as long as m is sufficiently large. However, we will need something slightly more precise than this for the following reason: While *on average* an outlier x will satisfy $\left|\|\text{Proj}_W(x - \mu)\|_2^2 - m\right| = \Omega(m)$, it might be that in reality only a small fraction of outliers satisfy this condition, and those that do have much larger discrepancies. What we will need in practice is a lemma that says that the total discrepancy coming from outliers exceeds that coming from inliers.

Lemma 3.19 *Let $W \subset \mathbf{R}^d$ be an m-dimensional subspace, for some $m \leq d$, and $X = \mathcal{N}(\mu, I)$. Then we have*

$$\mathbf{E}_{x \sim X}\left[\mathbf{1}\left\{\left|\|\text{Proj}_W(x - \mu)\|_2^2 - m\right| > m/10\right\} \|\text{Proj}_W(x - \mu)\|_2^2\right] = \exp(-\Omega(m)).$$
$$(3.4)$$

Furthermore, if S is a set of $\text{poly}(d/\epsilon)$ i.i.d. samples from X, for some sufficiently large constant degree polynomial, (3.4) holds for $x \sim_u S$ for all subspaces W of dimension $O(\log(1/\epsilon))$ with high probability.

Proof The first statement is a simple computation, and the latter statement can be proved by an application of the VC-inequality (Theorem A.12). The details are left as an exercise. □

Lemma 3.19 motivates our robust mean estimation algorithm for both subtractive and additive contamination.

Subtractive Contamination. Lemma 3.19 implies that for subtractive errors the covariance matrix of T, $\mathbf{Cov}[T]$, cannot have more than $\Omega(\log(1/\epsilon))$ eigenvalues of magnitude less than $1 - 3\epsilon$. For the sake of contradiction, suppose that $\mathbf{Cov}[T]$ has $m = \Theta(\log(1/\epsilon))$ eigenvalues less than $1 - 3\epsilon$, and let W be the span of the corresponding m eigenvectors, and let W' be the subspace of W orthogonal to $\mu_T - \mu$. Then we have

$$\mathbf{Cov}[T] = \frac{1}{|T|} \sum_{x \in T} (x - \mu)(x - \mu)^\top - (\mu_T - \mu)(\mu_T - \mu)^\top$$

$$\geq \mathbf{Cov}[S] - \frac{1}{|T|} \sum_{x \in S \setminus T} (x - \mu)(x - \mu)^\top - (\mu_T - \mu)(\mu_T - \mu)^\top.$$

For a matrix M and a subspace W, define the trace of M over W to be

$$\mathrm{tr}_W(M) := \mathrm{tr}(\Pi_W \, M \, \Pi_W),$$

where Π_W is the corresponding projection matrix. With this notation, the above gives

$$(1 - 3\epsilon)m \geq \mathrm{tr}_{W'}(\mathbf{Cov}[T]) \geq \mathrm{tr}_{W'}(\mathbf{Cov}[S]) - \frac{1}{|T|} \sum_{x \in S \setminus T} \|\mathrm{Proj}_{W'}(x - \mu)\|_2^2$$

$$\geq m(1 - \epsilon/2) - \frac{1}{|T|} \sum_{x \in S \setminus T} \|\mathrm{Proj}_{W'}(x - \mu)\|_2^2.$$

This in turn gives

$$\frac{1}{|T|} \sum_{x \in S \setminus T} \|\mathrm{Proj}_{W'}(x - \mu)\|_2^2 \geq 5m\epsilon/2.$$

Since $|S \setminus T| \leq 2\epsilon|T|$, by Lemma 3.19, the left-hand side of the above equation is at most

$$2\epsilon(1.1)m + \frac{2}{|S|} \sum_{x \in S} \mathbf{1}\{|\|\mathrm{Proj}_{W'}(x - \mu)\|_2^2 - m| > m/10\}\|\mathrm{Proj}_{W'}(x - \mu)\|_2^2$$

$$= 2.2\epsilon m + \exp(-\Omega(m)).$$

The right-hand side of the above equation fails to be large enough for m to be a sufficiently large constant multiple of $\log(1/\epsilon)$, which provides the desired contradiction.

Therefore, the robust mean estimation algorithm for dealing with subtractive contamination is surprisingly simple: Let V be the span of all eigenvectors of $\mathbf{Cov}[T]$ with eigenvalue less than $1 - 3\epsilon$. With high probability $\dim(V)$ will be less than $O(\log(1/\epsilon))$. Use Lemma 3.18 to compute the projection of μ onto V and use the sample mean for the projection onto $V^\perp$.

Additive Contamination. For the case of additive outliers, it will not necessarily be the case that $\mathbf{Cov}[T] - \mathbf{Cov}[S]$ will have few small eigenvalues. When the dimension is large, the existence of many large eigenvalues means that we have many outliers with large projection onto the relevant subspace. This property turns out to be sufficient for some sort of filtering. More specifically, we have

$$\mathbf{Cov}[T] \preceq \frac{1}{|T|} \sum_{x \in T} (x - \mu)(x - \mu)^\top$$

$$\preceq \mathbf{Cov}[S] + (\mu_S - \mu)(\mu_S - \mu)^\top + \frac{1}{|T|} \sum_{x \in T \backslash S} (x - \mu)(x - \mu)^\top.$$

Considering the trace on a subspace W of dimension m, we have

$$\mathrm{tr}_W(\mathbf{Cov}[T])$$

$$\leq \mathrm{tr}_W(\mathbf{Cov}[S]) + O(\epsilon) + \frac{1}{|T|} \sum_{x \in T \backslash S} \|\mathrm{Proj}_W(x - \mu)\|_2^2$$

$$\leq m + O(\epsilon m) + \frac{1}{|T|} \sum_{x \in T \backslash S} \mathbf{1}\left\{ \left| \|\mathrm{Proj}_W(x - \mu)\|_2^2 - m \right| > m/10 \right\} \|\mathrm{Proj}_W(x - \mu)\|_2^2.$$

This means that the trace of $\mathbf{Cov}[T]$ on W is at most $m(1 + O(\epsilon))$, unless the expectation over $x \sim_u T$ of the quantity

$$\mathbf{1}\left\{ \left| \|\mathrm{Proj}_W(x - \mu)\|_2^2 - m \right| > m/10 \right\} \|\mathrm{Proj}_W(x - \mu)\|_2^2$$

is more than ϵ. However, we know from Lemma 3.19 that the expectation of this quantity over $x \sim_u S$ is at most $\exp(-\Omega(m))$.

Suppose that $\mathbf{Cov}[T]$ has at least m eigenvectors whose eigenvalue is each at least $1 + C\epsilon$, where C is a sufficiently large constant. Then, if m is itself a sufficiently large constant multiple of $\log(1/\epsilon)$, we can let W be the span of these eigenvectors. Applying the above, we find that the expectation of the function

$$f(x) := \mathbf{1}\left\{ \left| \|\mathrm{Proj}_W(x - \mu)\|_2^2 - m \right| > m/10 \right\} \|\mathrm{Proj}_W(x - \mu)\|_2^2$$

over $x \sim_u T$ is more than ϵ, but the expectation over $x \sim_u S$ is less than ϵ^2. Using $f(x)$ as a score function for a randomized filter, we have that in expectation the number of good samples removed is at most an ϵ-fraction of the number of bad samples removed.

One caveat here is that the algorithm does not know the exact value of μ, and thus cannot compute the function $f(x)$ as provided. However, one can compute an $O(\epsilon)$-approximation of the projection of μ onto W, and it is not hard to show that computing f using this approximation suffices.

This allows us to create a filter-based algorithm. The algorithm will repeatedly compute the sample covariance of the remaining samples. If there are fewer than $C \log(1/\epsilon)$ eigenvalues larger than $1 + C\epsilon$, for C some sufficiently large constant, then we let V be the span of the eigenvectors with large eigenvalues, and compute an approximation to $\mathrm{Proj}_V(\mu)$ (using the algorithm of Lemma 3.18) and approximate $\mathrm{Proj}_{V^\perp}(\mu)$ by $\mathrm{Proj}_{V^\perp}(\mu_T)$. Otherwise, if there are many large eigenvalues, we let W be the span of the $C\log(1/\epsilon)$ top eigenvectors and define the function f as above, using it to create a randomized filter.

The analysis of this algorithm is relatively straightforward, with the caveat that we need all of the above arguments to still work even if we have potentially removed an $O(\epsilon^2)$-fraction of the original good samples. Fortunately, this is not difficult as if S' is any subset of S of size at least $(1 - \epsilon^2)|S|$, we will still have that $\mathbf{Cov}[S'] = I + O(\epsilon I)$ and $\mu_{S'} = \mu + O(\epsilon)$.

3.5 Robust Estimation via Nonconvex Optimization

Although the algorithms that we have presented until this point can be quite efficient, they are also somewhat complicated and have several constants that must be pinned down in order to actually implement them. It turns out that there is a fairly simple optimization framework that can be used in a black box-manner in order to efficiently solve robust mean estimation problems. Although this formulation is likely not as computationally efficient (especially compared to the near-linear time algorithm presented in Section 3.3), its simplicity and lack of extra parameters to tune makes it desirable in some settings.

To motivate our approach, we note that by the analysis of Section 2.2.2 if T is an ϵ-corrupted version of a $(3\epsilon, \delta)$-stable set S, then if we can find a set of weights w on T such that $0 \le w_x \le \frac{1}{(1-\epsilon)|T|}$ and $\sum_x w_x = 1$ for which the weighted covariance matrix $\Sigma_w := \sum_{x \in T} w_x(x - \mu_w)(x - \mu_w)^\top$ has maximum eigenvalue $1 + O(\delta^2/\epsilon)$, then we can conclude that $\|\mu_w - \mu_S\|_2 = O(\delta)$, giving us a good approximation to the mean of S.

A natural way to attempt to compute such a set of weights is to formulate it as an optimization problem. In particular, we would like to solve the following optimization problem:

$$\text{Find} \quad w\colon T \to \mathbf{R} \text{ such that} \qquad\qquad (3.5)$$

$$0 \le w_x \le \frac{1}{(1 - \epsilon)|T|} \text{ for all } x \in T$$

$$\sum_{x \in T} w_x = 1,$$

$$\text{Minimizing:} \quad \|\Sigma_w\|_2.$$

A first observation is that there exists a reasonably good set of weights. Specifically, by taking w^* to assign $\frac{1}{|S \cap T|}$ to $x \in S \cap T$ and 0 to other x, we know by the stability condition that $\|\Sigma_{w^*}\|_2 = 1 + O(\delta^2/\epsilon)$. The question is if can we efficiently find such a w.

We note that the optimization problem (3.5) is quite nice. The constraints are convex and the objective function is *almost* convex. In particular, the function

$$\left\| \sum_{x \in T} w_x (x - \mu)(x - \mu)^\top \right\|_2$$

for some *fixed* vector μ is convex in the weights w_x. Unfortunately, as μ_w depends on w, our actual objective will not in general be convex. This means that we cannot simply use convex optimization to find a global minimum of our objective function. Fortunately, it turns out that we do not have to do this. Specifically, we will show that *any* local minimum will suffice for our purposes. In particular, we show.

Theorem 3.20 *If T is an ϵ-corruption of a $(3\epsilon, \delta)$-stable set S for some ϵ sufficiently small and w is any local minimum of (3.5), then it holds that $\|\Sigma_w\|_2 \leq 1 + O(\delta^2/\epsilon)$.*

In particular, this means that in order to robustly estimate the mean of S, we do not necessarily need to find a global minimum of (3.5) (which might be hard), but merely a local minimum. This can be done much more generally. In particular, any gradient-descent type algorithm should allow one to find an approximate local minimum. While there are some technicalities involved with this strategy (in particular, the objective is not always differentiable, however one can solve a linear program to find a direction of decrease if it exists), they can be resolved by more-or-less standard methods. See Exercise 3.6 for more details.

Instead, we will work toward a proof of Theorem 3.20. To begin with, we want to understand the derivative of Σ_w. Since w is constrained, we cannot vary it in all directions. So we will consider the derivative in the direction of another weight vector u.

Lemma 3.21 *Let T be a set of points in $\mathbf{R}^d$. Let u and w be weight vectors satisfying the constraints of (3.5). Then, for $0 \leq t \leq 1$, we have*

$$\Sigma_{(1-t)w+tu} = (1 - t)\Sigma_w + t\Sigma_u + t(1 - t)(\mu_w - \mu_u)(\mu_w - \mu_u)^\top.$$

In particular, the derivative in the $u - w$ direction of Σ_w at w is

$$D_{u-w}\Sigma_w = \Sigma_u - \Sigma_w + (\mu_w - \mu_u)(\mu_w - \mu_u)^\top.$$

Proof The proof follows by noting that the distribution defined by $(1-t)w+tu$ is a mixture of the distributions defined by u and w. Applying the standard formula for the covariance of a mixture then yields

$$\Sigma_{(1-t)w+tu} = (1 - t)\Sigma_w + t\Sigma_u + t(1 - t)(\mu_w - \mu_u)(\mu_w - \mu_u)^\top.$$

Taking the derivative of this quantity with respect to t at $t = 0$ gives the second statement of the lemma, concluding our proof.   □

To prove Theorem 3.20, we need to show that for any weight vector with $\|\Sigma_w\|_2$ large, there exists another weight vector u such that moving in the u direction causes $\|\Sigma_w\|_2$ to decrease. We note that Lemma 3.21 is quite promising for this. If we take u to be a weight with $\|\Sigma_u\|_2$ small, then the $-\Sigma_w$-term in the derivative will cause the largest eigenvalues of Σ to decrease substantially, while the Σ_u term will only cause them to increase by a small amount. Unfortunately, we also have to deal with the remaining $(\mu_w - \mu_u)(\mu_w - \mu_u)^{\mathsf{T}}$ term.

For this, we note that the measure defined by w is 3ϵ-close to the uniform distribution over S. This and Lemma 2.10 imply that

$$\|\mu_w - \mu_S\|_2 = O(\delta + \sqrt{\epsilon}\|\Sigma_w - I\|_2).$$

By taking $u = w^*$ to be the uniform distribution over $S \cap T$, we therefore obtain $\|\mu_{w^*} - \mu_S\|_2 = O(\delta)$. Combining these we find that

$$\|\mu_w - \mu_{w^*}\|_2^2 = O(\delta^2 + \epsilon\|\Sigma_w - I\|_2).$$

In particular, if Σ_w has largest eigenvalue $1 + \lambda$, for some $\lambda > 0$, we have

$$\begin{aligned}
\|\Sigma_{(1-t)w+tw^*}\|_2 &= \|(1-t)\Sigma_w + t\Sigma_{w^*} + t(1-t)(\mu_w - \mu_{w^*})(\mu_w - \mu_{w^*})^{\mathsf{T}}\|_2 \\
&\leq (1-t)\|\Sigma_w\|_2 + t\|\Sigma_{w^*}\|_2 + t(1-t)\|(\mu_w - \mu_{w^*})\|_2^2 \\
&\leq (1-t)(1+\lambda) + t(1 + O(\delta^2/\epsilon)) + tO(\delta^2 + \epsilon\lambda) \\
&\leq \|\Sigma_w\|_2 - t(\lambda + O(\delta^2/\epsilon + \epsilon\lambda)).
\end{aligned}$$

Therefore, so long as λ is at least a sufficiently large constant multiple of δ^2/ϵ and ϵ is less than a sufficiently small constant, then for any $1 > t > 0$ (and in particular for any sufficiently small $t > 0$) we have that $(1 - t)w + tw^*$ has a smaller value of the objective of (3.5) than w does. This shows that w can only be a local minimum if $\lambda = O(\delta^2/\epsilon)$ or in other words, if $\|\Sigma_w\|_2 \leq 1 + O(\delta^2/\epsilon)$.

This completes the proof of Theorem 3.20.   □

Theorem 3.20 gives us our simple robust mean algorithm. We can use standard optimization methods to find any (approximate) local minimum of (3.5). We can then return $\hat{\mu} = \sum_{x \in T} w_x x$. This will then give an $O(\delta)$ approximation of the true mean by Lemma 2.6.

3.6 Robust Sparse Mean Estimation

Leveraging sparsity in high-dimensional datasets is a fundamental problem of significant practical importance. Various formalizations of this problem have been investigated in statistics and machine learning for at least the past two decades. Specifically, sparse mean estimation is arguably one of the most fundamental sparse estimation tasks and is closely related to the Gaussian sequence model.

In this section, we study sparse mean estimation in the strong contamination model. In *robust* sparse mean estimation, we are given an ϵ-corrupted set of samples from a structured distribution, where the unknown mean $\mu \in \mathbf{R}^d$ is k-sparse (i.e., supported on an unknown subset of k coordinates), and we want to compute a good approximation $\widehat{\mu}$ close to μ. Importantly, we want to achieve this using many fewer samples than in the dense case – namely, poly($k, \log(d)$) instead of poly(d) samples.

We will require the following notation to describe vectors and matrices subsets of their coordinates.

Definition 3.22 If $x \in \mathbf{R}^d$ and $C \subseteq [d]$, let x_C denote the vector in $\mathbf{R}^{|C|}$ obtained by taking the coordinates of x whose indices lie in C. For a matrix $M \in \mathbf{R}^{d \times d}$, we let M_C denote the $|C| \times |C|$ submatrix given by keeping the rows and columns corresponding to the elements of C.

Arguably, the simplest version of robust sparse mean estimation is the following: One is given ϵ-corrupted samples from the Gaussian $\mathcal{N}(\mu, I_d)$ with the guarantee that μ is a k-sparse vector, and the goal is to approximate μ in ℓ_2 norm. Of course, ignoring the sparsity assumption, we can efficiently obtain an $O(\epsilon \sqrt{\log(1/\epsilon)})$-approximation of μ with $O(d/\epsilon^2)$ samples. However, with the sparsity assumption, we can hope to significantly improve the sample complexity of this algorithm.

This improvement is readily apparent in the uncorrupted setting. In particular, if one takes N samples, with N a sufficiently large constant multiple of $k\log(d)/\epsilon^2$, it is not hard to show that with high probability the sample mean, $\widehat{\mu}$, approximates the true mean to error at most $\epsilon/\sqrt{k}$ in each coordinate. Of course, this leads to ℓ_2 error on the order of $\epsilon\sqrt{d/k}$; but this is mostly because we keep the errors from coordinates not in the support of μ. To overcome this issue, we can truncate $\widehat{\mu}$ to its top k coordinates. In particular, letting $t_k(x)$ be the vector obtained from x by setting all but the k coordinates with largest absolute value to 0, it is not hard to see that $t_k(\widehat{\mu})$ will be $O(\epsilon)$-close to μ. This holds because on $\text{Supp}(\mu) \cup \text{Supp}(t_k(\widehat{\mu}))$ we have that μ and $\widehat{\mu}$ are close, where $\text{Supp}(x)$ denotes the set of coordinates i where $x_i \neq 0$.

In fact, μ and $\widehat{\mu}$ are close on *every* set of small support. This in particular motivates the following definition.

Definition 3.23   For $x \in \mathbf{R}^d$ define the $\ell_{2,k}$-norm of x, denoted $\|x\|_{2,k} :=$ $\|t_k(x)\|_2$, to be the ℓ_2-norm over the k biggest coordinates of x. Equivalently, we have that $\|x\|_{2,k} \overset{\text{def}}{=} \sup_{\|v\|_2=1, |\text{Supp}(v)| \le k} v \cdot x$.

For k-sparse vectors, finding an approximation in $\ell_{2,k}$-norm is sufficient to find an approximation in ℓ_2-norm. In particular, we have the following simple structural result.

Lemma 3.24   *For $x, y \in \mathbf{R}^d$ with y a k-sparse vector, we have*

$$\|t_k(x) - y\|_2 \le \sqrt{6}\|x - y\|_{2,k}.$$

Proof   We consider the contributions to $\|t_k(x) - y\|_2$ coming from three sets of coordinates: (i) $C_1 = \text{Supp}(y) \cap \text{Supp}(t_k(x))$, (ii) $C_2 = \text{Supp}(t_k(x)) \backslash \text{Supp}(y)$, and (iii) $C_3 = \text{Supp}(y) \backslash \text{Supp}(t_k(x))$.

For the first of these, we note that $(t_k(x) - y)_{C_1} = (x - y)_{C_1}$. Since $|C_1| \le k$, we have that $\|(t_k(x) - y)_{C_1}\|_2 \le \|x - y\|_{2,k}$. A similar argument holds for the C_2, because $|C_2| \le k$ and $(t_k(x) - y)_{C_2} = (x - y)_{C_2}$.

To analyze C_3, we bound $\|(t_k(x) - y)_{C_3}\|_2 \le \|(x-y)_{C_3}\|_2 + \|(t_k(x) - x)_{C_3}\|_2$. Once again, we have that $\|(x-y)_{C_3}\|_2 \le \|x-y\|_{2,k}$. We also claim that $\|(t_k(x)-x)_{C_3}\|_2 \le \|x - y\|_{2,k}$. This is because t_k truncates x to the k-*largest* coordinates. In particular, this means that

$$\|(t_k(x) - x)_{C_3}\|_2 = \|x_{C_3}\|_2 \le \|x_{C_2}\|_2 = \|(t_k(x) - y)_{C_2}\|_2 \le \|x - y\|_{2,k}.$$

Note that $t_k(x) - y$ is supported on the three sets of coordinates above. The ℓ_2-norm on the first and second sets are at most $\|x - y\|_{2,k}$ and on the third set is at most twice this bound. Therefore, we have

$$\|t_k(x) - y\|_2^2 \le \|x - y\|_{2,k}^2 + \|x - y\|_{2,k}^2 + (2\|x - y\|_{2,k})^2 = 6\|x - y\|_{2,k}^2.$$

This completes our proof. $\square$

Lemma 3.24 and the above discussion show that in the uncorrupted case we can estimate μ to $\ell_{2,k}$-error ϵ (and thus to ℓ_2-error $O(\epsilon)$) using $O(k \log(d)/\epsilon^2)$ samples. Achieving a qualitatively similar guarantee in the robust setting requires additional work.

We start with an information-theoretic argument. If we take a set S of $N > k \log(2d/k)/\epsilon^2$ samples from $\mathcal{N}(\mu, I_d)$, Proposition 3.3 implies that for some $\delta = O(\epsilon \sqrt{\log(1/\epsilon)})$, for any given set $C \subset [d]$ with $|C| = k$, with probability $1 - \exp(-k \log(2d/k))$, the set of samples $\{x_C : x \in S\}$ is (ϵ, δ)-stable with respect to μ_C. Taking a union bound over C, with high probability, for each C

we can compute a $\widehat{\mu}(C)$ such that $\|\widehat{\mu}(C) - \mu_C\|_2 \leq \delta$. Thus, if we can find a single vector $\widehat{\mu}$ such that for every such C it holds $\|\widehat{\mu}(C) - \widehat{\mu}_C\|_2 \leq \delta$, we will have $\|\widehat{\mu} - \mu\|_{2,k} \leq 2\delta$. Clearly, such a $\widehat{\mu}$ exists (since μ is such a vector). It is thus information-theoretically possible to estimate μ to $\ell_{2,k}$ error $O(\epsilon \sqrt{\log(1/\epsilon)})$ with $O(k \log(2d/k)/\epsilon^2)$ samples.

The question is whether or not we can make some version of the above information-theoretic argument algorithmic. A first attempt at doing so would be to use a standard filtering method. Given a set T of ϵ-corrupted samples, one can try to find a subset $T' \subset T$ that still contains most of the inliers and has bounded covariance. We of course cannot expect that the full covariance matrix $\Sigma_{T'}$ will be bounded, as not even the covariance of the set of inlier samples will be (unless we take at least d of them). However, we can hope that $\|(\Sigma_{T'})_C\|_2 \leq 1 + O(\epsilon \log(1/\epsilon))$ for every subset $C \subset [d]$ of size k. If this holds, by Lemma 2.7 applied to $\{x_C : x \in T'\}$, we will have that $\|(\mu_{T'} - \mu)_C\|_2 = O(\epsilon \sqrt{\log(1/\epsilon)})$ for every $|C| \leq k$, or equivalently that $\|\mu_{T'} - \mu\|_{2,k} = O(\epsilon \sqrt{\log(1/\epsilon)})$.

Unfortunately, it appears quite challenging to make the above approach computationally efficient for the following reason. The required condition (i.e., that $\|(\Sigma_{T'})_C\|_2 \leq 1 + O(\epsilon \log(1/\epsilon))$ for all $|C| \leq k$) is equivalent to the bound $v^\top \Sigma_{T'} v \leq 1 + O(\epsilon \log(1/\epsilon))$ for all k-sparse vectors v with $\|v\|_2 \leq 1$. It turns out that this condition is not checkable in polynomial time, even approximately (under plausible complexity assumptions).

In order to obtain a computationally efficient algorithm, we will need to relax the aforementioned condition. Note that $v^\top \Sigma_{T'} v = \text{tr}(\Sigma_{T'} v v^\top)$, where $v v^\top$ is a matrix satisfying: (i) $v v^\top$ is symmetric, (ii) $v v^\top \succeq 0$, (iii) $\text{tr}(v v^\top) \leq 1$, (iv) $\|v v^\top\|_F \leq 1$, (v) the ℓ_1-norm of the ℓ_2-norms of the rows/columns of $v v^\top$ is at most $\sqrt{k}$, and (vi) $\|v v^\top\|_1 \leq k$, where by $\|v v^\top\|_1$ we denote the ℓ_1-norm of the coefficients of $v v^\top$. These last two conditions hold because k-sparsity implies $\|v\|_1 \leq \sqrt{k}\|v\|_2 \leq \sqrt{k}$.

Using these conditions, we define a convex relaxation (obtained by dropping the rank-1 requirement). Let $C(H)$ be the set of matrices satisfying the following conditions: (i) H is symmetric, (ii) $H \succeq 0$, (iii) $\text{tr}(H) \leq 1$, (iv) $\|H\|_F \leq 1$, (v) the ℓ_1-norm of the ℓ_2-norms of the rows/columns of H is at most $\sqrt{k}$, and (vi) $\|H\|_1 \leq k$.

We now consider the following natural convex relaxation:

$$\sup_{\|v\|_2 \leq 1, |\text{Supp}(v)| \leq k} v^\top \Sigma v \leq \sup_{C(H)} \text{tr}(\Sigma H). \tag{3.6}$$

Inequality (3.6) is useful for us because the right-hand side can be efficiently approximated using semidefinite programming. Thus, our new plan is to use the filtering method in order to find some $T' \subseteq T$ such that

$$\sup_{C(H)} \text{tr}(\Sigma_{T'} H) \le 1 + O(\epsilon \log(1/\epsilon)). \tag{3.7}$$

This will imply the necessary bounds on $\|(\Sigma_{T'})_C\|_2$ and give our result. Unfortunately, finding such a T' might not be possible unless we take more samples. In particular, using $o(k^2)$ samples it might not even be the case that $\sup_{C(H)} \text{tr}(\Sigma_S H)$ is small (see Exercise 3.8).

This problem can be resolved by drawing more samples. In particular, if we take $N \gg k^2 \log(d)/\epsilon^2$ samples, then with high probability each coordinate of $(\Sigma_S - I_d)$ will have absolute value $O(\epsilon/k)$. In such a case, for H satisfying the necessary conditions, we have

$$\text{tr}(\Sigma_S H) = \text{tr}(H) + \text{tr}((\Sigma_S - I_d)H) \le 1 + \|\Sigma_S - I_d\|_\infty \|H\|_1 \le 1 + O(\epsilon).$$

Furthermore, for any subset $S' \subseteq S$ with $|S'| \ge (1 - \epsilon)|S|$, we have $\Sigma_{S'} \preceq (1 + O(\epsilon))\Sigma_S$. Combined with the fact that H is positive semidefinite, we conclude that $\text{tr}(\Sigma_{S'} H) \le 1 + O(\epsilon)$.

Our next goal is to efficiently find a large subset T' of T such that Condition (3.7) holds. A convenient way to formulate this is by using the unknown convex programming approach for robust estimation (explained in Section 2.3). In particular, let Δ^T be the set of probability distributions W on T satisfying $W(x) \le \frac{1}{(1-\epsilon)|T|}$ for all x. Let W^* be the uniform distribution on $T \cap S$. We need to show that if we have a $W \in \Delta^T$ for which Σ_W does not satisfy (3.7), we can find a linear function L with $L(W) > L(W^*)$.

Toward this end, we note that we have a positive semidefinite, trace 1 matrix H with $\|H\|_1 \le k$ and $\text{tr}(\Sigma_W H) = 1 + \lambda$, where $\lambda > C\epsilon \log(1/\epsilon)$, for C a sufficiently large constant. We can rewrite the left-hand side as

$$\text{tr}(\Sigma_W H) = \sum_{x \in T} W(x)\text{tr}((x - \mu_W)(x - \mu_W)^\top H).$$

As this quantity is abnormally large, this suggests that we define the function

$$L(U) := \sum_{x \in T} U(x)\text{tr}((x - \mu_W)(x - \mu_W)^\top H).$$

That is, $L(W) \ge 1 + C\epsilon \log(1/\epsilon)$. On the other hand, we have

$$
\begin{aligned}
L(W^*) &= \sum_{x \in T} W^*(x)\text{tr}((x - \mu_W)(x - \mu_W)^\top H) \\
&= \text{tr}\left(\mathbf{E}_{x \sim W^*}[(x - \mu_W)(x - \mu_W)^\top]H\right) \\
&= \text{tr}\left(\left(\Sigma_{W^*} + (\mu_{W^*} - \mu_W)(\mu_{W^*} - \mu_W)^\top\right)H\right) \\
&= 1 + O(\epsilon) + (\mu_{W^*} - \mu_W)^\top H(\mu_{W^*} - \mu_W).
\end{aligned}
$$

To deal with the last term in the above equation, we note that for any k-sparse unit vector v we have $v^\top \Sigma_W v \leq 1 + \lambda$. Thus, applying Lemma 2.7 to $(\Sigma_W)_C$ for any $|C| \leq k$, we find that $\|(\mu_W - \mu)_C\|_2 = O(\epsilon \sqrt{\log(1/\epsilon)} + \sqrt{\epsilon\lambda})$. Thus, we have $\|\mu_W - \mu\|_{2,k} = O(\epsilon \sqrt{\log(1/\epsilon)} + \sqrt{\epsilon\lambda})$. By stability of the restrictions to each set of k coordinates, we have $\|\mu_{W^*} - \mu\|_{2,k} = O(\epsilon \sqrt{\log(1/\epsilon)})$. Combining the above, we have $\|\mu_W - \mu_{W^*}\|_{2,k} = O(\sqrt{\epsilon\lambda})$. This means that the top-k coordinates of $(\mu_W - \mu_{W^*})$ have ℓ_2-norm at most $O(\sqrt{\epsilon\lambda})$, and that the other coordinates are all smaller than $O(\sqrt{\epsilon\lambda/k})$. In particular, this means that we can write $(\mu_W - \mu_{W^*}) = v + w$, where $\|v\|_2 = O(\sqrt{\epsilon\lambda})$ and $\|w\|_\infty = O(\sqrt{\epsilon\lambda/k})$.

Thus, we have

$$(\mu_{W^*} - \mu_W)^\top H(\mu_{W^*} - \mu_W) = (v+w)^\top H(v+w) = v^\top Hv + v^\top Hw + w^\top Hv + w^\top Hw.$$

By the ℓ_2-bound on v and the Frobenius bound on H, we have $|v^\top Hv| \leq \|v\|_2^2 \|H\|_F = O(\epsilon\lambda)$. Since the ℓ_1-norm of the ℓ_2-norms of the rows of H is at most $\sqrt{k}$, we have $\|Hv\|_1 = O(\sqrt{\epsilon k \lambda})$, and thus $|w^\top Hv| = O(\epsilon\lambda)$. We bound $v^\top Hw$ similarly. Finally, we have $|w^\top Hw| \leq \|w\|_\infty^2 \|H\|_1 = O(\epsilon\lambda)$. Thus, combining with the above we have

$$L(W^*) = 1 + O(\epsilon) + O(\epsilon\lambda) < L(W).$$

In summary, we have shown the following theorem.

Theorem 3.25 *Let $d, k > 0$ be integers and $\epsilon > 0$ sufficiently small. Let N be a sufficiently large constant multiple of $k^2 \log(d)/\epsilon^2$. There exists a polynomial-time algorithm that given ϵ and N ϵ-corrupted samples from $N(\mu, I_d)$ computes a $\widehat{\mu}$ such that with high probability $\|\widehat{\mu} - \mu\|_{2,k} = O(\epsilon \sqrt{\log(1/\epsilon)})$.*

A few remarks are in order about Theorem 3.25. First, the final error of $O(\epsilon \sqrt{\log(1/\epsilon)})$ achieved by our algorithm is the best known guarantee even in the nonsparse case. Interestingly, there does appear to be an inherent gap in the sample complexity. Specifically, we showed that $O(k \log(d/k)/\epsilon^2)$ samples information-theoretically suffice; but we gave an efficient algorithm when given $\Omega(k^2 \log(d)/\epsilon^2)$ samples. While we can do better than this when $k \geq \sqrt{d}$ (since the dense algorithm only uses $O(d/\epsilon^2)$ samples), there is some evidence (see Chapter 8) that this information-computation trade-off is inherent.

3.7 Exercises

3.1 (Sample Complexity for Subexponential Tails) Let X be a distribution on $\mathbf{R}^d$ with identity covariance and $\mathbf{Pr}[X \cdot v > t] \ll \exp(-ct)$ for some constant $c > 0$ and any unit vector v. Let $x_1, x_2, \ldots, x_N$ be i.i.d. samples from X.

(a) Use a cover to show that for some $N = \tilde{O}(d^2/\epsilon^2)$, with high probability over the choice of x_i, the multiset $\{x_i\}_{i=1}^N$ is $(\epsilon, O(\epsilon \log(1/\epsilon))$-stable.

> *Note:* A simple cover cannot do much better than this, as it is not hard to show that for smaller values of N, the *expected* number of v's in our cover for which the stability condition is violated will be more than 1. The next few parts will show how to improve the sample complexity.

(b) Show that with high probability we have that $\|x_i\|_2 \ll \sqrt{d} \log(N)$ for all i.

> (Hint: Note that for a fixed x and v a random unit vector, it holds that $|v \cdot x| \gg \|x\|_2/\sqrt{d}$ with probability at least $1/2$.)

(c) Show that for any positive integer $m < N/2$ with high probability over our samples, the following holds: For any $2m$ distinct samples $y_1, y_2, \ldots, y_m$ and $z_1, z_2, \ldots, z_m$ in $\{x_1, x_2, \ldots, x_N\}$, if v_z is the unit vector in the direction of $(z_1 + z_2 + \cdots + z_m)$, then

$$v_z \cdot (y_1 + y_2 + \cdots + y_m) \ll m \log(N).$$

> (Hint: Show that for y_i, z_i, i.i.d. samples from X that this happens except with probability N^{-2m}. Note that v_z is some unit vector so $v_z \cdot X$ is stochastically dominated by an exponential distribution.)

(d) Show that if the conditions from parts (b) and (c) hold for every m, then for any m distinct samples $y_1, y_2, \ldots, y_m$ in $\{x_1, \ldots, x_N\}$ we have

$$\left\| \sum_{i=1}^m y_i \right\|_2 \ll \sqrt{dm} \log(N) + m \log(N).$$

> (Hint: Use induction on m a power of 2. Write $\sum_{i=1}^m y_i = \sum_{i=1}^{m/2} y_i + \sum_{i=m/2+1}^m y_i$ and use the condition from (c) to bound the inner product of the two halves.)

(e) Show that for $N = \tilde{\Omega}(d/\epsilon^2)$ (with sufficiently large implied constants) the set $\{x_1, \ldots, x_N\}$ is $(\epsilon, O(\epsilon \log(1/\epsilon))$-stable with high probability.

> (Hint: Assume that the condition from part (d) holds. Use a cover argument, but use part (d) to bound the contribution from terms with $|v \cdot x_i| \gg \log(N)$.)

3.2 (Bounded Covariance Sample Complexity) Let X be a random variable with $\mathbf{Cov}[X] \preceq I_d$. For constant ϵ_0, there is a polynomial-time algorithm that given $O(d)$ ϵ_0-corrupted samples from X computes and $O(1)$ approximation to $\mathbf{E}[X]$. Given this, show that for any $\epsilon_0 > \epsilon > 0$ there exists a polynomial time algorithm that given $O(d/\epsilon)$ ϵ-corrupted samples from X computes an $O(\sqrt{\epsilon})$ approximation to $\mathbf{E}[X]$.

3.3 (Robust Estimation in Small Space) The robust mean estimation algorithms described in the current and the previous chapters require essentially the entire dataset in memory. That is, the standard implementation of these algorithms requires memory scaling quadratically in the dimension d. Provide an algorithm that performs robust mean estimation, in the total variation contamination model, using $d$polylog(d/ϵ) bits of storage (in addition to read-only access to the data). How many passes over the dataset does your algorithm require? Can you develop an algorithm with similar guarantees in the strong contamination model?

(Hint: The near-linear time algorithm of Section 3.3 can be used as a starting point to achieve this goal.)

Remark 3.26 The reader is referred to [60] for a systematic investigation of robust statistics in the streaming model.

3.4 (Sample Complexity for the Huber Noise Algorithm) Show that the robust mean estimation algorithm for obtaining $O(\epsilon)$-error with Huber contamination (for spherical Gaussians) can be made to work with high probability with $\tilde{O}(d/\epsilon^2)$ samples.

3.5 (Nonconvex Optimization for Huber Noise) Show that we can get an efficient algorithm to obtain $O(\epsilon)$ error with Huber contamination using nonconvex optimization.

(Hint: Find a weight function that is a local minimum of the sum of the top $O(\log(1/\epsilon))$ eigenvalues of the covariance matrix. Show that this has the sum of these eigenvalues $O(\epsilon \log(1/\epsilon))$.)

3.6 (Finding Stationary Points) It is not quite trivial to find an approximate stationary point of the optimization problem (3.5), as the objective function is not smooth. Show however that given a nonstationary point w, it is possible to efficiently find a direction v in which the objective function decreases. Use this to give an efficient algorithm to find an approximate stationary point.

3.7 (Smooth Formulation of Nonconvex Optimization) Show that the nonconvex optimization technique for robust mean estimation also works if the objective function in (3.5) is replaced by

$$\mathrm{tr}\left((\Sigma_w - (1 - C\delta^2/\epsilon)I)^{\log(d)}\right),$$

for $C > 0$ a sufficiently large constant. This has the slight advantage of the objective function being smooth, and thus allowing one to use simple gradient descent.

3.8 (Sample Complexity of Robust Sparse Estimation) Show that for $k \leq \sqrt{d}$ if one takes S to be a set of k^2 i.i.d. samples from $\mathcal{N}(0, I_d)$, then with high probability

$$\sup_{C(H)} \mathrm{tr}(\Sigma_S H) > 1 + \Omega(1).$$

(Hint: Consider H a $k^2 \times k^2$ submatrix.)

3.8 Discussion and Related Work

The sample upper bounds given in Section 3.2 were established in the works by [45, 46, 59]. In more detail, for the case of identity covariance (sub)-Gaussians, the optimal sample complexity for the stability condition was given in [45]. For the case of bounded covariance distributions, a near-optimal sample upper bound was implicitly shown in [46] for the constant probability error regime. For the high probability regime, a nearly tight bound was given in [59]. Section 3.2 gives a unified and simplified exposition of these results. The reader is also referred to [145] for related sample size upper bounds.

The design of near-linear time algorithms for robust mean estimation was initiated in [30]. That work gave a robust mean estimation algorithm for bounded covariance distributions on $\mathbf{R}^d$ that has near-optimal sample complexity, achieves the optimal ℓ_2-error guarantee of $O(\sqrt{\epsilon})$, and runs in time $\tilde{O}(nd)/\mathrm{poly}(\epsilon)$, where n is the sample size and ϵ is the fraction of outliers. That is, the algorithm of [30] has the same (optimal) sample complexity and error guarantee as previous polynomial-time algorithms [45, 46], while running in near-linear time when the fraction of outliers ϵ is a small constant.

At the technical level, [30] builds on the convex programming approach of Section 2.3. Specifically, the algorithm of [30] reduces robust mean estimation to the task of solving a polylogarithmic number of covering/packing SDPs. Combined with the fact that such SDPs can be solved in near-linear time, using techniques from continuous optimization [2, 125], [30] obtain the desired near-linear time algorithm. Roughly speaking, their algorithm starts by fixing a guess v for the true mean. Given this guess, they consider an SDP whose solution gives a good set of weights (assuming the guess is sufficiently accurate). Even though this guess v may not be correct, [30] establish a win–win phenomenon: Either v is a good guess of the target mean μ in which case we get a good set of weights, or v is far from μ and we can efficiently find a new guess v' that is closer to μ by a constant factor.

Subsequent work [42] observed that a simple preprocessing step allows one to reduce to the case when the fraction of corruptions is a small universal constant. As a corollary, a simple modification of the [30] algorithm obtains the same guarantees in $\tilde{O}(nd)$ time. More importantly, [42] gave a probabilistic analysis that leads to a fast mean estimation algorithm that is simultaneously outlier-robust and achieves optimal sample complexity in the high success probability regime. Independently and concurrently to [42], [71] used the matrix multiplicative weights (MMW) method to develop a filtering-based algorithm with $\tilde{O}(nd)$ runtime. The near-linear time algorithm of Section 3.3 was inspired by the MMW-based approach of [71] and can be viewed as a simplification of their work. At a high level, a conceptual commonality of these works [30, 42, 71] is that they leverage algorithmic techniques from continuous optimization in order to develop iterative methods (with each iteration taking near-linear time) that are able to deal with multiple directions *in parallel*.

The $O(\epsilon)$-error robust mean estimator for spherical Gaussians under additive contamination presented in Section 3.4 was developed in [47]. The corresponding algorithm for subtractive contamination is based on the same ideas and first appears in this chapter.

The connection between nonconvex optimization given in Section 3.5 and robust mean estimation was first established in [32]. The reader is referred to [144] for a similar approach and generalizations to other estimation tasks, and to [31] for a refinement of these ideas in the context of robust sparse estimation. In this chapter, we presented a simplified proof of the main structural result of [32]. Finally, the reader is referred to [37] for a nonconvex gradient method in the context of heavy-tailed mean estimation.

The study of robust estimation under sparsity constraints (and robust sparse mean estimation in particular) was initiated in [10]. The latter work employed the unknown convex programming method to obtain sample-efficient and polynomial-time robust estimators for a number of sparse estimation tasks, including mean estimation for spherical Gaussians and sparse PCA in the spiked covariance model. Subsequent work developed practical provable algorithms for these tasks, under weaker distributional assumptions, by adapting the filtering technique [69] and the aforementioned connection to nonconvex optimization [31].

4

Robust Covariance Estimation

4.1 Introduction

In the previous chapters, we developed algorithmic techniques for robust mean estimation when the inlier distribution has known or bounded covariance matrix. These results suffice for example to robustly learn an unknown mean and identity covariance Gaussian to within small total variation distance. The immediate next question is how to efficiently and robustly learn an unknown mean *and unknown covariance* Gaussian in small total variation distance. More generally, the techniques of the previous chapters suffice to robustly estimate the mean of a distribution, assuming we have some prior knowledge about the covariance. It is natural to ask if this assumption is inherent or whether it is possible to robustly estimate the mean without a priori bounds on the covariance matrix.

Such results do not follow from the techniques we have developed so far. In particular, not knowing the covariance matrix makes the robust learning problem significantly more challenging. In fact, it is not immediately clear in what metric one should robustly learn the covariance to obtain total variation distance error guarantees, even in the Gaussian setting.

In this chapter, we develop efficient algorithms for robust covariance estimation of high-dimensional Gaussians and other distributions satisfying appropriate moment bounds. As an immediate corollary, we obtain the desired near-optimal total variation distance guarantees.

At a high-level, the basic idea underlying robust covariance estimation algorithms is fairly simple: If X is a centered random variable (i.e., satisfies $\mathbf{E}[X] = 0$), then the covariance of X is exactly the expectation of the random variable $Y = XX^\top$. That is, robustly estimating the covariance matrix of X is equivalent to robustly estimating the mean of the random variable $Y = XX^\top$. In other words, the problem of robust covariance estimation can be "reduced" to the problem of robust mean estimation of a more complicated random variable.

Given this observation, one might hope to use robust mean estimation algorithms directly. Unfortunately, it will typically not be quite this easy for the following reason: Our algorithms for robustly estimating the mean of a random variable require that we have an a priori upper bound (or, better yet, an approximation to) on its covariance (or equivalently its second moments). Since robustly learning the covariance of X can be thought of as learning the second moments of X, we would require knowing some kind of bound on the fourth moments of X (i.e., $\mathbf{Cov}[Y]$). If we knew an a priori upper bound on $\mathbf{Cov}[Y]$, we could use it directly with our robust mean estimation techniques to learn the covariance of X. Unfortunately, such bounds do not hold for the random variable $Y = XX^{\top}$, even if X is a Gaussian distribution. To handle this issue, we need to use additional structural properties of X.

Specifically, if $X \sim \mathcal{N}(0, \Sigma)$, we can leverage the fact that the covariance of Y, $\mathbf{Cov}[Y]$, can be expressed as a known function of the covariance of X, $\mathbf{Cov}[X]$. An upper bound on Σ will give us an upper bound on the covariance of Y, which can then be used to obtain a better approximation of Σ. Applying this idea iteratively will allow us to bootstrap better and better approximations, until we end up with an approximation to Σ with error close to the information-theoretic optimum.

In this chapter, we develop in detail the techniques alluded to above for estimating the covariance of a random variable. We will assume throughout that the random variables we work with have mean zero. A more critical assumption is that the random variables in question have a Gaussian-like relationship between their second and fourth moments. The reader is encouraged to consider the prominent special case of learning the covariance of a single Gaussian, although these assumptions will apply more generally.

Note that although these techniques can be used to learn the covariance of a Gaussian even if that covariance is degenerate, for the sake of ease of exposition, throughout this chapter we will be assuming that the covariance Σ is nondegenerate. See Remark 4.11 for more details.

4.2 Efficient Algorithm for Robust Covariance Estimation

Notation Before we begin, we introduce some additional notation. Our algorithm will make use of linear algebraic tools in order to transform our datasets into appropriate spaces. In order to notate this cleanly, if f is a function on $\mathbf{R}^d$ and S a set of points in $\mathbf{R}^d$, we will use $f(S)$ to denote the set $\{f(x) \colon x \in S\}$.

4.2.1 Additional Intuition and Basic Facts

Before we proceed with a detailed outline of our technique, we should clarify the metric we will use to approximate the covariance matrix. Recall that for mean estimation we used the ℓ_2-norm between vectors. Natural choices for the case of the covariance matrix could be either the spectral norm or the Frobenius norm.

In this chapter, we will use a stronger metric, known as Mahalanobis (or relative Frobenius) distance. This is an affine invariant metric that corresponds to multiplicative approximation.

Definition 4.1 (Mahalanobis Distance) Let $\Sigma_1, \Sigma_2 \in \mathbf{R}^{d \times d}$ be invertible PSD matrices. We define the Mahalanobis distance between these matrices to be $\|\Sigma_2^{-1/2} \Sigma_1 \Sigma_2^{-1/2} - I\|_F$.

We note that the Mahalanobis distance does *not* define a metric, though it does satisfy the identity axiom along with weak versions of the symmetry and transitivity axioms.

Definition 4.2 (Robust Covariance Estimation) Fix $0 < \epsilon < 1/2$. Given access to an ϵ-corrupted set of samples from a distribution X on $\mathbf{R}^d$ with unknown covariance Σ, the goal of a robust covariance estimation algorithm is to compute $\widehat{\Sigma}$ such that $\|\Sigma^{-1/2} \widehat{\Sigma} \Sigma^{-1/2} - I\|_F$ is small.

To understand the need to define a more complicated notion of distance as in Definition 4.1, we note that, unlike robust mean estimation, covariance estimation does not have a natural scale to it. Specifically, if one wants to estimate the mean of a Gaussian $X = \mathcal{N}(\mu, \sigma^2 I)$, there is a natural scale to the problem. As differences between points in X are proportional to σ, we expect that the achievable error should also be proportional to σ (and, in fact, the information-theoretically optimal error is $\Theta(\sigma\epsilon)$). On the other hand, if one wants to estimate the covariance of a Gaussian $X = \mathcal{N}(0, \Sigma)$, the situation is rather different. More precisely, there *is* a natural scale to the problem, but that scale is given by the unknown covariance Σ itself! This suggests that one should measure the error between Σ and $\widehat{\Sigma}$ only after normalizing both of them. This can be done by replacing Σ by $\Sigma^{-1/2} \Sigma \Sigma^{-1/2} = I$ and $\widehat{\Sigma}$ by $\Sigma^{-1/2} \widehat{\Sigma} \Sigma^{-1/2}$. This leaves open the question of *what* metric we want to use to compare these matrices. While it might be natural to use something like the spectral norm in some settings, the Frobenius norm turns out to be more useful in our context. This is because the Frobenius norm is in fact the strongest norm that one can expect to learn in, and in particular because it is proportional to the total variation distance between the underlying Gaussians.

Fact 4.3 *Let $\Sigma_1, \Sigma_2 \in \mathbf{R}^{d \times d}$ be positive-definite matrices such that*

$$\|\Sigma_2^{-1/2} \Sigma_1 \Sigma_2^{-1/2} - I\|_F = \delta.$$

Then we have

$$d_{\mathrm{TV}}(\mathcal{N}(0, \Sigma_1), \mathcal{N}(0, \Sigma_2)) = \Theta(\min(\delta, 1)).$$

In particular, as it is usually impossible to robustly learn a distribution to total variation distance better than ϵ, we cannot expect to learn the covariance to Mahalanobis distance better than $\Omega(\epsilon)$. As we will see, it is possible to efficiently learn to Mahalanobis distance $\tilde{O}(\epsilon)$. This shows that this algorithmic result is close to the strongest that one could hope for.

Let $X = \mathcal{N}(0, \Sigma)$. Since our goal is to robustly learn the mean of the random variable $Y = XX^\top$, we first need to understand the relationship between $\mathbf{Cov}[Y]$ and $\Sigma = \mathbf{Cov}[X]$. Toward this objective, it will be useful to consider the random variables $X' = \Sigma^{-1/2} X \sim \mathcal{N}(0, I)$ and $Y' = (X')(X')^\top = \Sigma^{-1/2} Y \Sigma^{-1/2}$.

By definition, to get a handle on $\mathbf{Cov}[Y']$, it suffices to understand the variance of the scalar random variable $\mathbf{Var}[\mathrm{tr}(AY')]$ for any $d \times d$ matrix A. Note that $\mathrm{tr}(AY')$ is a homogeneous degree-2 polynomial in X'. It is not hard to see that an orthonormal basis for the homogeneous degree-2 polynomials in X' (with respect to the inner product given by $\langle p, q \rangle := \mathbf{Cov}(p(X'), q(X'))$) is the set consisting of $X'_i X'_j$ for $i \neq j$ and $(X'_i)^2 / \sqrt{2}$.

Using the above, it is easy to see that

$$\mathbf{Var}[\mathrm{tr}(AY')] = 2 \left\| \frac{A + A^\top}{2} \right\|_F^2. \tag{4.1}$$

Making a change of variables, we can see that

$$\mathbf{Var}[\mathrm{tr}(AY)] = \mathbf{Var}[\mathrm{tr}((\Sigma^{1/2} A \Sigma^{1/2})Y')] = 2 \left\| \Sigma^{1/2} \left(\frac{A + A^\top}{2} \right) \Sigma^{1/2} \right\|_F^2. \tag{4.2}$$

We note that in some very real sense Equation (4.2) gives the covariance of Y, in that it gives the quadratic form that maps a linear function, $L(Y)$, of Y to its variance.

Writing this covariance matrix explicitly is somewhat more challenging. In particular, Y is naturally valued in matrices rather than vectors. This means that the covariance "matrix" of Y should most naturally be viewed as a 4-tensor, or a matrix over matrices, which is somewhat more difficult to think about. In order to turn the covariance of Y into a matrix, one would first need to associate the space of $d \times d$ symmetric matrices with vectors in some space. It turns out that there is a nice way to do this, at least for Y'.

In particular, we need to find the correct way of flattening matrices into vectors. To this end, we introduce the following definition.

Definition 4.4 (Flattening Operator)   Let e_{ij} denote the $d \times d$ matrix with a 1 in the (i, j)-entry and 0's elsewhere. We define L_d to be the linear transformation taking $d \times d$ symmetric matrices to elements of $\mathbf{R}^{\binom{d+1}{2}}$, such that L_d maps the elements $(e_{ij} + e_{ji})/2$ (for $1 \le i < j \le d$) and $e_{ii}/\sqrt{2}$ (for $1 \le i \le d$) to the standard basis vectors in $\mathbf{R}^{\binom{d+1}{2}}$. Likewise, it's inverse, L_d^{-1} is a bijection from $\binom{d+1}{2}$-dimensional vectors to $d \times d$ symmetric matrices.

It is not hard to see that for any symmetric matrix A we have $2\|A\|_F^2 = \|L_d(A)\|_2^2$. Given this fact, it is easy to see that Equation (4.1) is equivalent to $\mathrm{Cov}[L_d(Y')] = 4I$.

4.2.2 Algorithm Description

As in our algorithms for robust mean estimation, we will introduce a set of deterministic conditions on the inliers. Our robust covariance estimation algorithm will be shown to succeed subject to these deterministic conditions. In the following section, we show that these conditions will be satisfied with high probability given a polynomial-sized sample from the inlier distribution.

Since our general strategy will be to leverage some version of a robust mean estimation algorithm on the random variable $Y = XX^\mathsf{T}$, we will require that the set of these points (properly normalized) satisfy some version of the standard stability condition (see Definition 2.1 in Chapter 2). To quantify our notion of "properly normalized," we need to use Equation (4.2). Formally, we introduce the following definition.

Definition 4.5 (Covariance Stability Condition)   Let $\delta \ge \epsilon > 0$. Let $S \subset \mathbf{R}^d$ be a multiset of points with $|S| > 1/\epsilon$. We say that S is (ϵ, δ)-*covariance stable* if for $\Sigma = \mathbf{E}_{x \sim_u S}[xx^\mathsf{T}]$ and $M_\Sigma(x) = L_d(\Sigma^{-1/2}xx^\mathsf{T}\Sigma^{-1/2})$, we have that the set $M_\Sigma(S)$ is (ϵ, δ)-stable (with respect to $L_d(I_d)$).

Given this definition, the main theorem of this section is as follows.

Theorem 4.6 (Robust Covariance Estimation Algorithm)   *Let $S \subset \mathbf{R}^d$ be an (ϵ, δ)-covariance stable set with ϵ and δ less than a sufficiently small constant. Let T be an ϵ-corrupted version of S. Let $\Sigma = \mathbf{E}_{x \sim_u S}[xx^\mathsf{T}]$. Then there exists an algorithm that given T, ϵ, and δ runs in $\mathrm{poly}(|T|d/\epsilon)$ time and returns a $\widehat{\Sigma}$ such that $\|\Sigma^{-1/2}(\widehat{\Sigma} - \Sigma)\Sigma^{-1/2}\|_F = O(\delta)$.*

Before we proceed with the proof of Theorem 4.6, a remark is in order. In several natural settings, the error guarantee achieved by this result is nearly sharp. For example, if S consists of i.i.d. samples from $\mathcal{N}(0, \Sigma)$, then (as we will show in the next section) with high probability we will be able to take $\delta = \tilde{O}(\epsilon)$. By Fact 4.3, the error metric $\|\Sigma^{-1/2}(\widehat{\Sigma} - \Sigma)\Sigma^{-1/2}\|_F$ is proportional to the total variation distance between the Gaussians $\mathcal{N}(0, \Sigma)$ and $\mathcal{N}(0, \widehat{\Sigma})$. This means that we are able to efficiently learn the target Gaussian to within total variation distance error $\tilde{O}(\epsilon)$. On the other hand, achieving total variation distance error smaller than $\Omega(\epsilon)$ is information-theoretically impossible. That is, for the case of Gaussians, our algorithm matches the best possible error within logarithmic factors.

We now proceed to describe and analyze our algorithm. The basic idea of our approach will be to use an adaptation of the filtering technique. This is fairly reasonable, since the goal is to approximate the expectation of $ZZ^\top$, where $Z \sim_u S$, and we know that the transformed version of $ZZ^\top$, namely $M_\Sigma(S)$, satisfies an appropriate stability condition. The obvious complication is that the necessary transformation involves knowledge of the real Σ, which is what we are trying to approximate in the first place. Instead, we can use the next best thing, that is, the empirical approximation to Σ. The key result here is that this approximation of the desired transform still produces a set of sufficiently good stability parameters.

In more detail, we establish the following.

Proposition 4.7 *Let S, T, ϵ, δ be as in the statement of Theorem 4.6. Let $\Sigma' = \mathbf{E}_{x \sim_u T}[xx^\top]$. Suppose that the largest eigenvalue of $\mathbf{Cov}[M_{\Sigma'}(T)]$ is $1 + \lambda$, for some $\lambda \geq 0$. Then the set $M_{\Sigma'}(S)$ is (ϵ, δ')-stable for*

$$\delta' = O\left(\delta + \min\left(\sqrt{\epsilon}, \epsilon^{3/4}\lambda^{1/4}\right)\right),$$

where the stability is taken with respect to the mean $L_d\left((\Sigma')^{-1/2}\Sigma(\Sigma')^{-1/2}\right)$.

Proof The basic idea of the proof will be to show that Σ' is not too far away from Σ. Since we know that applying the transformation M_Σ to S yields a stable set, it is not hard to show that the related transform $M_{\Sigma'}$ also gives a stable set. To show that Σ is close to Σ', we will take advantage of the fact that the largest eigenvalue of $\mathbf{Cov}[M_\Sigma(T)]$ is not too large along with Lemma 2.7 to show that

$$L_d(\Sigma^{-1/2}\Sigma'\Sigma^{-1/2}) = \mathbf{E}[M_\Sigma(T)] \approx \mathbf{E}[M_\Sigma(S)] = L_d(I).$$

Unfortunately, this requires knowing that $M_{\Sigma'}(S)$ is already stable, so we need somewhere to get started. We begin with the following lemma.

Lemma 4.8 *Suppose that $\Sigma' \geq \Sigma/2$, then we have that $M_{\Sigma'}(S)$ is (ϵ, δ')-stable for*

$$\delta' = O\left(\delta + \sqrt{\epsilon \min\left(1, \left\|(\Sigma')^{-1/2}\Sigma(\Sigma')^{-1/2} - I\right\|_2\right)}\right).$$

Proof We know that $M_\Sigma(S)$ is stable by the covariance stability of S. We would like to understand the stability of $M_{\Sigma'}(S)$. We do this by noting that $M_\Sigma(S)$ and $M_{\Sigma'}(S)$ are linearly related, namely that $M_{\Sigma'}(S) = C_{\Sigma'}^\Sigma(M_\Sigma(S))$, where $C_{\Sigma'}^\Sigma : \mathbf{R}^{\binom{d+1}{2}} \to \mathbf{R}^{\binom{d+1}{2}}$ is given by

$$C_{\Sigma'}^\Sigma(v) := L_d\left((\Sigma')^{-1/2}\Sigma^{1/2}L_d^{-1}(v)\Sigma^{1/2}(\Sigma')^{-1/2}\right),$$

since $C_{\Sigma'}^\Sigma(L_d(\Sigma^{-1/2}xx^\top\Sigma^{-1/2})) = L_d((\Sigma')^{-1/2}xx^\top(\Sigma')^{-1/2})$. Using the notation $H(A) = L_d(\Sigma^{-1/4}A\Sigma^{-1/4})$, for symmetric $d \times d$ matrices A, the above equation can be rewritten as

$$C_{\Sigma'}^\Sigma(v) = H\left((\Sigma^{1/4}(\Sigma')^{-1/2}\Sigma^{1/4})H^{-1}(v)(\Sigma^{1/4}(\Sigma')^{-1/2}\Sigma^{1/4})\right).$$

Note that this means that $C_{\Sigma'}^\Sigma$ is conjugate (via H) to the operator

$$A \mapsto \left(\Sigma^{1/4}(\Sigma')^{-1/2}\Sigma^{1/4}\right)A\left(\Sigma^{1/4}(\Sigma')^{-1/2}\Sigma^{1/4}\right), \tag{4.3}$$

and therefore has the same eigenvalues.

Suppose that the matrix $B = (\Sigma')^{-1/2}\Sigma(\Sigma')^{-1/2}$ has eigenvalues v_i. Then the matrix $C = (\Sigma^{1/4}(\Sigma')^{-1/2}\Sigma^{1/4})$ (which is conjugate to $B^{-1/2}$) has eigenvalues $v_i^{-1/2}$. Writing A in the eigen-basis of C, we find that the operator in Equation (4.3) multiplies the (i, j)-entry of A by $(v_i v_j)^{-1/2}$. Therefore, the eigenvalues of the operator in (4.3), and thus of $C_{\Sigma'}^\Sigma$, are $(v_i v_j)^{-1/2}$.

Let S' be a subset of S of size at least $(1 - \epsilon)|S|$. By the covariance stability condition, we have that $\mathbf{Cov}[M_\Sigma(S')]$ has eigenvalues $1 + O(\delta^2/\epsilon)$. To establish stability of $M_{\Sigma'}(S)$, we need to bound the eigenvalues of

$$\mathbf{Cov}[M_{\Sigma'}(S')] = \mathbf{Cov}\left[C_{\Sigma'}^\Sigma M_\Sigma(S')\right] = C_{\Sigma'}^\Sigma \mathbf{Cov}[M_\Sigma(S')](C_{\Sigma'}^\Sigma)^\top.$$

Using our knowledge of the eigenvalues of each term in the above product, we obtain that the eigenvalues of $\mathbf{Cov}[M_{\Sigma'}(S')]$ are between $\min_i(v_i)^{-1}(1 - O(\delta^2/\epsilon))$ and $\max_i(v_i)^{-1}(1 + O(\delta^2/\epsilon))$. Moreover, it is clear that the biggest distance from 1 of any of these eigenvalues is

$$O\left(\delta^2/\epsilon + \min\left(1, \max_i(|v_i - 1|)\right)\right).$$

This implies that $M_{\Sigma'}(S)$ is $(\epsilon, O(\delta + \sqrt{\epsilon \min(1, \|\Sigma^{-1/2}\Sigma'\Sigma^{-1/2} - I\|_2)}))$-stable, completing the proof of Lemma 4.8. $\qquad\square$

Once again, applying Lemma 4.8 requires that we already know that Σ' is not too far from Σ. However, we note that as long as we have a lower bound, this is not too hard to show.

Lemma 4.9 *With the above notation, we have that $\Sigma' \succeq \Sigma(1 - O(\delta))$.*

Proof Define $S_0 = S \cap T$. Since $T \supset S_0$ and $|S_0| \geq (1 - \epsilon)|T|$, we have

$$\Sigma' = \mathbf{E}_{x \sim_u T}[xx^\top] \geq (1 - \epsilon)\mathbf{E}_{x \sim_u S_0}[xx^\top] := \Sigma_0.$$

We will show that $\Sigma_0 \geq \Sigma(1 - O(\delta))$. By the (ϵ, δ)-stability of $M_\Sigma(S)$, we have

$$\|\mathbf{E}_{x \sim_u S_0}[M_\Sigma(x)] - \mathbf{E}_{x \sim_u S}[M_\Sigma(x)]\|_2 = O(\delta).$$

For the second term above, we can write that

$$\mathbf{E}_{x \sim_u S}[M_\Sigma(x)] = L_d\left(\Sigma^{-1/2}\mathbf{E}_{x \sim_u S}[xx^\top]\Sigma^{-1/2}\right) = L_d\left(\Sigma^{-1/2}\Sigma\Sigma^{-1/2}\right).$$

Similarly, we can express the first term as follows:

$$\mathbf{E}_{x \sim_u S_0}[M_\Sigma(x)] = L_d\left(\Sigma^{-1/2}\mathbf{E}_{x \sim_u S_0}[xx^\top]\Sigma^{-1/2}\right) = L_d\left(\Sigma^{-1/2}\Sigma_0\Sigma^{-1/2}\right).$$

Combining the above, we obtain

$$O(\delta) = \left\|L_d\left(\Sigma^{-1/2}(\Sigma_0 - \Sigma)\Sigma^{-1/2}\right)\right\|_2 = \sqrt{2}\left\|\Sigma^{-1/2}(\Sigma_0 - \Sigma)\Sigma^{-1/2}\right\|_F$$
$$\geq \sqrt{2}\left\|\Sigma^{-1/2}(\Sigma_0 - \Sigma)\Sigma^{-1/2}\right\|_2.$$

This implies that

$$\Sigma^{-1/2}(\Sigma - \Sigma_0)\Sigma^{-1/2} \geq O(\delta)\,I,$$

and rearranging we get $\Sigma_0 \leq \Sigma(1 - O(\delta))$. This completes the proof of Lemma 4.9. $\square$

Combining Lemmas 4.8 and 4.9, it follows that $M_{\Sigma'}(S)$ is $(\epsilon, O(\sqrt{\epsilon}))$-stable.

To do better than this, we need to show that Σ' is likely already a good approximation Σ, which we can achieve by leveraging Lemma 2.7.

Lemma 4.10 *Suppose* $\Sigma' \geq \Sigma/2$ *and that* $M_{\Sigma'}(S)$ *is* (ϵ, η)-*stable. Then it is* (ϵ, η')-*stable for*

$$\eta' = O\left(\delta + \min(\sqrt{\epsilon}, \sqrt{\epsilon\eta} + \epsilon^{3/4}\lambda^{1/4})\right).$$

Proof We apply Lemma 2.7 to the sets $M_{\Sigma'}(S)$ and $M_{\Sigma'}(T)$, which are ϵ-corrupted versions of each other. Since $M_{\Sigma'}(S)$ is (ϵ, η)-stable by assumption, and since $\mathbf{Cov}[M_{\Sigma'}(T)]$ has eigenvalues bounded by $1 + \lambda$ by assumption, we can apply Lemma 2.7 to show that the means of $M_{\Sigma'}(S)$ and $M_{\Sigma'}(T)$ have ℓ_2-distance of at most $O(\eta + \sqrt{\epsilon\lambda})$. Moreover, we can express each mean as follows:

$$\mathbf{E}[M_{\Sigma'}(S)] = L_d\left((\Sigma')^{-1/2}\mathbf{E}_{x \sim_u S}[xx^\top](\Sigma')^{-1/2}\right) = L_d\left((\Sigma')^{-1/2}\Sigma(\Sigma')^{-1/2}\right),$$

and

$$\mathbf{E}[M_{\Sigma'}(T)] = L_d\left((\Sigma')^{-1/2}\mathbf{E}_{x \sim_u T}[xx^\top](\Sigma')^{-1/2}\right) = L_d\left((\Sigma')^{-1/2}\Sigma'(\Sigma')^{-1/2}\right).$$

Therefore, we have

$$O(\eta + \sqrt{\epsilon\lambda}) = \left\| L_d\left((\Sigma')^{-1/2}(\Sigma - \Sigma')(\Sigma')^{-1/2} \right) \right\|_2 = \sqrt{2} \left\| (\Sigma')^{-1/2}(\Sigma - \Sigma')(\Sigma')^{-1/2} \right\|_F.$$
(4.4)

This implies that the eigenvalues of $(\Sigma')^{-1/2}\Sigma(\Sigma')^{-1/2}$ are within $O(\eta + \sqrt{\epsilon\lambda})$ of 1. Applying Lemma 4.8 gives Lemma 4.10. $\qquad\Box$

To apply Lemma 4.10, we need to know that $\Sigma' \succeq \Sigma/2$. However, we have that

$$\Sigma' = \mathbf{E}_{x\sim_u T}[xx^\top] \succeq (2/3)\mathbf{E}_{x\sim_u S\cap T}[xx^\top] \succeq \Sigma/2,$$

where the last inequality is by the covariance-stability of S.

We note that $\eta' < \eta$ in Lemma 4.10, unless $\eta = O(\delta + \min(\sqrt{\epsilon}, \epsilon^{3/4}\lambda^{1/4}))$. Therefore, iterating Lemma 4.10 yields Proposition 4.7. $\qquad\Box$

We are now prepared to prove Theorem 4.6.

Proof The basic strategy of our algorithm will be to iteratively apply a filter to $M_{\Sigma'}(T)$. More specifically, at any stage in our algorithm, we will maintain a set R (initially taken to be T) that is an $O(\epsilon)$-noisy version of S. We compute $\Sigma' = \mathbf{E}_{x\sim_u R}[xx^\top]$ and $\mathbf{Cov}[M_{\Sigma'(R)}]$ letting it have largest eigenvalue $1 + \lambda$.

By Proposition 4.7, $M_{\Sigma'}(S)$ is $(O(\epsilon), O(\delta'))$-stable with

$$\delta' = O(\delta + \min(\sqrt{\epsilon}, \epsilon^{3/4}\lambda^{1/4})).$$

Unless λ is bounded above by a constant multiple of $(\delta')^2/\epsilon$, we can apply the universal filter to R and obtain a new set R' that is closer to S than R was.

If this is not the case, it means that

$$\lambda \le O(\delta^2/\epsilon + \min(1, \sqrt{\epsilon\lambda})),$$

which implies that $\lambda \le O(\delta^2/\epsilon)$. Therefore, applying Equation (4.4), we have

$$\|(\Sigma')^{-1/2}(\Sigma - \Sigma')(\Sigma')^{-1/2}\|_F = O(\delta).$$

Given this, it is easy to see that $\|\Sigma^{-1/2}(\Sigma - \Sigma')\Sigma^{-1/2}\|_F = O(\delta)$. Indeed, since Σ and Σ' must agree to within a factor of 2 (in Loewner order), the two different normalizations only change things by a constant factor.

Thus, at each stage, our algorithm can either find an R' closer to S than R was, or can return Σ', which will have an appropriate error. By iterating this technique, our algorithm will eventually land in the latter case and return an appropriate approximation.

In particular, the pseudocode of our algorithm is as follows:

Algorithm Robust-Covariance

Input: Dataset $T \subset \mathbf{R}^d$ that is an ϵ-corruption of an (ϵ, δ)-covariance stable set S.

1. Let C be a sufficiently large constant.
2. Let $R = T$, and $\Sigma' = \mathbf{E}_{x \sim_u T}[xx^\top]$.
3. While $\mathbf{Cov}[M_{\Sigma'}(R)]$ has largest eigenvalue $1 + \lambda$ for $\lambda > C^4\delta^2/\epsilon$:
   1. Let $\delta' = C(\delta + \min(\sqrt{\epsilon}, \epsilon^{3/4}\lambda^{1/4}))$.
   2. Noting that $M_{\Sigma'}(R)$ is (ϵ, δ')-stable, and that $C(\delta')^2/\epsilon < \lambda$, apply a randomized universal filter to R obtaining $R' \subseteq R$.
   3. Set $R \leftarrow R'$ and $\Sigma' \leftarrow \mathbf{E}_{x \sim_u R}[xx^\top]$.
4. Return Σ'.

To analyze this algorithm, we note that so long as R is an $O(\epsilon)$-corrupted version of S, by Proposition 4.7, the set $M_{\Sigma'}(R)$ is (ϵ, δ')-stable. Thus, since $\lambda > C(\delta')^2/\epsilon$, our universal filter will remove in expectation fewer elements of $R \cap S$ than elements of $R \setminus S$. Combining these with the martingale arguments from the proof of Theorem 2.17, we have that with probability at least $2/3$, the size of the symmetric difference between R and S will remain $O(\epsilon|S|)$ throughout the algorithm.

If this holds, we will eventually find such an R where $\mathbf{Cov}[M_{\Sigma'}(R)]$ has largest eigenvalue $O(\delta^2/\epsilon)$. By Proposition 4.7, this implies that $M_{\Sigma'}(R)$ is $(\epsilon, O(\delta))$-stable, and thus by Equation (4.4), we have

$$\|(\Sigma')^{-1/2}(\Sigma - \Sigma')(\Sigma')^{-1/2}\|_F = O(\delta),$$

which implies the desired bound. □

Remark 4.11 (Handling Degenerate Covariances) Note that the algorithm just presented only works when Σ is nonsingular. This is because when renormalizing vectors, we need to multiply by $\Sigma^{-1/2}$. In fact, we need to be able to multiply by $\Sigma^{-1/2}$ to even define our notion of covariance stability. However, there is a reasonable notion of covariance stability for sets S that are not full-rank. One can think about this by first restricting S to the subspace given by its span and then checking covariance stability on this subspace (over which Σ is full-rank).

Using this notion, the aforementioned algorithm can be shown to still work with the slight modification that $(\Sigma')^{-1/2}$ be replaced by the square root of a pseudo-inverse of Σ' in the definition of $M_{\Sigma'}$. The rest of the analysis follows

110 Robust Covariance Estimation

mutatis mutandis. This allows us to learn an ϵ-corrupted Gaussian $\mathcal{N}(0, \Sigma)$ to error $O(\epsilon \log(1/\epsilon))$ in total variation distance, even if Σ is degenerate.

Although this generalization is not particularly difficult, the additional complications interrupt the clarity of the key ideas; so throughout this chapter, we will assume that the covariances we are trying to learn are nondegenerate.

4.3 Applications to Concrete Distribution Families

Theorem 4.6 tells us that we can efficiently and robustly learn the covariance of a distribution from samples that satisfy the covariance stability condition. We have yet to show that this condition is satisfied (with reasonable probability) for sample sets from specific families. In this section, we will show that this is in fact the case. In particular, in Section 4.3.1, we show that a polynomial number of samples from a zero-mean Gaussian suffice with high probability. In Section 4.3.2, we show that this even holds for a mixture of Gaussians as long as the components are not too far apart.

4.3.1 Robustly Learning the Covariance of a Gaussian

Perhaps the most natural application of Theorem 4.6 is that of robustly learning the covariance of a Gaussian $G = \mathcal{N}(0, \Sigma)$. For this basic case, our algorithm achieves Mahalanobis distance $O(\epsilon \log(1/\epsilon))$, which is within a logarithmic factor from the information-theoretic optimum of $\Theta(\epsilon)$.

It is clear that by taking sufficiently many i.i.d. samples from $\mathcal{N}(0, \Sigma)$, we can ensure that the sample covariance matrix is arbitrarily close to Σ. The question is for what values of δ will a set of random samples be (ϵ, δ)-covariance stable. This is quantified in the following proposition.

Proposition 4.12 *Let $\epsilon > 0$ be sufficiently small. Let $G = \mathcal{N}(0, \Sigma)$ and let S be a set of a sufficiently large polynomial number of i.i.d. samples from G. Then, with high probability, S is (ϵ, δ)-covariance stable for some $\delta = O(\epsilon \log(1/\epsilon))$.*

Proof We start by noting that this problem is invariant under linear transformations. This allows us to take $\Sigma = I$. Moreover, it is easy to see that with sufficiently many samples, we can ensure with high probability that the empirical expectation $\mathbf{E}_{x \sim_u S}[xx^\top]$ is $1/\text{poly}(d)$-close to the identity matrix, in Frobenius norm. Given these observations, it suffices to show that with high probability the set of points $\{L_d(xx^\top): x \in S\}$ is (ϵ, δ)-stable.

To establish this using the alternative characterization of stability from Lemma 3.1, it suffices to show that for any $S' \subseteq S$ with $|S'| \geq (1 - \epsilon)|S|$ and for any unit vector $v \in \mathbf{R}^{\binom{d+1}{2}}$, the following holds:

$$\left| \frac{1}{|S|} \sum_{x \in S \setminus S'} \left(v \cdot L_d(xx^\top - I) \right)^2 \right| = O(\epsilon \log^2(1/\epsilon)). \tag{4.5}$$

We define the truncation function

$$f(x) = \begin{cases} (v \cdot L_d(xx^\top - I))^2, & \text{if } |v \cdot L_d(xx^\top - I)| > C \log(1/\epsilon), \\ 0, & \text{otherwise} \end{cases}$$

for some large universal constant $C > 0$. Then it suffices to show that

$$\frac{1}{|S|} \sum_{x \in S} f(x) = O(\epsilon \log^2(1/\epsilon)).$$

We can bound the LHS above as follows:

$$\int_{C \log(1/\epsilon)}^{\infty} 2t \mathbf{Pr}_{x \sim_u S} [|v \cdot L_d(xx^\top - I)| > t] dt$$
$$+ (C^2 \log^2(1/\epsilon)) \mathbf{Pr}_{x \sim_u S} [|v \cdot L_d(xx^\top - I)| > C \log(1/\epsilon)].$$

With high probability, no point $x \in S$ has norm more than $B = \sqrt{d}\text{polylog}(d/\epsilon)$. Thus, we can bound the upper range of the integral by B instead of at ∞. Furthermore, given sufficiently many samples, we will have that for each t and v, the empirical probability $\mathbf{Pr}_{x \sim_u S} [|v \cdot L_d(xx^\top - I)| > t]$ will approximate $\mathbf{Pr}[|v \cdot (L_d(GG^\top) - I)| > t]$. Note that $v \cdot (L_d(GG^\top) - I)$ is a quadratic polynomial in G with mean 0 and variance 1. To bound from above the corresponding tail probability, we use the following standard concentration inequality for low-degree polynomials over Gaussians (see Theorem A.9). In particular,

Fact 4.13 *For any quadratic polynomial p and a Gaussian $G \sim \mathcal{N}(0, 1)$, we have that $\mathbf{Pr}[|p(G)| > t \|p(G)\|_2] < 2e^{-\Omega(t)}$.*

Fact 4.13 immediately implies that $\mathbf{Pr}[|v \cdot L_d(GG^\top - I)| > t] < 2e^{-\Omega(t)}$. Plugging this in to the bounds above gives Proposition 4.12. $\qquad \square$

4.3.2 Robustly Learning the Covariance of Gaussian Mixtures

Another important application of these techniques is for Gaussian mixture models, that is, distributions of the form $X = \sum_{i=1}^{k} w_i \mathcal{N}(\mu_i, \Sigma_i)$. Robustly estimating the covariance of X is an important ingredient when trying to robustly learn mixtures of Gaussians.

While general mixtures of Gaussians do not necessarily satisfy the covariance stability condition, it turns out that if the component Gaussians are not too far from each other, this will be the case. Specifically, we show the following.

Proposition 4.14 *Let* $X = \sum_{i=1}^{k} w_i \mathcal{N}(\mu_i, \Sigma_i)$ *be a mixture of Gaussians with* $\mathbf{E}[X] = 0$ *and* $\mathbf{Cov}[X] = I$. *Then a set of sufficiently large polynomial number of samples from* X *is* (ϵ, δ)-*covariance stable with high probability for*

$$\delta = O\left(\sqrt{\epsilon} \max_i (1 + \|\Sigma_i - I\|_F + \|\mu_i\|_2^2) \right).$$

Two remarks are in order about this proposition. First, the assumption that $\mathbf{Cov}[X] = I$ is simply a normalization assumption. In particular, for any mixture of Gaussians X with $\mathbf{Cov}[X] = \Sigma$, we can reduce to this case by considering $\Sigma^{-1/2}$. This has the effect of replacing the $\|\mu_i\|_2$ terms with $\sqrt{\mu_i^\top \Sigma^{-1} \mu_i}$ and the $\|\Sigma_i - \Sigma_j\|_F$ terms with $\|\Sigma^{-1/2}(\Sigma_i - \Sigma_j)\Sigma^{-1/2}\|_F$. Second, we note that the parameter δ will be small so long as the component Gaussians of X are not too far apart in total variation distance from each other.

Proof First, note that since $\mathbf{Cov}[X] = I$ and $\delta^2/\epsilon > 1$, it suffices to show that for a polynomially large sample set S, the following holds

$$\|\mathbf{Cov}_{x \sim_u S}[xx^\top]\|_2 \leq \delta^2/\epsilon.$$

This is because restricting S to a subset will not increase the covariance by much, that is, the covariance will still be bounded above by $O(\delta^2/\epsilon)$, and because Chebyshev's inequality implies that removing any ϵ-fraction of S will change the mean by at most $O(\sqrt{\epsilon(\delta^2/\epsilon)}) = O(\delta)$. As $\mathbf{Cov}_{x \sim_u S}[xx^\top]$ will approximate $\mathbf{Cov}[XX^\top]$ with enough samples, it suffices to show that $\|\mathbf{Cov}[XX^\top]\|_2 \leq \delta^2/(2\epsilon)$.

To show this, we recall that the covariance of a mixture $Y = \sum_{i=1}^{k} w_i Y_i$ is given by

$$\mathbf{Cov}[Y] = \sum_{i=1}^{k} w_i \mathbf{Cov}[Y_i] + \mathbf{Cov}[m],$$

where m is the random variable that has value $\mathbf{E}[Y_i]$ with probability w_i. In our case, we take Y_i to be $(\mu_i + Z_i)(\mu_i + Z_i)^\top$, where $Z_i \sim \mathcal{N}(0, \Sigma_i)$. We note that $Z_i Z_i^\top$ has covariance corresponding to the operator $A \mapsto 2\|\Sigma_i((A + A^\top)/2)\Sigma_i\|_F^2$, which has operator norm $O(\|\Sigma_i\|_F^2)$. The other terms, $\mu_i Z_i^\top$, $Z_i \mu_i^\top$ and $\mu_i \mu_i^\top$, have covariances with norms bounded by $O(\|\mu_i\|_2 + \|\Sigma_i\|_F)^2$. Therefore, the sum, Y_i, has covariance bounded by $O(\|\mu_i\|_2 + \|\Sigma_i\|_F)^2$.

For the other terms, we note that $\mathbf{E}[Y_i] = \mu_i \mu_i^\top + \Sigma_i$. Therefore, the remaining term, $\mathbf{Cov}[m]$, is given by

$$\frac{1}{2} \sum_{i,j} w_i w_j ((\mu_i \mu_i^\top + \Sigma_i) - (\mu_j \mu_j^\top + \Sigma_j))((\mu_i \mu_i^\top + \Sigma_i) - (\mu_j \mu_j^\top + \Sigma_j))^\top.$$

The spectral norm of this matrix is bounded above by the maximum value of $\|(\mu_i \mu_i^\top + \Sigma_i) - (\mu_j \mu_j^\top + \Sigma_j)\|_F^2$, which in turn is clearly $O(\max_i(\|\Sigma_i - I\|_F + \|\mu_i\|_2^2))^2$.

Thus, our set will be (ϵ, δ)-covariance stable so long as δ^2/ϵ is at least a sufficiently large multiple of

$$\max_i (1 + \|\mu_i\|_2 + \|\Sigma_i\|_F + \|\Sigma_i - I\|_F + \|\mu_i\|_2^2)^2.$$

It is not hard to see that it suffices to replace this with $\max_i(1 + \|\Sigma_i - I\|_F + \|\mu_i\|_2^2)$, which gives our result. $\qquad\square$

4.4 Reduction to Zero-Mean Case

Throughout this chapter, we have been restricting ourselves to the case where X is centered, that is, $\mathbf{E}[X] = 0$. In this case, computing the covariance of X becomes equivalent to computing the expectation of the variable $Y = XX^\top$. While many cases that we would like to consider do not satisfy this assumption, there is a relatively simple reduction to this case.

In particular, given a random variable X, we can define a new random variable $X' = (X_1 - X_2)/\sqrt{2}$, where X_1 and X_2 are two independent copies of X. The following important properties are all easy to verify:

1. $\mathbf{E}[X'] = 0$.
2. $\mathbf{Cov}[X'] = \mathbf{Cov}[X]$.
3. A sample from X' can be computed from two samples of X. Furthermore, if we have access to a source of ϵ-corrupted samples from X, we can use this to obtain a source of 2ϵ-corrupted samples from X'.

This means that if we want to robustly estimate the covariance of X, it suffices to robustly estimate the covariance of X' instead. Since the mean of X' is 0, the techniques of this chapter will apply. For example, if $X = \mathcal{N}(\mu, \Sigma)$, then we have that $X' = \mathcal{N}(0, \Sigma)$, which we can learn robustly.

The following proposition shows that we can efficiently and robustly learn an arbitrary Gaussian $\mathcal{N}(\mu, \Sigma)$ within small total variation distance.

Proposition 4.15 *Let $d \in \mathbf{Z}_+$ and ϵ at most a sufficiently small universal constant. There is an algorithm that given $n = \text{poly}(d/\epsilon)$ ϵ-corrupted samples from an arbitrary Gaussian distribution X on $\mathbf{R}^d$, runs in $\text{poly}(n)$ time, and learns X to error $O(\epsilon \log(1/\epsilon))$ in total variation distance.*

Proof Let $X \sim \mathcal{N}(\mu, \Sigma)$. First, we consider the variable X' as described above. Given 2ϵ-corrupted samples from X', we can use Proposition 4.12 and Theorem 4.6 to learn a $\widehat{\Sigma}$ with

$$\|\Sigma^{-1/2}(\widehat{\Sigma} - \Sigma)\Sigma^{-1/2}\|_F = O(\epsilon \log(1/\epsilon)).$$

Note that $\widehat{\Sigma}^{-1/2}X \sim \mathcal{N}(\widehat{\Sigma}^{-1/2}\mu, \widehat{\Sigma}^{-1/2}\Sigma\widehat{\Sigma}^{-1/2})$ has covariance $\widehat{\Sigma}^{-1/2}\Sigma\widehat{\Sigma}^{-1/2}$, and that

$$(1 - O(\epsilon \log(1/\epsilon)))I \leq \widehat{\Sigma}^{-1/2}\Sigma\widehat{\Sigma}^{-1/2} \leq (1 + O(\epsilon \log(1/\epsilon)))I.$$

From this it is easy to see that taking sufficiently many samples from $\widehat{\Sigma}^{-1/2}X$ gives an (ϵ, δ)-stable set with $\delta = O(\epsilon \log(1/\epsilon))$. We can then use our standard mean estimation techniques to compute a $\widehat{\mu}$ so that $\|\widehat{\Sigma}^{-1/2}(\mu - \widehat{\mu})\|_2 = O(\epsilon \log(1/\epsilon))$. Since $\widehat{\Sigma}$ is close to Σ, this implies that $\|\Sigma^{-1/2}(\mu - \widehat{\mu})\|_2 = O(\epsilon \log(1/\epsilon))$.

Using standard facts, it is easy to see that $d_{\mathrm{TV}}(\mathcal{N}(\widehat{\mu}, \widehat{\Sigma}), \mathcal{N}(\mu, \Sigma)) = O(\epsilon \log(1/\epsilon))$.   □

One potential issue with this reduction technique is that computing the moments of $(X')(X')^\top$ might be nontrivial. Fortunately, there is a relatively simple formula for it.

Lemma 4.16 *Let X be a random variable with finite fourth moments, where $\mathbf{E}[X] = \mu$ and $\mathbf{Cov}[X] = \Sigma$. Let $X' = (X_1 - X_2)/\sqrt{2}$, where X_i are independent copies of X. Finally, let $Y = (X - \mu)(X - \mu)^\top$ and $Y' = (X')(X')^\top$. Then for any symmetric matrix A we have*

$$\mathbf{Var}[\mathrm{tr}(AY')] = \frac{\mathbf{Var}[\mathrm{tr}(AY)] + 2\|\Sigma^{1/2}A\Sigma^{1/2}\|_F^2}{2}.$$

In other words, the covariance of Y' is the average of what it would need to be in order to be covariance stable, and the covariance of Y. This allows us for example to take the results on the covariance of a mixture of Gaussians from Section 4.3.2, and show that under similar conditions we can robustly learn the covariance of a mixture of Gaussians even if the mean is not 0.

Proof Note that $X' = (X_1 - \mu) - (X_2 - \mu)$. Therefore, we can equivalently rewrite

$$Y' = ((X_1 - \mu)(X_1 - \mu)^\top - 2(X_1 - \mu)(X_2 - \mu)^\top + (X_2 - \mu)(X_2 - \mu)^\top)/2.$$

Therefore, $\mathbf{Var}[\mathrm{tr}(AY')]$ equals

$$\frac{1}{4}\mathbf{Var}\Big[\mathrm{tr}((X_1 - \mu)(X_1 - \mu)^\top A) - 2\mathrm{tr}((X_1 - \mu)(X_2 - \mu)^\top A)$$
$$+ \mathrm{tr}((X_2 - \mu)(X_2 - \mu)^\top A)\Big].$$

We claim that the three terms in the variance above are pairwise uncorrelated. Indeed, the random variables $\mathrm{tr}((X_1 - \mu)(X_1 - \mu)^\top A)$ and $\mathrm{tr}((X_2 - \mu)(X_2 - \mu)^\top A)$

are clearly independent. Also, we have that the mean of the random variable $\text{tr}((X_1 - \mu)(X_2 - \mu)^{\mathsf{T}}A)$ is 0 (since the term inside the trace has mean 0), and

$$\mathbf{E}[\text{tr}((X_1 - \mu)(X_1 - \mu)^{\mathsf{T}}A)\text{tr}((X_1 - \mu)(X_2 - \mu)^{\mathsf{T}}A)] = 0,$$

since for any X_1, the expectation over X_2 is 0. The third comparison follows similarly. Therefore,

$$\mathbf{Var}[\text{tr}(AY')] = \mathbf{Var}[\text{tr}((X_1 - \mu)(X_1 - \mu)^{\mathsf{T}}A)]/4 + \mathbf{Var}[\text{tr}((X_1 - \mu)(X_2 - \mu)^{\mathsf{T}}A)]$$
$$+ \mathbf{Var}[\text{tr}((X_2 - \mu)(X_2 - \mu)^{\mathsf{T}}A)]/4.$$

The first and last terms are clearly each equal to $\mathbf{Var}[\text{tr}(YA)]$. The middle term equals

$$\mathbf{E}[\text{tr}((X_2 - \mu)^{\mathsf{T}}A(X_1 - \mu))^2] = \mathbf{E}[\text{tr}((X_2 - \mu)^{\mathsf{T}}A(X_1 - \mu)(X_1 - \mu)^{\mathsf{T}}A(X_2 - \mu))]$$
$$= \mathbf{E}[\text{tr}((X_2 - \mu)(X_2 - \mu)^{\mathsf{T}}A(X_1 - \mu)(X_1 - \mu)^{\mathsf{T}}A)]$$
$$= \text{tr}(\Sigma A \Sigma A)]$$
$$= \text{tr}(\Sigma^{1/2}A\Sigma A\Sigma^{1/2})$$
$$= \text{tr}((\Sigma^{1/2}A\Sigma^{1/2})(\Sigma^{1/2}A\Sigma^{1/2})^{\mathsf{T}})$$
$$= \|\Sigma^{1/2}A\Sigma^{1/2}\|_F^2.$$

This completes the proof of Lemma 4.16. □

4.5 Exercises

4.1 (Robust PCA) Suppose that one has access to ϵ-corrupted samples from $X = \mathcal{N}(0, \Sigma)$, a Gaussian in $\mathbf{R}^d$ with unknown covariance Σ, but instead of learning all of Σ one merely wants to learn (an approximation to) the principal eigenvector of Σ. In particular, if $\lambda = \|\Sigma\|_2$ is the largest eigenvalue, one wants to compute a unit vector v such that $v^{\mathsf{T}}\Sigma v \geq \lambda(1 - O(\epsilon \log(1/\epsilon)))$. Give an efficient algorithm for this task using $\tilde{O}(d/\epsilon^2)$ samples.

(Hint: Compute the principal eigenvector $\widehat{v}$ of $\widehat{\Sigma}$ and filter in the $\widehat{v}$ direction if necessary.)

4.2 (Sample Complexity of Robust Covariance Estimation) Let $d \in \mathbf{Z}_+, \epsilon > 0$. Show that there is an $N = \tilde{O}(d^2/\epsilon^2)$ such that if one takes N i.i.d. samples from a d-dimensional Gaussian $X = \mathcal{N}(0, \Sigma)$, the resulting set is $(\epsilon, \epsilon \text{polylog}(d/\epsilon))$-covariance stable with high probability.

(Hint: Assuming $\Sigma = I$, you will need to bound $\sum_{x \in S'} x^{\mathsf{T}}Mx$ for symmetric matrices M and any $S' \subset S$ of size at most ϵN. Try writing M as a linear combination of projections onto subspaces of dimension 2^k for various values of k. You can use the fact that a cover of the set of such projections will have size roughly $2^{O(dk)}$ along with the Hanson-Wright inequality, which states that for a degree-2 polynomial p and $t > 0$, $\mathbf{Pr}[|p(X)| > t] \ll \exp(-\min(t^2/\mathbf{E}[p^2(X)], t/\lambda))$, where λ is the largest absolute value of an eigenvalue of the quadratic form associated to p.)

4.3   (Sample Complexity of Robust Covariance Estimation in Relative Operator Norm) This chapter discussed attempts to estimate the covariance Σ of a distribution to small error in relative Frobenius norm. Namely, to compute a $\widehat{\Sigma}$ such that $\|\Sigma^{-1/2}\widehat{\Sigma}\Sigma^{-1/2} - I\|_F$ is small. Although this is a natural error metric, there are other reasonable ones to consider. For example, one could instead try to find a good estimator in the *relative operator norm*. That is, computing a $\widehat{\Sigma}$ such that $\|\Sigma^{-1/2}\widehat{\Sigma}\Sigma^{-1/2} - I\|_2$ is small.

Show that if $X = \mathcal{N}(0, \Sigma)$ is a zero-mean Gaussian in $\mathbf{R}^d$, there is an (inefficient) algorithm that given $N = O(d/\epsilon^2)$ ϵ-corrupted samples from X (for some $\epsilon < 1/3$) learns Σ to relative operator norm $O(\epsilon)$.

(Hint: Robustly estimate $\mathbf{Var}(v \cdot X)$ for each v in a cover of the unit sphere.)

Remark 4.17   This sample complexity is better than the complexity of $\Omega(d^2/\epsilon^2)$ that is needed to learn Σ to relative Frobenius norm $O(\epsilon)$, even without any corruptions. Unfortunately, while information-theoretically $O(d/\epsilon^2)$ samples suffice to learn to error $O(\epsilon)$ in relative operator norm, it is believed that any computationally efficient estimator may well require $\Omega(d^2/\epsilon^2)$ samples (see Exercise 8.12).

4.4   (Robustly Learning the Mean and Covariance Simultaneously) While considering samples from $X - X'$ in order to reduce to the zero-mean case is convenient, it is not necessary. Show how one can robustly learn the mean and covariance of an unknown Gaussian simultaneously. In particular, if we have an upper bound $\widehat{\Sigma}$ on Σ, we can use it to learn an estimate $\widehat{\mu}$ of μ. We can then robustly estimate $\mathbf{E}[(x - \widehat{\mu})(x - \widehat{\mu})^\top]$ to get a better estimate for Σ and iterate. Formalize and analyze this algorithm.

4.5   (Higher Moments of Gaussian Mixtures) Let X be as in Proposition 4.14. For $m \in \mathbf{Z}_+$, let $h_m(x)$ be the rank-m tensor whose $(j_1, j_2, \ldots, j_m)$-entry is $\prod_{i=1}^d h_{a_i}(x_i)$, where a_i is the number of j's equal to i, and h_{a_i} are the Hermite polynomials (see Chapter A.2). Show that $\mathbf{Cov}[h_m(X)]$ has spectral norm bounded by $\mathrm{poly}(1 + \max(\|\mu_i\|_2 + \|\Sigma_i - I\|_F)^m)$. Use this to show that one can robustly estimate $\mathbf{E}[h_m(X)]$ for mixtures of Gaussians that are all close to $\mathcal{N}(0, I)$.

(Hint: For the first part you might want to note that $h_m(x)$ is proportional to the sum of all possible tensor products of x and $-I$ that leave a rank-m tensor.)

Note: This procedure is a useful step toward developing an efficient algorithm to robustly learn arbitrary Gaussian mixtures.

4.6 (Learning Finite Markov Chains) Consider the following finite Markov chain. One obtains samples $X \in \{0,1\}^d$ generated in the following way: $X_1 = 1$ with probability p_1, and then one sequentially generates random variables $X_1, X_2, \ldots, X_d \in \{0,1\}$, where $X_i = 1$ with probability $p_{0,i}$ if $X_{i-1} = 0$ and probability $p_{1,i}$ if $X_{i-1} = 1$. For simplicity, we assume that these probabilities are balanced, in particular that $p_1, p_{j,i}$ are all in $[1/3, 2/3]$. Give a polynomial-time algorithm that given poly(d/ϵ) ϵ-corrupted samples from X computes the vector of $p_{j,i}$'s to ℓ_2-error $\tilde{O}(\epsilon)$.

(Hint: Ideally, one would like to produce a (noisy) random variable whose mean is the vector of $p_{j,i}$. Conditioned on $X_{i-1} = j$, X_i is an unbiased estimator of $p_{j,i}$. How do we handle the case of $X_{i-1} \neq j$? One strategy would be to use our current best guess $\widehat{p_{j,i}}$. Of course, this introduces some error if $\widehat{p_{j,i}} \neq p_{j,i}$. However, by iterating this technique one can obtain better and better approximations.)

4.6 Discussion and Related Work

The robust covariance estimation algorithm under relative Frobenius norm given in this chapter was essentially developed in [45, 46] for the case of Gaussian distributions. This algorithm was improved in [33], where new techniques were developed to obtain a faster runtime, again in the Gaussian case. The reader is also referred to the work of [115] for an algorithm whose runtime dependence on d matches [33] and improved runtime dependence on ϵ. The application of Section 4.3.2 on robustly estimating the covariance of Gaussian mixtures was obtained in [104], and the overall approach of this chapter is based on that work; the more precise statements of the stability condition are new.

The work by [114] gave a robust covariance estimation algorithm with respect to the Frobenius norm under explicit upper bounds on certain moments of degree up to eight of the inlier distribution X. Their algorithm computes an estimate $\widehat{\Sigma}$ of the target covariance that with high probability satisfies $\|\widehat{\Sigma} - \Sigma\|_F = O(\epsilon^{1/2} \sqrt{\log(d)} \|\Sigma\|_2)$, where the hidden constant in the $O(\cdot)$ depends on the assumed moment upper bound. Their covariance estimation algorithm amounts to an application of a robust mean estimator from that work to the random variable $XX^\top$. We note that using the robust mean estimation for bounded covariance distributions from Chapter 2 instead, one can obtain an error guarantee of $O(\epsilon^{1/2} \|\Sigma\|_2)$ under an analogous fourth moment assumption.

The robust covariance estimation algorithm presented in this chapter achieves error guarantee of $O(\epsilon \log(1/\epsilon))$ with respect to the (relative) Frobenius norm in the strong contamination model. On the other hand, it is information-theoretically possible to achieve error $O(\epsilon)$. Similarly to the case of robust mean estimation, there is evidence (in the form of a Statistical Query lower bound) that this gap may be inherent for computationally efficient algorithms, and in particular that any improvement over the $O(\epsilon \log(1/\epsilon))$ error requires super-polynomial time. These developments are described in Chapter 8. In the presence of additive contamination, [47] gave a robust covariance estimation algorithm achieving the optimal error of $O(\epsilon)$ using poly(d/ϵ) samples and running in time poly(d)$2^{\text{polylog}(1/\epsilon)}$. Whether the quasi-polynomial dependence in $1/\epsilon$ can be improved to polynomial remains an interesting open problem.

Finally, it is worth mentioning that [112] used the sum-of-squares method to develop robust covariance estimation algorithms with respect to a relative version of the spectral norm for a broader class of sub-Gaussian distributions satisfying additional properties. Interestingly, for the distribution class considered in [112], obtaining distribution-independent error with respect to the (relative) Frobenius norm is information-theoretically impossible. Using a similar methodology, [8] developed alternative robust covariance estimation algorithms in relative Frobenius norm for a subclass of the aforementioned class, which includes Gaussian distributions.

5

List-Decodable Learning

5.1 Introduction

5.1.1 Background and Motivation

In the previous chapters, we focused on the classical robust statistics setting, where the outliers constitute the minority of the dataset, quantified by the proportion of contamination $\epsilon < 1/2$, and the goal is to obtain estimators whose error scales as a function of ϵ (and, in particular, is independent of the dimension d). A related setting of interest focuses on the regime where the fraction α of clean data (inliers) is small – at most $1/2$.

There are several settings of practical interest where these kinds of highly noisy datasets might be expected to appear. For example, in many settings there is a trade-off between the amount and the quality of the collected data. A prototypical application domain is crowdsourcing. For a fixed budget, it may be possible to collect either a very small clean dataset or a large and highly noisy dataset. A concrete scenario is when we collect a large dataset of customer evaluations of products, and we are interested on the preferences of a small demographic of customers.

Perhaps surprisingly, it turns out that even with an overwhelming majority of the samples being outliers, strong positive results are still possible given reasonable assumptions on the clean data. Moreover, as we will see later in Section 5.4, robust learning with a minority of inliers can be used as a crucial ingredient for learning mixture models of various kinds.

The setting studied in this chapter is the following: We observe n points in $\mathbf{R}^d$, an α-fraction of which (for some $0 < \alpha \leq 1/2$) are samples from an unknown distribution X in a known family $\mathcal{D}$. The goal is to estimate the mean μ of X. As is standard in robust statistics, no assumptions are made about the remaining $(1 - \alpha)$-fraction of the points. The major difference with what we

119

have previously studied is that in the current setting the outliers constitute the *majority* of the dataset.

A first observation is that it is information-theoretically impossible to estimate the mean with a single hypothesis. Indeed, an adversary can produce $\Omega(1/\alpha)$ clusters of points, each drawn from a distribution $D_i \in \mathcal{D}$ such that the D_i's have very different means. In this case, even if we could learn the distribution of the samples *exactly*, it still would not be possible to identify which of the clusters is the "correct" one (see Lemma 5.3). Interestingly, it turns out that this "symmetry breaking" is essentially the only real bottleneck. To circumvent this issue, we relax the definition of learning by allowing the algorithm to return *a small list of hypotheses* with the guarantee that *at least one* of the hypotheses is reasonably close to the true mean (see Definition 5.4). We will call this the *list-decodable learning* model. It follows from the above example that the list of hypotheses must have size at least $\Omega(1/\alpha)$. As we will see, one can typically construct estimators for many problems that output a list of size $O(1/\alpha)$.

Another notable difference here from the classical robust statistics setting has to do with the size of the errors. In particular, while robust statistics questions with bounded error rates ϵ usually allow one to produce estimators with bounded error for all ϵ, in the list decoding setting this is usually not the case. In particular, suppose that given a sufficiently large dataset, with an α-fraction of inliers, one can find a list of $O(1/\alpha)$ many hypotheses, at least one of which is within distance $f(\alpha)$ of the true mean. For many problems, this will be impossible unless the function $f(\alpha)$ goes to ∞ as α goes to 0. This being said, finding the optimal asymptotic form for $f(\alpha)$ is often an interesting question and usually depends on the distributional assumptions made on the good data-points.

The algorithmic frameworks developed in previous chapters do not suffice to obtain efficient estimators in the presence of a minority of inliers. In this chapter, we build on these algorithmic ideas to develop methodologies for efficient robust estimation in the list-decodable setting.

5.1.2 Problem Formulation and Basic Facts

The setup for the problems studied in this chapter is similar to what we have been studying thus far. Given corrupted samples from a distribution X, we want to estimate a pre-specified statistic of the distribution (e.g., the mean). The major difference with the previous chapters is that instead of the contamination parameter ϵ being some small constant (less than 1/2), we have $\epsilon = 1 - \alpha$, for some $\alpha \leq 1/2$ representing the fraction of clean samples in the dataset.

Similarly to our corruption models in previous chapters, the contamination can be additive, subtractive, or both. Moreover, the adversary can be adaptive or oblivious, as before.

The literature on list-decodable learning has focused on the case of additive contamination. Throughout this chapter, we study the following model of adaptive additive contamination.

Definition 5.1 (Additive Contamination Model)   Given a parameter $0 < \alpha \leq 1/2$ and a distribution family $\mathcal{D}$ on $\mathbf{R}^d$, the adversary operates as follows: The algorithm specifies a number of samples n, and $\lfloor \alpha n \rfloor$ samples are drawn from some unknown distribution $D \in \mathcal{D}$. The adversary is allowed to inspect these samples and adds a multiset of $n - \lfloor \alpha n \rfloor$ many arbitrary points to the dataset. This modified dataset of n points is then given as input to the algorithm. We say that a set of samples is *additively* $(1 - \alpha)$-*corrupted* if it is generated by the above process.

Remark 5.2   Some works in the literature instead use n for the number of inliers samples (and $\lceil n/\alpha \rceil$) for the total number of samples. This mostly reflects a philosophical difference about whether or not the algorithm should be "charged" for the bad samples or just for the clean ones. In the end, the theory is largely the same, though the sample complexity bounds will of course differ by a factor of α.

In the corruption model of Definition 5.1 the adversary is not allowed to alter the clean samples (inliers). One can consider an even more powerful adversary that is allowed to remove an arbitrary $(1 - \alpha)$ fraction of the clean samples as well. We note that in some cases such an adversary can be reduced to the additive adversary. For example, suppose we want to estimate the mean of a distribution X with bounded covariance $\Sigma \leq \sigma^2 I$. Then, after removing a $(1 - \alpha)$-fraction of the clean samples, we obtain a new distribution X' whose mean is within distance $O(\sigma/\sqrt{\alpha})$ of the mean of X and whose covariance is $\Sigma' \leq (\sigma^2/\alpha) I$, essentially reducing the learning problem to learning a distribution with covariance bounded by $(\sigma^2/\alpha) I$ with only additive noise.

A qualitatively similar contamination model is the following: One obtains i.i.d. samples from a distribution X of the form $X = \alpha D + (1 - \alpha)E$, for an unknown $D \in \mathcal{D}$ and some adversarially chosen distribution E. This is essentially a weaker model than that of Definition 5.1, as roughly an α-fraction of the points will be taken i.i.d. from D. More formally, if one takes $n \gg 1/(\alpha' - \alpha)^2$ samples from $X' = \alpha'D + (1 - \alpha')E$ for some $\alpha' > \alpha$, it is likely that this will include αn i.i.d. samples from G. This model may in fact be weaker than that of Definition 5.1 as it is nonadaptive, that is, the adversary must pick their distribution over the outliers before seeing the clean samples chosen. That said, this is a model worth considering, especially when proving lower bounds.

This chapter will focus on list-decodable mean estimation. The algorithms presented here succeed under appropriate deterministic conditions on the clean data, analogous to the stability conditions in previous chapters. We start with a simple lemma, establishing that even very weak approximations to the mean are impossible without relaxing our definition of learning.

Lemma 5.3 *Let $G = \mathcal{N}(\mu, I)$ be an identity covariance, unknown mean Gaussian and $0 < \alpha \leq 1/2$. Let X be a distribution of the form $\alpha G + (1 - \alpha)E$, where E is an adversarially chosen distribution. Then, for any $M \in \mathbf{R}_+$ and $N \in \mathbf{Z}_+$ there is no algorithm that given N i.i.d. samples from X returns an estimate $\widehat{\mu}$ satisfying $\|\widehat{\mu} - \mu\|_2 \leq M$ with probability greater than $1/\lfloor 1/\alpha \rfloor$.*

Lemma 5.3 implies that no algorithm given any number of $(1 - \alpha)$-corrupted samples from $\mathcal{N}(\mu, I)$ can learn an M-approximation to μ with probability better than $1/\lfloor 1/\alpha \rfloor$ (though when $1/\alpha$ is an integer, a slightly different argument is needed to ensure that exactly an α-fraction of samples come from each cluster).

Proof First assume for simplicity that $1/\alpha$ is an integer. We choose the noise distribution E such that $E = \sum_{i=1}^{k}(1/k)\mathcal{N}(\mu^{(i)}, I)$, where $k = 1/\alpha - 1$, and the pairwise ℓ_2-distances between the $\mu^{(i)}$'s, $i = 0, 1, \ldots, k$ (where $\mu^{(0)} = \mu$) are each greater than $2M$, as shown in Figure 5.1.

That is, X is a mixture of $1/\alpha$ many identity covariance Gaussians whose means are pairwise far from each other. Then, even if the algorithm knows the distribution of X exactly (with the corresponding mean vectors $\mu^{(i)}$), it will not be able to determine which of these $1/\alpha$ candidate means is the true μ. It is easy to see that the best thing an algorithm can do in this case is guess the correct mean from this set; this succeeds with probability α. If $1/\alpha$ is not an integer, we can replace α by $1/\lfloor 1/\alpha \rfloor \geq \alpha$ in the previous argument. Since we have increased the fraction of inliers, this step only makes the problem easier. $\square$

Lemma 5.3 is not specific to the Gaussian distribution. It is easily seen to hold for any class of distributions without an a priori bound on their mean. The lemma implies that it is impossible to obtain a nontrivial estimator of the mean with a single hypothesis that succeeds with probability better than $1/2$. The essential problem here is that if the corrupted distribution consists of several clusters, then the algorithm may have no way of knowing which cluster is the correct one to output. One way around this is to allow the algorithm to instead return a small list of hypotheses with the guarantee that at least one is close to

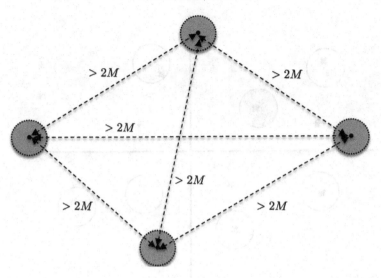

Figure 5.1 Illustration of a hard instance for Lemma 5.3 when $\alpha = 1/4$. Notice that each of the four equal clusters of points could be the set of "good" points. However, since their means are pairwise separated by more than $2M$, any guess the algorithm provides will be within distance M of at most one of the cluster means.

the target (see Figure 5.2 for an illustration). We formalize this idea with the following definition.

Definition 5.4 (List-Decodable Mean Estimation) A *list-decoding algorithm* for mean estimation with error β, failure probability δ, and list size s is an algorithm that given a multiset of $(1 - \alpha)$-corrupted samples from a distribution X with unknown mean μ returns a list H of hypotheses of size $|H| \leq s$ such that with probability at least $1 - \delta$ there exists $h \in H$ such that $\|h - \mu\|_2 \leq \beta$.

Note that there is a natural trade-off between the size of the output list and the best attainable error. For example, if the list size is allowed to be very large (e.g., exponential in the dimension), we can make the error very small by returning a fine cover of an appropriately chosen region. Arguably, allowing for very large list size trivializes the problem and we will not be interested in this regime. On the other hand, if the list size is sufficiently small, no nontrivial error guarantees are possible.

We have the following corollary of Lemma 5.3.

Corollary 5.5 *Let* $0 < \alpha \leq 1/2$. *Any list-decoding algorithm that learns the mean of* $(1 - \alpha)$-*corrupted, identity-covariance Gaussians within finite error*

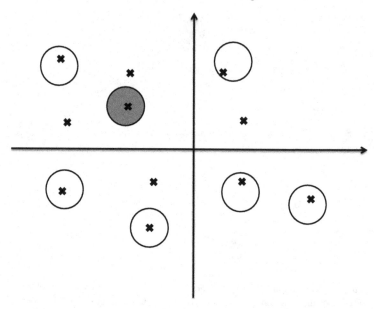

Figure 5.2 An example of a distribution consisting of several clusters (circles) and a list of hypotheses (crosses). Note that at least one hypothesis is close to the mean of the cluster of inlier samples (in gray), thus satisfying the guarantee of Definition 5.4.

must either return at least $s \geq \lfloor 1/(2\alpha) \rfloor$ hypotheses or have error probability $\delta \geq 1/2$.

Proof If the algorithm returns a list $(h_1, h_2, \ldots, h_s)$ of hypotheses, by Lemma 5.3, the probability that h_i is close to the true mean is at most $1/\lceil 1/\alpha \rceil$ for each i. Therefore, by a union bound, the probability that *any* hypothesis is close is at most $s/\lceil 1/\alpha \rceil \leq 1/2$. □

It turns out that the most interesting regime is the case that the list size is a polynomially bounded function of $1/\alpha$. As we will see later in this chapter, it usually suffices to take $s = O(1/\alpha)$.

Chapter Organization The structure of this chapter is as follows: In Section 5.2, we explore the information-theoretic limits of list-decodable mean estimation. In Section 5.3, we develop our algorithmic techniques for list-decodable mean estimation. In Section 5.4, we show how to use a list-decodable mean estimator to learn mixture models.

5.2 Information-Theoretic Limits of List-Decodable Learning

5.2.1 Information-Theoretic Upper Bounds

In this section, we present list-decodable mean estimators whose error guarantees are information-theoretically optimal (within constant factors), assuming the distribution of the inliers satisfies certain concentration or bounded moment properties. We note that these estimators are not computationally efficient. In particular, they correspond to algorithms whose runtime is exponential in the dimension. In Section 5.3, we will discuss some efficient algorithms with worse error guarantees.

The high-level intuition for our information-theoretically optimal estimators is the following: Since the underlying distribution family $\mathcal{D}$ is assumed to have good concentration, with high probability the set of inliers S will be concentrated around the target mean μ. In more detail, the target mean μ satisfies the following property: It is associated with a subset S of the input dataset T of size $|S| \geq \alpha|T|$ such that S is concentrated around μ.

Therefore, any reasonable candidate hypothesis h in our list should be associated with a subset (cluster) S_h of the input dataset T of size $|S_h| \geq \alpha|T|$, such that S_h is similarly concentrated around h. If two of these clusters are close to each other, then they can share the same hypothesis. On the other hand, if two such clusters are sufficiently separated, then (because of the assumed concentration) they will necessarily have small overlap (see, for example, Claim 5.8). Using this fact along with a simple counting argument, one can show that the number of pairwise separated clusters will be small. For example, in Lemma 5.7 we show that there are at most $O(1/\alpha)$ such clusters. Indeed, if we had many separated clusters, then we would run out of datapoints. Our estimator then returns one hypothesis for each such cluster.

More formally, we establish the following proposition.

Proposition 5.6 *Let $\mathcal{D}$ be a distribution family on $\mathbf{R}^d$ and let $0 < \alpha \leq 1/2$. Suppose that there exists $t > 0$ such that for every $G \in \mathcal{D}$ and every unit vector v it holds $\Pr[v \cdot (G - \mu_G) > t] \leq \alpha/20$.*

Then there exists an (inefficient) algorithm with the following guarantee: Given a multiset of $N \geq Cd/\alpha^3$ additively $(1 - \alpha)$-corrupted points from an unknown $G \in \mathcal{D}$, where $C > 0$ is a sufficiently large constant, the algorithm returns a list of $O(1/\alpha)$ many hypotheses such that with high probability at least one such hypothesis is within ℓ_2-distance $2t$ from the target mean μ_G of G.

The proof of Proposition 5.6 makes essential use of the following geometric lemma.

Lemma 5.7 *Let $T \subset \mathbf{R}^d$ be a set of points, $t > 0$, $0 < \alpha \le 1/2$, and $k \in \mathbf{Z}_+$. Suppose that there exist potentially overlapping subsets $S_1, S_2, \ldots, S_k \subseteq T$ with $|S_i| \ge \alpha|T|$ with the following property: For each S_i, $i \in [k]$, there is an associated vector $\mu_i \in \mathbf{R}^d$ such that for any unit vector $v \in \mathbf{R}^d$, it holds*

$$\Pr_{x \sim_u S_i} [v \cdot (x - \mu_i) > t] \le \alpha/10. \tag{5.1}$$

If the set of μ_i's are pairwise separated by ℓ_2-distance at least $2t$, then we have that $k \le 2/\alpha$.

Furthermore, this holds even if Condition (5.1) is satisfied only for unit vectors v in the direction of $\mu_i - \mu_j$ for all pairs $i \ne j$.

Proof The proof proceeds by contradiction. Suppose that there exist sets $S_1, \ldots, S_k$ and points $\mu_1, \ldots, \mu_k \in \mathbf{R}^d$ with $k > 2/\alpha$ so that $\|\mu_i - \mu_j\|_2 \ge 2t$, for all $i \ne j$. By ignoring some of these points if necessary, we can assume that $k = \lceil 2/\alpha \rceil$.

By definition, each S_i satisfies $|S_i| \ge \alpha|T|$ and for any unit vector v, it holds that $\Pr_{x \sim_u S_i}[v \cdot (x - \mu_i) > t] \le \alpha/10$. Our first key claim is that the pairwise intersection between the S_i's is small. Specifically, we show the following.

Claim 5.8 *For each $i \ne j$, $i, j \in [k]$, we have that $|S_i \cap S_j| \le (\alpha/10)(|S_i| + |S_j|)$.*

Proof Since $\|\mu_i - \mu_j\|_2 \ge 2t$, if v_{ij} is the unit vector in the direction of $\mu_i - \mu_j$, every point $y \in \mathbf{R}^d$ must satisfy (i) $|v_{ij} \cdot (y - \mu_i)| \ge t$, or (ii) $|v_{ij} \cdot (y - \mu_j)| \ge t$. By the assumed concentration property (5.1) of the μ_i's, at most $\alpha/10$-fraction of points $y \in S_i$ satisfy (i) and at most $\alpha/10$-fraction of points $y \in S_j$ satisfy (ii). If L is the subset of points $y \in S_i \cap S_j$ satisfying (i), then we have that $|L| \le (\alpha/10)|S_i|$. Similarly, if R is the subset of points $y \in S_i \cap S_j$ satisfying (ii), then it holds that $|R| \le (\alpha/10)|S_j|$. Therefore, it follows that $|S_i \cap S_j| \le (\alpha/10)(|S_i| + |S_j|)$, proving the claim. □

Given Claim 5.8, the proof of Lemma 5.7 follows by a simple counting argument. In particular, by the approximate inclusion-exclusion formula, we have

$$|T| \ge |\cup_{i=1}^k S_i| \ge \sum_{i=1}^k |S_i| - \sum_{1 \le i < j \le k} |S_i \cap S_j|$$

$$\ge \sum_{i=1}^k |S_i| - \sum_{1 \le i < j \le k} (\alpha/10)(|S_i| + |S_j|)$$

$$= \sum_{i=1}^k |S_i| - (\alpha/10)(k-1) \sum_{i=1}^k |S_i|$$

$$\geq (1 - (k-1)\alpha/10) \sum_{i=1}^{k} |S_i|$$

$$\geq (4/5) \sum_{i=1}^{k} \alpha|T| = (4/5)(k\alpha)|T| \geq (8/5)|T|,$$

where the second line follows from Claim 5.8, the third line follows from the elementary fact that $\sum_{1 \leq i < j \leq k}(|S_i| + |S_j|) = (k-1)\sum_{i=1}^{k}|S_i|$, and the last line uses the assumption that $|S_i| \geq \alpha|T|$ and the definition of k. This yields the desired contradiction, proving Lemma 5.7. □

With this lemma in hand, we can show that there can only be $O(1/\alpha)$ many clusters of plausible means.

Proof of Proposition 5.6 Let T be a set of N additively $(1-\alpha)$-corrupted samples from an unknown distribution $G \in \mathcal{D}$, where $N \geq Cd/\alpha^3$ for C is a sufficiently large constant. By definition, there exists a set $S \subseteq T$ of i.i.d. samples from G with $|S| = \alpha|T| \gg d/\alpha^2$.

We claim that the set S is a representative sample of the distribution G in the sense that, with high probability over the randomness in S, for any unit vector v we have

$$\Pr_{X \sim_u S}[|v \cdot (X - \mu_G)| > t] \leq \alpha/10, \tag{5.2}$$

where μ_G is the mean of G. Recall that we have $\Pr[v \cdot (G - \mu_G) > t] \leq \alpha/20$, by assumption. Condition (5.2) then follows by an application of the VC inequality (Theorem A.12), given our assumption on N and the fact that the class of halfspaces has VC-dimension $O(d)$. We henceforth condition on this event.

Let H be the set of all points in $\mathbf{R}^d$ with the following property: A point $x \in \mathbf{R}^d$ is in H if there exists a subset $S_x \subseteq T$ of cardinality $|S_x| \geq \alpha|T|$ such that, in any direction, all but an $\alpha/10$-fraction of the points in S_x are within distance t of x. That is, for any unit vector v, we have

$$\Pr_{X \sim_u S_x}[|v \cdot (X - x)| \geq t] \leq \alpha/10. \tag{5.3}$$

By the above conditioning, we have $\mu_G \in H$. Consider a maximal subset, C, of elements of H that are pairwise separated by a distance of at least $2t$. By Lemma 5.7, $|C| \leq 2/\alpha$. On the other hand, every element of H must be within distance $2t$ of some element in C, as otherwise it could be added to C, contradicting maximality.

The list-decoding algorithm now merely needs to return the set C. As $\mu_G \in H$, we know that the true mean μ_G must be within distance $2t$ of some element in C. This completes the proof of Proposition 5.6. □

Proposition 5.6 yields tight error upper bounds for a number of distribution families. We explicitly state its implications for the following families: sub-Gaussian distributions, distributions with bounded covariance, and distributions with bounded low-degree moments.

Corollary 5.9 *Let $0 < \alpha \leq 1/2$. Given a sufficiently large multiset of additively $(1 - \alpha)$-corrupted samples from a distribution $G \in \mathcal{D}$, there exists a list-decodable mean estimation algorithm for G that outputs a list of size $O(1/\alpha)$ whose error guarantee is at most:*

- $O(\sqrt{\log(1/\alpha)})\sigma$, *if $\mathcal{D}$ is the family of sub-Gaussian distributions with parameter σ.*
- $O(1/\sqrt{\alpha})\sigma$, *if $\mathcal{D}$ is the family of distributions with covariance matrix $\Sigma \preceq \sigma^2 I$.*
- $O((C/\alpha)^{1/k})$, *if $\mathcal{D}$ is the family of distributions whose kth central moments in any direction, for some even $k > 0$, are at most C.*

Proof These statements follow from Proposition 5.6 using the appropriate concentration inequality.

Recall that if G is sub-Gaussian on $\mathbf{R}^d$ with mean vector μ and parameter $\sigma > 0$, then for any unit vector $v \in \mathbf{R}^d$ we have $\Pr_{X \sim G}[|v \cdot (X - \mu)| \geq t] \leq \exp(-t^2/(2\sigma^2))$. By taking $t = \Theta(\sqrt{\log(1/\alpha)})\sigma$, the assumption in the statement of Proposition 5.6 is satisfied.

If G has covariance matrix $\Sigma \preceq \sigma^2 I$, by Chebyshev's inequality, we can apply Proposition 5.6 for $t = \Theta(1/\sqrt{\alpha})\sigma$.

Finally, if $\mathbf{E}[(v \cdot (X - \mu))^k] \leq C$, then $\Pr[|v \cdot (X - \mu)| \geq t] = \Pr[(v \cdot (X - \mu))^k \geq t^k] \leq C/t^k$. Therefore, if G has its first k central moments bounded, we can take $t = (20C/\alpha)^{1/k}$ in Proposition 5.6. This completes the proof. $\square$

5.2.2 Information-Theoretic Lower Bounds

In this section, we show that upper bounds on the errors for list decoding algorithms proved in Corollary 5.9 are information-theoretically optimal to within constant factors. Specifically, we will establish lower bounds of the following form: Any list-decodable mean estimator that returns a small list of hypotheses (i.e., of size poly($1/\alpha$), independent of d) will inherently have either large error or large failure probability. In particular, this statement implies that the required error will necessarily go to infinity as α goes to 0.

It is interesting to note that the lower bounds we give in this section do not depend on the number of samples drawn from the underlying distribution. In particular, these lower bounds apply even if the learner is allowed to take an unlimited number of samples and spend an unlimited amount of computation time. In order to achieve this goal, we will ensure that the lower bounds hold even if the algorithm is able to successfully learn the complete distribution X that the samples in question are being drawn from.

The proof will be along the same lines as the proof of Lemma 5.3. In particular, we will construct a distribution X consisting of many possible clusters, any one of which could be the good distribution. However, while in Lemma 5.3 our goal was to have $\lfloor 1/\alpha \rfloor$ many clusters that were pairwise separated by an arbitrarily large distance, here we want to have a much larger number of clusters separated by a large but bounded distance.

Our results will make essential use of the following fundamental lemma.

Lemma 5.10 *Let $\mathcal{D}$ be a class of distributions on $\mathbf{R}^d$, $0 < \alpha \leq 1/2$, and $s \in \mathbf{Z}_+$. Suppose that there is a distribution X on $\mathbf{R}^d$ and distributions $G_1, G_2, \ldots, G_s$ in $\mathcal{D}$ such that (i) $\alpha G_i \leq X$ for each $i \in [s]$, and (ii) $\|\mu_{G_i} - \mu_{G_j}\|_2 > 2\beta$ for all $i \neq j$. Then any list-decodable mean estimation algorithm for $\mathcal{D}$ that is given access to an $(1 - \alpha)$-additively corrupted set of samples and achieves error at most β with failure probability at most $1/2$ must return a list of size at least $s/2$.*

Proof We construct an adversarial distribution as follows: The distribution G of the inliers is defined to be equal to G_i, for a uniformly random $i \in [s]$. The distribution of the outliers E is defined by $E = (X - \alpha G)/(1 - \alpha)$. The assumption that $X \geq \alpha G_i$, for all $i \in [s]$, implies that E is a well-defined probability distribution. By construction, we note that the underlying distribution of the data is equal to $X = \alpha G + (1 - \alpha)E$. Since X is independent of the choice of i, and since the output of the algorithm correlates with i only through its samples (which in turn depend only on X), we have that the output of the algorithm is independent of i.

Let H be the list of hypotheses output by a list-decodable mean estimator for $\mathcal{D}$. To prove the lemma, we need to bound from above the probability that there exists an $h \in H$ such that $\|h - \mu_G\|_2 \leq \beta$, where μ_G is the target mean. Since the μ_{G_i}'s are pairwise separated by at least 2β in ℓ_2-distance, any $h \in H$ can be within ℓ_2-distance β of at most one μ_{G_i}. This means that for any given $h \in H$ the probability that $\|h - \mu_G\|_2 \leq \beta$ is at most $1/s$. Given that $|H| \leq s/2$, a union bound implies that with probability at least $1/2$ the distance between μ_G and the closest element of h is more than β. This completes the proof of the lemma. □

Given Lemma 5.10, proving explicit lower bounds for a given class of distributions reduces to finding an appropriate distribution X. We perform this step for two natural distribution families in the following sections.

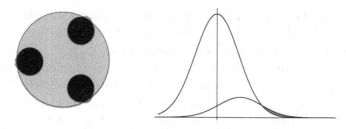

Figure 5.3 Illustration of hard instance given in Proposition 5.11. The diagram on the left shows the overall plan for the distribution. The large Gaussian X_0 (shown in gray) is nearly above each of the αY_μ (shown in black). By adding a small amount of extra mass to accommodate the difference, we end up with a distribution X such that $X \geq \alpha Y_\mu$ for many Gaussians Y_μ with widely separated means. The diagram on the right shows a one-dimensional projection of X_0 and one of the αY_μ. The shaded gray region denotes the small gap between the two.

5.2.2.1 Lower Bounds in the Gaussian Setting

For identity covariance Gaussian distributions, we show:

Proposition 5.11 *Let $\mathcal{D}$ be the class of identity covariance Gaussians on $\mathbf{R}^d$ and let $0 < \alpha \leq 1/2$. Then any list-decoding algorithm that learns the mean of an element of $\mathcal{D}$, with failure probability at most $1/2$, given access to $(1 - \alpha)$-additively corrupted samples, must either have error bound $\beta = \Omega(\sqrt{\log(1/\alpha)})$ or return $\min\{2^{\Omega(d)}, (1/\alpha)^{\omega(1)}\}$ many hypotheses.*

See Figure 5.3 for an illustration of the hard distribution on points.

We note that as long as $d = \omega(\log(1/\alpha))$, Proposition 5.11 along with Corollary 5.9 imply a tight error bound for this problem. That is, assuming that the learner is only allowed to output a list of size poly$(1/\alpha)$, an error bound of $\Theta(\sqrt{\log(1/\alpha)})$ is both necessary and sufficient.

Proof We assume throughout that α is sufficiently small. Let X_0 be the pseudo-distribution (i.e., a positive measure) $X_0 = \mathcal{N}(0, I)/2$. Consider $G = \mathcal{N}(\mu, I)$ for some μ with $\|\mu\|_2 = c\sqrt{\log(1/\alpha)}$, where $c < 1$ is sufficiently small. We note that X_0 is already *nearly* larger than αG for any such choice of G. In particular, the ratio of their probability density functions is

$$\frac{X_0}{\alpha G} = \frac{1}{2\alpha} e^{(-\|x\|_2^2 + \|x - \mu\|_2^2)/2} = \frac{1}{2\alpha} e^{-x \cdot \mu + \|\mu\|_2^2/2}.$$

We note that the RHS above is more than 1, unless $|x \cdot \mu| \gg \log(1/\alpha)$, or if the projection of x in the μ-direction is at least some sufficiently large multiple of $c^{-1}\sqrt{\log(1/\alpha)}$. The latter event happens with probability at most poly$(\alpha^{c^{-2}})$ with respect to either X_0 or G. Therefore, there is another pseudo-distribution $Y_\mu = \max(0, \alpha G - X_0)$ with total mass poly$(\alpha^{c^{-2}})$ such that $X_0 + Y_\mu \geq \alpha G$.

Let N be an integer such that $N = \min\{2^{cd}, 1/(2\|Y_\mu\|_1)\}$, where μ is any vector with $\|\mu\|_2 = c\sqrt{\log(1/\alpha)}$ as described above. For $1 \le i \le N$, we define $G_i = \mathcal{N}(\mu_i, I)$, where $\|\mu_i\|_2 = c\sqrt{\log(1/\alpha)}$, such that $\|\mu_i - \mu_j\|_2 \gg c\sqrt{\log(1/\alpha)}$, for all $i \ne j$. The latter constraint can be ensured since $N \le 2^{cd}$ and Theorem A.10 implies that one can find N unit vectors in $\mathbf{R}^d$ with pairwise distances at least a constant. Multiplying these vectors by $c\sqrt{\log(1/\epsilon)}$ yields our μ_i's.

Let X be any distribution satisfying $X \ge X_0 + \sum_{i=1}^{N} Y_{\mu_i}$. We note that since $N \le 1/(2\|Y_{\mu_i}\|_1)$ for any such μ_i, the RHS has total probability mass at most 1 and therefore such a distribution X exists.

For such a choice of X, it is easy to see that $X \ge \alpha G_i$ for each $i \in [N]$. Thus, by Lemma 5.10, any list-decodable mean estimation algorithm will need to either output a list of size $N/2 = (1/2)\min\{2^d, \text{poly}(\alpha^{-c^{-2}})\}$ or incur error at least $\Omega(c\sqrt{\log(1/\alpha)})$. This completes our proof.   □

5.2.2.2 Lower Bounds for Distributions with Bounded Moments

In this section, we establish tight error lower bounds for distributions with bounded moments. Recall that we say that a distribution G has kth central moments bounded by C, if for every unit vector v we have $\mathbf{E}[|v \cdot (G - \mu_G)|^k] \le C$. For this class of distributions, we show:

Proposition 5.12 *Let $\mathcal{D}$ be the class of distributions on $\mathbf{R}^d$ whose kth central moments are at most 1 for some positive even integer k, and let $2^{-k-1} > \alpha > 0$. Then any list-decoding algorithm that learns the mean of an element of $\mathcal{D}$ with failure probability at most $1/2$, given access to $(1 - \alpha)$-additively corrupted samples, must either have error bound $\beta = \Omega(\alpha^{-1/k})$ or return a list of at least d hypotheses.*

Proposition 5.12 along with Corollary 5.9 imply a tight error bound for distributions in this class. In particular, if the list-decodable mean estimation algorithm for distributions with bounded kth central moments is required to output a list whose size is independent of the dimension, an error bound of $\Theta(\alpha^{-1/k})$ is necessary and sufficient.

Note also that if we scale the distributions by $C^{1/k}$, we find that for distributions whose kth moments are bounded by C, we obtain a lower bound of $\Omega((C/\alpha)^{1/k})$. By taking $k = 2$, we get a lower bound of $\sigma/\sqrt{\alpha}$ for distributions with covariance bounded by $\sigma^2 I$.

Proof We start by constructing an appropriate one-dimensional distribution. Our family of high-dimensional distributions will simply be the product of d independent copies from this family.

For $1 \leq i \leq d$, we define X_i to be the distribution on the real line such that $X_i = 0$ with probability $1 - 2\alpha$, $X_i = (2\alpha)^{-1/k}$ with probability α, and $X_i = -(2\alpha)^{-1/k}$ with probability α. Note that the kth central moment of X_i is equal to 1.

Let $X = \prod_{i \in [d]} X_i$, that is, X is the product distribution with marginals X_i. We will show that X satisfies the kth bounded central moments property. For any unit vector v, we have

$$\mathbf{E}[|v \cdot X|^k] = \sum_{a_1, \dots, a_d \geq 0, \sum a_i = k} \binom{k}{a_1, \dots, a_d} \prod_{i=1}^{d} v_i^{a_i} \mathbf{E}\left[\prod_{i=1}^{d} X_i^{a_i}\right].$$

Since the X_i's are symmetric and independent, we note that the quantity

$$\mathbf{E}\left[\prod_{i=1}^{d} X_i^{a_i}\right] = \prod_{i=1}^{d} \mathbf{E}\left[X_i^{a_i}\right]$$

is equal to 0 unless all of the a_i's are even. If all the a_i's are even, let $b_i = a_i/2$ and let c be the number of nonzero b_i's. Then we have $\mathbf{E}\left[\prod_{i=1}^{d} X_i^{a_i}\right] = (2\alpha)^{c-1}$. Therefore, we can write

$$\mathbf{E}[|v \cdot X|^k] = \sum_{\sum_i b_i = k/2} \binom{k}{2b_1, \dots, 2b_d} \prod_{i=1}^{d} v_i^{2b_i} (2\alpha)^{c-1}.$$

We proceed to compare this quantity to

$$1 = (\|v\|_2^2)^{k/2} = \sum_{\sum_i b_i = k/2} \binom{k/2}{b_1, \dots, b_d} \prod_{i=1}^{d} v_i^{2b_i}.$$

Noting that $\binom{k}{2b_1, \dots, 2b_d} \leq c^k$, it is easy to see that the latter expression dominates termwise. Hence, we have $\mathbf{E}[|v \cdot X|^k] \leq 1$.

We will now construct $2d$ distributions G_j satisfying $\alpha G_j \leq X$ such that the means of the G_j's differ by $\Omega(\alpha^{-1/k})$. We let G_j be the product of the X_i's in all dimensions except for $i = j$. The jth coordinate of G_j will either be the constant $(2\alpha)^{1/k}$ or the constant $-(2\alpha)^{1/k}$. By the above, it is easy to see that G_j's has bounded kth central moments (as G_j is a translation of a $(d-1)$-dimensional version of X), and that $\alpha G_j \leq X$. Note that there are $2d$ different G_j's, as there are d possibilities for the coordinate j and two possibilities for the sign. Finally, it is clear that each G_j has mean $\pm(2\alpha)^{-1/k} e_j$, and that these means differ pairwise by ℓ_2-distance $\Omega(\alpha^{-1/k})$. The proposition now follows directly from Lemma 5.10. □

5.3 Efficient Algorithms for List-Decodable Mean Estimation

Given our understanding of the information-theoretic possibilities and limitations of list-decodable mean estimation, in this section we consider the more challenging question of what can actually be achieved in a computationally efficient manner. A number of algorithmic techniques for list-decodable learning have been developed in the literature. Here we focus on two distinct such techniques. In Section 5.3.1, we develop efficient algorithms based on a technique we will call multifiltering, a generalization of the filtering technique of Chapter 2. In Section 5.3.2, we present a different algorithmic technique for the problem that is arguably simpler and can be advantageous in certain settings.

5.3.1 List-Decodable Learning via Multifiltering

Recall the regime where the outliers constitute a minority of the dataset. The goal of a filtering algorithm is quite simple. By iterative outlier removal, we wish to find a subset T' of the original sample set T such that T' still contains a large fraction of inliers, and so that the covariance of T' is not too large. This condition suffices to ensure that the sample mean of T' is close to the true mean. Interestingly, this structural result still qualitatively holds with a *majority* of outliers. Specifically, we have the following simple lemma.

Lemma 5.13 *Let $T \subset \mathbf{R}^d$ be a multiset such that $\mathbf{Cov}[T]$ has maximum eigenvalue λ. Then for any $S \subset T$ with $|S| \geq \alpha|T|$ we have that $\|\mu_S - \mu_T\|_2 \leq \sqrt{\lambda/\alpha}$.*

Proof Let $R = T \setminus S$. Noting that the uniform distribution on T is a mixture of the uniform distributions over S and R, we can write:

$$\mathbf{Cov}[T] = \frac{|S|}{|T|}\mathbf{Cov}[S] + \frac{|R|}{|T|}\mathbf{Cov}[R] + \frac{|S|}{|T|}(\mu_S - \mu_T)(\mu_S - \mu_T)^\top$$
$$+ \frac{|R|}{|T|}(\mu_R - \mu_T)(\mu_R - \mu_T)^\top \qquad (5.4)$$
$$\geq \alpha(\mu_S - \mu_T)(\mu_S - \mu_T)^\top,$$

where we used the assumption that $|S|/|T| \geq \alpha$ and the fact that the remaining terms in the right-hand side of Equation (5.4) are PSD. Since by assumption $\mathbf{Cov}[T]$ has no eigenvalue bigger than λ, it follows that the largest eigenvalue of the rank-one term, $\alpha(\mu_S - \mu_T)(\mu_S - \mu_T)^\top$, is at most λ. That is, we have that $\alpha\|\mu_S - \mu_T\|_2^2 \leq \lambda$, which completes the proof. □

Lemma 5.13 is the basis of the list-decoding algorithms in this section. Specifically, if we can find a subset T' of the input dataset T that still contains at least an α-fraction of inliers and has bounded covariance, then we can use it to approximate the true mean of our distribution (by outputting the empirical mean of T'). A natural attempt to achieve this is via a filtering algorithm. The basic strategy here is the same as in the minority-outlier regime: Given a set T of samples, if $\mathbf{Cov}[T]$ is small, we return the sample mean of T. Otherwise, we project the sample points onto the direction of largest variance and use the structure of projected points to remove outliers.

At a high-level, it turns out that this strategy still works in the list-decodable setting. Of course, in the list-decodable setting, the "outlier removal" step is necessarily more complicated. Recall the main idea of the outlier removal step in the minority-outlier regime. After projecting the points on a large-variance direction, the true mean in this direction must not be very far from the empirical mean. Since the inliers exhibit tight concentration around their mean, we can conclude that points that lie far from the sample mean (which must exist due to the large variance in this direction) are almost all outliers. Therefore, removing these points will increase the fraction of inliers. Unfortunately, this basic strategy breaks down in the first step. Although Lemma 5.13 implies that the true mean cannot be *too* far from the empirical mean, the bound it provides will be qualitatively too weak for our purposes. In particular, the true mean might be many standard deviations away from the sample mean, and thus, removing samples far from the sample mean will risk throwing away the inliers.

The following examples illustrate the difficulties that can arise in our setting.

Example 5.14   Consider the case where after projecting the set T onto the largest variance direction we are left with a dataset approximating the uniform distribution over an interval of length $\Theta(1/\alpha)$. If the inlier distribution is known to have identity covariance, then the true mean could plausibly be almost anywhere in this interval, as any unit length subinterval will consist of an α-fraction of points with appropriate concentration. Therefore, only points whose projections onto this direction lie far from this interval can confidently be declared to be outliers. Unfortunately, there might not be any such points, leaving us with a direction of variance $\Theta(1/\alpha^2)$, but no way to filter.

Example 5.15   An arguably worse example arises when the projected samples form two distinct clusters that are at very large distance from each other. An algorithm can potentially determine that the true mean must be within one of these clusters and that the other cluster will consist almost entirely of outliers. However, there is no way for the algorithm to determine *which* cluster is the correct one. This example illustrates the necessity of list-decoding. If

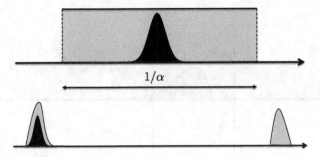

Figure 5.4 Illustration of instances in Example 5.14 (top) and Example 5.15 (bottom). In both bases, the black graphs correspond to plausible locations for the set of inliers.

our algorithm is going to succeed in this setting, it will need to consider both clusters as possible hypotheses.

See Figure 5.4 for an illustration of Examples 5.14 and 5.15.

Intuition The question that needs to be addressed is how to adapt the basic filtering idea into a principled method that can return multiple hypotheses. The basic filtering method maintains a single set of samples that eventually allows it to return a single hypothesis. In order to develop a list-decoding algorithm, we will need a method that maintains several sets of samples. A natural solution to Example 5.15 is the following: If the projection of the points contains two clusters of points, our algorithm will produce two sets of samples (one corresponding to each cluster), each of which will lead to an eventual hypothesis (after potentially being further refined in subsequent iterations).

Alas, it is less clear how to address Example 5.14. If the samples are approximately uniform within a short interval, there is not a straightforward way to partition them into subsets. Simply cutting the interval in two pieces might cause an issue in the case that the true mean lies near the boundary of this division. Indeed, in such a case, we may lose roughly half of the inliers on either side; and it may well be the case that neither side has a higher fraction of inliers than our original set of samples. To resolve this, we allow the algorithm to split our sample set into two *overlapping* subsets. By ensuring that our sets have sufficient overlap on the boundary, we can ensure that no matter where the true mean is, at least one of the two new sets contains almost all of the inliers, as shown in Figure 5.5.

One wrinkle with this strategy is that if we split our dataset into *multiple* subsets, we may need to divide the two initial subsets into smaller subsets,

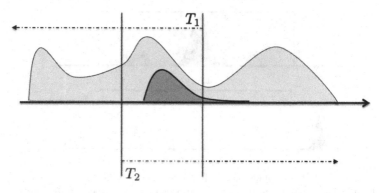

Figure 5.5 Example of sets T_1 and T_2 produced by a multifilter. The projected samples here are given by the light gray curve with the inlier samples given by the dark gray curve. Note that almost all of the inlier samples are contained in T_2. However, the overlap between T_1 and T_2 is sufficiently large here that no matter where the inlier samples were located (so long as they have similar concentration properties), at least one of T_1 and T_2 would contain almost all of the inliers.

and so on. If we do this poorly, we may end up with potentially exponentially many subsets in total, which will imply both that our number of hypotheses will be very large and that our final runtime is exponential. To avoid this potential problem, we will ensure that whenever we subdivide, the corresponding subsets are not too large. One way of achieving this is by enforcing the condition that whenever a set T is divided into subsets T_1 and T_2, we have $|T_1|^2 + |T_2|^2 \leq |T|^2$. This condition guarantees that, no matter how many subdivisions we perform, the sum of the squares of the sizes of the sets does not increase.

Algorithm Description We are now ready to present the basic version of our multifilter step. In the proceeding discussion, we consider the points after they have been projected onto one dimension. We use T to denote the set of all (projected) samples and S to denote the set of good samples (inliers). As is typically the case, we will make some concentration assumptions on S and will only be able to apply the multifiltering step if $\mathbf{Var}[T]$ is sufficiently large. Our algorithm considers two cases. If the points of T are mostly concentrated enough that we can identify the approximate location of the true mean, we will be able to run a vanilla filtering step, where we remove a few likely outliers. For technical reasons (that will make the later analysis of our algorithm easier), we design this step to remove only a single likely outlier point. If we cannot identify a small interval that must contain the true mean, we instead split the dataset into two overlapping sets, as described in the previous paragraph.

A basic version of our multifiltering step is the following.

Proposition 5.16 *Let $S, T \subset \mathbf{R}$ and let $M, \alpha, \beta, t > 0$ be parameters with $\alpha \leq 1/2$ sufficiently small such that $|S \cap T| \geq \max\{|S|/2, \alpha|T|\}$. Furthermore, assume that (i) $\mathbf{Var}[S] \leq 2$, (ii) $\mathbf{Var}[T]$ is at least a sufficiently large multiple of $[(t \log \log(1/\alpha) + 8)^2 + M]$, and (iii) all but a β-fraction of the points in S lie in an interval of length t. Then there exists a computationally efficient algorithm that given $T, \alpha, \beta, t,$ and M returns either:*

1. *a point $x \in T$ such that $x \in S$ with probability at most $\frac{2|S|}{M|T|}$ or*
2. *a pair of subsets $T_1, T_2 \subset T$ such that (i) $|T_1|^2 + |T_2|^2 \leq |T|^2$, and (ii) for at least one value of $i \in \{1, 2\}$, we have*

$$\frac{|S \cap (T \setminus T_i)|}{|T \setminus T_i|} \leq O\left(\frac{\beta|S|}{\alpha|T|}\right). \tag{5.5}$$

Before we proceed with the proof of Proposition 5.16, some comments are in order. First, we note that the set S is assumed to be highly concentrated and contains at least an α-fraction of the points of T. The algorithm either finds a point that is almost certainly an outlier (i.e., not in S) or divides the set T into two (not too large) subsets T_1, T_2 such that for at least one of the T_i's almost all of the points in $T \setminus T_i$ are not in S (i.e., almost all of the points removed are outliers).

Proof The pseudocode for the algorithm is given below:

Algorithm Basic-Multifilter

Input: Dataset $T \subset \mathbf{R}$, $0 < \alpha \leq 1/2$, parameters $\beta, t, M > 0$.

1. Let a be the $\alpha|T|/4$th smallest element of T and b the $\alpha|T|/4$th largest element.
2. If $b - a \leq Ct \log \log(1/\alpha)$:

   Return a random element of T with $x \in T$ selected with probability proportional to

$$f(x) := \min_{t \in [a-4, b+4]} (x - t)^2 = \begin{cases} (a - 4 - t)^2, & \text{if } t < a - 4, \\ 0, & \text{if } a - 4 \leq t \leq b + 4, \\ (t - b - 4)^2, & \text{if } t > b + 4. \end{cases}$$

3. Otherwise:

   (a) Find a real number $x \in [a, b-t]$ such that for $T_1 := T \cap (-\infty, x+t]$ and $T_2 := T \cap [x, \infty)$ we have $|T_1|^2 + |T_2|^2 \leq |T|^2$.

   (b) Return T_1, T_2.

Our algorithm starts by computing $I = [a, b]$, the interval spanning the distance between the $\alpha|T|/4$th smallest element of T to the $\alpha|T|/4$th largest element of T. We consider two cases based on whether the length of I is larger than $L = Ct \log \log(1/\alpha)$, for a sufficiently large constant $C > 0$.

If the length of I is at most L, we will be in the situation where we remove a single outlier. We begin by observing that the mean of S cannot be far outside of I. In particular, by Chebyshev's inequality, all but a $1/4$ fraction of the elements of S are within distance 4 of its mean. Since $|S \cap T| \geq |S|/2$, at least half of the points of $S \cap T$ are within distance 4 of the mean of S. Note that this set contains at least $\alpha|T|/4$ points. That is, the mean of S cannot be less than $a - 4$ or more than $b + 4$, since otherwise there would not be enough points.

This means that points far away from the interval I are likely to be outliers. In order to make this rigorous, we will want to define a weight function that assigns large weight to the points far away. In particular, we define the function

$$f(x) := \min_{t \in [a-4, b+4]} (x - t)^2 = \begin{cases} (a - 4 - t)^2, & \text{if } t < a - 4, \\ 0, & \text{if } a - 4 \leq t \leq b + 4, \\ (t - b - 4)^2, & \text{if } t > b + 4. \end{cases}$$

We note that $f(x) \leq (x - \mu_S)^2$, and therefore we have

$$\mathbf{E}_{x \sim_u S}[f(x)] \leq \mathbf{E}_{x \sim_u S}[(x - \mu_S)^2] = \mathbf{Var}(S) \leq 2.$$

On the other hand, it is not hard to see that

$$f(x) \geq (x - (a + b)/2)^2/4 - (b - a + 8)^2.$$

This is because if $|x - (a + b)/2| \leq (b - a + 8)$, the right-hand side is negative and f is not; and otherwise, $|x - t| \geq |x - (a + b)/2|/2$ for any $t \in [a - 4, b + 4]$, and so $f(x) \geq (x - (a + b)/2)^2/4$. Therefore, we have

$$\mathbf{E}_{x \sim_u T}[f(x)] \geq \mathbf{E}_{x \sim_u T}[(x-(a+b)/2)^2/4-(b-a+8)^2] \geq \mathbf{Var}(T)/4-(b-a+8)^2 \geq M.$$

The algorithm now picks a point $x \in T$ with probability proportional to $f(x)$. The probability that a point in S is selected is

$$\frac{\sum_{x \in S \cap T} f(x)}{\sum_{x \in T} f(x)} \leq \frac{\sum_{x \in S} f(x)}{\sum_{x \in T} f(x)} = \frac{|S| \mathbf{E}_{x \sim_u S}[f(x)]}{|T| \mathbf{E}_{x \sim_u T}[f(x)]} \leq \frac{2|S|}{M|T|}.$$

Next we consider the remaining case, where $I = [a, b]$ has length at least $L = Ct \log \log(1/\alpha)$. In this case, our algorithm will find a point $x \in \mathbf{R}$ such that $a \leq x \leq b - t$ and corresponding sets $T_1 = T \cap (-\infty, x + t], T_2 = T \cap [x, \infty)$. We will argue that this condition suffices to guarantee that the fraction of good points removed from one of the T_i's is small. In particular, we know that all but a β-fraction of the points in S lie in some interval J of length t. It is not hard to see that no matter what J is, we have that either $J \subset (-\infty, x + t]$ or $J \subset [x, \infty)$. In the former case, we have that $|S \cap (T \setminus T_1)| \le \beta|S|$, and in the latter case we have that $|S \cap (T \setminus T_2)| \le \beta|S|$. In either case, it holds that $|T \setminus T_i| \ge \alpha|T|/4$, since $|T \cap (-\infty, a)| = |T \cap (b, \infty)| = \alpha|T|/4$. This suffices to verify Condition (5.5).

It remains to ensure that $|T_1|^2 + |T_2|^2 \le |T|^2$. We claim that this is always possible as long as the length of I is at least a sufficiently large constant multiple of $t \log\log(1/\alpha)$. To facilitate our analysis, we define the function $g(x) = |T \cap (-\infty, x]|/|T|$ to be the fraction of the points in T that are at most x. In order for our sets to have appropriate size, we need to find an x such that $g(x+t)^2 + (1 - g(x))^2 \le 1$. We assume for sake of contradiction that there is no $a \le x \le b - t$ that satisfies this condition.

Note that if $g(x) \le 1/2$ and $x + t \le b$, we have $g(x + t)^2 + (1 - g(x))^2 = 1 - \Omega(g(x)) + g(x+t)^2$. This is more than 1 only if $g(x) = O(g(x+t))^2$, or equivalently $g(x + t) = \Omega(g(x))^{1/2}$. Recall we know that $g(a) = \alpha/4$. If the above holds for all x, we will have $g(a + t) = \Omega(\alpha^{1/2})$ and $g(a + 2t) = \Omega(\alpha^{1/4})$. Repeating this process, we find that $g(a + kt) = \Omega(\alpha^{1/2^k})$. Setting k to be $\log\log(1/\alpha)$, we obtain that $g(a + kt)$ must be constant sized; from this point, it is not hard to see that the median m of T (i.e., the value for which $g(m) = 1/2$) satisfies $m - a = O(t \log\log(1/\alpha))$. Similarly, we obtain that $b - m = O(t \log\log(1/\alpha))$. This means that if there is no x for which our set sizes are sufficient, it must be the case that $b - a = O(t \log\log(1/\alpha))$, which yields a contradiction.

Thus, our algorithm can always find an $x \in [a, b - t]$ such that $g^2(x + t) + (1 - g(x))^2 \le 1$. Using this x, we obtain appropriate sets T_1 and T_2. This completes the proof of Proposition 5.16. □

Proposition 5.16 is the basis of our list-decodable mean estimation algorithm. We will require the following definition of a good set.

Definition 5.17 Given $t, \alpha > 0$, we call a set $T \subset \mathbf{R}^d$ (t, α)-*good* if there exists a subset $S \subseteq T$ such that (i) $|S| \ge \alpha|T|$, and (ii) S is $(\beta, t\beta)$-stable, where β is a sufficiently small constant multiple of $\alpha/\log(1/\alpha)$.

We are ready to describe our list-decodable mean estimator based on the multifilter technique.

Theorem 5.18 *There exists an algorithm that given a (t, α)-good set $T \subset \mathbf{R}^d$ runs in time* $\mathrm{poly}(|T|, d)$ *and returns a set H of hypotheses with $|H| = O(1/\alpha^2)$ such that with high constant probability at least one $h \in H$ satisfies*

$$\|\mu_S - h\|_2 = O((t \log\log(1/\alpha) + \sqrt{\log(1/\alpha)})/\sqrt{\alpha}).$$

Proof The pseudocode for our algorithm is as follows:

Algorithm `List-Decoding-Multifilter`
Input: (t, α)-good set $T \subset \mathbf{R}^d$, $0 < \alpha \leq 1/2$, $t > 0$.

1. Let C be a sufficiently large constant, and $M = C \log(1/\alpha)$.
2. Let $\mathcal{T} = \{T\}$.
3. While there exists a $T' \in \mathcal{T}$ with $|T'| > (\alpha/2)|T|$ and $\mathbf{Cov}[T']$ having an eigenvalue more than $C[((t \log \log(1/\alpha)) + 4)^2 + M]$:

   (a) Compute a direction v of variance at least
   $$C[((t \log \log(1/\alpha)) + 4)^2 + M]/2.$$

   (b) Run the algorithm from Proposition 5.16 on $v \cdot T'$.
   (c) If it returns an element $v \cdot x$, replace T' in $\mathcal{T}$ with $T' \setminus \{x\}$.
   (d) If it returns subsets $v \cdot T_1, v \cdot T_2$, replace T' in $\mathcal{T}$ with T_1 and T_2.

4. Return the set $\{\mathbf{E}_{x \in_u T_i}[x] : T_i \in \mathcal{T}, |T_i| \geq \alpha |T|/2\}$.

Note that any univariate projection of the set S satisfies the hypotheses of Proposition 5.16. In particular, let v be any unit vector. Since $\mathbf{Cov}[S]$ is close to the identity, it follows that $\mathbf{Var}(v \cdot S) \leq 2$. Moreover, the stability condition implies that all but a β-fraction of the points in $v \cdot S$ lie in an interval of length at most $4t$. Indeed, since by removing a β-fraction of the points of S cannot move the mean by more than $t\beta$, all but a β-fraction of the points in $v \cdot S$ must be within distance $2t$ of the mean of $v \cdot S$. Otherwise, removing a $\beta/2$-fraction of the points from the same side will move the mean by too much.

To analyze the runtime, we note that at every step $\sum_{T' \in \mathcal{T}}(|T'|^2 - 1)$ decreases by at least 1. This implies that the overall algorithm terminates after a polynomial number of iterations. Moreover, $|\mathcal{T}|$ is polynomially bounded at each step, and thus the total runtime is polynomial. Finally, at the end of the algorithm, the collection $\mathcal{T}$ contains at most $4/\alpha^2$ sets of size at least $\alpha|T|/2$, and thus the algorithm returns at most polynomially many hypotheses.

It remains to prove that with reasonable probability at least one output hypothesis is close to the true mean.

Suppose that at the end of the algorithm there exists $T' \in \mathcal{T}$ with $|T' \cap S| \geq |S|/2$. Then, by Lemma 5.13, we have

$$\|\mu_S - \mu_{T'}\|_2 \leq \|\mu_S - \mu_{S \cap T'}\|_2 + \|\mu_{S \cap T'} - \mu_{T'}\|_2 \leq O(1) + \sqrt{\lambda/\alpha}$$
$$= O((t \log \log(1/\alpha) + \sqrt{\log(1/\alpha)})/\sqrt{\alpha}),$$

where λ is the largest eigenvalue of $\mathbf{Cov}[T']$. Here, we used the fact that since $|S \cap T'| \geq |S|/2$ and since $\mathbf{Cov}[S] = O(I)$, by Lemma 5.13, we have $\|\mu_S - \mu_{S \cap T'}\|_2 = O(1)$.

It remains to show that with high constant probability, there exists $T' \in \mathcal{T}$ with $|T' \cap S| \geq |S|/2$. To that end, for a subset $T' \subset T$, we define the potential function

$$\Delta(T') := 2 \log_2(2/\alpha) \log_2 \left(\frac{|S \cap T'|}{|S|} \right) - \log_2 \left(\frac{|T'|}{|T|} \right),$$

and

$$\Delta(\mathcal{T}) := \max_{T' \in \mathcal{T}} \Delta(T').$$

We observe that $\Delta(T') \leq \log_2(1/\alpha)$ for any $T' \subset T$. This follows from the elementary inequality $\log_2(|T'|/|T|) \geq (|S \cap T'|/|S|) - \log_2(1/\alpha)$.

The main claim we need is the following.

Claim 5.19 *Assuming* $\Delta(\mathcal{T}) \geq -\log_2(2/\alpha)$, $\Delta(\mathcal{T})$ *is a submartingale.*

Proof To show that $\Delta(\mathcal{T})$ is a submartingale, we need to show that if T' (the element of $\mathcal{T}$ currently attaining the maximum) is replaced by our algorithm, then on average the maximum of the Δ's of the new sets increases. If T' is replaced by two sets T'_i, we have that for at least one i Condition (5.5) holds. For this i, we have

$$\Delta(T') - \Delta(T_i) = 2 \log_2(2/\alpha) \log \left(1 - \frac{|S \cap (T' \setminus T'_i)|}{|S \cap T'|} \right) - \log \left(1 - \frac{|T' \setminus T'_i|}{|T'|} \right).$$

Condition (5.5) gives

$$\frac{|S \cap (T' \setminus T'_i)|}{|S \cap T'|} = O \left(\left(\frac{|T' \setminus T'_i|}{|T'|} \right) \beta/\alpha \right).$$

Since β/α is less than a small constant multiple of $1/\log(2/\alpha)$, this suffices to ensure that Δ increases.

In the case that a single point x is removed from T', the expected difference between $\Delta(T')$ and $\Delta(T' - \{x\})$ is

$$\log_2 \left(1 + \frac{1}{|T'| - 1} \right) - 2 \log_2(2/\alpha) \log_2 \left(1 + \frac{1}{|S \cap T'| - 1} \right) \mathbf{Pr}(x \in S)$$

$$\leq \log_2 \left(1 + \frac{1}{|T'| - 1} \right) - 2 \log_2(2/\alpha) \log_2 \left(1 + \frac{1}{|S \cap T'| - 1} \right) \left(\frac{2|S \cap T'|}{M|T'|} \right).$$

For M a sufficiently large constant multiple of $\log(1/\alpha)$, it is easy to see that this quantity is nonnegative. Thus, $\Delta(\mathcal{T}')$ is a submartingale, as desired. $\quad\square$

By the upper bound $\Delta(\mathcal{T}) \leq \log_2(1/\alpha)$, it follows that with constant probability $\Delta(\mathcal{T})$ never goes below $-\log_2(2/\alpha)$ during the execution of our algorithm. This implies that for at least one $T' \in \mathcal{T}$, we will have $|S \cap T'| \geq |S|/2$, which completes the proof. $\quad\square$

Note that the failure probability in Theorem 5.18 can be made arbitrarily small simply by running the algorithm several times independently and returning the union of the resulting hypothesis sets.

Discussion We conclude this section by discussing a few implications of Theorem 5.18. First, if we have sufficiently many corrupted samples from an identity covariance Gaussian, the set of good samples S is $(\beta, O(\sqrt{\log(1/\beta)}\beta))$-stable with high probability. This means that the multifilter algorithm of Theorem 5.18 efficiently obtains error guarantee of $\tilde{O}(\alpha^{-1/2})$. This error bound is quite far from the information-theoretically optimal error of $O(\sqrt{\log(1/\alpha)})$, and this is inherent in the described algorithm. In particular, the use of Lemma 5.13 essentially guarantees that our error will be $\Omega(\alpha^{-1/2})$. In Section 5.3.2, we will give a different algorithm for the Gaussian case with the same error guarantee. Obtaining better error requires a stronger correctness certificate and leads to somewhat more complicated algorithms. This is achieved in Chapter 6.

Another natural application is for bounded covariance distributions. If we have sufficiently many corrupted samples from a bounded covariance distribution, the set of inliers S is $(\beta, O(\sqrt{\beta}))$-stable with high probability. Applying Theorem 5.18, gives us an approximation to the true mean with error $\tilde{O}(1/\alpha)$. This is again somewhat worse than the optimal bound of $\Theta(1/\sqrt{\alpha})$.

5.3.2 List-Decodable Learning via Subspace Isotropic Filtering

In this section, we develop a different technique for list-decodable mean estimation that is arguably simpler than the multifiltering technique of the previous section. Additionally, this new technique naturally leads to near-optimal error bounds for the class of bounded covariance distributions. Recall that for the case of bounded covariance distributions, the multifilter algorithm achieved error of $\tilde{O}(\alpha^{-1})$, which is quite far from the information-theoretic optimum of $O(\alpha^{-1/2})$. While it is possible to close this gap (to within logarithmic factors) with a careful modification to the basic multifilter algorithm, the technique of the current section provides a much simpler method to achieve the optimal error of $O(\alpha^{-1/2})$.

SIFT (Subspace Isotropic Filtering) We start with an intuitive explanation of this algorithmic technique, which we term SIFT. The major difficulty with list-decoding algorithms is that it is not possible in general to find a single collection of points guaranteed to be tightly clustered around the true mean. The samples may consist of as many as $\lfloor 1/\alpha \rfloor$ distinct clusters. The multifilter

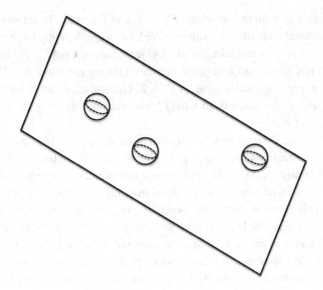

Figure 5.6 Example of the output of the SIFT algorithm. Note that all of the remaining points are well-concentrated about the subspace V.

algorithm deals with this issue by maintaining several clusters of samples and trying to guarantee that at least one of them has the desired properties. Unfortunately, the bookkeeping involved with this approach adds a lot of complication to the final algorithm.

In contrast, SIFT tries to maintain a *single* set of samples, only throwing away obvious outliers. Rather than trying to produce a single cluster of good points, SIFT attempts to find a subset T' containing almost all of the good points with the guarantee that T' is well-concentrated about an $O(1/\alpha)$-dimensional *subspace* V containing the true mean, as shown in Figure 5.6. Intuitively, we can hope to accomplish this goal, as if our sample set actually consisted of $1/\alpha$ clusters, we could simply let V be the span of the cluster means.

On the flip side, if we have such a subspace V, we know that the true mean must lie close to V. The remaining question is how to locate the projection of the mean into V. Fortunately, since V is low-dimensional, if the set of inliers has bounded covariance, then a random good sample projected onto V will have distance approximately $\sqrt{\dim(V)}$ from the true mean, giving us error $O(1/\sqrt{\alpha})$.

In more detail, our goal will be to identify a subspace V of dimension $O(1/\alpha)$ and a set $S \subset T$ of points such that (i) a large fraction of the inliers lie in T', and (ii) the variance of T' in directions orthogonal to V is small.

This leaves us with the question of how to find V and T'. To achieve this, a more traditional filter-like idea suffices. We let k be a sufficiently large constant multiple of $1/\alpha$, and consider the top-k eigenvalues of $\mathbf{Cov}[T]$. We note that if $\mathbf{Cov}[T]$ has fewer than k large eigenvalues, then we can simply let V be the span of the large eigenvalues and let $T' = T$. Otherwise, we let W be the span of the k largest eigenvectors of $\mathbf{Cov}[T]$, and consider the projections of the points in T on W.

By definition, W represents k directions of large variance. However, at most $1/\alpha$ of these directions can be due to the differences in mean between plausible clusters. Morally speaking, the outliers must contribute to this large variance in all k directions, while the potential inliers will only contribute in $1/\alpha$ many directions. This allows us to assign a score to each point (essentially the squared distance from the sample mean after projecting onto W, and renormalizing so that the variance in each direction is the same) for which it is not hard to show that the outliers have higher average score than the good points. Given these scores, we construct a weighted filter that will clean-up our dataset.

We need to handle an additional complication that does not appear in the minority-outlier regime. The standard filter step guarantees that the fraction of inliers removed is at most a *small constant multiple* of the fraction of points removed overall. If the initial fraction of inliers is large, this suffices to guarantee that the algorithm never removes more than a small fraction of the inliers. In the majority-outlier regime, this is no longer the case.

Concretely, suppose that a filter step replaces a set T by a set T', and for some set of points S we can guarantee that

$$\frac{|S \cap (T - T')|}{|S \cap T|} \le c \left(\frac{|T - T'|}{|T|} \right)$$

for some constant $c < 1$. That is, the fraction of inliers removed in each step is at most c times the fraction of total points removed. It is not hard to see that this implies that

$$\log(|S \cap T|) - c \log(|T|)$$

decreases in every step. If $|S \cap T|$ is almost as large as $|T|$, it is not hard to see that if this invariant is maintained, then $|T|$ cannot decrease very much before $|T| < |S \cap T|$, which is impossible. However, if $|T|$ is much larger than $|S \cap T|$, this is not necessarily the case. In particular, every time that $|T|$ decreases by a factor of $2^{1/c}$, we could have $|S \cap T|$ decreasing by a factor 2. This is a problem for two reasons. First, if the final set of points that we end up with has small intersection with the original set of inliers, the mean of $S \cap T$ need no longer necessarily be close to S. Second, in order for a filter step to satisfy the appropriate guarantees, we often need to assume that a large fraction of the original inliers are still remaining.

The multifilter step of the previous section deals with this issue by letting c be a small constant multiple of $1/\log(1/\alpha)$. This ensures that even after $|T|$ decreases by a factor of α (and thus has roughly the same size as S), the size of $|S \cap T|$ can only decrease by a small constant multiple. This suffices to ensure that, throughout the course of the entire algorithm, $|S \cap T|$ never decreases by more than a constant factor. While this is a relatively simple solution to the problem above, unfortunately, setting c to be so small loses polylogarithmic terms in $1/\alpha$ in the final error, which we cannot afford.

The SIFT algorithm will instead make do with letting c be some constant less than $1/2$. In particular, this means that once we have reached the point where we are left with only a β-fraction of the original samples, for some $\beta > 0$, we will still have at least a $\beta^{1/2}$-fraction of the inliers (or perhaps β^c, for some $c \leq 1/2$). This suffices to guarantee termination, as when $\beta < \alpha^2$ we would have fewer points remaining overall than inliers remaining, a contradiction.

Unfortunately, the above step introduces a new complication. Our filtering technique relied on the fact that among the set of remaining inliers the covariance was $O(I)$. However, if we have reduced to a γ-fraction of the original inliers, the covariance of the remaining inlier set could be as large as $O(\gamma^{-1} I)$. This defect can be corrected by rescaling the remaining points by a factor of $\gamma^{1/2}$. This rescaling step will multiply our final error (after un-rescaling) by a factor of $\gamma^{-1/2}$. This increase to the error is compensated for by the fact that the fraction of inliers is now larger. In particular, if we have reduced to a set $T' \subset T$, where $|T'| = \beta|T|$ and the set of remaining inliers has size at least $\beta^{1/2}\alpha|T|$, then we have a set where an $\alpha\beta^{-1/2}$-fraction of the samples are inliers, and the set of inliers has variance bounded above by $\beta^{-1/2}$. Applied recursively, this means that we should be able to attain a final error of $O(\sqrt{\beta^{-1/2}/(\alpha\beta^{-1/2})}) = O(1/\sqrt{\alpha})$, as desired.

In practice, rather than explicitly rescaling the points in our distribution every time we remove samples (to deal with the above issue), the algorithm will dynamically adjust what it considers to be a "large eigenvalue" when trying to construct a filter, leaving the rest of the algorithm unchanged.

Formal Description and Analysis of SIFT   After our intuitive explanation, we are ready to provide a formal description of SIFT and its proof of correctness.

We will assume that the true (inlier) distribution has bounded (unknown) covariance, that is, $\Sigma \leq I$. Our algorithm will work under the following deterministic condition.

Assumption 5.20 There exists a subset $S \subseteq T \subseteq \mathbf{R}^d$ with $|S| = \alpha|T|$ such that $\frac{1}{|S|} \sum_{x \in S} (x - \mu^*)(x - \mu^*)^\top \preceq I$.

If S consists of $\Omega(d \log(d))$ i.i.d. samples from a distribution with covariance bounded above by $I/2$ and mean μ^*, S will contain a set of size $|S|/2$ satisfying Assumption 5.20 with high probability by Proposition 3.9.

The simplest version of the SIFT algorithm that we will describe uses weighted outlier-removal. For this, we need to define a condition under which the current weights still satisfy our necessary invariants. In particular, we must develop a weighted version of the condition that $|S \cap T|$ decreases by a factor that is at most the square root of the fraction by which $|T|$ has decreased overall. Here our set T is maintained by a vector w of weights with $\|w\|_1$ being our proxy for $|T|$ and $\|w_S\|_1$ being our proxy for $|S \cap T|$.

Using the notation $\Delta^T := \{w : T \to \mathbf{R}_+ : \|w\|_\infty \leq 1/|T|\}$, we define a condition under which our weight function assigns enough of its mass to S.

Definition 5.21 (Saturated Weights) We call the weight vector $w \in \Delta^T$ *saturated* if and only if $\|w_S\|_1 \geq \alpha \sqrt{\|w\|_1}$.

Essentially, a weight vector is saturated if the "weight" of $S \cap T$ is at least α times the square root of the total "weight" of T.

As with other weighted outlier-removal algorithms, each round of filtering will assign a nonnegative score τ_x to each point $x \in T$, and we will decrease the weight of x by an amount proportional to $w_x \tau_x$. We will need these scores to satisfy a condition in order to ensure that this outlier-removal process maintains the condition of saturated weights. This condition will need to roughly be that the fraction of inliers removed is at most half the fraction of total points removed. In particular, we define:

Definition 5.22 (Safe Scores) We call scores $\{\tau_x\}_{x \in T} \in \mathbf{R}^n_{\geq 0}$ *safe with respect to* $w \in \Delta^T$ if $\sum_{x \in S} \frac{w_x}{\|w_S\|_1} \tau_x \leq (1/2) \sum_{x \in T} \frac{w_x}{\|w\|_1} \tau_x$. When the weights w are clear from context, we will simply call the scores τ *safe*.

The intuition behind this is that if we remove weight from x by an amount proportional to $w_x \tau_x$, then the fraction of its weight that S loses will be at most half the fraction of mass lost by T. This says roughly that the amount that $\log(\|w_S\|_1)$ decreases by is at most half of the decrease in $\log(\|w_T\|_1)$ or that $\log(\|w_S\|_1 / \sqrt{\|w_T\|_1})$ only increases. Hence this procedure should produce a new set of saturated weights.

In particular, we show that using safe scores in our weight removal process maintains saturated weights.

Lemma 5.23 *Consider a set of saturated weights w, and an update of the form:*

1. *Let $\{\tau_x\}_{x \in T}$ be safe with respect to w.*
2. *Update for all $x \in T$,*

$$w'_x \leftarrow (1 - \tau_x/\tau_{\max}) w_x, \text{ where } \tau_{\max} := \max_{x \in T | w_x \neq 0} \tau_x. \tag{5.6}$$

Then, the result of the updates w' is also saturated.

Proof It is easy to see that $\|w'_S\|_1 = \|w_S\|_1 - (1/\tau_{\max}) \sum_{x \in S} w_x \tau_x$ and $\|w'\|_1 = \|w\|_1 - (1/\tau_{\max}) \sum_{x \in T} w_x \tau_x$. Since τ is safe, we have that $\frac{\sum_{x \in S} w_x \tau_x}{\|w_S\|_1} \leq \frac{\sum_{x \in T} w_x \tau_x}{2\|w\|_1}$. In particular, this means that

$$\frac{\|w_S\|_1 - \|w'_S\|_1}{\|w_S\|_1} \leq \frac{\|w\|_1 - \|w'\|_1}{2\|w\|_1}.$$

The above together with the fact $\|w_S\|_1 \geq \alpha \sqrt{\|w\|_1}$ implies that $\|w'_S\|_1 \geq \alpha \sqrt{\|w'\|_1}$.

In particular, if $\|w_S\|_1^2 = \beta \|w_T\|$ for some $\beta \geq \alpha$, we have:

$$\begin{aligned}
\|w'_S\|_1^2 &= \|w_S\|_1^2 - 2\|w_S\|_1 (\|w_S\|_1 - \|w'_S\|_1) + (\|w_S\|_1 - \|w'_S\|_1)^2 \\
&\geq \|w_S\|_1^2 - (\|w_S\|_1^2/\|w\|_1)(\|w\|_1 - \|w'\|_1) \\
&= \beta\|w\|_1 - \beta(\|w\|_1 - \|w'\|_1) \\
&= \beta\|w'\|_1 \geq \alpha\|w'\|_1.
\end{aligned}$$

This completes our proof. $\qquad\square$

For any weight vector w and subset $R \subseteq T$, w defines a probability distribution on R by assigning the point $x \in R$ probability proportional to w_x. It will be useful to be able to talk about the mean and covariance of such a distribution, particularly when $R = S$ or $R = T$. We define:

Definition 5.24 Let $w \in \Delta^T$ and let $R \subset T$ be such that w_R is nonzero. Then we define

$$\mu_w[R] := \frac{1}{\|w_R\|_1} \sum_{x \in R} w_x x$$

and

$$\mathbf{Cov}_w[R] := \frac{1}{\|w_R\|_1} \sum_{x \in R} w_x (x - \mu_w[R])(x - \mu_w[R])^\top.$$

The analogue of Lemma 5.13 is the following.

Lemma 5.25 *We have that* $(\mu_w[S] - \mu_w[T])(\mu_w[S] - \mu_w[T])^\top \leq \frac{\|w\|_1}{\|w_S\|_1} \mathbf{Cov}_w[T]$.

Proof Let X_S be the probability distribution that assigns $x \in S$ probability $w_x/\|w_S\|_1$, and let X_T be the distribution that assigns $x \in T$ probability $w_x/\|w_T\|_1$. Note that $\mu_w[S]$ and $\mu_w[T]$ are the means of X_S and X_T, respectively, and that $\mathbf{Cov}_w[T]$ is the covariance of X_T. Furthermore, note that X_T is a mixture of X_S with mixing weight $\frac{\|w_S\|_1}{\|w\|_1}$ and some other distribution X_R. It follows that $\mathbf{Cov}_w[T]$ is equal to

$$\frac{\|w_S\|_1(\|w\|_1 - \|w_S\|_1)}{\|w\|_1^2}(\mathbf{E}[X_S] - \mathbf{E}[X_R])(\mathbf{E}[X_S] - \mathbf{E}[X_R])^\top + \frac{\|w_S\|_1}{\|w\|_1}\mathbf{Cov}[X_S]$$

$$+ \frac{\|w\|_1 - \|w_S\|_1}{\|w\|_1}\mathbf{Cov}[X_R].$$

Noting that $\mathbf{Cov}[X_S], \mathbf{Cov}[X_R] \geq 0$ and that $\mu_w[S] - \mu_w[T] = \frac{(\|w\|_1 - \|w_S\|_1)}{\|w\|_1}(\mathbf{E}[X_S] - \mathbf{E}[X_R])$ yields the result. □

We would next like to know that if $\mathbf{Cov}_w[T]$ is small, then $\mu_w[T]$ is close to μ^*. This follows relatively easily from Lemma 5.25.

Lemma 5.26 *Let* $w \in \Delta^T$, *then*

$$\|\mu_w[T] - \mu^*\|_2 \leq \sqrt{\|\mathbf{Cov}_w[T]\|_2 \frac{\|w\|_1}{\|w_S\|_1}} + \sqrt{\frac{\alpha}{\|w_S\|_1}}.$$

Proof Taking the spectral norm of both sides in Lemma 5.25, we get that

$$\|\mu_w[S] - \mu_w[T]\|_2 \leq \sqrt{\|\mathbf{Cov}_w[T]\|_2 \frac{\|w\|_1}{\|w_S\|_1}}. \tag{5.7}$$

We next need to bound $\|\mu_w[S] - \mu^*\|_2$. We have by Assumption 5.20 that

$$\mathbf{E}_{x \sim_u S}(x - \mu^*)(x - \mu^*)^\top \leq I.$$

Letting X_S be the distribution over S weighted by w, we note that X_S is X conditioned on an event with probability $\|w_S\|_1/\alpha$. Therefore, we have that

$$\mathbf{E}_{x \sim X_S}(x - \mu^*)(x - \mu^*)^\top \leq (\alpha/\|w_S\|_1)I.$$

On the other hand, since the left-hand side is $\mathbf{Cov}[X_S] + (\mu_w[S] - \mu^*)(\mu_w[S] - \mu^*)^\top$, we have that $\|\mu_w[S] - \mu^*\|_2 \leq \sqrt{\alpha/\|w_S\|_1}$.

Combining this with Condition (5.7) yields the result. □

We will also need one final lemma.

Lemma 5.27 *Let $w \in \Delta^T$, then*

$$\mathbf{Cov}_w[S] \preceq \frac{1}{\|w_S\|_1} \sum_{x \in S} w_x (x - \mu^*)(x - \mu^*)^\top \preceq \frac{\alpha}{\|w_S\|_1} I.$$

Proof This follows by noting that $\mathbf{Cov}_w[S]$ is at most

$$\frac{1}{\|w_S\|_1} \sum_{x \in S} w_x (x - \mu^*)(x - \mu^*)^\top \preceq \left(\frac{\alpha}{\|w_S\|_1}\right) \frac{|T|}{|S|} \sum_{x \in S} (1/n)(x - \mu^*)(x - \mu^*)^\top \preceq \left(\frac{\alpha}{\|w_S\|_1}\right) I.$$

□

With this setup, we are ready to develop our main algorithmic tool. In particular, we show that given a set of saturated weights, either $\mathbf{Cov}_w[T]$ has few large eigenvalues (in which case, we can let V be the span of the large eigenvalues, producing an appropriate subspace) or we can find a collection of safe scores.

Proposition 5.28 *Let T be a set of points in $\mathbf{R}^d$ with a subset S satisfying Assumption 5.20. Let w be a saturated weight vector with $\|w\|_1 = \beta$. Let $C \geq 8$ be a constant, and suppose that $\mathbf{Cov}_w[T]$ has at least $C\beta^{1/2}/\alpha$ eigenvectors with eigenvalue more than $C/\beta^{1/2}$. Then there exists a polynomial-time algorithm that given T, w, α, β computes a set of safe scores.*

Proof Let W be the span of the eigenvectors of $\mathbf{Cov}_w[T]$ with eigenvalues more than $C/\beta^{1/2}$ and let $k > C\beta^{1/2}/\alpha$ be the dimension of W. The basic idea of our algorithm comes from the following simple observation. Let P be the projection matrix onto W. Then we can write

$$\mathrm{tr}(P\mathbf{Cov}_w[T]P) = \frac{1}{\|w\|_1} \sum_{x \in T} w_x \mathrm{tr}(P(x - \mu_w[T])(x - \mu_w[T])^\top P)$$

$$= \frac{1}{\|w\|_1} \sum_{x \in T} w_x \|P(x - \mu_w[T])\|_2^2,$$

and similarly

$$\mathrm{tr}(P\mathbf{Cov}_w[S]P) = \frac{1}{\|w_S\|_1} \sum_{x \in S} w_x \|P(x - \mu_w[S])\|_2^2.$$

That is, the average value (weighted by w_x) of $\|P(x - \mu_w[T])\|_2^2$ is equal to $\mathrm{tr}(P\mathbf{Cov}_w[T]P)$, which is at least $kC\beta^{-1/2}$ by assumption. Similarly, the average value over $x \in S$ (weighted by w_x) of $\|P(x - \mu_w[S])\|_2^2$ is equal to $\mathrm{tr}(P\mathbf{Cov}_w[S]P)$. By an application of Lemma 5.27, we have that $\mathbf{Cov}_w[S] \preceq \frac{\alpha}{\|w_S\|_1} I \preceq \frac{\alpha}{\alpha\sqrt{\beta}} I = \beta^{-1/2} I$. Thus, we have $\mathrm{tr}(P\mathbf{Cov}_w[S]P) \leq k\beta^{-1/2}$.

To summarize the above, the average value over T of $\|P(x - \mu_w[T])\|_2^2$ is substantially larger than the average value over S of $\|P(x - \mu_w[S])\|_2^2$. Were it not for the fact that one of these expressions uses $\mu_w[T]$ and the other uses $\mu_w[S]$, this would imply that $\tau_x := \|P(x - \mu_w[T])\|_2^2$ would be a safe score.

To complete the proof, it is important to understand how the use of the different means affects things. By Condition (5.7), it follows that

$$\|\mu_w[T] - \mu_w[S]\|_2 \leq \sqrt{\|\mathbf{Cov}_w[T]\|_2(\beta^{1/2}/\alpha)} \leq \sqrt{\|\mathbf{Cov}_w[T]\|_2 k/C}.$$

This means that the average value over $x \in S$ of $\|P(x - \mu_w[T])\|_2^2$ is at most twice the average value of $\|P(x - \mu_w[S])\|_2^2$ plus twice $\|\mu_w[S] - \mu_w[T]\|_2^2$ or

$$2k\beta^{-1/2} + 2\|\mathbf{Cov}_w[T]\|_2 k/C. \tag{5.8}$$

If it were the case that $\mathbf{Cov}_w[T]$ had just k eigenvalues of size approximately $C/\beta^{1/2}$, and none much larger, then (5.8) would be $O(k\beta^{-1/2})$, while the corresponding average over T is at least $kC\beta^{-1/2}$. Unfortunately, if $\mathbf{Cov}_w[T]$ has a single much larger eigenvalue, this analysis might fail.

To handle this issue, we need a way to regularize the points so that the eigenvalues of $\mathbf{Cov}_w[T]$ along W are approximately the same. An easy way to do this is via a simple pre-processing step. In particular, let $\mathbf{Cov}_w[T]$ have eigenvalue decomposition $\mathbf{Cov}_w[T] = \sum_i \lambda_i v_i v_i^\top$, where the v_i's form an orthonormal basis of $\mathbf{R}^d$. Then let $M := \sum_i e_i v_i v_i^\top$, where

$$e_i = \begin{cases} \sqrt{(C\beta^{-1/2})/\lambda_i}, & \text{if } \lambda_i \geq C\beta^{-1/2}, \\ 1, & \text{otherwise.} \end{cases}$$

We then note that letting T' be obtained by multiplying each point of T by M, and letting w' be the weight function corresponding to w, T' has exactly k eigenvectors with eigenvalue $C\beta^{-1/2}$ and none larger. Meanwhile, letting $S' \subseteq T'$ be the set of points Mx for $x \in S$, it is easy to see that since $M \leq I$ that S' satisfies Assumption 5.20 (with $M\mu^*$ replacing μ^*). Therefore, the above analysis shows that letting $\tau'_x := \|P(x - \mu_{w'}(T'))\|_2^2$, the average value of τ'_x over $x \in S'$ is at most $4k\beta^{-1/2}$; while the average value over $x \in T'$ is at least $kC\beta^{-1/2}$. Thus, if $C \geq 8$, this gives a set of safe scores over T'.

Translating the definitions back to S and T, it is not hard to see that this implies that

$$\tau_x := \|PM(x - \mu_w[T])\|_2^2$$

is a safe set of scores. As a final note, it is also not hard to see that τ_x is proportional to $\|P\mathbf{Cov}_w[T]^{-1/2}(x - \mu_w[T])\|_2^2$, and so the latter can be used more conveniently as scores. □

The following theorem encapsulates the guarantees of our algorithm.

Theorem 5.29 *If Algorithm SIFT is run on a set T satisfying Assumption 5.20, then it runs in polynomial-time and with probability $\Omega(\alpha)$ it returns a point x so that $\|x - \mu^*\|_2 = O(\alpha^{-1/2})$.*

The success probability in Theorem 5.29 is small, but that is because it returns only a single hypothesis. If instead we run the algorithm a large constant multiple of $\log(1/\delta)/\alpha$ times (and note that the separate runs only differ in their random choice of x in the next-to-last step), then we will obtain a list of $O(\log(1/\delta)/\alpha)$ many hypotheses such that with probability at least $1 - \delta$, at least one of the chosen hypotheses will be within distance $O(\alpha^{-1/2})$ of μ^*.

Note that for sets S on which we only assume bounded covariance, this error is information-theoretically optimal. Furthermore, if we take δ to be a constant, the list size is optimal as well.

The pseudocode of our list-decoding algorithm SIFT is as follows:

Algorithm SIFT

Input: $T \subset \mathbf{R}^d$ with $|T| = n$ satisfying Assumption 5.20 for some $\alpha > 0$

1. $w^{(0)} := \frac{1}{n}\mathbf{1}_T, t := 0, \beta := 1$.
2. While $\mathbf{Cov}_{w^{(t)}}[T]$ has at least $8\beta^{1/2}/\alpha$ eigenvalues of size at least $8\beta^{-1/2}$:
   (a) Let W be the subspace spanned by the eigenvectors of $\mathbf{Cov}_{w^{(t)}}[T]$ with eigenvalue at least $8\beta^{-1/2}$.
   (b) Let P be the projection matrix onto W and $\tau_x^{(t)} := \|P\mathbf{Cov}_{w^{(t)}}[T]^{-1/2}(x - \mu_{w^{(t)}}[T])\|_2^2$ for $x \in T$. Let $\tau_{\max}^{(t)}$ be the maximum value of $\tau_x^{(t)}$ over all $x \in T$ with $w_x^{(t)} \neq 0$.
   (c) For each $x \in T$, let $w_x^{(t+1)} := w_x^{(t)}(1 - \tau_x^{(t)}/\tau_{\max}^{(t)})$.
   (d) $\beta := \|w^{(t+1)}\|_1, t := t + 1$.
3. Let V be the span of the eigenvectors of $\mathbf{Cov}_{w^{(t)}}[T]$ with eigenvalue at least $8\beta^{-1/2}$.
4. Let V' be the affine subspace given by the translation of V passing through $\mu_{w^{(t)}}[T]$.
5. Pick a uniform random point $x \in T$.
6. Return the projection of x onto V'.

Proof of Theorem 5.29 First, we claim that each $w^{(t)}$ is saturated. The proof is by induction on t. In particular, as a base case we can see that $w^{(0)}$ is saturated. For the inductive step, if $w^{(t)}$ is saturated, then by Proposition 5.28, $\tau^{(t)}$ are safe scores, so by Lemma 5.23, $w^{(t+1)}$ is saturated.

Next we note that each iteration of the while loop sets at least one of the w_x's to 0, and that once a w_x is set to 0, it will stay that way. Therefore, the algorithm will exit after at most $|T|$ iterations through the loop. At the end of the loop, we have a saturated set of weights $w = w^{(t)}$ such that with $\beta = \|w\|_1$ we have that $\mathbf{Cov}_w[T]$ has at most $8\beta^{1/2}/\alpha$ eigenvalues of size at least $8\beta^{-1/2}$. In particular, this means that $\dim(V) \leq 8\beta^{1/2}/\alpha$. Moreover, letting $T_{V^\perp}$ be the set of the projections of the points of T onto $V^\perp$, we have that the eigenvalues of $\mathbf{Cov}_w[T_{V^\perp}]$ are all at most $8\beta^{-1/2}$. In particular, applying Lemma 5.26 to $T_{V^\perp}$, we find that:

$$
\begin{aligned}
\|\mathrm{Proj}_{V^\perp}(\mu_w[T]) - \mathrm{Proj}_{V^\perp}(\mu^*)\|_2 &\leq \sqrt{(8\beta^{-1/2})\frac{\|w\|_1}{\|w_S\|_1}} + \sqrt{\frac{\alpha}{\|w_S\|_1}} \\
&\leq \sqrt{(8\beta^{-1/2})(\beta)/(\alpha\beta^{-1/2})} + \sqrt{\alpha/(\alpha\beta^{1/2})} \\
&= \sqrt{8/\alpha} + \sqrt{\beta^{-1/2}}.
\end{aligned}
$$

Noting that for saturated weights we must have $\|w\|_1 \geq \|w_S\|_1$, we have $\beta \geq \alpha\beta^{1/2}$ and thus, $\beta \geq \alpha^2$. Therefore, the above is $O(\alpha^{-1/2})$.

This means in particular that the distance between μ^* and its projection onto V' is at most $O(\alpha^{-1/2})$.

Finally, we note that with probability at least α we have $x \in S$. Recalling that the expectation over $x \in S$ of $(x - \mu^*)(x - \mu^*)^\top$ is at most I, we can write

$$
\begin{aligned}
\mathbf{E}_{x\sim_u S}[\|\mathrm{Proj}_{V'}(x) - \mathrm{Proj}_{V'}(\mu^*)\|_2^2] &= \mathbf{E}_{x\sim_u S}[\|\mathrm{Proj}_V(x) - \mathrm{Proj}_V(\mu^*)\|_2^2] \\
&= \mathbf{E}_{x\sim_u S}[\mathrm{tr}(\mathrm{Proj}_V(x - \mu^*)(x - \mu^*)^\top \mathrm{Proj}_V)] \\
&\leq \mathrm{tr}(\mathrm{Proj}_V I \mathrm{Proj}_V) \leq \dim(V) = O(\alpha^{-1}).
\end{aligned}
$$

Thus, by Markov's inequality, conditioned on x being in S, with probability at least $1/2$, we have that $\|\mathrm{Proj}_{V'}(x) - \mathrm{Proj}_{V'}(\mu^*)\|_2 = O(\alpha^{-1/2})$. Thus, this happens with probability at least $\alpha/2$.

If this holds, we have

$$
\|\mathrm{Proj}_{V'}(x) - \mu^*\|_2 \leq \|\mathrm{Proj}_{V'}(x) - \mathrm{Proj}_{V'}(\mu^*)\|_2 + \|\mu^* - \mathrm{Proj}_{V'}(\mu^*)\|_2 = O(\alpha^{-1/2}).
$$

This completes the proof. $\qquad\square$

Remark 5.30 A final note about the SIFT algorithm is the use of the weighted filter. While it should be possible to convert this algorithm to work with an appropriate randomized filter, the analysis becomes somewhat subtle as we need to ensure that at all points during the execution of the algorithm, the fraction of remaining inliers is related appropriately to the fraction of remaining points overall. As these fractions are varying over a much wider range than before, this analysis becomes somewhat more complicated.

5.3.3 Reducing the Set of Hypotheses

Note that the multifilter algorithm of Section 5.3.1 can return as many as $\Omega(\alpha^{-2})$ hypotheses, while the SIFT algorithm of Section 5.3.2 may need to return a large multiple of $1/\alpha$ if we want small failure probability. This is in contrast to the fact that information-theoretically $O(1/\alpha)$ many hypotheses suffice to achieve the information-theoretically optimal error, even with high probability. In this section, we provide a simple general method to post-process a list of hypotheses in order to produce a smaller list of size $O(1/\alpha)$ without significantly increasing the error.

We start with the assumption that each hypothesis comes with an associated subset satisfying the hypotheses of Lemma 5.7. We note that the output of the multifilter algorithm satisfies this property automatically.

Proposition 5.31   *There exists an algorithm that, given a set T along with s candidate means μ_i and subsets S_i satisfying the assumptions of Lemma 5.7 and such that at least one of the candidates is within error E of the true mean μ, runs in time* $\mathrm{poly}(d, s, 1/\alpha)$ *and returns a list of $O(1/\alpha)$ hypotheses such that at least one of the hypotheses is within $O(E + t)$ of μ.*

Proof   The algorithm establishing Proposition 5.31 is quite simple. We begin by finding a maximal subset of our hypotheses that are pairwise separated by at least $2t$. This can be done by starting with an empty set H of hypotheses and for each hypothesis in our set comparing it to each of the hypotheses currently in H and adding it to H if it is not too close to any of them. It is clear that the runtime of this algorithm is $O(d|H|s)$. Moreover, if the original list of hypotheses contained a point μ_0, then H will contain a point $\tilde{\mu}$ with $\|\tilde{\mu} - \mu_0\|_2 < 2t$. Therefore, if our original set contained a μ_0 with $\|\mu_0 - \mu\|_2 \le E$, then by the triangle inequality, H will contain a $\tilde{\mu}$ with $\|\tilde{\mu} - \mu\|_2 = O(E + t)$.

It remains to show that $|H| = O(1/\alpha)$; but this follows from Lemma 5.7.   □

The algorithm of Proposition 5.31 works for reducing the set of hypotheses from the multifilter algorithm, as each such hypothesis comes with an appropriate subset S_i. Unfortunately, for SIFT, this will not necessarily be the case. However, there is an algorithmic way to get around this, essentially by finding such sets S_i if they exist, and removing hypotheses for which they do not exist.

Theorem 5.32 *Let $T \subset \mathbf{R}^d$ be a multiset of points such that there is an unknown $\mu \in \mathbf{R}^d$ and $S \subset T$ with $|S| \geq \alpha|T|$ satisfying Condition (5.1). Furthermore, let $H \subset \mathbf{R}^d$ be a finite list of hypotheses such that there exists $h \in H$ with $\|h - \mu\|_2 \leq E$. Then there exists an algorithm that given T, H, E, t, α runs in time $\mathrm{poly}(d, |T|, |H|)$, and returns a set of $O(1/\alpha)$ hypotheses, at least one of which is within distance $O(E + t)$ of μ.*

Proof Let $\mathcal{D}$ be the set of unit vectors in the direction of $h - h'$ for $h, h' \in H$. We note that if $h \in H$ satisfies $\|h - \mu\|_2 \leq E$, then for all $v \in \mathcal{D}$ we have $\mathbf{Pr}_{x \sim_u S}[v \cdot (x - h) > t + E] \leq \alpha/10$. Let H' be the set of $h \in H$ such that there exists a set $S' \subset T$ with $|S'| \geq \alpha|T|$ such that for all $v \in \mathcal{D}$ we have $\mathbf{Pr}_{x \sim_u S'}[v \cdot (x - h) > t + E] \leq \alpha/10$. We note that there is an $h \in H'$ with $\|h - \mu\|_2 \leq E$, and furthermore, given H' we could run the algorithm from Proposition 5.31 to produce a list of $O(1/\alpha)$ hypotheses such that at least one of them is guaranteed to be within $O(t + E)$ of μ.

Thus, it is sufficient to have an algorithm for determining whether or not an $h \in H$ is in H'. Unfortunately, determining whether or not an S' exists is nontrivial. Fortunately, there is a linear programming relaxation that we can solve. In particular, we want to find weights w_x for each $x \in T$ satisfying the following relations:

1. $0 \leq w_x \leq 1/(\alpha|T|)$ for all $x \in T$.
2. $\sum_{v \cdot (x-h) > t + E} w_x \leq \alpha/10$ for all $v \in \mathcal{D}$.
3. $\sum_x w_x = 1$.

The above system of linear inequalities can be efficiently solved using an LP solver. Furthermore, it is not hard to see that the existence of such a w is equivalent to the existence of a set S' with the desired properties contained in a multiset consisting of a large number of copies of T.

Thus, our final algorithm is fairly simple. We let h' be the set of elements $h \in H$ for which the above system has a solution, and then run the algorithm from Proposition 5.31 on H'. This completes the proof. $\square$

5.4 Application: Learning Mixture Models

In this section, we show that the problem of learning mixture models can often be efficiently reduced to list-decoding. Specifically, we focus on the following setting: We are given i.i.d. samples from a uniform k-mixture of identity covariance Gaussians $X = \sum_{i=1}^k (1/k)\mathcal{N}(\mu_i, I)$ and we additionally assume that the component means μ_i are pairwise separated in distance by an appropriately large quantity Δ. Our goal is to accurately cluster the samples and/or approximate the unknown component means.

Since a Gaussian mixture model (GMM) can simultaneously be thought of as a mixture of any one of its components with some error distribution, applying a list-decodable mean estimation algorithm to samples from a GMM will return a list of hypotheses so that *every* mean in the mixture is close to some hypothesis in the list. We can then use this list to cluster our samples by component. The main result of this section is the following proposition.

Proposition 5.33 *Let $X = \sum_{i=1}^{k}(1/k)\mathcal{N}(\mu_i, I)$ be a uniform k-mixture of identity covariance Gaussians in $\mathbf{R}^d$ with the component means separated by 7Δ, where $\Delta \gg \sqrt{\log(k/\delta)}$, for some $0 < \delta < 1/2$. Suppose that we are given a set of points $H \subset \mathbf{R}^d$ such that for each $i \in [k]$, there exists $h \in H$ with $\|h - \mu_i\|_2$ at most a sufficiently small constant multiple of Δ. There exists an algorithm that draws $n = O(dk/\delta^2)$ samples from X, runs in $\mathrm{poly}(d, |H|, n)$ time, and with probability at least $9/10$ learns a distribution $\tilde{X}$ so that $d_{\mathrm{TV}}(X, \tilde{X}) \leq \delta$.*

Proof We start with an overview of the algorithm and its analysis. First, we can apply Theorem 5.32 to reduce to the case where $|H| = O(k)$, and where for each $i \in [k]$, there exists $h_j \in H$ with $\|h_i - \mu_j\|_2 \leq \Delta/10$. We start by drawing a set T of $n = O(dk/\delta^2)$ samples from X. We denote by S_i the subset of T drawn from the component $\mathcal{N}(\mu_i, I)$. Given T and H, we associate each sample $x \in T$ with its closest point in H. We then cluster points based on which means they are associated to and use this to learn the correct components.

Given samples from a Gaussian $G = \mathcal{N}(\mu, I)$ and a list of m hypothesis means, $h_1, \ldots, h_m$, we consider the process of associating a sample x from G with the nearest h_i. Note that x is closer to h_j than h_i if and only if the projection of x onto the line defined by h_i and h_j is closer to h_j than to h_i. If h_i is substantially closer to μ than h_j is, then this projection will be far from its mean, which happens with very small probability. Thus, by a union bound, as long as our list contains some h_i that is close to μ, the closest hypothesis to x with high probability is not much further. If the separation between the means in our mixture is much larger than the separation between the means and the closest hypotheses, this implies that almost all samples from the mixture are associated with one of the hypotheses near their component mean, and this will allow us to cluster samples by component.

We will show that, with high probability, almost every sample $x \in S_i$ will be associated with a point in H that is close to the corresponding component mean μ_i. The key lemma is as follows:

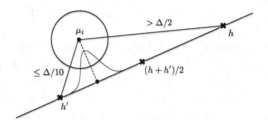

Figure 5.7 Illustration of the proof of Lemma 5.34. Note that because there is a hypothesis h' much closer to μ_i than h, the projection of samples onto the line between h and h' will almost all lie closer to h'. This implies that almost all of the samples from this cluster will be closer to h' than h, and thus are not associated with h.

Lemma 5.34 *Fix $i \in [k]$ and a point $h \in H$ with $\|h - \mu_i\|_2 > \Delta/2$. Assuming that $|H| = O(k)$, the probability that a random sample $x \sim N(\mu_i, I)$ is associated with h is at most $\exp(-\Omega(\Delta^2))$.*

Proof Let $h' \in H$ be such that $\|h' - \mu_i\|_2 \le \Delta/10$. To prove the lemma, we will show that a sample $x \sim N(\mu_i, I)$ is closer to h than to h' with probability at most $\exp(-\Omega(\Delta^2))$. See Figure 5.7 for a summary of the proof idea.

Let v be the unit vector in the direction of $h - h'$. Recall that x can be associated to h only if $\|x - h\|_2 \le \|x - h'\|_2$. We will bound from above the probability of this event.

By basic linear algebra, $\|x - h\|_2 \le \|x - h'\|_2$ if and only if we have that $v \cdot x \ge v \cdot (h + h')/2$. Observe that for any unit vector u, we have $u \cdot (\mu_i - h') \le \|h' - \mu_i\|_2 \le \Delta/10$. This implies that

$$v \cdot \mu_i \le v \cdot h' + \Delta/10. \tag{5.9}$$

By the definition of v and the triangle inequality, we have

$$v \cdot h = v \cdot h' + \|h - h'\|_2 \ge v \cdot h' + \|h - \mu_i\|_2 - \|h' - \mu_i\|_2 \ge v \cdot h' + 2\Delta/5. \tag{5.10}$$

From (5.9) and (5.10), we get $v \cdot (h + h')/2 \ge v \cdot \mu_i + \Delta/10$. Therefore,

$$\mathbf{Pr}_{x \sim N(\mu_i, I)} [v \cdot x \ge v \cdot (h + h')/2] \le \mathbf{Pr}_{x \sim N(\mu_i, I)} [v \cdot x \ge v \cdot \mu_i + \Delta/10]$$
$$= \exp(-\Omega(\Delta^2)),$$

where the last inequality follows from the Gaussian concentration. This completes the proof.   □

Algorithm `Learn-Identity-Covariance-GMM`

Input: Parameters $k \in \mathbf{Z}_+$, $\delta > 0$ and sample access to X on $\mathbf{R}^d$.

1. Apply the algorithm from Theorem 5.32 on H and a set of Ckd i.i.d. samples from X (for some large constant C), and let H be the smaller list of hypotheses it returns.

2. Let $H \subset \mathbf{R}^d$ be the list of hypotheses satisfying the assumption of Proposition 5.33.

3. Draw a multiset T of $n = \Omega(dk/\delta^2)$ i.i.d. samples from X. For each $x \in T$ associate x to its closest hypothesis of H (in ℓ_2-distance) breaking ties arbitrarily.

4. Let H' be the set of $h \in H$ such that at least a $2/(3k)$-fraction of the points in T are associated to a point in H at distance at most Δ from h.

5. Define the binary relation "$\sim$" on H' defined as follows: $h \sim h'$ if and only if $\|h - h'\|_2 \le 3\Delta$. If this does not define an equivalence relation on H', return "FAIL."

6. For each equivalence class C_i of H', let T_{C_i} be the set of points in T that are associated to points in C_i. Assign T_{C_i} to the ith component.

7. For each equivalence class C_i, run `Robust-Mean` on T_{C_i}, and let μ_{C_i} be the approximation of the mean obtained. Return the list of these means.

See Figure 5.8 for an illustration of the algorithm.

As an immediate corollary, we obtain.

Corollary 5.35 *With probability $1 - \exp(-\Omega(\Delta^2))$ over the samples from S_i, a $(1 - \exp(-\Omega(\Delta^2)))$-fraction of the points in S_i are associated with points in H within distance $\Delta/2$ of μ_i.*

Proof Fix $h \in H$ with $\|h - \mu_i\|_2 > \Delta/2$. By Lemma 5.34, any $x^{(j)} \in S_i$ is associated with h with probability $p \le \exp(-\Omega(\Delta^2))$. Let $Z_{i,j}$ be the indicator random variable of this event and $\bar{Z}_i = (1/n_i) \sum_{j=1}^{n_i} Z_{i,j}$, where $n_i = |S_i|$. It is clear that $\mathbf{E}[\bar{Z}_i] = p$. By Markov's inequality, we have $\mathbf{Pr}_{S_i}\left[\bar{Z}_i \ge p^{1/2}\right] = \mathbf{Pr}_{S_i}\left[\bar{Z}_i \ge p^{-1/2}\,\mathbf{E}[\bar{Z}_i]\right] \le p^{1/2}$. That is, the probability that more than a $p^{1/2}$-fraction of the points in S_i are associated to h is at most $p^{1/2}$. Taking a union bound over all $h_j \in H$ such that $\|h_j - \mu_i\|_2 > \Delta/2$, it follows that the probability that more than a $p^{1/2}$-fraction of the points in S_i are associated to some such h_j is at most $|H| \, p^{1/2} \le \text{poly}(k) \, p^{1/2}$. By our assumption that $\Delta \gg \sqrt{\log(k/\delta)}$, it follows that $\text{poly}(k) \, p^{1/2} \le \exp(-\Omega(\Delta^2))$ with suitably small constant in the $\Omega(\cdot)$. This completes the proof. $\qquad \square$

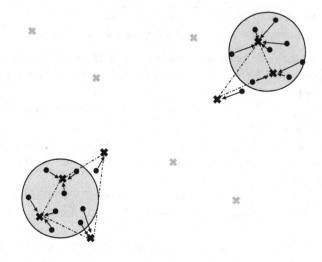

Figure 5.8 Illustration of algorithm Learn-Identity-Covariance-GMM. Each sample (small dot) is associated with its nearest hypothesis (cross). The hypotheses with few samples associated to nearby hypotheses are removed from H' (and grayed out). The remaining hypotheses can then be easily clustered based on their distances to each other; this allows us to reliably cluster our original samples based on which component they came from.

By a union bound over the k components and Corollary 5.35, the event that there exists $i \in [k]$ such that more than a $p^{1/2}$-fraction of the points in S_i are associated to some point in H at distance more than $\Delta/2$ from μ_i is at most $k|H|p^{1/2} \leq \mathrm{poly}(k)p^{1/2} = \exp(-\Omega(\Delta^2))$. Equivalently, with probability at least $1 - \exp(-\Omega(\Delta^2))$, for all components $i \in [k]$ simultaneously, at least a $1 - p^{1/2} = (1 - \exp(-\Omega(\Delta^2)))$ fraction of the points in S_i are associated with elements in H within distance $\Delta/2$ of μ_i. By a Chernoff bound, with probability at least $1 - k\exp(-\Omega(|T|/k))$ over the samples from the mixture X, we have that $(3/(4k))|T| \leq |S_i| \leq (4/(3k))|T|$, for all $i \in [k]$. We henceforth condition on these two events, whose intersection has probability at least $9/10$.

The next claim shows that any point in H that is sufficiently close to some μ_i is in H'.

Claim 5.36 *Let $h \in H$ be such that $\|h - \mu_i\| \leq \Delta/2$, for some $i \in [k]$. Then $h \in H'$.*

Proof By our above conditioning, for all $i \in [k]$, $|S_i| \geq (3/(4k))|T|$ and at least a $9/10$-fraction of points in S_i are associated with points $h_j \in H$ such that $\|h_j - \mu_i\| \leq \Delta/2$. By the triangle inequality, each such h_j satisfies $\|h_j - h\|_2 \leq \Delta$. Therefore, at least $(9/10)(3/(4k))|T| \geq (2/(3k))|T|$ points in T are associated with hypotheses $h_j \in H$ within distance Δ of h. Hence, $h \in H'$. $\qquad\square$

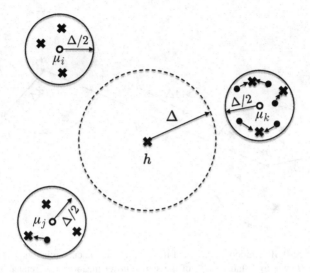

Figure 5.9 Illustration of the proof of Claim 5.37. The hypothesis h is $3\Delta/2$-far from any μ_i, which makes it Δ-far from any hypothesis within distance $\Delta/2$ of any μ_i. However, since almost all samples have a closest hypothesis within distance $\Delta/2$ of their cluster mean, very few will be associated to hypotheses within distance Δ of h. Therefore, $h \notin H'$.

By assumption, for each $i \in [k]$, there exists $h \in H$ such that $\|h - \mu_i\|_2 \leq \Delta/10$. Claim 5.36 therefore implies that $H' \neq \emptyset$. Since the μ_i's are separated by 7Δ, it follows that $|H'| \geq k$.

Conversely, we show that any point in H' will be relatively close to some μ_i.

Claim 5.37   *For any $h \in H'$ there exists some $i \in [k]$ such that $\|h-\mu_i\| \leq 3\Delta/2$.*

Proof   Let $h \in H'$ and $\{h_j\} \subset H$ be the subset of points in H that satisfy $\|h_j - h\|_2 \leq \Delta$. We will show that there exists $i \in [k]$ such that at least one of the h_j's satisfies $\|h_j - \mu_i\|_2 \leq \Delta/2$. The claim will then follow from the triangle inequality.

By definition of H', each such point $h_j \in H$ will be associated to a subset $T_j \subset T$ of points in T and moreover $|\cup_j T_j| \geq (2/(3k))|T|$. Suppose, for the sake of contradiction that each h_j is Δ-far from all μ_i's, that is, it satisfies the condition $\min_{i \in [k]} \|h_j - \mu_i\|_2 > \Delta/2$. By our conditioning, at most an $\exp(-\Omega(\Delta^2)) \ll \delta/k$ fraction of the points in $T = \cup_i S_i$ are associated with the union of h_j's. Since $\delta/k < 2/(3k)$, we obtain a contradiction, completing the proof.

See Figure 5.9 for an illustration of the argument. $\square$

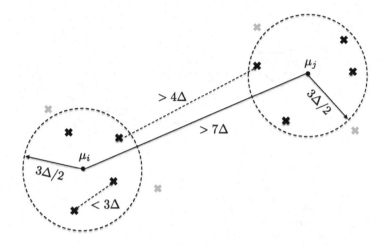

Figure 5.10 Illustration of the proof that ~ is an equivalence relation. Hypotheses in H' within distance $3\Delta/2$ of the same cluster mean will be related, while hypotheses within distance $3\Delta/2$ of different means will not.

Claim 5.37 and the assumed separation between the μ_i's implies that the relation "~" on H' is an equivalence relation. We show this as follows: Let $h, h' \in H'$ be close to component means μ_i, μ_j with $i \neq j$, that is, $\|h-\mu_i\| \leq 3\Delta/2$ and $\|h' - \mu_j\| \leq 3\Delta/2$. Then, by the triangle inequality, we get

$$\|h - h'\|_2 \geq \|\mu_i - \mu_j\| - \|h - \mu_i\| - \|h' - \mu_j\| \geq 7\Delta - 3\Delta = 4\Delta.$$

That is, if $\|h-h'\|_2 < 4\Delta$, h and h' are $3\Delta/2$-close to the same μ_i. Let $h_1, h_2, h_2 \in H'$ be such that $h_1 \sim h_2$ and $h_2 \sim h_3$. Since $\|h_1 - h_2\| \leq 3\Delta$, there exists $i \in [k]$ such that $\|h_1 - \mu_i\| \leq 3\Delta/2$ and $\|h_2 - \mu_i\| \leq 3\Delta/2$. Similarly, there exists $j \in [k]$ such that $\|h_2 - \mu_j\| \leq 3\Delta/2$ and $\|h_3 - \mu_j\| \leq 3\Delta/2$. Therefore, $\mu_i = \mu_j$, as otherwise

$$\|\mu_i - \mu_j\|_2 \leq \|\mu_i - h_2\|_2 + \|h_2 - h_3\|_2 + \|h_3 - \mu_j\|_2 \leq 3\Delta/2 + 3\Delta + 3\Delta/2 = 6\Delta,$$

a contradiction. This implies that $\|h_1 - h_3\| \leq 3\Delta$, that is, $h_1 \sim h_3$, which shows that "~" is an equivalence relation on H'. See Figure 5.10 for an illustration of this argument.

Also note that each equivalence class consists of all the points in H' within distance $3\Delta/2$ of some particular component mean μ_i. In particular, there is exactly one equivalence class C_i for each μ_i, that is, we have k equivalence classes. This allows us to accurately cluster the samples in T.

By our conditioning, for each $i \in [k]$, an $(1 - \exp(-\Omega(\Delta^2)))$-fraction of the points in S_i are associated with elements of H' in the equivalence class C_i

corresponding to μ_i. Therefore, at most an $\exp(-\Omega(\Delta^2)) \ll \delta/k$-fraction of the points in T are misclassified.

Since the points associated with C_i are a δ-corrupted sample from $\mathcal{N}(\mu_i, I)$ (in the worst case they get a δ/k-fraction of the points from each other cluster), Robust-Mean returns a mean v_i with $\|v_i - \mu_i\|_2 = \tilde{O}(\delta/k)$. This completes the proof of Proposition 5.33. □

Combining Proposition 5.33 with the algorithms of Section 5.3, we obtain efficient clustering algorithms for learning mixtures of spherical Gaussians, under the assumption that their pairwise mean separation is $\Delta = \Omega(k^{1/2})$. This reduction-based approach can be extended to bounded covariance distributions under similar separation assumptions. While these guarantees are not difficult to obtain using other methods, in Chapter 6 we will see how to design list-decoding algorithms with near-optimal error guarantees, which can in turn be used to obtain learning algorithms for mixtures under near-optimal separation.

Remark 5.38 Given the warm-start achieved by the above algorithm, a number of known local search methods (see, e.g., [113, 131]) can be used to efficiently obtain an ϵ-approximate solution, for any desired accuracy $\epsilon > 0$.

5.5 Exercises

5.1 (More General List-Decoding) Our list-decoding algorithms in this chapter have focused on learning the mean of a distribution, but more general statistical tasks can be considered. In particular, let $\mathcal{X}$ be a set and $\mathcal{D}$ be a family of distributions on $\mathcal{X}$. Let $\mathcal{C}$ be the collection of sets of the form $\{x : p(x) > q(x)\}$, where there are distributions in $\mathcal{D}$ with densities p and q. Suppose that $\mathcal{C}$ has VC-dimension d.

Let T be a set of n samples of G that are $(1 - \alpha)$-corrupted for some unknown $G \in \mathcal{D}$. Show that there is an (inefficient) algorithm that given these samples for some appropriately large $n = \text{poly}(d/\alpha)$ returns a list of $O(1/\alpha)$ many $G_i \in \mathcal{D}$ such that with high probability there is at least one i with $d_{\text{TV}}(G, G_i) < 1 - \alpha/10$.

5.2 (Trade-offs between Number of Hypotheses and Error) Let $1/\alpha$ be an integer k. Suppose that one wants to list-decode the mean of a distribution G in $\mathbf{R}^d$ with a $(1 - \alpha)$-fraction of corruptions using at most $k + m$ hypotheses for some positive integer m. Note that Proposition 5.6 shows that this is possible when $m \geq k$. Here we will consider what happens when $m < k$.

(a) Suppose that if it is known that for some t for any unit vector v, it holds $\Pr[v \cdot (G - \mu_G) > t] < m/(10k^2)$. Show that there is an (inefficient) algorithm that given $\text{poly}(d, k)$ many $(1-\alpha)$-corrupted samples from G with high probability returns a list of $m+k$ hypotheses at least one of which is within $2t$ of μ_G.

(b) Show that the bound in part (a) is tight in the following sense: Show that if $d \geq m+k$ no algorithm given any number of $(1-\alpha)$-corrupted samples from a distribution G with covariance bounded by I can return a list of $m+k$ hypotheses such that with probability better than $1 - 1/(m+k+1)$ at least one of the hypotheses is within $k/(10\sqrt{m})$ of μ_G.

5.3 (Bounds for List-Decoding of Logconcave Distributions)

(a) Show that it is information-theoretically possible, given an appropriately large number of $(1 - \alpha)$-corrupted samples from an unknown mean and identity covariance logconcave distribution to find a list of $O(1/\alpha)$ many hypotheses such that with high probability at least one of them is within distance $O(\log(1/\alpha))$ of the true mean.

(b) Show that it is information-theoretically *impossible* to find a list of $\text{poly}(1/\alpha)$ hypotheses such that at least one is within $o(\log(1/\alpha))$ of the mean.

5.4 (Fast Multifilter Step) Show how to implement the `Basic-Multifilter` subroutine on a set $T \subset \mathbf{R}$ in time $\tilde{O}(|T|)$.

5.5 (List-Decoding Gaussian Covariances) Let $G \sim \mathcal{N}(0, \Sigma)$ be a zero-mean Gaussian in $\mathbf{R}^d$ with unknown covariance Σ and $\alpha > 0$. Design an algorithm that given a set of $\text{poly}(d/\alpha)$ $(1 - \alpha)$-corrupted samples from G runs in $\text{poly}(d/\alpha)$ time and returns a list of $\text{poly}(1/\alpha)$ hypotheses $\widehat{\Sigma}_i$ such that with constant probability at least one hypothesis $\widehat{\Sigma}$ satisfies

$$\|\widehat{\Sigma}^{-1/2}\Sigma\widehat{\Sigma}^{-1/2} - I\|_F = \text{poly}(1/\alpha).$$

(Hint: Some version of a multifilter should suffice. If T contains an α-fraction of inliers, use some multiple of $\mathbf{Cov}[T]$ as an upper bound on Σ. Show that Σ must be fairly close to $\mathbf{Cov}[T]$, unless there is a degree-2 polynomial p with $\mathbf{Var}[p(T)]$ much larger than $\mathbf{Var}[p(\mathcal{N}(0, \mathbf{Cov}(T)))]$. If such a p exists, use it to construct a multifilter.)

Remark 5.39 Ideally, one would want a list-decoding algorithm where additionally one has that Σ and $\widehat{\Sigma}$ are comparable in the Loewner ordering (i.e., that for some $C(\alpha)$ we have that $\Sigma/C(\alpha) \preceq \widehat{\Sigma} \preceq C(\alpha)\Sigma$). This would imply that the Gaussians $\mathcal{N}(0, \Sigma)$ and $\mathcal{N}(0, \widehat{\Sigma})$ have some reasonable (i.e., a function of α) overlap between them. Unfortunately, there are Statistical Query (SQ) lower bounds suggesting that this kind of list-decoding, although information-theoretically possible (for example, by Exercise 5.1), is computationally intractable. The reader is referred to Exercise 8.9 in Chapter 8.

5.6 (SIFT Isotropy) Give an example of a set of points where if a round of SIFT is run without isotropization (in particular, if $\|P(x - \mu)\|_2^2$ is used as the weight function) the fraction of inliers removed is higher than the fraction of outliers removed.

5.7 (Necessity of Separation Assumptions) Here we show that the $\Omega(\sqrt{\log(k)})$ pairwise separation we have been assuming for clustering mixtures of spherical Gaussians is actually necessary. In particular, we show that with only a slightly weaker separation assumption, clustering may be information-theoretically impossible.

   (a) Let $G = \mathcal{N}(\mu, I_d)$ be a Gaussian in $\mathbf{R}^d$ with mean μ such that $\|\mu\|_2 = \sqrt{d}$. Let $C > 0$ be a sufficiently large constant and t be an integer with $t > Cd$. Show that if the probability density function of G is approximated by its degree-t Taylor expansion around 0 truncated to a ball of radius $\sqrt{t}$, then the resulting function will be $\exp(-\Omega(t))$-close to the true probability density function in L_1-distance.

   (b) Let $K > \binom{t+d}{d}$. Let $x_1, x_2, \ldots, x_K$ be distinct points in $\mathbf{R}^d$ with $\|x_i\|_2 = \sqrt{d}$. Show that there exist two mixtures M_1, M_2, where M_i is a mixture of Gaussians of the form $\mathcal{N}(x_j, I_d)$ whose components are distinct and such that $d_{\mathrm{TV}}(M_1, M_2) = \exp(-\Omega(t))$.

   (Hint: Find mixtures such that the degree-t Taylor approximations to their densities at 0 agree.)

   (c) Show that for any integers $A, k > 0$, there exists a constant $C_A > 0$ and two mixtures of spherical Gaussians in $\mathbf{R}^{d'}$ for any $d' > \log(k)$ such that the mixtures are k^{-A}-close in total variation distance, but the means of the mixtures are pairwise separated by at least $\sqrt{\log(k)}/C_A$.

5.8 (Elementary Algorithms for Learning Mixtures of Gaussians) Here we present an elementary algorithm for learning mixtures of k uniformly weighted spherical Gaussians with pairwise separation roughly $k^{1/4}$. In particular, let $X = (1/k) \sum_{i=1}^{k} \mathcal{N}(\mu_i, I)$ be an equally weighted mixture of k spherical Gaussians and let $\epsilon > 0$ be a parameter.

(a) Give an algorithm that given poly(dk/ϵ) i.i.d. samples from X runs in polynomial time and with high probability computes a k-dimensional subspace H such that each of the μ_i's is within ϵ of H.

(Hint: Consider the k largest eigenvalues of $\mathbf{Cov}[X]$.)

(b) Suppose additionally that $\min_{i \neq j} \|\mu_i - \mu_j\|_2 > Ck^{1/4} \sqrt{\log(k/\epsilon)}$, for some sufficiently large constant $C > 0$. Suppose that poly(k/ϵ) samples are drawn from X and that for each pair x, y of samples one computes $\|\mathrm{Proj}_H(x) - \mathrm{Proj}_H(y)\|_2$. Show that with high probability the distance computed from every pair of samples coming from the same component is smaller than the distance computed from every pair of samples taken from different components.

(c) Devise an algorithm that under the assumptions in Part (b) learns X to total variation distance ϵ using poly(dk/ϵ) time and samples.

5.6 Discussion and Related Work

The list-decodable learning model was introduced by [11] in the context of clustering (without generative model assumptions on the inliers) and was first studied by [25] in the context of high-dimensional mean estimation. The latter work gave the first polynomial-time algorithm for list-decoding the mean of bounded covariance distributions achieving near-optimal error of $\tilde{O}(\alpha^{-1/2})$. Their algorithm is based on black-box convex optimization. Moreover, [25] first pointed out the connection between list-decodable mean estimation and clustering well-separated mixture models. Additional applications of list-decodable learning to stochastic block models and crowdsourcing were explored in [25] and [122], respectively.

The information-theoretic bounds on list-decodable mean estimation presented in Section 5.2 were established in [65]. The multifilter technique of Section 5.3.1 was developed in [65] for identity covariance sub-Gaussian distributions. The work of [53] gave a refinement of the multifilter technique that achieves near-optimal error guarantees for bounded covariance distributions. The SIFT algorithm presented in Section 5.3.2 was developed in [54]. The technique of efficiently reducing the list size presented in Section 5.3.3 is implicit in [65]. The efficient reduction of clustering to list-decoding for spherical Gaussians presented in Section 5.4 was given in [65]. As shown in [65], a slight adaptation of this reduction suffices to obtain a robust clustering algorithm, namely: one that tolerates a fraction of outliers proportional to the relative size of the smallest true cluster. Reference [55] extends this reduction to bounded covariance distributions under a separation of $\tilde{\Omega}(\sqrt{k})$, which is information-theoretically near-optimal.

A standard implementation of the multifilter method in Section 5.3.1 leads to an algorithm with runtime $\tilde{O}(n^2 d/\alpha^2)$. Similarly, the SIFT algorithm of Section 5.3.2 has runtime $\tilde{O}(n^2 d/\alpha)$. A related line of work focused on developing faster list-decodable mean estimators for sub-Gaussian and, more generally, bounded covariance distributions. Specifically, [38] gave an SDP-based algorithm with runtime $\tilde{O}(nd/\alpha^6)$ achieving the optimal error of $O(\alpha^{-1/2})$. Subsequent work by [54] combined the SIFT algorithm with techniques from continuous optimization to obtain an algorithm with near-optimal error and runtime $\tilde{O}(nd/\alpha)$. More recently, [55] obtained an algorithm with similar error guarantees that runs in almost linear time, namely: $O_c(n^{1+c}d)$, for any fixed $c > 0$. Similarly, the latter algorithm combines the multifilter technology with techniques from continuous optimization. At a high-level, both of these algorithms achieve their faster runtimes by reducing the number of iterations from linear in n to polylogarithmic, using ideas similar in spirit to those in Chapter 3. As an application, [55] gave the first almost-linear time algorithm for learning well-separated mixtures with near-optimal statistical guarantees. This improves a long line of work that had developed spectral algorithms for learning well-separated mixture models, see, for example, [1, 4, 22, 41, 105, 143].

Finally, it should be noted that the list-decoding algorithms we have presented in this chapter can at best achieve error guarantee of $\Omega(\alpha^{-1/2})$, even for the class of spherical Gaussians. We remind the reader that this bound is very far from the information-theoretic limit of $\Theta(\sqrt{\log(1/\alpha)})$. Consequently, the implications for learning uniform mixture models require mean separation of $\Delta = \Omega(\sqrt{k})$. Clustering mixtures of spherical Gaussians with this kind of separation can be achieved by elementary methods. In fact, [143] gives an algorithm for clustering such mixtures with separation $\tilde{O}(k^{1/4})$ (see Exercise 5.8). For mixtures of bounded covariance distributions, [55] obtains a learning algorithm under near-optimal separation of $\tilde{\Omega}(\sqrt{k})$.

In Chapter 6, we will present list-decoding algorithms for structured distributions including Gaussians (and their applications to learning mixtures) that achieve significantly better error guarantees. At a high-level, this is achieved by leveraging higher moment information about the clean data [65, 112].

6

Robust Estimation via Higher Moments

6.1 Introduction

The robust estimation algorithms that have been developed in the previous chapters work by considering only the low-degree moments of the underlying distributions. Specifically, the robust mean estimation algorithms of Chapter 2 and list-decodable mean estimation algorithms of Chapter 5 make use of only the first and second moments. The algorithm for robust covariance estimation of Chapter 4 leverages the fourth moments; however, these can be thought of as second moments of the tensor $X \otimes X$.

In a number of learning applications (much) higher degree moments need to be considered in order to obtain either meaningful or quantitatively better results. Leveraging higher moments in robust statistics requires new techniques that come with a number of complications. In this chapter, we will discuss when these techniques are useful and how to apply them.

The structure of this chapter is as follows: We begin in Section 6.2 by motivating the use of higher degree moments in the context of list-decodable mean estimation of spherical Gaussians. Here there are two known techniques: one making use of the known variances of higher degree polynomials, and a more flexible one making use of the sum-of-squares (SoS) method. We describe these techniques in Sections 6.3 and 6.4, respectively. In the subsequent sections, we discuss two related settings where higher moment techniques can be applied. In Section 6.5, we describe how to use higher moments in robust mean estimation in order to take advantage of bounded central moments of the inlier distribution. In Section 6.6, we describe how higher moment techniques can be leveraged in robust clustering of mixture models.

6.2 Leveraging Higher-Degree Moments in List-Decodable Learning

In Chapter 5, we gave an algorithm for list decoding the mean of an identity covariance Gaussian achieving ℓ_2-error of $\tilde{O}(1/\sqrt{\alpha})$. On the other hand, as we showed in that chapter, the information-theoretically optimal error is exponentially smaller, namely: $\Theta(\sqrt{\log(1/\alpha)})$. It is worth understanding why we have such a large gap and to ask whether it is possible to overcome it.

One way to see where the suboptimal error guarantee comes from is to recall the basic multifilter algorithm. At the end of the algorithm, we are left with a list of subsets S_i with the guarantee that (i) each S_i has bounded covariance, and (ii) at least one of the S_i's has at least an α-fraction of the points in S_i coming from the inlier distribution. Given these properties, it is shown that the sample mean of the particular subset S_i satisfying (ii) gives a good approximation to the true mean. This holds because the covariance bounds from (i) imply *concentration* bounds on S_i. In particular, since S_i has bounded covariance, it follows that any α-fraction of the points of S_i (including the subset of clean points in S_i) cannot have mean more than $\Omega(1/\sqrt{\alpha})$-far from the mean of S_i.

Unfortunately, the above quantitative bound is the best concentration that bounded covariance implies. In particular, it is not hard to construct a set T with covariance bounded by $O(I)$, such that an α-fraction of the points of T are i.i.d. samples from a Gaussian distribution $\mathcal{N}(\mu, I)$ and the sample mean of T is $\Omega(1/\sqrt{\alpha})$-far from μ (see Exercise 6.1). If such a set S is the set of (corrupted) samples given as input, the multifilter algorithm, as the covariance is already bounded, will simply return the mean of S.

6.2.1 The Usefulness of Higher Moments

As follows from the preceding discussion, ensuring that a set of samples has bounded covariance does not imply sufficiently strong concentration bounds. To circumvent this obstacle, we would need a filtering algorithm to enforce some stronger condition on the sets S_i, which will in turn would imply stronger concentration. The pressing issue here – and one that we will need to return to a few times – is how do we find a condition that allows us to computationally efficiently *verify* concentration bounds. For example, if we were able to ensure that our final sets S_i satisfied Gaussian-like tail bounds, it is not hard to see that this would imply that the mean of the good subset S_i will be within distance

$O(\sqrt{\log(1/\alpha)})$ of the true mean. However, enforcing this condition on our subsets is challenging for the following reason: Given a set S, it is believed to be computationally hard to even verify whether or not it satisfies Gaussian tail bounds (see Theorem 8.30 for an example of a result in this direction).

A natural tool for obtaining concentration bounds is the use of higher moments of a distribution. In particular, we consider the higher *central* moments of the distribution, namely $\mathbf{E}[(v \cdot (X - \mu_X))^{2k}]$, for v a unit vector and k a positive integer. We introduce the following definition.

Definition 6.1   We say that a set $S \subset \mathbf{R}^d$ with mean $\mu \in \mathbf{R}^d$ has $2k$th *central moments* bounded by $M \in \mathbf{R}_+$, if for any unit vector $v \in \mathbf{R}^d$ we have that $\mathbf{E}_{x \sim_u S}[(v \cdot (x - \mu))^{2k}] \leq M$.

The following simple lemma shows that bounded central moments imply the strong desired concentration.

Lemma 6.2   *Let S be a set of points in $\mathbf{R}^d$ with $2k$th central moments bounded by M and $0 < \alpha < 1$. Let $T \subset S$ be any subset such that $|T| \geq \alpha|S|$. Letting μ_S and μ_T be the means of S and T respectively, we have that $\|\mu_S - \mu_T\|_2 \leq (M/\alpha)^{-1/(2k)}$.*

Proof   Let v be the unit vector in the direction of $\mu_T - \mu_S$. In particular, we have that $\|\mu_S - \mu_T\|_2 = v \cdot (\mu_T - \mu_S)$. On the other hand, by the bounded central moments assumption, we have

$$M \geq \mathbf{E}_{x \sim_u S}[(v \cdot (x - \mu_S))^{2k}]$$
$$\geq \alpha \mathbf{E}_{x \sim_u T}[(v \cdot (x - \mu_S))^{2k}]$$
$$\geq \alpha(v \cdot (\mu_T - \mu_S))^{2k}$$
$$= \alpha\|\mu_S - \mu_T\|_2^{2k},$$

where the second line holds because $|T| \geq \alpha|S|$ and the third line follows by Jensen's inequality (see Theorem A.6). From the above, we conclude that $\|\mu_S - \mu_T\|_2 \leq (M/\alpha)^{-1/(2k)}$, as desired.   □

6.2.2 Computationally Inefficient Higher Moments Filter

Lemma 6.2 motivates an idea for a multifilter-type algorithm. Specifically, we would like a multifilter algorithm which ensures that our final sets of points have bounded central moments as opposed to just bounded covariance. At a high level, to achieve this, one can try to repeatedly filter in the direction of the large moment until this is the case. Roughly speaking, this scheme gives rise to the following procedure.

Algorithm `Basic-Higher-Moments-Filter`

Input: Dataset $S \subset \mathbf{R}^d$ that contains an unknown $T \subseteq S$ with $|T| \geq \alpha|S|$ and T has bounded central moments.

1. Compute the first $2k$ empirical moments of the sample set S.
2. Determine whether or not S has bounded $2k$th central moments.
3. If S has bounded central moments, return the mean of S.
4. If S does not have bounded central moments:
   (a) Find a unit vector v such that $\mathbf{E}_{x \sim_u S}[(v \cdot (x - \mu_S))^{2k}]$ is large.
   (b) Compute the projections $v \cdot x$ for $x \in S$.
   (c) Run a multifilter on these projections, producing a small list of new sets S_i.
   (d) Run Basic-Higher-Moments-Filter recursively on each S, returning the set of all returned hypotheses.

By applying the above procedure, we will eventually obtain a collection of sets of samples each of which has bounded $2k$th central moments, at least one of which contains a large fraction of the original set of clean points. Applying Lemma 6.2, we can show that the mean of this subset is close to the mean of T. In particular, given roughly d^k/α samples, this algorithm should return a polynomial-size list of hypotheses, at least one of which is $O(\alpha^{1/2k})$-close to the true mean. This is a substantial improvement over the previous algorithms which obtained roughly $1/\sqrt{\alpha}$ error.

The description of this algorithm is somewhat sketchy and in particular there are a few points to be clarified. An obvious deficiency is the design of the necessary multifilter under only the assumption that the $2k$th moment in the v-direction is large. It turns out that this step can be performed without much difficulty (see Exercise 6.2). A deeper problem with this approach is that of computing the desired vector v, or even determining whether or not a set S has bounded central moments for any $k > 1$. As we will explain in Chapter 8, there is strong evidence that this problem is computationally intractable. In fact, for general sets S, it is believed to be computationally difficult to distinguish between the cases where S has k bounded central moments, for any constant k, and the case where the fourth central moment is large.

Given this computational bottleneck, to obtain an efficient algorithm we will instead need to find a new surrogate condition for concentration bounds which can be efficiently verified. To achieve this, we will need to assume that the inlier samples satisfy certain conditions stronger than just having bounded central moments.

There are two known methods in the literature for doing this. The first method, which we will call *the variance of polynomials method*, succeeds, for example, in the basic case that the inliers are drawn from the Gaussian distribution – when the higher moments of the clean data distribution are *known ahead of time*. For example, if it is assumed that the inlier distribution is of the form $\mathcal{N}(\mu, I)$, we can try to check if

$$\mathbf{E}_{x \sim_u S}[p^2(x - \mu_S)] \leq 2\mathbf{E}[p^2(\mathcal{N}(0, I))] \tag{6.1}$$

for *every* degree at most k polynomial p. We note that this condition is efficiently verifiable, as it is merely comparing two different quadratic forms in p and can be checked with an eigenvalue computation. Furthermore, by applying Equation (6.1) with $p(x) = (v \cdot x)^k$, one can verify that the central moments of S are not too large.

One disadvantage of the aforementioned technique is that it requires a priori knowledge of the higher order central moments of the inlier distribution. Ideally, we would like to obtain efficient list-decodable learners in more general settings, where the higher central moments are bounded but unknown, for example, when the inlier distribution is a Gaussian with unknown but bounded covariance. This brings us back to our original issue of how to efficiently verify that the central moments of the empirical distribution are in fact bounded. A general way to do this is to employ sum-of-squares proofs. This gives rise to a technique making use of the sum-of-squares method.

6.3 List-Decodable Learning via Variance of Polynomials

The high-level idea for the variance of polynomials technique is fairly natural: Check whether or not Equation (6.1) (or an equivalent, depending on the underlying inlier distribution) is satisfied for all low-degree polynomials p. If so, then we have obtained a certificate of bounded central moments, and we can return the sample mean of S. Otherwise, we find a violating polynomial p and use it to create a multifilter, where we appropriately remove points x such that $|p(x - \mu_S)|$ is too large.

Unfortunately, this simple idea quickly runs into technical issues. These stem from the problem that creating a multifilter requires having a bound on the variance of $p(x - \mu_S)$ over the inlier points x. Unfortunately, for a Gaussian $G = \mathcal{N}(\mu, I)$, the variance of $p(G)$ depends on the value of μ (note that this does *not* happen for degree-1 polynomials p, which explains why this issue did not arise in the "linear" multifilter of Chapter 5). As a result, the filtering step required becomes difficult to implement. Initial work on the variance of polynomials technique dealt with this issue by considering multilinear polynomials evaluated at collections of samples from our set. Since these polynomials were linear in each sample, this circumvented the issue above. Unfortunately, the solution thus obtained is somewhat technically involved. In this section, we will present a different, arguably simpler, method of dealing with it. This so-called *difference-of-pairs method* leads to slightly less efficient algorithms, but is technically simpler and easily generalizes to other settings.

6.3.1 Differences-of-Pairs Filter

As follows from the preceding discussion, the technical issue at hand is the following: For the inlier distribution X, we know what the variances of $p(X - \mu_X)$ ought to be, but not the variances of $p(X)$. One way to deal with this issue is to renormalize the samples to have mean 0. A simple and convenient way to do this is to consider differences of pairs of samples instead of individual samples. This suffices because if, for example, $X \sim \mathcal{N}(\mu, I)$, for some unknown μ, we know that $X - X' \sim \mathcal{N}(0, 2I)$.

To formalize this idea, let S be the multiset of corrupted samples given as input to our algorithm and let S_{good} be the inlier samples drawn from X. We define

$$\mathcal{P} := \{x - y : x, y \in S\} \quad \text{and} \quad \mathcal{P}_{\text{good}} := \{x - y : x, y \in S_{\text{good}}\}.$$

It is not hard to see (see Exercise 6.3) that if the size of S is sufficiently large, then, with high probability, for all polynomials p of degree at most k, we have

$$\mathbf{E}_{z \sim_u \mathcal{P}_{\text{good}}}[p^2(z)] \le 2\mathbf{E}_{X, X' \sim \mathcal{N}(0, I)}[p^2(X - X')]. \tag{6.2}$$

We note that if Equation (6.2) held for the average over *all* $z \in \mathcal{P}$, we would be done. This is because taking $p(x) = (v \cdot x)^k$ for some unit vector v, we can write

$$\begin{aligned}
\mathbf{E}_{z \sim_u \mathcal{P}}[p^2(z)] &= \mathbf{E}_{x, x' \sim_u S}[(v \cdot (x - x'))^{2k}] \\
&\ge (|S_{\text{good}}|/|S|) \, \mathbf{E}_{x \sim_u S, x' \sim_u S_{\text{good}}}[(v \cdot (x - x'))^{2k}] \\
&\ge \alpha (v \cdot (\mathbf{E}_{x \sim_u S}[x] - \mathbf{E}_{x' \sim_u S_{\text{good}}}[x']))^{2k} \\
&= \alpha (v \cdot (\mu_S - \mu_{S_{\text{good}}}))^{2k},
\end{aligned}$$

where the next-to-last line above follows from Jensen's Inequality. This means that if the expectation of $p^2(z)$ is bounded, for $p(x) = (v \cdot x)^k$ with v the unit vector in the direction of $\mu_S - \mu_{S_{\text{good}}}$, we can bound $\|\mu_S - \mu_{S_{\text{good}}}\|_2$.

Of course, in the presence of corruptions, the expectation of $p^2(z)$ over all of $\mathcal{P}$ might not be particularly small. However, it is not difficult to construct a filter to find a subset of $\mathcal{P}$ for which this will be the case. This is established in the following lemma.

Lemma 6.3 (Basic Difference-of-Pairs Filter)   *Let $\mathcal{P}$ be a multiset of points in $\mathbf{R}^d$ for which there exists a subset $\mathcal{P}_{good} \subset \mathcal{P}$ with $|\mathcal{P}_{good}| \geq \alpha^2|\mathcal{P}|$, for some $\alpha > 0$. Furthermore, assume that there is an explicit quadratic form Q on the space of degree-at-most-k polynomials p on $\mathbf{R}^d$ (for example, given a basis of the set of such polynomials, Q could be presented by a symmetric matrix) such that $\mathbf{E}_{z\sim_u\mathcal{P}_{good}}[p^2(z)] \leq Q(p)$. Then there exists a randomized algorithm that, given Q and $\mathcal{P}$, runs in $\mathrm{poly}(d^k, |\mathcal{P}|)$ time, and returns a subset $T \subseteq \mathcal{P}$ such that:*

1. *For all degree at most k polynomials p, it holds $\sum_{z\in T} p^2(z) = O(|\mathcal{P}|)Q(p)$.*
2. *With probability at least $2/3$, we have $|T \cap \mathcal{P}_{good}| \geq |\mathcal{P}_{good}|/2$.*

Before we give the proof, we note that we will apply this lemma with $Q(p) := 2\mathbf{E}[p^2(X - X')]$.

Proof   The algorithm is quite simple. For $C > 0$ a sufficiently large universal constant, we have the following procedure.

Algorithm `Difference-Of-Pairs-Filter`
Input: Dataset $\mathcal{P} \subset \mathbf{R}^d$ and a quadratic form Q on the space of degree-k polynomials, $C > 0$ a sufficiently large constant.

1. Let $T = \mathcal{P}$.
2. While there exists a degree-at-most k polynomial p such that $\sum_{z\in T} p^2(z) > (C|\mathcal{P}|)Q(p)$:
   (a) Find a degree-at-most k polynomial p such that $\sum_{z\in T} p^2(z) > (C|\mathcal{P}|/2)Q(p)$.
   (b) Filter elements of T as follows: $z \in T$ is removed with probability proportional to $p^2(z)$.
3. Return T.

Note that this procedure can deterministically remove the point $z \in T$ with the largest value of $p^2(z)$. Doing so means that we remove at least one point in each iteration. Thus, the overall algorithm will terminate in $\mathrm{poly}(|\mathcal{P}|, d^k)$ time.

It is clear that this algorithm runs until it finds a set T such that $\sum_{z\in T} p^2(z) \leq (C|\mathcal{P}|)Q(p)$ for all p, proving our first condition. For the second condition, we first observe that, by increasing α, we may assume that $|\mathcal{P}_{good}| = \alpha^2|\mathcal{P}|$. We next note that in each iteration the expected number of elements of $\mathcal{P}_{good}$ that are removed by the above filter is proportional to

$$\sum_{z \in \mathcal{P}_{\text{good}} \cap T} p^2(z) \leq \sum_{z \in \mathcal{P}_{\text{good}}} p^2(z) \leq \alpha^2 |\mathcal{P}| \mathbf{E}_{z \sim_u \mathcal{P}_{\text{good}}} [p^2(z)] \leq \alpha^2 |\mathcal{P}| Q(p),$$

while the expected number of total elements removed is proportional to

$$\sum_{z \in T} p^2(z) \geq C(|\mathcal{P}|/2) Q(p).$$

The ratio of these expectations is at most $2\alpha^2/C < \alpha^2/6$, since C was selected to be sufficiently large. This means that if we consider the potential function

$$\Delta := |T| + (6/\alpha^2)(|\mathcal{P}_{\text{good}}| - |\mathcal{P}_{\text{good}} \cap T|),$$

it will be a supermartingale. Since Δ is nonnegative, with probability $2/3$ it will never increase to more than three times its initial value of $|\mathcal{P}|$. If this holds, then it will be the case that $|\mathcal{P}_{\text{good}} \cap T| \geq \alpha^2 |\mathcal{P}|/2 = |\mathcal{P}_{\text{good}}|/2$. This completes the proof. $\qquad\square$

6.3.2 Efficient Rounding

Applying Lemma 6.3 to our set of differences of samples yields a set of points that satisfy strong concentration bounds. If we had a set of our original sample points that contained a decent fraction of the good points and satisfied similar concentration bounds, we could return the mean of that set. Lemma 6.2 would then imply that we are done. Unfortunately, with sets of differences this does not work, as the average of our set of differences will likely be close to 0 regardless of the true mean. Instead, we will try to use this information about pairs to find subsets of our original samples that have appropriate concentration bounds.

We will require the following definition.

Definition 6.4 (Bounded Moments Graph) Let $S \subset \mathbf{R}^d$. A graph $G = (V, E)$ with $V = S$ is said to have its $2k$th moments bounded by M, if for every unit vector v we have that $\sum_{(x,y) \in E} (v \cdot (x - y))^{2k} \leq M|S|^2$.

It is not hard to see that if we take the set T returned by the algorithm from Lemma 6.3, then letting G be the graph with vertex set S and an edge between (x, y) if $x - y$ or $y - x$ is in T, then G will have bounded $2k$th moments. In particular, we have the following Corollary of Lemma 6.3.

Corollary 6.5 *Let S be a set of points in $\mathbf{R}^d$ containing a subset S_{good}. Furthermore, suppose that there is an explicit quadratic form Q on degree-k polynomials such that $\mathbf{E}_{s,s' \sim_u S_{\text{good}}} [p^2(s - s')] \leq Q(p)$ for all p, and that $Q((v \cdot x)^k) \leq M\|v\|_2^{2k}$ for all vectors v. Then there exists an algorithm that given*

Q and S runs in polynomial time and with probability at least 2/3 *returns a graph G in S such that:*

1. *G has 2kth moments bounded by* $O(M)$.
2. *At least half of the pairs of elements in* S_{good} *are connected in G.*

We already know that if G is the complete graph, then the sample mean of S will be a good estimator. It is not hard to show that it also suffices if we have a clique in G containing a large fraction of the points in S_{good}.

Lemma 6.6 *Let S be a set of points in* $\mathbf{R}^d$ *and G be a graph on S with 2kth moments bounded by M. Let* $C \subseteq S$ *be a clique in G and let* $C_{\text{good}} \subseteq C$ *be a subset with* $|C_{\text{good}}| \geq \alpha|S|$. *Then, letting* μ_C *and* μ_g *be the means of C and* C_{good}, *respectively, we have* $\|\mu_C - \mu_g\|_2 \leq (2M/\alpha^2)^{1/(2k)}$.

In applications, we will use Lemma 6.6 with $C_{\text{good}} = S_{\text{good}} \cap C$. As long as $S_{\text{good}} \cap C$ is reasonably large, and as long as the points in S_{good} are concentrated, the means of S_{good} and C_{good} will be close.

Proof Let v be a unit vector in the direction of $\mu_C - \mu_g$. Then we have that $\|\mu_C - \mu_g\|_2 = v \cdot (\mu_C - \mu_g)$. On the other hand, by the bounded moments property, we have

$$
\begin{aligned}
M|S|^2 &\geq \sum_{(x,y)\in E} (v \cdot (x - y))^{2k} \\
&\geq \frac{1}{2} \sum_{x,y\in C} (v \cdot (x - y))^{2k} \\
&\geq \frac{1}{2} \sum_{x\in C, y\in C_{\text{good}}} (v \cdot (x - y))^{2k} \\
&\geq \frac{1}{2}|C_{\text{good}}||C|(v \cdot (\mu_C - \mu_g))^{2k} \\
&\geq |S|^2(\alpha^2/2)\|\mu_C - \mu_g\|_2^{2k},
\end{aligned}
$$

from which the result follows. Note that the second line in this equation follows from the fact that C is a clique and the fourth line follows from Jensen's Inequality. This completes the proof. $\square$

Unfortunately, it is unlikely that G will contain an actual clique. Furthermore, even if G does, finding this clique may not be computationally feasible. Therefore, we will need a more flexible method of finding our final set of points. A useful fact here is the triangle inequality. We note that $|v \cdot (x - y)| \leq |v \cdot (x - a)| + |v \cdot (y - a)|$ for any a. Thus, if two vertices x and y have many neighbors a in common, it is likely that they are not too separated. To formalize this observation, we define the notion of the *overlap graph*.

Definition 6.7 (Overlap Graph)   Let $G = (V, E)$ be a graph and $\gamma > 0$ be a parameter. The *overlap graph* $R_\gamma(G)$ is defined to be the graph with vertex set V, where (x, y) is an edge in the graph if and only if $|N_G(x) \cap N_G(y)| \geq \gamma|V|$, where $N_G(x)$ and $N_G(y)$ are the neighborhoods of x and y in G. In other words, there is an edge between x and y in $R_\gamma(G)$ if and only if x and y share at least $\gamma|V|$ neighbors in G.

The following key lemma shows that if G has bounded moments, then so does $R_\gamma(G)$.

Lemma 6.8   *Let S be a set of points in $\mathbf{R}^d$ and G be a graph on S that has $2k$th moments bounded by M. Then, for any $\gamma > 0$, the overlap graph $R_\gamma(G)$ has $2k$th moments bounded by $(2 \cdot 4^k M/\gamma)$.*

Proof   Let v be a unit vector. We wish to bound $\sum_{x,y \text{ neighbors in } R_\gamma(G)} (v \cdot (x-y))^{2k}$. We note that for any such x, y, we have

$$(v \cdot (x - y))^{2k} = \frac{1}{|N_G(x) \cap N_G(y)|} \sum_{a \in N_G(x) \cap N_G(y)} (v \cdot (x - a) - v \cdot (y - a))^{2k}$$

$$\leq \frac{1}{\gamma|S|} \sum_{a \in N_G(x) \cap N_G(y)} 4^k[(v \cdot (x - a))^{2k} + (v \cdot (y - a))^{2k}].$$

Summing this over all edges in $R_\gamma(G)$, we have

$$\sum_{x,y \text{ neighbors in } R_\gamma(G)} (v \cdot (x - y))^{2k}$$

$$\leq \frac{4^k}{\gamma|S|} \sum_{x,y \text{ neighbors in } R_\gamma(G)} \sum_{a \in N_G(x) \cap N_G(y)} [(v \cdot (x - a))^{2k} + (v \cdot (y - a))^{2k}]$$

$$= \frac{2 \cdot 4^k}{\gamma|S|} \sum_{(a,x) \in E} \sum_{\substack{y \text{ neighbor of } x \text{ in } R_\gamma(G) \\ \text{and neighbor of } a \text{ in } G}} (v \cdot (x - a))^{2k}$$

$$\leq \frac{2 \cdot 4^k|S|}{\gamma|S|} \sum_{(a,x) \in E} (v \cdot (x - a))^{2k}$$

$$\leq (2 \cdot 4^k M/\gamma)|S|^2.$$

This completes the proof.   □

Unfortunately, the overlap graph $R_\gamma(G)$ might still not have any large cliques. However, it is guaranteed at least to have some fairly dense subgraphs, as shown in the following lemma.

Lemma 6.9   *Let $G = (V, E)$ be a graph and $\gamma > 0$. If x is a randomly selected vertex of G, then the expected number of pairs $y, z \in N(x)$ such that y and z are not neighbors in $R_\gamma(G)$ is at most $\gamma|V|^2$.*

Proof   The expectation in question is equal to $1/|V|$ times the number of triples $x, y, z \in V$ such that y and z are not neighbors in $R_\gamma(G)$, but are both neighbors of x in G. By the definition of $R_\gamma(G)$, if y and z are not neighbors in $R_\gamma(G)$, they have at most $\gamma|V|$ common neighbors in G. Thus, the number of such triples is at most $\gamma|V|^3$, which implies that the expectation in question is at most $\gamma|V|^2$.   □

Similarly, this dense subgraph may not be a clique, but if we are willing to prune a few points and take another overlap graph, we can find one.

Lemma 6.10 (Densification Lemma)   *Let $G = (V, E)$ be a graph and let $W \subset V$ be a set of vertices with $|W| = \beta|V|$ and all but $\gamma|V|^2$ pairs of vertices in W connected in G, for some $\beta, \gamma > 0$ with $\gamma \leq \beta^2/36$. There exists an algorithm that given G, W, β, γ runs in polynomial time, and returns a subset $W' \subseteq W$ such that $|W'| \geq |W| - (6\gamma/\beta)|V|$ and such that W' is a clique in $R_{\beta/3}(G)$.*

Proof   The algorithm is quite simple. We begin with $W' = W$, and then while there is some $x \in W'$ where x is not neighbor with at least $2|W'|/3$ other elements of W', we remove x from W'.

We note that, so long as $|W'| \geq 5|W|/6$, each such x removed decreases the number of pairs of unconnected elements in W' by at least $|W|/6 = (\beta/6)|V|$. This can happen at most $(6\gamma/\beta)|V|$ times before we run out of unconnected pairs of elements in W'. However, since $(6\gamma/\beta)|V| \leq (\beta/6)|V| = |W|/6$, this must happen before $|W'|$ drops below $5|W|/6$. Therefore, when this procedure terminates, we will have $|W'| \geq |W| - (6\gamma/\beta)|V|$.

On the other hand, each element of W' is connected to at least $2|W'|/3$ other elements of W' in G. From here it is easy to see that any pair of elements of W' have at least $|W|/3$ common neighbors, and thus are adjacent in $R_{\beta/3}(G)$. This completes the proof.   □

We are now ready to prove our main result on rounding.

Proposition 6.11 (Efficient Rounding)   *Let S be a set of points in $\mathbf{R}^d$ and let G be a graph on S with $2k$th moments bounded by M. Suppose that there is a subset $S_{\text{good}} \subseteq S$ with $|S_{\text{good}}| \geq \alpha|S|$ and at least half of the pairs of points in S_{good} are connected by an edge of G. Suppose furthermore that the points of S_{good} have covariance matrix bounded by a constant multiple of the identity and mean μ_{good}. There exists a randomized algorithm that given G, S, and α*

runs in polynomial time and returns a $\widehat{\mu} \in \mathbf{R}^d$ such that with probability $\Omega(\alpha)$ it will be the case that $\|\widehat{\mu} - \mu_{\text{good}}\|_2 = O(M^{1/(2k)}\alpha^{-3/k} + 1)$.

We note that the small probability of success here is necessary. Indeed, it could be the case that G is a disjoint union of $\Omega(1/\alpha)$ cliques, one of which corresponds to S_{good}. In such a case, the algorithm will have no better recourse than to guess one of the cliques and return the sample mean.

On the other hand, this small probability of success is sufficient to obtain a list-decoding algorithm. Simply running our rounding algorithm $O(1/\alpha)$ times on the same S, G, α will produce a list of $O(1/\alpha)$ many hypotheses that with constant probability contains an element close to μ_{good}.

Proof   The rounding algorithm establishing the proposition is quite simple.

Algorithm Difference-of-Pairs-Rounding

1. Let $\delta = \alpha^3/4608$.
2. Pick a random $x \in S$.
3. Let W be the neighborhood of x in G, and let $G' = R_\delta(G)$.
4. If the number of pairs of points in W that are not connected in G' is more than $(8\delta/\alpha)|V|^2$ or if $|W| \leq (\alpha/4)|V|$, return FAIL.
5. Otherwise, run the algorithm from Lemma 6.10 on G' and W with $\gamma = (8\delta/\alpha)$ and $\beta = |W|/|V|$ to obtain W'.
6. Return $\widehat{\mu}$ as the sample mean of W'.

It is clear that this algorithm runs in polynomial time. In order to prove correctness, we claim that the algorithm succeeds as long as x satisfies the following conditions:

- $x \in S_{\text{good}}$.
- x has at least $|S_{\text{good}}|/4$ neighbors in S_{good}.
- The number of pairs of neighbors of x that are not neighbors in G' is at most $(8\delta/\alpha)|V|^2$.

First, we show that these conditions hold with probability at least $\Omega(\alpha)$. Indeed, the first condition holds with probability at least α over the choice of x. Conditioned on $x \in S_{\text{good}}$, the expected number of nonneighbors that x has in S_{good} is at most $|S_{\text{good}}|/2$. Thus, by Markov's inequality, the probability that it has more than $3|S_{\text{good}}|/4$ nonneighbors is at most $2/3$. Therefore, the first two conditions both hold with probability at least $\alpha/3$. Finally, the expected number of pairs of neighbors of x that are nonneighbors in G' is at most $\delta|V|^2$ by

Lemma 6.9. Thus, by Markov's inequality, there will be more than $(8\delta/\alpha)|V|^2$ such nonconnected neighbors with probability at most $\alpha/8$. Combining the above, all three conditions hold with probability at least $\alpha/24$.

Given these assumptions, it follows that $|W| \geq |S_{good}|/4 \geq (\alpha/4)|V|$, and at most $(8\delta/\alpha)|V|^2$ of pairs in W are not connected in G'. This implies that we pass the conditions in Line 4. Given these definitions, we have that $\gamma \leq \beta^2/36$, satisfying the assumptions of Lemma 6.10. We can write

$$|W| - |W'| \leq (6\gamma/\beta)|V| \leq (48\delta/\alpha)/(\alpha/4)|V| \leq (\alpha/24)|V|,$$

which gives $|W' \cap S_{good}| \geq |S_{good}|/4 - (\alpha/24)|V| \geq |S_{good}|/6$.

On the other hand, we know that G has $2k$th moments bounded by M by assumption. Lemma 6.8 implies that G' has moments bounded by $O(4^k M/\alpha^3)$. Applying Lemma 6.8 again implies that $R_{\beta/3}(G')$ has moments bounded by $O(16^k M/(\alpha^3\beta)) = O(16^k M/\alpha^4)$. Since W' is a clique in $R_{\beta/3}(G')$, we have by Lemma 6.6 that if $\mu_\cap$ is the sample mean of $S_{good} \cap W'$, then

$$\|\widehat{\mu} - \mu_\cap\|_2 = O(M^{1/(2k)}\alpha^{-3/k}).$$

Since $|W' \cap S_{good}| \geq |S_{good}|/6$ and since S_{good} has bounded covariance, we have that $\|\mu_\cap - \mu_{good}\|_2 = O(1)$. Combining with the above completes the proof. □

Combining the rounding algorithm with the difference-of-pairs filter gives us a list-decoding algorithm for spherical Gaussians with near-optimal error.

Theorem 6.12 *Let $d, k \in \mathbf{Z}_+$, $0 < \alpha < 1$, and $C > 0$ a sufficiently large constant. Let N be an integer larger than $(d + 1)^{Ck}/\alpha$. Let S be a collection of N points in $\mathbf{R}^d$, an α-fraction of which are i.i.d. samples from $\mathcal{N}(\mu, I)$ and the rest are chosen adversarially. There exists a randomized algorithm that given S, α, k runs in $\mathrm{poly}(N)$ time, and returns a list of $O(1/\alpha)$ hypotheses μ_i such that with constant probability $\min_i \|\mu - \mu_i\|_2 = O(\sqrt{k}\alpha^{-3/k})$.*

Proof Let $S_{good} \subset S$ be the collection of samples drawn from $\mathcal{N}(\mu, I)$. It is not hard to see that with high probability S_{good} has covariance bounded by $2I$ and mean $\tilde{\mu}$ with $\|\tilde{\mu} - \mu\|_2 = O(1)$.

We define the quadratic form on degree-k polynomials

$$Q(p) := 2\mathbf{E}[p^2(\mathcal{N}(0, 2I))].$$

It is not hard to see that with high probability over the samples we have $\mathbf{E}_{x,y \sim_u S_{good}}$ $[p^2(x - y)] \leq Q(p)$ for all p. Applying the algorithm from Lemma 6.3 to $S \times S$ and Q, with constant probability we obtain a graph G on S such that at least half of the pairs in S_{good} are connected by edges and for any degree-k polynomial

p we have $\sum_{(x,y)\in G} p^2(x-y) = O(|S|^2)Q(p)$. Applying this to the polynomial $p(x) = (v \cdot x)^k$ for unit vector v, we find that

$$\sum_{(x,y)\in G} (v \cdot (x-y))^{2k} = O(k)^{k/2}|S|^2.$$

In other words, G has $2k$th moments bounded by $M = O(k)^{k/2}$.

Running the algorithm from Proposition 6.11 gives with probability $\Omega(\alpha)$ a hypothesis $\widehat{\mu}$ such that $\|\widehat{\mu} - \tilde{\mu}\|_2 = O(M^{1/(2k)}\alpha^{-3/k}) = O(\sqrt{k}\alpha^{-3/k})$. This implies that $\|\widehat{\mu} - \mu\|_2 = O(\sqrt{k}\alpha^{-3/k})$. Running the algorithm of Proposition 6.11 $O(1/\alpha)$ times, we have a constant probability that this holds for at least one of our hypotheses. This completes the proof. □

Remark 6.13 Some remarks are in order about the algorithm of Theorem 6.12:

- Taking $k = \Theta(\log(1/\alpha))$, we obtain an algorithm with quasi-polynomial sample complexity and runtime, achieving the information-theoretically optimal error of $O(\sqrt{\log(1/\alpha)})$.
- The algorithm exhibits a trade-off between its sample complexity and its achieved error. In particular, to get error $\alpha^{-1/t}$, the algorithm requires $d^{O(t)}$ samples. There is reason to believe that this kind of trade-off is intrinsic. See Chapter 8 for more details.
- Unfortunately, the difference-of-pairs filter is a slightly inefficient way of achieving the above trade-off. Ideally, with roughly d^k samples, one can ensure that the set of inliers has bounded $2k$th central moments. By enforcing this with some kind of multifilter, one could potentially obtain a final error of $O_k(\alpha^{-1/(2k)})$ – rather than the $O_k(\alpha^{-3/k})$ achieved here. In fact, there exist more complicated algorithms for this problem in the literature that do achieve this better trade-off.
- One can straightforwardly generalize this algorithm to any distribution with bounded central moments for which the algorithm knows ahead of time all of the first $2k$ moments of $X - X'$. This latter restriction is unfortunately necessary for this approach, in order to know what quadratic form Q to use.

6.4 List-Decodable Learning via Sum of Squares

Unfortunately, the variance of polynomials method in its current form only works when one knows ahead of time exactly what the low-degree central moments of the inliers distribution are supposed to be. That is, the method is not applicable if we do not know exactly what these moments are, even if they are guaranteed to be bounded above. For example, if the clean samples are known to come from a normal distribution $\mathcal{N}(\mu, \Sigma)$, where the covariance matrix Σ is bounded but unknown, the variance of polynomials method will not work.

If we do not know the higher moments, this again leaves us with the computationally intractable question of determining whether or not the central moments of the distribution in question are actually bounded. In particular, if we have a multiset T of differences-of-pairs, we would like an efficient way to verify that for all unit vectors v it holds that $\sum_{z \in T} (v \cdot z)^{2k} \leq M|T|$. Homogenizing the latter inequality, we can equivalently ask to verify that for all vectors v we have

$$\sum_{z \in T} (v \cdot z)^{2k} \leq M|T| \|v\|_2^{2k}. \tag{6.3}$$

As already mentioned, there is evidence that given an arbitrary set T, determining whether or not Equation (6.3) holds for all v is computationally intractable. In our setting, we do not need an exact characterization of the complexity of this task. It suffices to be able to efficiently verify that Equation (6.3) holds in some practically relevant cases.

To this end, we observe that Equation (6.3) is equivalent to the polynomial inequality

$$P(v) := M|T| \|v\|_2^{2k} - \sum_{z \in T} (v \cdot z)^{2k} \geq 0.$$

A standard way to show that a polynomial is always nonnegative is by what is known as a *sum-of-squares proof*. In particular, if we can find polynomials $f_1, f_2, \ldots, f_n$ such that the identity

$$P(v) = \sum_{i=1}^{n} f_i^2(v) \tag{6.4}$$

holds, it is clear that this implies that $P(v) \geq 0$ for all v.

In particular, we give the following definition.

Definition 6.14 (SoS-Certifiable-Bounded Central Moments)   We say that a set T has $2k$th moments SoS-certifiably bounded by M if the polynomial

$$M|T| \|v\|_2^{2k} - \sum_{z \in T} (v \cdot z)^{2k}$$

can be written as a sum of squares of polynomials.

This of course leaves open the question of whether or not a set does have certifiably bounded moments; remarkably, this *can* be efficiently determined.

6.4.1 Simple Sum-of-Squares Proofs

Given a polynomial P of degree $2k$, we want to determine whether or not it is possible to write P as a sum of squares of lower-degree polynomials f_i. If this is possible, it must be the case that the f_i's are themselves polynomials of degree at most k. Indeed, if the maximum degree were d, the degree-$2d$ part of $\sum_i f_i^2$ would be the sum of the squares of the degree-d parts of the f_i's, which would necessarily be nonzero (as a sum of squares of nonzero polynomials cannot be identically zero).

Thus, our computational problem reduces to determining whether or not P can be written as a convex combination of squares of polynomials of degree at most k. We note that the latter condition is equivalent to asking whether or not there is a linear function $F \colon \{\text{Polynomials of degree at most } 2k\} \to \mathbf{R}$ such that $F(f^2) \geq 0$, for f any polynomial of degree at most k, and $F(P) < 0$. This function F is often called a *pseudo-expectation* and is denoted $\widetilde{\mathbf{E}}$. To justify this terminology, we note that if X is any distribution over $\mathbf{R}^n$, then the function $F(f) := \mathbf{E}[f(X)]$ will satisfy all the conditions except perhaps $F(P) < 0$ (it will also necessarily satisfy $F(1) = 1$, which is a commonly used normalization condition). Morally speaking, this pseudo-expectation behaves (at least as far as degree-k sum-of-squares proofs are concerned) like the expectation of f over some distribution on points where P is negative.

Fortunately, there is an efficient algorithm to determine whether or not such a pseudo-expectation exists. By definition, the desired pseudo-expectation is a linear function satisfying certain linear inequalities (namely, $\widetilde{\mathbf{E}}(f^2) \geq 0$ and $\widetilde{\mathbf{E}}[P] < 0$). If this were a *finite* set of conditions, we would have an LP that is of course solvable in polynomial time. As it stands, this is *nearly the case*. We can still hope to solve this system using the ellipsoid algorithm, so long as we have a separation oracle – that is, an algorithm that given a putative pseudo-expectation $\widetilde{\mathbf{E}}$ determines whether or not it violates one of our constraints, and if so finds such a constraint. To this end, it is easy to check whether or not $\widetilde{\mathbf{E}}[P] < 0$. The more difficult problem is to determine whether or not there is any degree at most k polynomial f such that $\widetilde{\mathbf{E}}[f^2] < 0$. However, note that $\widetilde{\mathbf{E}}[f^2]$ is just a quadratic form in f, and so a singular value decomposition allows us to efficiently determine whether or not there are any f's for which it takes negative values, and to demonstrate such an f if it exists. This gives us the desired efficient algorithm.

Remark 6.15 The above description glosses over some important technical details. In particular, in order for the ellipsoid algorithm to run in polynomial time, one needs to know that the solution (if it exists) will be appropriately bounded. Moreover, one needs to slightly relax the constraints so that the set of solutions has at least some minimal volume. These issues are usually not too difficult to work out in most cases, but they are fairly technical and will interfere with a clean presentation. We will therefore ignore these issues for the rest of this chapter, and instead assume that pseudo-expectations (when they exist) can always be efficiently computed in time poly(d^k).

6.4.2 Sum-of-Squares Proofs of Bounded Moments

To make use of a sum-of-squares proof to verify that our final sets of points have bounded central moments, it will need to be the case that the set of inliers not only have bounded central moments, but bounded central moments *provable by a sum-of-squares proof*. While this condition is not trivially satisfied, it can be shown to hold in a fairly wide variety of cases. For example, the fact that the central moments of $\mathcal{N}(0, \Sigma)$ for $\Sigma \leq I$ are bounded can be proved by a low-degree Sum-of-Squares proof. In particular, we have

$$\mathbf{E}_{X \sim \mathcal{N}(0, \Sigma)}[(v \cdot x)^{2k}] = (2k - 1)!! \, (v^{\top} \Sigma v)^k.$$

By diagonalizing Σ, we can write $v^{\top} \Sigma v$ as $\sum_{i=1}^{d} \lambda_i (v \cdot w_i)^2$, for some orthonormal basis w_i and some $0 \leq \lambda_i \leq 1$. This allows us to write $v^{\top} \Sigma v$ as a sum of squares. Similarly, the quantity $v \cdot v - v^{\top} \Sigma v = \sum_{i=1}^{d} (1 - \lambda_i)(v \cdot w_i)^2$ is also a sum of squares. This lets us write

$$(2k - 1)!!(v \cdot v)^k = (2k - 1)!!(v^{\top} \Sigma v + (v \cdot v - v^{\top} \Sigma v))^k$$

$$= (2k - 1)!! \sum_{t=0}^{k} \binom{k}{t} (v^{\top} \Sigma v)^t (v \cdot v - v^{\top} \Sigma v)^{k-t}.$$

We note that the $t = k$ term above gives $\mathbf{E}_{X \sim \mathcal{N}(0, \Sigma)}[(v \cdot x)^{2k}]$, and the other terms can be written as sums of squares. Therefore,

$$(2k - 1)!!(v \cdot v)^k - \mathbf{E}_{X \sim \mathcal{N}(0, \Sigma)}[(v \cdot x)^{2k}]$$

can be written as a sum of squares of polynomials.

The above can be easily adapted to handle the case of the empirical moments of a sufficiently large set of samples from $\mathcal{N}(0, \Sigma)$ or another distribution with SoS-certifiably bounded moments. In this case, the higher moments of the sample set will probably not exactly match the higher moments of the original distribution. However, given sufficiently many samples, with high probability the moments of the sample set will be sufficiently close that any Sum-of-Squares proofs of bounded moments will transfer over. In particular, let us assume that we have a distribution X on $\mathbf{R}^d$ with mean μ for which there exists an SoS proof that for any vector v it holds

$$\mathbf{E}[(v \cdot (X - \mu))^{2k}] \leq M(v \cdot v)^k.$$

Suppose furthermore that the $4k$th central moments of X are bounded. Let S be a set of N i.i.d. samples from X. We would like to be able to find a Sum-of-Squares proof of bounded moments for the distribution of $x - \mu$, for x chosen uniformly at random from S. To do this, we note that

$$\mathbf{E}_{x \sim_u S}[(v \cdot (x - \mu))^{2k}] = \sum_{m \text{ monomial of degree } 2k} c_m m(v) \mathbf{E}_{x \sim_u S}[m(x - \mu)].$$

where c_m is a constant depending on m between $(2k)!$ and 1. Due to the bound on the $4k$th central moments of X, we have that $m(X - \mu)$ is a distribution with bounded covariance. Thus, the empirical average of this (i.e., the average value over S) will be $\mathbf{E}[m(X - \mu)]$ plus an error with expectation $O(1/\sqrt{N})$. Thus, if N is at least a sufficiently large multiple of d^{2k} (with the constant depending on the bounds on the $4k$th moments of X), then with high probability we have that $\mathbf{E}_{x \sim_u S}[(v \cdot (x - \mu))^{2k}]$ is

$$\sum_{m \text{ monomial of degree } 2k} m(v)(\mathbf{E}[m(X - \mu)] + err_m) = \mathbf{E}[(v \cdot (X - \mu))^{2k}] + p(v),$$

where $p(v)$ is some homogeneous degree-$2k$ polynomial such that the sum of the squares of its coefficients is at most 1.

By assumption, $M(v \cdot v)^k - \mathbf{E}[(v \cdot (X-\mu))^{2k}]$ can be written as a sum of squares. We claim that $(v \cdot v)^k - p(v)$ can also be written as a sum of squares. Adding these together would imply that we can write $(M+1)(v \cdot v)^k - \mathbf{E}_{x \sim_u S}[(v \cdot (x-\mu))^{2k}]$ as a sum of squares. The proof of this fact comes from noting that we can write $p(v)$ as $(v^{\otimes k})^\top A v^{\otimes k}$, for some $d^k \times d^k$ matrix A with Frobenius norm at most 1. Since $I \succeq A$, by diagonalizing we can write $(v^{\otimes k})^\top I v^{\otimes k} - (v^{\otimes k})^\top A v^{\otimes k}$ as a sum of squares; but this is just $(v \cdot v)^k - p(v)$.

Finally, to adapt the difference-of-pairs technique to this setting, we require an SoS proof not for the uniform distribution over S, but instead for the uniform distribution over differences of pairs of points in S. In particular, given an SoS proof that

$$\mathbf{E}_{x \sim_u S}[(v \cdot (x - \mu))^{2k}] \leq M(v \cdot v)^k,$$

we want to have an SoS proof that

$$\mathbf{E}_{x,y \sim_u S}[(v \cdot (x - y))^{2k}] \leq M'(v \cdot v)^k$$

for some appropriately chosen value of M'. For this, we note that

$$(v \cdot (x-y))^{2k} = ((v \cdot (x-\mu)) + (v \cdot (y-\mu)))^{2k} \leq 4^k[(v \cdot (x-\mu))^{2k} + (v \cdot (y-\mu))^{2k}].$$

Additionally, this inequality can be expressed as a sum of squares. In fact, *any true inequality between homogeneous polynomials in two variables (in this* case, $v \cdot (x - \mu)$ and $v \cdot (y - \mu))$ can be proved by Sum-of-Squares (see Exercise 6.4(c)). This allows us to write the difference

$$2 \cdot 4^k \mathbf{E}_{x \sim_u S}[(v \cdot (x - \mu))^{2k}] - \mathbf{E}_{x,y \sim_u S}[(v \cdot (x - y))^{2k}]$$

as a sum of squares. Recalling that by assumption we have that the quantity $M(v \cdot v)^k - \mathbf{E}_{x \sim_u S}[(v \cdot (x - \mu))^{2k}]$ is a sum of squares, we have a Sum-of-Squares proof that

$$\mathbf{E}_{x,y \sim_u S}[(v \cdot (x - y))^{2k}] \leq 2 \cdot 4^k M(v \cdot v)^k.$$

6.4.3 Sum-of-Squares-Based Filter for List-Decodable Mean Estimation

In this section, we build on the machinery of the two previous sections to develop an efficient list-decodable mean estimation algorithm for distributions with SoS-certifiable low-degree moment bounds. Suppose that we have a set of samples S for which there is some subset S_{good} with $|S_{\text{good}}| \geq \alpha|S|$ and for which there is an SoS proof of bounded $2k$th central moments. We would like to develop a filter along the lines of Lemma 6.3 that removes outliers and produces a set of differences-of-pairs that does have bounded central moments.

Let $\mathcal{P}$ be the multiset of differences of elements of S and $\mathcal{P}_{\text{good}}$ the multiset of differences of elements from S_{good}. We have the following lemma.

Lemma 6.16 (SoS Difference-of-Pairs Filter)   *Let $\mathcal{P}$ be a multiset of points in $\mathbf{R}^d$ for which there exists a subset $\mathcal{P}_{\text{good}} \subset \mathcal{P}$. Furthermore, assume that for some $M > 0$ the polynomial $M(v \cdot v)^k - \mathbf{E}_{z \sim_u \mathcal{P}_{\text{good}}}[(v \cdot z)^{2k}]$ can be written as a sum of squares. Then there exists a randomized $\mathrm{poly}(d^k, |\mathcal{P}|)$-time algorithm that given $\mathcal{P}, M, k$ returns a subset $T \subseteq \mathcal{P}$ such that:*

1. *We have*

$$6M|\mathcal{P}|(v \cdot v)^k - \sum_{z \in T}(v \cdot z)^{2k} \tag{6.5}$$

   can be written as a sum of squares.
2. *With probability at least $2/3$, we have $|T \cap \mathcal{P}_{\text{good}}| \geq |\mathcal{P}_{\text{good}}|/2$.*

We note that the first condition above implies that T has bounded moments. In particular, if $\mathcal{P}$ is the set of pairwise differences from a set S, then interpreting T as a graph on S, it will have $2k$th moments bounded by $O(M)$, and we can apply Proposition 6.11 to it in order to get a list-decoding algorithm for the sample mean of S_{good}.

Proof   The algorithm is a fairly straightforward filter. We maintain a subset $T \subseteq \mathcal{P}$, initially setting $T = \mathcal{P}$. In each round, we check if (6.5) can be written as a sum of squares. If it can, we return T and are done. Otherwise, we can find a pseudo-expectation $\widetilde{\mathbf{E}}$ such that $\widetilde{\mathbf{E}}[f^2] \geq 0$ for all f, but $\widetilde{\mathbf{E}}[(6.5)] < 0$.

By the linearity of the $\widetilde{\mathbf{E}}$ operator, this means that

$$\sum_{z \in T} \widetilde{\mathbf{E}}[(v \cdot z)^{2k}] > 6M|\mathcal{P}|\widetilde{\mathbf{E}}[(v \cdot v)^k]. \tag{6.6}$$

On the other hand, we know that

$$M(v \cdot v)^{2k} - \mathbf{E}_{z \sim_u \mathcal{P}_{\text{good}}}[(v \cdot z)^{2k}]$$

can be written as a sum of squares. Applying $\widetilde{\mathbf{E}}$ and noting that $\widetilde{\mathbf{E}}$ is nonnegative on sums of squares, we have

$$M\,\widetilde{\mathbf{E}}[(v \cdot v)^{2k}] \geq \frac{1}{|\mathcal{P}_{\text{good}}|} \sum_{z \in \mathcal{P}_{\text{good}}} \widetilde{\mathbf{E}}[(v \cdot z)^{2k}] \geq \frac{\alpha^{-2}}{|\mathcal{P}|} \sum_{z \in \mathcal{P}_{\text{good}} \cap T} \widetilde{\mathbf{E}}[(v \cdot z)^{2k}],$$

where the second inequality comes from the fact that $(v \cdot z)^{2k}$ is a sum of squares, and thus $\widetilde{\mathbf{E}}[(v \cdot z)^{2k}] \geq 0$. Comparing this to Equation (6.6), we have

$$\frac{\sum_{z \in \mathcal{P}_{\text{good}} \cap T} \widetilde{\mathbf{E}}[(v \cdot z)^{2k}]}{\sum_{z \in T} \widetilde{\mathbf{E}}[(v \cdot z)^{2k}]} \leq \alpha^2/6.$$

This means that if we remove each element z from T with probability proportional to $\widetilde{\mathbf{E}}[(v \cdot z)^{2k}]$, on average only an $\alpha^2/6$-fraction of the points removed are from $\mathcal{P}_{\text{good}}$.

The pseudocode of the algorithm is as follows:

Algorithm `Difference-of-Pairs-SoS-Filter`

Input: Dataset $\mathcal{P} \subset \mathbf{R}^d$ containing an unknown subset $\mathcal{P}_{\text{good}}$ whose $2k$th moment is SoS-cerifiably bounded by M for given values k and M.

1. Let $T = \mathcal{P}$.
2. While (6.5) cannot be written as a sum of squares:
   (a) Find a pseudo-expectation $\widetilde{\mathbf{E}}$ for which $\widetilde{\mathbf{E}}[(6.5)] < 0$.
   (b) Remove each $z \in T$ with probability proportional to $\widetilde{\mathbf{E}}[(v \cdot z)^{2k}]$.
3. Return T.

For the analysis, we note that since $(v \cdot z)^{2k}$ is a sum of squares, $\widetilde{\mathbf{E}}[(v \cdot z)^{2k}] \geq 0$, so the probabilities of removing elements are well-defined. If the probabilities are properly normalized, we can ensure that the single z with largest value of $\widetilde{\mathbf{E}}[(v \cdot z)^{2k}]$ is always removed, guaranteeing that the algorithm will terminate in polynomial time. It is clear that once the algorithm terminates, (6.5) can be written as a sum of squares.

Finally, we need to analyze the size of $T \cap \mathcal{P}_{\text{good}}$. By the above analysis, the expected number of samples in $\mathcal{P}_{\text{good}}$ that are removed is at most $\alpha^2/3$ times the expected number of total samples removed. Thus, the potential function

$$\Delta = |T| + (6/\alpha^2)(|\mathcal{P}_{\text{good}}| - |\mathcal{P}_{\text{good}} \cap T|)$$

is a supermartingale. Since Δ is initially equal to $|\mathcal{P}|$ and is always nonnegative, with probability at least $2/3$, at the end of the algorithm we have $\Delta \leq 3|\mathcal{P}|$, implying that $|\mathcal{P}_{\text{good}} \cap T| \geq |\mathcal{P}_{\text{good}}|/2$. □

Combining this with Proposition 6.11 yields the following theorem.

Theorem 6.17 *Let S be a set of points in $\mathbf{R}^d$ containing a subset S_{good} with $|S_{\text{good}}| \geq \alpha|S|$ and such that S_{good} has covariance bounded by the identity and has $2k$th central moments SoS-certifiably bounded by M, for some positive integer k and $M > 0$ (i.e., the polynomial $M\|v\|_2^{2k} - \mathbf{E}_{x \sim_u S_{\text{good}}}[(v \cdot (x - \mu_{S_{\text{good}}}))^{2k}]$ can be written as a sum of squares of polynomials in v). Then there exists an algorithm that given $S, k, M,$ and α, runs in time $\text{poly}(d^k, |S|)$ and with probability $\Omega(\alpha)$ returns a $\widehat{\mu}$ with $\|\widehat{\mu} - \mu_{S_{\text{good}}}\|_2 = O(M^{1/(2k)}\alpha^{-3/k} + 1)$.*

Proof Letting $\mathcal{P}$ be the set of pairwise differences of elements of S and $\mathcal{P}_{\text{good}}$ the set of pairwise differences of points in S_{good}, we note that $|\mathcal{P}_{\text{good}}| \geq \alpha^2|\mathcal{P}|$ and for vectors v

$$
\begin{aligned}
\mathbf{E}_{x \sim_u \mathcal{P}_{\text{good}}}[(v \cdot x)^{2k}] &= \mathbf{E}_{y,y' \sim_u S_{\text{good}}}[(v \cdot (y - y'))^{2k}] \\
&\leq 4^k \mathbf{E}_{y,y' \sim_u S_{\text{good}}}[(v \cdot (y - \mu_{S_{\text{good}}}))^{2k} + (v \cdot (y' - \mu_{S_{\text{good}}}))^{2k}] \\
&\leq 2 \cdot 4^k \mathbf{E}_{y \sim_u S_{\text{good}}}[(v \cdot (y - \mu_{S_{\text{good}}}))^{2k}] \\
&\leq 2 \cdot 4^k M\|v\|_2^{2k}.
\end{aligned}
$$

Furthermore, it is not hard to see that the above can be formalized as a Sum-of-Squares proof. Therefore, $\mathcal{P}_{\text{good}}$ has $2k$th moments SoS-certifiably bounded by $2 \cdot 4^k M$. Applying the algorithm from Lemma 6.16 gives (with probability $2/3$) a graph G on S with $2k$th moments bounded by $12 \cdot 4^k M$ such that at least half of the pairs of elements of S_{good} are connected in G. Applying Proposition 6.11 completes the proof. □

6.5 Leveraging Higher Moments in Robust Mean Estimation

In this section, we show how to leverage higher moment information in "vanilla" robust mean estimation with a minority of outliers.

The fact that bounds on the higher moments imply concentration bounds can already be taken advantage of in our algorithms.

Lemma 6.18 *Let S be a set of points in $\mathbf{R}^d$ with identity covariance and with $2k$th central moments bounded by $M > 0$. Then, for any $0 < \epsilon < 1/3$, S is $(\epsilon, O(M^{1/(2k)}\epsilon^{1-1/(2k)}))$-stable.*

Proof Consider a set $T \subset S$ with $|T| \le \epsilon|S|$. We need to show that the mean of $S \setminus T$ is within δ of the mean of S, and that the variance of $S \setminus T$ in any direction is within δ^2/ϵ of 1, for some $\delta = O(M^{1/(2k)}\epsilon^{1-1/(2k)})$. For the first of these, by Lemma 6.2, it follows that if $|T| = \epsilon|S|$, then $\|\mu_T - \mu_S\|_2 = O(M^{1/(2k)}/\epsilon^{1/(2k)})$. Therefore, removing T from S changes the mean by $O(M^{1/(2k)}\epsilon^{1-1/(2k)})$.

The argument for the variance is as follows. It suffices to show that for any unit vector v we have that $\sum_{x \in T} |(v \cdot (x - \mu_S))^2 - 1| \le (\delta^2/\epsilon)|S|$. Since $|(v \cdot (x - \mu_S))^2 - 1| \le (v \cdot (x - \mu_S))^2 + 1$ and the sum over T of 1 is not too large, it suffices to bound the sum of $(v \cdot (x - \mu_S))^2$. However, by the bounded central moments property, we have

$$\sum_{x \in T} (v \cdot (x - \mu_S))^{2k} \le \sum_{x \in S} (v \cdot (x - \mu_S))^{2k} \le M|S|.$$

Applying Holder's Inequality, we have

$$\sum_{x \in T} (v \cdot (x - \mu_S))^2 \le (M|S|)^{1/k}|T|^{(k-1)/k} = M^{1/k}\epsilon^{1-1/k}|S| \le (\delta^2/\epsilon)|S|.$$

This completes the proof.   □

As a corollary of Lemma 6.18, *if* the covariance matrix of the inlier points is known, then bounded $2k$th central moments suffice for the existing universal filter to efficiently and robustly estimate the mean of the distribution to error $O(\epsilon^{1-1/(2k)})$. An immediate natural question is what happens if the covariance of the set of inliers is *unknown*.

It is not hard to see that, under the bounded moment assumption we considered, it is information-theoretically possible to learn the mean robustly within error $O(\epsilon^{1-1/(2k)})$ (see Chapter 1). In particular, suppose we have two sets of points S and S_{good} with $|S|, |S_{\text{good}}| \le (1 + \epsilon)|S \cap S_{\text{good}}|$, that is, one can obtain S from S_{good} by modifying an $O(\epsilon)$-fraction of the elements. Assume furthermore that S_{good} has bounded central moments. Then if T is any large subset of S with bounded central moments (for example, $T = S \cap S_{\text{good}}$), then the mean of T is close to the mean of S. Specifically, we have the following lemma.

Lemma 6.19 *Let T and S be sets of points in $\mathbf{R}^d$ each with $2k$th central moments bounded by M. Suppose furthermore that $|S|, |T| \le (1 + O(\epsilon))|S \cap T|$, for some $\epsilon > 0$ sufficiently small. Then we have $\|\mu_S - \mu_T\|_2 = O(M^{1/(2k)}\epsilon^{1-1/(2k)})$.*

Proof Let $R = S \cap T$. Note that $|R| = (1 - O(\epsilon))|S|$ and $|R| = (1 - O(\epsilon))|T|$. By Lemma 6.2, we have that the mean of $T \setminus R$ differs from the mean of

R by $O((M/\epsilon)^{1/(2k)})$. Therefore, $\|\mu_R - \mu_T\|_2 = O(M^{1/(2k)}\epsilon^{1-1/(2k)})$. Similarly, $\|\mu_R - \mu_S\|_2 = O(M^{1/(2k)}\epsilon^{1-1/(2k)})$. The lemma now follows from the triangle inequality. □

Lemma 6.19 implies that if we can find *any* subset $T \subseteq S$ with size $|T| = (1 - O(\epsilon))|S|$ for which T has bounded central moments, then the mean of T will be close to the mean of S_{good}. Thus, information-theoretically, the mean of S_{good} can be robustly estimated to error $O(M^{1/(2k)}\epsilon^{1-1/(2k)})$.

Similarly to the list-decodable learning setting, there is a natural way to try to build a filtering algorithm to find such a set T. We start with $T = S$. As long as T does not have appropriately bounded central moments, we find a direction v such that the central moments in the v-direction are too large, and using the knowledge of v we create a filter. The difficulty with making this idea work of course is that it may be computationally challenging to find the vector v (or even to determine whether or not one exists). Thus, once again, instead of merely requiring that our set of inliers have bounded moments, we will need to make a stronger assumption that allows us to efficiently certify that it has bounded central moments. Specifically, we will need to assume that the set of inliers has bounded central moments that can be proved via Sum-of-Squares. The following lemma shows that under this assumption there is a computationally efficient filter.

The pseudocode for this filtering algorithm is given below followed by its proof of correctness.

Algorithm SoS-Filter

Input: Dataset $S \subset \mathbf{R}^d$, and $k, M, \epsilon > 0$ such that S is an ϵ-corruption of an unknown set S_{good} with $2k$th central moments SoS-certifiably bounded by M.

1. Let $T = S$.
2. While (6.8) (found below) is not a sum of squares:
   (a) Find the (approximately) largest value M' such that

   $$M'(v \cdot v)^k|S| - \sum_{x \in T}(v \cdot (x - \mu_T))^{2k} \qquad (6.7)$$

   cannot be written as a sum of squares (this can be found via binary search).
   (b) Find a pseudo-expectation $\widetilde{\mathbf{E}}$ such that $\widetilde{\mathbf{E}}[(6.7)] < 0$.
   (c) Remove each x from T with probability proportional to

   $$\widetilde{\mathbf{E}}[(v \cdot (x - \mu_T))^{2k}].$$

3. Return T.

Proposition 6.20 *Let S and S_{good} be sets of points in $\mathbf{R}^d$, where S_{good} has 2kth central moments SoS-certifiably bounded by M, and $|S|, |S_{\text{good}}| \leq (1 + \epsilon)|S \cap S_{\text{good}}|$, for some $\epsilon > 0$ with $\epsilon \ll 1/k$. There exists a randomized algorithm running in time $\text{poly}(d^k, |S|)$ that given S and M returns a subset $T \subseteq S$ such that:*

1. The polynomial

$$2M(v \cdot v)^k|S| - \sum_{x \in T}(v \cdot (x - \mu_T))^{2k} \tag{6.8}$$

can be written as a sum of squares (i.e., T has bounded central moments provable via Sum-of-Squares).

2. With probability at least 2/3, we have $|T| \geq |S|(1 - O(\epsilon))$.

Proof The algorithm is a conceptually simple filter similar to that of Lemma 6.16. This algorithm runs in polynomial time and returns a set T such that (6.8) is a sum of squares. It remains to show that the expected value of $|T|$ is sufficiently large. In order to do this, consider the set $R = T \cap S_{\text{good}}$. We know that

$$M|S_{\text{good}}|(v \cdot v)^k - \sum_{x \in S}(v \cdot (x - \mu_{S_{\text{good}}}))^{2k}$$

can be written as a sum of squares, and therefore

$$2M|S|(v \cdot v)^k - \sum_{x \in R}(v \cdot (x - \mu_{S_{\text{good}}}))^{2k}$$

can as well.

We would like to bound the sum over $x \in R$ of $(v \cdot (x - \mu_T))^{2k}$. We know that

$$(v \cdot (x - \mu_T))^{2k} \geq (1/4)(v \cdot (x - \mu_{S_{\text{good}}}))^{2k} - k^{2k}(v \cdot v)^k \|\mu_{S_{\text{good}}} - \mu_T\|_2^{2k},$$

and it is not hard to see that the difference can be written as a sum of squares. By Lemma 6.19, since both S_{good} and T have 2kth moments bounded by M, we have that $\|\mu_{S_{\text{good}}} - \mu_T\|_2 = O((M')^{1/(2k)}\eta^{1-1/(2k)})$, where $\eta = 1 - |T \cap S_{\text{good}}|/|S_{\text{good}}|$. Thus, as long as η is sufficiently small, we have

$$8M|S|(v \cdot v)^k - \sum_{x \in R}(v \cdot (x - \mu_T))^{2k} + |S|O(k)^{2k}(M')\eta^{2k-1}(v \cdot v)^k$$

can be written as a sum of squares. In particular, so long as η is less than a sufficiently small constant multiple of $1/k$, we have

$$\sum_{x \in R}\widetilde{\mathbf{E}}[(v \cdot (x - \mu_T))^{2k}] \leq O(M')|S|\widetilde{\mathbf{E}}[(v \cdot v)^k],$$

with an arbitrarily small constant in the big-O term. On the other hand, since $\widetilde{\mathbf{E}}[(6.7)] < 0$, it must be the case that

$$\sum_{x \in T} \widetilde{\mathbf{E}}[(v \cdot (x - \mu_T))^{2k}] = \Omega(M') \, |S| \, \widetilde{\mathbf{E}}[(v \cdot v)^k].$$

Together these imply that the expected number of elements of R that are removed from T in the filter step is at most a small constant multiple of the number of elements of T that are removed. Since initially T contains only an $O(\epsilon)$-fraction of points not in S_{good}, a standard martingale argument shows that with probability at least $2/3$ the total number of removed points never exceeds $O(\epsilon)|S|$. This completes the proof. □

Combining Proposition 6.20 with Lemma 6.19, we have that the sample mean of the set returned by the algorithm in Proposition 6.20 is, with probability at least $2/3$, within distance $O(M^{1/(2k)}\epsilon^{1-1/(2k)})$ of the mean of S_{good}. Therefore, we can robustly learn the mean of a set S_{good} to error $O(\epsilon^{1-1/(2k)})$ without knowing the covariance, assuming that S_{good} has bounded $2k$th moments that can be certified by a low-degree sum-of-squares proof.

In particular, we have the following theorem.

Theorem 6.21 *Let S and S_{good} be sets of points in $\mathbf{R}^d$, where S_{good} has $2k$th central moments SoS-certifiably bounded by M, and we have that $|S|, |S_{\text{good}}| \le (1 + \epsilon)|S \cap S_{\text{good}}|$, for some $\epsilon > 0$ with $\epsilon \ll 1/k$. There exists a randomized algorithm running in time $\text{poly}(d^k, |S|)$ that given S and M returns a $\widehat{\mu}$ such that with probability at least $2/3$*

$$\|\widehat{\mu} - \mu_{S_{\text{good}}}\|_2 = O(M^{1/(2k)}\epsilon^{1-1/(2k)}).$$

6.6 Clustering Mixture Models via Higher-Degree Moments

In this section, we show how to leverage higher-degree moments for (robust) clustering of mixture models. The focus of our technical description will be on the problem of (robust) clustering uniform mixtures of identity covariance Gaussians, that is, distributions of the form $X = (1/m)\sum_{i=1}^{m} \mathcal{N}(\mu_i, I)$. Specifically, given a multiset of N points in $\mathbf{R}^d$, where a $(1 - \epsilon)$-fraction of the points are i.i.d. samples from an unknown mixture X and the remaining can be arbitrary, the goal is to split the samples into k clusters such that most of the pairs of clean samples come from the same cluster if and only if these samples came from the same component Gaussian.

For this clustering task to be information-theoretically possible, we need some sort of separation assumption. Specifically, we will assume that there exists a parameter $\Delta > 0$ such that $\|\mu_i - \mu_j\|_2 \ge \Delta$ for all $i \ne j$.

As discussed in Chapter 5, several such clustering problems can be solved using a list-decodable mean estimation algorithm. Specifically, one can attempt to cluster points based on which of the hypotheses the sample is closest to, and indeed this suffices under our separation assumptions. In this section, we develop direct algorithms for clustering using the filtering method and the Sum-of-Squares method.

6.6.1 Clustering with High-Degree Filtering

Here we show how to construct a filter for the clustering task using the difference-of-pairs technique. Let S be the set of points given to our clustering algorithm with S_i being the set of samples from the ith Gaussian component. Letting $\mathcal{P}$ be the set of pairwise differences, we can run the algorithm of either Lemma 6.3 or Lemma 6.16. We note that we can take $\mathcal{P}_{\text{good}}$ as the set of pairwise differences of samples from S_i for any i. Thus, on average, the resulting set T will contain a constant fraction of the differences of pairs of samples from the same S_i. On the other hand, it is not hard to show that T will contain relatively few pairs of samples from different clusters.

In particular, we know that for any unit vector v we have $\sum_{z \in T}(v \cdot z)^{2k} = O_k(|S|^2)$. If we let v be the unit vector in the direction of $\mu_i - \mu_j$, we note that for all but a δ-fraction of pairs $x \in S_i, y \in S_j$ we have $|v \cdot (x-y)| > \Delta - O(\sqrt{\log(1/\delta)})$. If we take δ to be such that this quantity is at least $\Delta/2$, each such pair of x, y with $(x - y)$ still in T will contribute at least $(\Delta/2)^{2k}$ to $\sum_{z \in T}(v \cdot z)^{2k}$. Therefore, the number of pairs $x \in S_i, y \in S_j$ with $(x - y) \in T$, for some given $i \neq j$, will be at most

$$O_k(|S|^2)[\Delta^{-2k} + \exp(-\Omega(\Delta^2))].$$

In other words, while a constant fraction of differences of points from the same component are kept, only a small fraction of points from different components are. If, for example, $\Delta \gg_k m^{1/(2k)}$, then most of the remaining pairs will be points from the same cluster. Given these properties, clustering will require some kind of rounding algorithm to obtain the clusters. Depending on what exactly the goal is, this could be as simple as picking a few random samples x and creating a cluster of the set of y such that $x - y$ is in T.

In this analysis, the set T only keeps a constant fraction of the differences from any given cluster. For some clustering algorithms, it may be required that we keep a larger fraction of the good samples. There are two ways one can accomplish this.

Perhaps the simplest method involves simply modifying the filtering algorithm by changing the threshold at which one is willing to terminate the algorithm. If, for example, one increases the value of C in the algorithm from

Lemma 6.3, it is not hard to see that this decreases the expected number of pairs of samples from the same cluster removed, at the expense of a corresponding increase in the bounds on the moments of the final set.

Another approach is to try to find a set T satisfying the desired moment conditions, while removing as few samples as possible. This can be done by using linear programming. Instead of letting T be a set that points are either in or out of, we instead assign a weight $w_z \in [0, 1]$ to each $z \in \mathcal{P}$. The condition on bounded central moments then becomes that for any degree k polynomial p the following holds:

$$\sum_{z \in \mathcal{P}} w_z p^2(z) \leq O(|\mathcal{P}|)Q(p). \tag{6.9}$$

We can then solve for the set of w_z's with $\sum_{z \in \mathcal{P}} w_z$ as large as possible using linear programming. In particular, we need to find a set of w_z's optimizing the linear objective $\sum_{z \in \mathcal{P}} w_z$, while satisfying the linear inequalities $0 \leq w_z \leq 1$ and (6.9) for all p. This gives us an infinite linear program, but it is not hard to find a separation oracle for it: If (6.9) is violated for some p, we can find it by linear algebra and there are only finitely many other constraints to check. Thus, we can solve for the optimal w_z's. We can then choose to let T be, for example, the set of all z's such that $w_z \geq 1/2$.

This new T will have many of the properties we desire. Since Equation (6.9) holds, it will be the case that

$$\sum_{z \in T} p^2(z) \leq O(|\mathcal{P}|)Q(p),$$

implying that T has bounded central moments. This in turn implies that we will have very few points corresponding to differences of pairs from different clusters.

Moreover, we know that the sum of the w_z's will be fairly large. In particular, letting w_z be 1 if $z = x - y$ with $x - y$ from the same cluster, and 0 otherwise satisfies Equation (6.9). Thus, the sum of the w_z's in our solution must be at least this large. Since very little weight comes from differences of pairs from different clusters and not much comes from pairs with corruptions (assuming that ϵ is substantially smaller than $1/k$), this implies that most of the pairs from the same cluster are kept.

Using these techniques, one can prove, for example, the following theorem.

Theorem 6.22 *Let X be a mixture of m equally weighted spherical Gaussians whose means are pairwise separated by at least Δ, and let k be a positive integer. There exists an algorithm that given m, k, Δ, and S, a sufficiently large number of i.i.d. samples from X runs in time* poly($|S|, d^k$) *and computes a graph*

G on S such that with high probability for $\epsilon = O_k(\Delta^{-2k} + \exp(-\Omega(\Delta^2)))$ *we have that at most an ϵ-fraction of the pairs of elements of S coming from different components of X are adjacent in G and at most an $m\epsilon$-fraction of the pairs of elements of S from the same cluster are nonadjacent in G.*

6.6.2 Clustering with Sum of Squares

In this section, we give an SoS-based algorithm for clustering mixtures of spherical Gaussians. In Section 6.6.2.1, we start by formulating our clustering problem as a nonconvex optimization problem. In Section 6.6.2.2, we show how to use sum-of-squares-based techniques to efficiently find an approximate clustering. Finally, in Section 6.6.2.3, we briefly summarize known generalizations.

6.6.2.1 Nonconvex Formulation

Given a set $x_1, x_2, \ldots, x_N$ of samples, one would like to assign most of the x_i's to one of m different groups, such that each group is roughly the same size and has low-order moments approximately matching those of a Gaussian (which will imply concentration). To state this more formally, we define weight variables $w_{i,j}$ for $1 \le i \le N$ and $1 \le j \le m$, where $w_{i,j}$ is 1 if x_i is in the jth group and 0 otherwise.

These weights would need to satisfy a number of constraints. Specifically, the fact that the $w_{i,j}$'s are binary and that each x_i is placed in at most one cluster is equivalent to the following conditions:

$$w_{i,j}(1 - w_{i,j}) = 0 \text{ for all } 1 \le i \le N \text{ and } 1 \le j \le m, \tag{6.10}$$

and

$$\sum_{j=1}^{m} w_{i,j} \le 1 \text{ for all } 1 \le i \le N. \tag{6.11}$$

To ensure that the groups are of the same size, we can add the constraint

$$\sum_{i=1}^{N} w_{i,j} = (1 - \epsilon)N/m \text{ for all } 1 \le j \le k. \tag{6.12}$$

Finally, to enforce that the central moments in each cluster agree with the central moments of a Gaussian, we can add the constraint:

$$-\delta \le \mathbf{E}[p(\mathcal{N}(0, 2I))] - [(1 - \epsilon)N/m]^{-2} \sum_{i,i'=1}^{N} w_{i,j} w_{i',j} p(x_i - x_{i'}) \le \delta, \tag{6.13}$$

for all monomials p of degree at most $2k$ and all $1 \le j \le m$.

Now suppose that a $(1 - \epsilon)$-fraction of these samples x_i came from a mixture of separated Gaussians. We will show that the clusters produced by a solution to the above system must correspond reasonably well to the original clustering. In fact, it can be shown that for each j, almost all of the nonzero $w_{i,j}$'s come from a single cluster.

Lemma 6.23 *Let $x_1, \ldots, x_N \in \mathbf{R}^d$. Let $S, T \subseteq [N]$ be such that the set $\{x_i : i \in S\}$ matches its first $2k$ moments with $\mathcal{N}(\mu_S, I)$ for some $\mu_S \in \mathbf{R}^d$, and $\{x_i : i \in T\}$ matches its first $2k$ moments with $\mathcal{N}(\mu_T, I)$ for some $\mu_S \in \mathbf{R}^d$ with $\|\mu_S - \mu_T\|_2 > \Delta$. Suppose that in addition we have $w_{i,j}$'s satisfying the relations above. Then, for any j we have*

$$\left(\sum_{i \in S} w_{i,j} \right) \left(\sum_{i \in T} w_{i,j} \right) \leq N^2 O(\sqrt{k}/\Delta)^{2k} + N^2 d^k \delta.$$

In particular, this shows that the jth cluster cannot have both many points from S and many points from T. If additionally the x_i's can be partitioned into k such sets, each cluster will contain almost entirely points from a single one of these sets, and therefore the learned clusters will correspond fairly well to the original sets.

Proof Let v be the unit vector in the direction of $\mu_S - \mu_T$. Let $S' = \{i \in S : |v \cdot (x_i - \mu_S)| < \Delta/3\}$ and $T' = \{i \in T : |v \cdot (x_i - \mu_T)| < \Delta/3\}$. Since S matches $2k$ moments with $\mathcal{N}(\mu_S, I)$, we have that the average value over $i \in S$ of $|v \cdot (x_i - \mu_S)|^{2k}$ is equal to $(2k - 1)!!$. Therefore, the number of i in S not in S' is at most $O(\sqrt{k}/\Delta)^{2k}N$. Similarly, we have that $|T \setminus T'| = O(\sqrt{k}/\Delta)^{2k}N$.

The above implies that

$$\left(\sum_{i \in S} w_{i,j} \right) \left(\sum_{i \in T} w_{i,j} \right) \leq O(\sqrt{k}/\Delta)^{2k}N^2 + \left(\sum_{i \in S'} w_{i,j} \right) \left(\sum_{i \in T'} w_{i,j} \right).$$

Let $p(x) = (v \cdot x)^{2k}$. Writing p as a linear combination of monomials (with sum of coefficients at most d^k), we find that

$$[(1 - \epsilon)N/m]^{-2} \sum_{i,i'=1}^{N} w_{i,j} w_{i',j} p(x_i - x_{i'}) \leq \mathbf{E}[p(\mathcal{N}(0, 2I))] + d^k \delta.$$

On the other hand, we have

$$\sum_{i,i'=1}^{N} w_{i,j} w_{i',j} p(x_i - x_{i'}) \geq \sum_{i \in S', i' \in T'} w_{i,j} w_{i',j} (\Delta/3)^{2k} = (\Delta/3)^{2k} \left(\sum_{i \in S} w_{i,j} \right) \left(\sum_{i \in T} w_{i,j} \right).$$

Combining with the above completes the proof of the lemma. $\qquad\square$

Lemma 6.23 shows that if our data includes k clusters of points whose low-order moments mimic those of separated Gaussians, it suffices for our algorithm to find weights $w_{i,j}$ that satisfy the above properties. Unfortunately, this is a computationally challenging task to accomplish directly. It is particularly challenging in that it is a discrete and nonconvex optimization problem. In order to efficiently find appropriate weights, we are going to need to develop an appropriate relaxation of the problem. This can be accomplished in a convenient way with sum of squares.

6.6.2.2 Clustering Mixtures of Spherical Gaussians via Sum-of-Squares

We will require some additional background on Sum-of-Squares proof systems. If one wants to show that a single polynomial f is everywhere nonnegative, one can try (as discussed in Section 6.4) to write it as a sum of squares. This suffices for unconstrained optimization problems. The constrained case is somewhat more subtle. Suppose we have a collection of polynomials $g_1, g_2, \ldots,$ g_n and want to know if $f(x)$ is nonnegative whenever all of the $g_i(x)$ are nonnegative. A natural generalization of writing f as a sum of squares would be to instead write f in the form:

$$f(x) = \sum_i h_i^2(x) + \sum_{i,j} h_{i,j}^2(x) g_j(x) \tag{6.14}$$

for some polynomials $h_i, h_{i,j}$. It is clear that if f can be written in the form of (6.14), it must be the case that $f(x)$ is nonnegative whenever all of the $g_j(x)$ are nonnegative. The more important question is whether we can determine whether or not it is possible to express f in the form given by (6.14). As in Section 6.4, one can attempt to do this by using linear programming, to find what is known as a "dual pseudo-expectation." Unfortunately, this comes with a restriction. In particular, for the analysis in Section 6.4, we showed that none of the h_i's needed to be degree more than $\deg(f)/2$. This allowed us to define a pseudo-expectation only on low-degree polynomials. This trick will not work here.

To deal with this issue, we will need to artificially restrict the degree. We say that we have a sum-of-squares proof of degree-t of the statement ($g_j(x) \geq 0$ for all j implies $f(x) \geq 0$) if f can be written as in Equation (6.14) for some polynomials h_i and $h_{i,j}$ with $\deg(h_i^2), \deg(h_{i,j}^2 g_j) \leq t$ for all i, j. This problem does have a tractable dual. In particular, such a sum-of-squares proof exists unless there exists a pseudo-expectation $\widetilde{\mathbf{E}}$, that is a linear function from the set of polynomials of degree at most t to $\mathbf{R}$, such that:

$$\widetilde{\mathbf{E}}[h^2(x)] \geq 0 \text{ for all polynomials } h \text{ of degree at most } t/2, \qquad (6.15)$$

$$\widetilde{\mathbf{E}}[h^2(x)g_j(x)] \geq 0 \text{ for all polynomials } h \text{ and all } j \text{ so that } \deg(h^2 g_j) \leq t,$$
$$\qquad (6.16)$$

$$\widetilde{\mathbf{E}}[f(x)] < 0. \qquad (6.17)$$

Fortunately, the ellipsoid algorithm *can* be used to determine whether or not such a pseudo-expectation exists, and exhibit one if it does.

In most concrete settings, we will often not even use this full system. We will often just search for a pseudo-expectation satisfying Equations (6.15) and (6.16) along with $\widetilde{\mathbf{E}}[1] = 1$. This will morally behave somewhat like an expectation over points x such that $g_j(x) \geq 0$ for all j. More precisely, for any polynomial f for which there is a degree at most t sum-of-squares proof that $g_j(x) \geq 0$ implies $f(x) \geq 0$, we will have $\widetilde{\mathbf{E}}[f] \geq 0$.

Sum-of-squares proofs of this form are a powerful tools in computer science, allowing one to solve (at least in terms of a pseudo-expectation) or disprove complicated polynomial systems. Generally, increasing the degree of the sum-of-squares proof will increase its power, but at the cost of runtime, as solving a degree-t sum-of-squares proof system will require time polynomial in d^t.

We now explain how the above can be used in our clustering setting. Suppose that we are in the setting of Lemma 6.23. We can solve for a pseudo-expectation using the $w_{i,j}$ as variables and with constraints given by Equations (6.10) through (6.13). If our data consists of k clusters of points whose first $2k$-moments mimic those of Gaussians with means separated by at least Δ, we know that a solution to these equations exists, and therefore so does a pseudo-expectation for our algorithm to find. Furthermore, it is not hard to see that Lemma 6.23 can be proven by a sum-of-squares proof of degree at most $2k$ (at least if k is a power of 2, see Exercise 6.4(f)). Specifically, if we have two real clusters given by S and T, then for some sufficiently large constant $C > 0$, the polynomial

$$N^2(C\sqrt{k}/\Delta)^{2k} + N^2 d^k \delta - \left(\sum_{i \in S} w_{i,j}\right)\left(\sum_{i \in T} w_{i,j}\right)$$

can be written as a sum of terms of the form h^2 with $\deg(h) \leq k$ or $h^2 g$ with $\deg(h^2 g) \leq 2k$ and $g \geq 0$ one of our constraints. In particular, since $\widetilde{\mathbf{E}}[h^2], \widetilde{\mathbf{E}}[h^2 g] \geq 0$, our pseudo-expectation will satisfy

$$\widetilde{\mathbf{E}}\left[\left(\sum_{i \in S} w_{i,j}\right)\left(\sum_{i \in T} w_{i,j}\right)\right] \leq N^2 O(\sqrt{k}/\Delta)^{2k} + N^2 d^k \delta.$$

Making use of Equation (6.12), it is not hard to see that we will have

$$\widetilde{\mathbf{E}}\left[w_{i_0,j}\left(\sum_{i \in T} w_{i,j}\right)\right] = (1 - \epsilon)N/k\widetilde{\mathbf{E}}[w_{i_0,j}].$$

This means that if we find i_0 for which $\widetilde{\mathbf{E}}[w_{i_0,j}]$ is reasonably large, then the average value of $\widetilde{\mathbf{E}}[w_{i_0,j}w_{i,j}]$ over various i's will be fairly large, but the total value over i's in different clusters likely will not be. This means that this pseudo-expectation can be used to cluster.

More precisely, we have the following result.

Theorem 6.24   *Let X be a mixture of m equally weighted spherical Gaussians whose means are pairwise separated by at least Δ, and let k be a power of 2. Let $\{x_i\}$ be a set of N i.i.d. samples from X for some N sufficiently large. Let $\widetilde{\mathbf{E}}$ be a degree-2k pseudo-expectation with variables $w_{i,j}$ for $1 \leq i \leq N$ and $1 \leq j \leq m$ satisfying Equations (6.10)–(6.13) and $\widetilde{\mathbf{E}}[1] = 1$. Construct the graph G on $[N]$, where there is an edge between vertices i and i' if and only if*

$$\widetilde{\mathbf{E}}\left[\sum_{j=1}^{m} w_{i,j}w_{i',j}\right] > 1/2.$$

Then with high probability over our samples, the fraction of pairs of elements (x_i, x_j) from different components of X that are adjacent in G is at most

$$O(\sqrt{k}/\Delta)^{2k} + d^k\delta,$$

and the fraction of such pairs from the same component of X that are not adjacent in G is at most

$$mO(\sqrt{k}/\Delta)^{2k} + md^k\delta + \epsilon.$$

6.6.2.3 Clustering General Mixture Models via Sum of Squares

The application given above for sum of squares for clustering is fairly simple. Essentially, considering the matrix with entries $\widetilde{\mathbf{E}}\left[\sum_j w_{i,j}w_{i',j}\right]$ gives us something with similar properties to what can be obtained using filtering techniques for this problem. As we have already mentioned, the advantage of sum of squares is in its flexibility.

More generally, given *any* clustering problem one can determine some polynomial inequalities that ought to be satisfied by the correct clustering, and then search for a pseudo-expectation that satisfies these inequalities. Then, if there are any properties of the clustering that can be established from the constraints via a low-degree sum-of-squares proof, the pseudo-expectation will also satisfy these properties. We are particularly interested in properties like the one in Lemma 6.23 that says that the clustering found by the pseudo-expectation corresponds in some sense to the true clustering.

This method has several applications, many of them too technical to develop in detail here. One particularly nice example is the following: Let m be an integer and let $\epsilon > 0$ be less than some sufficiently small constant c_m. Let $X = (1/m) \sum_{i=1}^{m} G_i$ be an equally weighted mixture of m (not-necessarily spherical) Gaussians in $\mathbf{R}^d$ such that these Gaussian components are pairwise separated (in particular, $d_{\text{TV}}(G_i, G_j) \geq 1 - \epsilon$ for all $i \neq j$). One is then given N samples, a $(1 - \epsilon)$-fraction of which are drawn i.i.d. from X. One can then attempt to find some clustering of these points such that the low-degree moments of the points from each cluster approximately agree with the corresponding moments of some Gaussian. It can be shown that these constraints imply via a sum-of-squares proof of degree $O_m(1)$ that the clustering found mostly agrees with the true clustering on points (i.e., assigning the points drawn from each component of X to their own cluster). With additional work, one can show that for some sufficiently large constant C_m, as long as $N > (d/\epsilon)^{C_m}$, there exists an algorithm that runs in time poly(N) and with high probability returns a distribution $\tilde{X}$ such that $d_{\text{TV}}(\tilde{X}, X) < \epsilon^{1/C_m}$.

In particular, we get the following result.

Theorem 6.25 *Let X be an equally weighted mixture of m Gaussians in $\mathbf{R}^d$ and C_m a sufficiently large constant. Suppose that any two components of X have total variation distance at least $1 - 1/C_m$. Let $k > C_m$ be an integer and let ϵ, δ be sufficiently small. Let $x_1, x_2, \ldots, x_N$ be i.i.d. samples from X and consider the system of inequalities in the variables $w_{i,j}$, for $1 \leq i \leq N$ and $1 \leq j \leq m$, and μ_j, Σ_j, for $1 \leq j \leq m$, satisfying Equations (6.10)–(6.12) and*

$$\left[\mathbf{E}[p(\mathcal{N}(\mu_j, \Sigma_j))] - [(1 - \epsilon)N/m]^{-2} \sum_{i,i'=1}^{N} w_{i,j} w_{i',j} p(x_i - x_{i'}) \right]^2$$
$$\leq \delta \mathbf{Var}[p(\mathcal{N}(\mu_j, \Sigma_j))]$$

for all polynomials p of degree at most $2k$.

Letting $\tilde{\mathbf{E}}$ be a pseudo-expectation (of degree $4k$) for the above system with $\tilde{\mathbf{E}}[1] = 1$, then with high probability over the samples such a $\tilde{\mathbf{E}}$ exists and if G is the graph on $[N]$ connecting i and i' if and only if

$$\tilde{\mathbf{E}}\left[\sum_{j=1}^{m} w_{i,j} w_{i',j} \right] > 1/2,$$

then for 99% of the pairs i, i' with x_i and $x_{i'}$ taken from the same cluster of X, the edge (i, i') is in G, and these comprise at least 99% of the edges of G.

6.7 Exercises

6.1 (Second Moment List-Decoding Counterexample) Show that if S is a set of points in $\mathbf{R}^d$ with $\mathbf{E}[S] = \mu$, $\mathbf{Cov}[S] \preceq I$, and $\alpha > 0$, there exists a superset of points $T \supset S$ in $\mathbf{R}^d$ with $|S| \ge \alpha|T|$, $\mathbf{Cov}[T] \preceq I$ and $\|\mu - \mathbf{E}[T]\|_2 = \Omega(1/\sqrt{\alpha})$. Note that a list-decoding algorithm that only checks for second moments will, when given T, produce an error of $\Omega(1/\sqrt{\alpha})$.

6.2 (Higher Moments Multifilter) Here we lay out in detail the rough algorithm from Section 6.2.2.

(a) Suppose S is a set containing a subset S_{good} with $|S_{\text{good}}| \ge \alpha|S|$, for some $1/2 > \alpha > 0$ and S_{good} having $2k$th central moments bounded by M. Suppose furthermore that one is given a unit vector v such that

$$\mathbf{E}_{x \sim_u S}[|v \cdot (x - \mu_S)|^{2k}] > M\alpha^{-1} \log^{C_k}(1/\alpha)$$

for C_k some sufficiently large constant. Devise an algorithm that given S, v, k, M, α computes at most two subsets $S_i \subset S$ such that:

- $\sum_i |S_i|^2 < |S|^2$.
- For at least one value of i, we have that (in expectation) $|S_{\text{good}} \setminus S_i| < (\alpha/2)|S \setminus S_i|$.

(b) Show that using the above algorithm and an oracle that given a set S determines the unit vector v maximizing $\sum_{x \in S}(v \cdot (x - \mu_S))^{2k}$, one can solve the list-decodable mean estimation problem when the set of inliers has $2k$th central moments bounded by M achieving error $\tilde{O}_k(M^{1/(2k)}\alpha^{-1/k})$.

6.3 (Sample Complexity for the Variance of Polynomials Filter) Show that, for some $N = \text{poly}((dk)^k)$, given a set S of N i.i.d. samples from $\mathcal{N}(0, I_d)$ with high probability for all degree at most d polynomials p, we have $\mathbf{E}_{x,y \sim_u S}[p^2(x - y)] < 2\mathbf{E}_{z \sim \mathcal{N}(0,2I_d)}[p^2(z)]$. Furthermore, show that this is not true if $N < d^{k/4}$.

6.4 (Basic Techniques for Sum-of-Squares Proofs) Here we discuss some basic techniques for proving inequalities by sum of squares.

(a) **Transitivity** Let $A \ge_{SoS} B$ denote that $A - B$ can be written as a sum of squares of polynomials. Show that if $A \ge_{SoS} B$ and $B \ge_{SoS} C$, then $A \ge_{SoS} C$.

(b) **Composability** Show that if $A \ge_{SoS} A'$ and $B \ge_{SoS} B'$ in the notation above, then $A + B \ge_{SoS} A' + B'$. Show that if additionally we have that $A', B' \ge_{SoS} 0$, then $AB \ge_{SoS} A'B'$.

(c) **One-variable Inequalities** Show that if f is a polynomial in one variable or a homogeneous polynomial in two variables that is nonnegative for all real inputs, then $f \geq_{SoS} 0$.
(Hint: Try factoring f.)

(d) **Triangle Inequality** Show that for any positive even integer k we have $2^{k-1}(x^k + y^k) \geq_{SoS} (x + y)^k$.

(e) **Cauchy-Schwartz** Show that $\left(\sum_{i=1}^n x_i^2\right)\left(\sum_{i=1}^n y_i^2\right) \geq_{SoS} \left(\sum_{i=1}^n x_i y_i\right)^2$.

(f) **Holder's Inequality** Show that if t is a power of 2, then the sum-of-squares proof system using the constraints $w_i = w_i^2$ and degree $2t$ can prove

$$\left(\sum_{i=1}^n w_i x_i\right)^t \leq \left(\sum_{i=1}^n w_i\right)^{t-1}\left(\sum_{i=1}^n x_i^t\right).$$

(Hint: Prove this by induction on t.)
Note: This inequality is particularly useful since it says that if the tth moment of the x_i's is bounded, then the sum of any small number of them will not be too big. In other words, this is a sum-of-squares proof of the fact that a distribution with bounded tth moments satisfies good concentration bounds.

6.5 (SoS Proofs of Bounded Central Moments) Here we will prove that some common distributions have SoS-certifiable bounded central moments.

(a) Let X be the uniform distribution over $\{0, 1\}^d$. Give a sum-of-squares proof that the $2k$th central moments of X are bounded by $O(k)^k$.

(b) Let X be a mixture of Gaussians with means $\|\mu_i\|_2 \leq 1$ and covariances $\Sigma_i \preceq I$. Give a sum-of-squares proof that the $2k$th central moments of X are bounded by $O(k)^k$.

6.6 (Clustering Mixtures of Separated Gaussians) Here we will consider Gaussian mixture models of the form $X = (G_1 + G_2)/2$, where $G_i = \mathcal{N}(\mu_i, \Sigma_i)$ is a d-dimensional Gaussian. Our goal will be given samples from X to cluster them based on which G_i the sample came from. We note that this is information-theoretically impossible unless we assume some separation, namely: $d_{\mathrm{TV}}(G_1, G_2) > 1 - \delta$ for some small $\delta > 0$.

(a) First, we need to understand what the separation assumption means. Show that $d_{\mathrm{TV}}(G_1, G_2) > 1 - \delta$ implies that one of the following holds:

– There exists a unit vector v such that

$$\mathbf{Var}(v \cdot G_1) + \mathbf{Var}(v \cdot G_2) = o_\delta(|v \cdot (\mu_1 - \mu_2)|^2),$$

that is, the means are separated in some direction.

– There exists a unit vector v such that either it holds that $\mathbf{Var}(v \cdot G_1) = o_\delta(\mathbf{Var}(v \cdot G_2))$ or we have $\mathbf{Var}(v \cdot G_2) = o_\delta(\mathbf{Var}(v \cdot G_1))$, that is, the covariance matrices are spectrally separated.

– $\left\| (\Sigma_1 + \Sigma_2)^{-1/2}(\Sigma_1 - \Sigma_2)(\Sigma_1 + \Sigma_2)^{-1/2} \right\|_F = \omega_\delta(1)$, that is, the covariances are far apart in relative Frobenius norm.

In the above, $o_\delta(x)$ denotes that the implied constant goes to 0 with δ and $\omega_\delta(x)$ means that the implied constant goes to ∞ as δ goes to 0. Note that it is also not hard to show that if any of the above hold with sufficiently large/small constants, this implies that $d_{\mathrm{TV}}(G_i, G_j) > 1 - \delta$.

(b) Let t be a sufficiently large constant and let $S = \{x_1, x_2, \ldots, x_N\}$ be a sufficiently large set of samples drawn i.i.d. from X. Suppose that S is split into two subsets, each with approximately $N/2$ elements, and each having t moments nearly agreeing with those of some Gaussian. Show using a sum-of-squares proof that each subset must have at least 99% of its points coming from a single Gaussian component.

(Hint: Use a different proof for each case of part (a).)

(c) Develop a sum-of-squares relaxation for the problem of splitting S into subsets. Show how to round any pseudo-expectation into an actual clustering of the points.

(d) Show how to make the clustering algorithm above work, even if a small constant fraction of the points of S are adversarially corrupted.

(Hint: If you ensure that each cluster approximately matches $2t$ moments with a Gaussian, this will imply, by something along the lines of Lemma 2.6, that the nonerroneous samples in the cluster approximately match t moments, and the argument from part (c) should apply when considering just the good points in each cluster.)

6.8 Discussion and Related Work

One of the earliest applications of high-degree methods in robust statistics involved applications to the list-decodable mean estimation problem as discussed in this chapter. In particular, the variance of polynomials technique was introduced in [65] and was first applied to the problem of list-decoding the mean of a spherical Gaussian. The original paper [65] develops a multifilter for this regime. A major technical hurdle in that work comes from the fact that the variance of degree at least two polynomials is a function of the unknown mean. To deal with this issue, [65] develops fairly complicated machinery. The difference-of-pairs technique presented in this chapter greatly simplifies this result. We note that the difference-of-pairs technique is new, as are its applications to list-decoding and robust mean estimation. The difference-of-pairs technique was leveraged to obtain efficient algorithms for list-decodable sparse mean estimation in [51].

Two independent and concurrent works [92, 112] initiated the use of the sum-of-squares method to leverage higher-order moments in robust statistics. Specifically, [92] gave robust algorithms for mean estimation under higher-moment assumptions as well as robust clustering of spherical Gaussians and other structured distributions. In addition to these tasks, [112] gave SoS-based algorithms for list-decodable mean estimation. More recently, [52] leveraged the SoS method to develop efficient algorithms for robust sparse mean estimation with near-optimal error in the unknown covariance regime. It should be noted that these works used the SoS method to construct a single semi-definite program (SDP) and a rounding scheme that directly yields the desired solution. In contrast, in this chapter, we use SoS only for the certification step and combine it with a filtering technique to find a solution. This SoS-based filtering method is new to this chapter.

Since the dissemination of [65, 92, 112], the variance of polynomials and sum-of-squares methods have been used to develop robust learners for a range of learning tasks. These include supervised PAC learning of geometric concepts [64], list-decodable linear regression [106, 130] learning more general mixture models [6, 7, 8, 43, 104, 118], and list-decodable covariance estimation [98]. Focusing on mixture models, the works [6, 8, 43] gave SoS-based algorithms for learning uniform mixtures of separated (not necessarily spherical) Gaussians. Subsequently, [7, 104, 118] developed algorithms for arbitrary Gaussian mixtures. In more detail, [104] gave the first efficient robust learner for the case of two components with equal weights; [118] gave an efficient algorithm for any constant number of components with certain assumptions on the weights and covariances; and [7] gave a robust learning algorithm for the general case, that is, robustly learning a mixture of any constant number of Gaussians in total variation distance.

It is also worth mentioning two recent works [49, 117] leveraging high-degree moments for learning mixture models. Specifically, [49] developed a framework motivated by algebraic geometry that leads to quasi-polynomial time density estimation algorithms for a range of mixture models, including mixtures of identity covariance Gaussians. More recently, [117] gave the first polynomial-time algorithm for mixtures of identity covariance Gaussians under near-optimal separation assumptions. Even though these works do not rely on a robust statistics framework, they share many ideas with these high-degree methods from robust statistics.

We conclude by noting that our description of the sum-of-squares method in this chapter is somewhat informal and focusing explicitly on robust statistics applications. For a systematic development of this topic, the reader is referred to [77] and the lecture notes [13]. For an overview of the sum-of-squares method in high-dimensional estimation, the reader is referred to [89, 129].

7

Robust Supervised Learning

7.1 Introduction

Throughout this book, we have so far focused on robust algorithms for unsupervised learning problems, that is, problems about learning some parameters like the mean or covariance of a distribution. In this chapter, we illustrate how the algorithmic ideas developed in this book can be applied to supervised problems as well. At a high level, supervised learning is the task of inferring a function from a set of labeled observations. The usual setting for supervised learning is that one observes pairs (x, y) drawn i.i.d. from some joint distribution satisfying certain properties, generally with the conceit that $y \approx f(x)$ for some function f that the algorithm wishes to learn. There has been an extensive amount of work on "robust" algorithms on supervised learning, for various noise models. The separation of the inputs into x and y "coordinates" allows for more complicated families of noise models. For example, one standard family of contamination models assumes that the adversary cannot corrupt the points x, but is allowed to corrupt the labels y in various ways (randomly, adversarially, or a combination thereof). In this chapter, we will focus on the strong contamination model that allows an ϵ-fraction of the (x, y) pairs to be corrupted arbitrarily.

In this chapter, we will study three main problems. First, we will discuss the problem of linear regression in a fairly simple setting (Section 7.2). Next we will consider the binary classification problem of learning halfspaces (Section 7.3). Finally, we will consider a substantial generalization of these problems and look into algorithms for robust stochastic optimization (Section 7.4).

One theme that runs through this chapter is that the algorithms for these supervised learning problems usually work by reducing them to the unsupervised problem of robustly learning some relevant parameter of the joint distribution over (x, y). Interestingly, while the initial approximation to this parameter is often not strong enough for what we need, it can often be improved by some kind of iterative method, using the first rough approximation to get better and better approximations to the desired parameter.

7.2 Outlier-Robust Algorithms for Linear Regression

Linear regression is arguably the prototypical supervised learning task. In the nonrobust setting, we are given i.i.d. samples of the form $(X, y) \in \mathbf{R}^{d+1}$ with the guarantee that $y = \beta \cdot X + \xi$ for some unknown vector $\beta \in \mathbf{R}^d$ (sometimes referred to as the "regressor" vector) and a zero-mean random variable $\xi \in \mathbf{R}$ modeling observation noise. It is typical to assume that ξ is independent of X. That is, y is a linear function of X up to some random noise. In the most fundamental setting, the covariate (i.e. the random vector $X \in \mathbf{R}^d$) is drawn from a standard Gaussian distribution $\mathcal{N}(0, I)$. For simplicity, in this section, we will focus on the Gaussian covariate case as well. The goal is to learn a good approximation to β in an appropriate metric (usually L^2).

In the above vanilla setting (without outliers), the classical least-squares estimator is sample-optimal and computationally efficient. In the outlier-robust setting, we want to be able to approximate β in the presence of an ϵ-fraction of arbitrary outliers, for some constant $\epsilon < 1/2$. That is, we are given an ϵ-corrupted set of labeled samples where the inliers are drawn from the above joint distribution (X, y) and the outliers are arbitrary.

Here we will focus on the simplest possible setting where $X \sim \mathcal{N}(0, I)$ is a standard Gaussian and $\xi \sim \mathcal{N}(0, \sigma^2)$ is a centered Gaussian independent of X. The following basic fact motivates our approach.

Fact 7.1 *Under the above assumptions, the joint distribution on (X, y) is a Gaussian on $\mathbf{R}^{d+1}$ with covariance matrix* $\begin{bmatrix} I & \beta^\top \\ \beta & \sigma^2 + \|\beta\|_2^2 \end{bmatrix}$.

Given Fact 7.1, it is easy to see that we can apply our robust covariance estimation algorithm from Chapter 4 to approximate β within ℓ_2-error of at most $O(\epsilon \log(1/\epsilon)\sigma)$. We note that this reduction to covariance estimation will at best lead to an algorithm with sample complexity $\Omega(d^2/\epsilon^2)$, since this is an information-theoretic lower bound for robust covariance estimation. Moreover, the approach is essentially restricted to Gaussian covariates.

In this section, we will present an algorithm that achieves similar error guarantees, and has two additional advantages: First, it can be implemented to work with $\tilde{O}(d/\epsilon^2)$ samples. Second, it can be easily extended to linear regression problems in somewhat greater generality.

7.2.1 Reduction to Robust Mean Estimation

At a high level, our robust learning algorithm is inspired by ordinary least-squares regression. The key observation is that

$$\mathbf{E}[yX] = \mathbf{E}[X(X^\top\beta + \xi)] = \mathbf{E}[XX^\top]\beta = \beta,$$

where we used the facts $\mathbf{Cov}[X] = I$ and ξ is independent of X.

Thus, our problem of robust linear regression can be reduced to the problem of robust mean estimation for the random variable yX.

Recalling our robust mean estimation algorithms from Chapter 2, it suffices to show that (sufficiently many) i.i.d. samples drawn from yX will satisfy an appropriate stability condition (with high probability). To achieve this, we begin by computing the covariance matrix of yX. Here one gets a multiple of the covariance of X in directions orthogonal to β with something more complicated going on in the β-direction. In particular, we have

$$\mathbf{E}[(yX)(yX)^\top] = \mathbf{E}[y^2 XX^\top] = \mathbf{E}[((\beta \cdot X)^2 + 2(\beta \cdot X)\xi + \xi^2)XX^\top]$$
$$= \mathbf{E}[(\beta \cdot X)^2 XX^\top] + \sigma^2 \mathbf{E}[XX^\top] = \mathbf{E}[(\beta \cdot X)^2 XX^\top] + \sigma^2 I.$$

To compute the expectation of $(\beta \cdot X)^2 XX^\top$, we proceed as follows: If the vector w is orthogonal to β, then $\mathbf{E}[(w \cdot X)^2(\beta \cdot X)^2] = \|w\|_2^2\|\beta\|_2^2$. On the other hand, if v is parallel to β and w is orthogonal, then we have $\mathbf{E}[(\beta \cdot X)^2(v \cdot X)(w \cdot X)] = 0$, since $w\cdot X$ is independent of the other terms. Finally, if v is a unit vector parallel to β, then $\mathbf{E}[(\beta \cdot X)^2(v \cdot X)^2] = \|\beta\|_2^2 \mathbf{E}[(v \cdot X)^4] = 3\|\beta\|_2^2$. Therefore, we have $\mathbf{E}[(yX)(yX)^\top] = (\sigma^2 + \|\beta\|_2^2)I + 2\beta\beta^\top$, which gives

$$\mathbf{Cov}[yX] = (\sigma^2 + \|\beta\|_2^2)I + \beta\beta^\top.$$

Unfortunately, the β-dependence in this covariance matrix implies that we do not have any a priori bound on the stability. To obtain such a bound, we need to assume some upper bound on the ℓ_2-norm of β. In particular, if we assume that $\|\beta\|_2 \leq B$, for some parameter B, then we get that the covariance matrix of the random variable yX/σ is bounded above (in Loewner ordering) by $O(1 + B/\sigma)^2 I$. Recalling the stability bound for bounded covariance distributions (Proposition 3.9), we have that $\tilde{O}(d/\epsilon)$ i.i.d. samples from yX/σ contain a large subset that is $(\epsilon, O(\sqrt{\epsilon}(1 + B/\sigma)))$-stable with respect to $\beta/\sigma = \mathbf{E}[yX/\sigma]$ with high probability. Thus, our standard robust mean estimation algorithm, applied to yX/σ, is sufficient to learn the mean of yX (i.e., the target vector β) to ℓ_2-error of $O(\sqrt{\epsilon}(\sigma + B))$.

The latter guarantee is quite far from the information-theoretic optimal error. Indeed, it is not difficult to show (see Exercise 7.2) that in our setting there exists an (inefficient) algorithm with error $O(\epsilon\sigma)$, and that this is best possible to within a constant factor. That is, the error bound of $O(\sqrt{\epsilon}(\sigma + B))$ is both quantitatively suboptimal (as a function of ϵ) and – more importantly – qualitatively suboptimal, as it scales with the parameter B. If we are only given a weak a priori bound B on the size of β, the final error to which we can robustly learn β will be quite high.

7.2.2 Removing the B-Dependence

A natural way to remove the B-dependence is via an iterative approach. The idea is to use the approximation $\widehat{\beta}$ that we learned in the first step and compute the residuals $y' = y - \widehat{\beta} \cdot X$. Note that $y' = \beta' \cdot X + \xi$, where $\beta' = \beta - \widehat{\beta}$. This allows us to reduce the problem of learning β to another robust linear regression problem (X, y').

One might ask if we have truly gained anything here having found a reduction from one robust linear regression problem to another. It turns out we have a subtle advantage this time. In particular, the bound B' that we have on $\|\beta'\|_2$ will likely be smaller than the bound on $\|\beta\|_2$. More precisely, we have

$$\|\beta'\|_2 = \|\beta - \widehat{\beta}\|_2 = O(\sqrt{\epsilon}(\sigma + B)).$$

This gives rise to an iterative algorithm. In particular, if we have some method of approximating β to ℓ_2 error at most B, we can use this robust mean estimation technique to obtain a new estimate with error only $O(\sqrt{\epsilon}(\sigma + B))$. It is easy to see that if ϵ is less than a sufficiently small constant, we can iterate this technique $O(\log(B/\sigma))$ times in order to learn β to error $O(\sqrt{\epsilon}\sigma)$ (see Exercise 7.1 for details).

7.2.3 Improving the ϵ-Dependence

One might ask if it is possible to obtain error that scales better than $\sqrt{\epsilon}$. Doing so would depend on proving better bounds on the stability condition satisfied by yX/σ. For large values of B, we note that the covariance of yX/σ is far from the identity, and so we cannot hope to get better bounds than what can be achieved by the covariance bounds. However, for smaller values of B, we note that $\mathbf{Cov}[yX/\sigma]$ has eigenvalues $1 + O(B/\sigma)^2$. In such cases, we can hope to obtain better stability if we also have concentration bounds on yX/σ. To establish such bounds, we note that every coordinate of yX/σ is a degree-2 polynomial in the multivariate Gaussian (X, y). Using Gaussian hypercontractivity (see Theorem A.9), this implies that yX/σ has exponential tails in each direction. Using this fact, it is easy to see that a sufficiently large number of i.i.d. samples from yX/σ will be $(\epsilon, O(\sqrt{\epsilon}B/\sigma) + O(\epsilon \log(1/\epsilon)))$-stable with high probability (see Exercise 3.1 for a tighter sample complexity analysis). Therefore, by Theorem 2.11, we can efficiently robustly learn β to ℓ_2-error $O(\sqrt{\epsilon}B + \epsilon\sigma \log(1/\epsilon))$.

By iteratively applying this technique, we can efficiently learn β to a final ℓ_2-error of $O(\sigma\epsilon \log(1/\epsilon))$. We present the final theorem here.

Theorem 7.2 (Efficient Robust Linear Regression) *Let* (X, y) *be a distribution on* $\mathbf{R}^{d+1}$ *given by* $X \sim N(0, I)$ *and* $y = \beta \cdot X + \xi$, *where* $\xi \sim N(0, \sigma^2)$ *is independent of* X. *Assume that* $\|\beta\|_2 \leq B$. *Suppose we have access to i.i.d. samples from a distribution* (X', y') *that is* ϵ-*close to* (X, y) *in total variation distance. There exists an algorithm that given* B, σ, *and* $\tilde{O}(d/\epsilon^2)O(\log(B/\sigma))$ *samples from* (X', y') *runs in sample polynomial time and with high probability approximates* β *to* ℓ_2-*error* $O(\sigma\epsilon \log(1/\epsilon))$.

Theorem 7.2 is unsatisfactory in two ways. First, note that the statement only applies in the case of total variation distance contamination and not against an adaptive adversary. This is essentially because given the iterative nature of the algorithm, it is important that the samples being fed into the algorithm in each iteration are independent of the current approximation $\widehat{\beta}$ being used to compute residuals. The second issue that one might want to improve is the $O(\log(B/\sigma))$-dependence in the sample complexity, which we know (at least for large B) is not information-theoretically necessary.

Both of these issues arise because of the need to draw independent samples at each round of our iterative procedure, and could be avoided if we could take a single set of samples that worked for every round of the algorithm. Unfortunately, this requires that our samples satisfy a somewhat stronger condition. Namely, we need a set S of samples (X_i, y_i) such that for any $\widehat{\beta}$ used by our algorithm, the set of residuals $(y_i - \widehat{\beta} \cdot X_i)X_i/\sigma$ is stable (with appropriate parameters) with respect to the distribution $(y - \widehat{\beta} \cdot X)X/\sigma$.

Establishing such a statement is somewhat technically complicated, but not especially difficult. It can be shown, for example, that for $N = \tilde{O}(d/\epsilon^2)$ large enough that N i.i.d. samples from (X, y) have the property that for every $\widehat{\beta}$ there is a subset of $(1 - \epsilon)N$ of our original samples that satisfy an appropriate stability condition. Note that restricting to a subset here is necessary, as otherwise letting $\widehat{\beta} = \beta - \sigma X_i/\sqrt{d}$, for some X_i in the sample set, leads to one of the $(y_j - \widehat{\beta} \cdot X_j)X_j/\sigma$ having norm on the order of d, which in turn means that $\Omega(d^2)$ samples will be needed to ensure that the sample covariance in this direction is not too big.

7.3 Robust Learning of Linear Separators

In this section, we develop robust algorithms for learning *linear threshold functions* (LTFs), also known as linear separators or halfspaces. An LTF is any Boolean-valued function $f: \mathbf{R}^d \to \{\pm 1\}$ of the form $f(x) = \text{sign}(w \cdot x - t)$, where $w \in \mathbf{R}^d$ is known as the weight vector and t is known as the threshold. The problem of learning LTFs is arguably the prototypical binary classification task and has been studied in machine learning since the beginning of the field.

In the noiseless (nonrobust) setting, the learning problem is the following: Given i.i.d. samples of the form $(X, y) \in \mathbf{R}^d \times \{\pm 1\}$, where $X \sim D$ (known as the *marginal distribution*) and $y = f(X)$ for an unknown LTF f, the goal is to output a hypothesis function $h: \mathbf{R}^d \to \{\pm 1\}$ such that with high probability the 0–1 loss, that is, $\text{Pr}_{X \sim D}[h(X) \neq f(X)]$, is small. This definition amounts to the well-known Probably Approximately Correct (PAC) learning model.

In the above setting, LTFs are efficiently learnable with *any* marginal distribution D using linear programming. Specifically, for any desired accuracy parameter $\epsilon > 0$, there is an algorithm that draws $\tilde{O}(d/\epsilon)$ labeled samples, runs in poly(d/ϵ) time, and returns an LTF hypothesis such that with high probability the 0–1 loss is at most ϵ.

Here we will study the efficient learnability of LTFs in the strong contamination model, that is, in the presence of an ϵ-fraction of adversarial outliers. Interestingly, the strong contamination model is known as *nasty noise* model in the binary classification setting. In contrast to robust mean estimation, which is information-theoretically impossible for some distributions, the robust learning problem of LTFs is information-theoretically solvable for any marginal distribution D. Specifically, there exists an (inefficient) algorithm that draws $\tilde{O}(d/\epsilon)$ ϵ-corrupted labeled samples and outputs a hypothesis with 0–1 error $O(\epsilon)$. Unfortunately, in this level of generality, known results show that the problem is computationally intractable. In particular, even if $\epsilon > 0$ is an arbitrarily small constant, it is computationally hard (given some standard complexity assumptions) to find any hypothesis with 0–1 error $1/2 - \gamma$, for any constant $\gamma > 0$.

To circumvent this intractability, it is reasonable to make some assumptions about the structure of the marginal distribution D. A number of such structural assumptions have been made in the literature, typically involving upper bounds on its moments/concentration and anti-concentration of D. The most basic such assumption is that D is the standard Gaussian distribution $\mathcal{N}(0, I)$. In this chapter, we will focus on the case of Gaussian marginals.

Throughout this section, for simplicity we will focus on homogeneous LTFs, that is, ones with zero threshold. While similar bounds are achievable for nonhomogeneous LTFs, the algorithms and analyses are somewhat more complicated.

7.3.1 Robustly Learning LTFs via Robust Mean Estimation

In this section, we give an efficient algorithm for robustly learning homogeneous LTFs under Gaussian marginals that achieves error $O(\epsilon \sqrt{\log(1/\epsilon)})$. The main theorem established in this section is as follows.

Theorem 7.3 *There exists an algorithm with the following behavior: Given $0 < \epsilon < \epsilon_0$, for some sufficiently small constant ϵ_0, and a set of $n = \text{poly}(d/\epsilon)$ samples with ϵ-contamination labeled samples from the distribution $(X, f(X)) \in \mathbf{R}^d \times \{\pm 1\}$, where $X \sim N(0, I)$ and f is an unknown homogeneous LTF, the algorithm runs in $\text{poly}(n)$ time and with high probability outputs a hypothesis LTF $h: \mathbf{R}^d \to \{\pm 1\}$ such that $\Pr_{X \sim N(0,I)}[h(X) \neq f(X)] = O(\epsilon \sqrt{\log(1/\epsilon)})$.*

Our algorithm is somewhat analogous to our basic algorithm for robust linear regression in the previous section. At a high level, the goal is to formulate the robust LTF learning problem as a robust mean estimation problem. The crucial quantities to achieve this goal are known as Chow parameters of a Boolean function.

Definition 7.4 (Chow Parameters) Let $f: \mathbf{R}^d \to \{\pm 1\}$ be a Boolean function and let D be a distribution over $\mathbf{R}^d$. The *Chow parameters* of f with respect to D are the d numbers $\mathbf{E}_{X \sim D}[f(X)X_i]$, $i \in [d]$. We will denote by $\vec{\chi}_f$ the d-dimensional vector $\mathbf{E}_{X \sim D}[f(X)X]$ of its Chow parameters.

The first question to understand is why the Chow parameters of an LTF are useful in our context. Indeed, for a general Boolean function f, the values of its Chow parameters may reveal little information about the function itself. Interestingly, if the function f is an LTF, its Chow parameters uniquely *characterize* the function. This is established in the following simple fact.

Fact 7.5 *Fix a distribution D on $\mathbf{R}^d$ such that $\Pr_{X \sim D}[v \cdot X = 0] = 0$ for any unit vector v. Let $f: \mathbf{R}^d \to \{\pm 1\}$ be a homogeneous LTF and $g: \mathbf{R}^d \to \{\pm 1\}$ be any Boolean-valued function. If $\vec{\chi}_f = \vec{\chi}_g$, then $\Pr_{X \sim D}[f(X) \neq g(X)] = 0$.*

Proof Let $f(X) = \text{sign}(w \cdot x)$, for some weight vector $w \in \mathbf{R}^d$ of unit norm. We can write

$$0 = \sum_{i=1}^{d} w_i \left(\mathbf{E}_{X \sim D}[f(X)X_i] - \mathbf{E}_{X \sim D}[g(X)X_i] \right) = \mathbf{E}_{X \sim D} \left[(f(X) - g(X))(w \cdot X) \right],$$

where the first equality follows from our assumption that $\vec{\chi}_f = \vec{\chi}_g$ and the second is linearity of expectation. Note that the RHS above is equal to

$$\mathbf{E}_{X \sim D} \left[(f(X) - g(X))(w \cdot X) \mid f(X) \neq g(X) \right] \Pr_{X \sim D} [f(X) \neq g(X)].$$

Under this conditioning, we have $f(X) - g(X) = 2f(X)$. If $f(x) = \mathrm{sign}(w \cdot X)$, we have $f(X)(w \cdot X) = |w \cdot X|$. Therefore, for this choice of w, the argument in the above expectation will be $2|w \cdot X|$. By our anti-concentration assumption on D, the latter quantity is strictly positive with probability 1. Therefore, the above conditional expectation will be positive, which in turn implies that $\Pr_{X \sim D}[f(X) \neq g(X)] = 0$, as otherwise we obtain a contradiction. This completes the proof. $\qquad \square$

Fact 7.5 shows that the *exact* values of the Chow parameters characterize an LTF for any distribution D that puts zero mass on any hyperplane. In the context of learning, since we only have sample access to the target function, we can only hope to approximately estimate the Chow parameters (even without outliers). As a result, even in the nonrobust setting, we would need a stronger ("robust") version of Fact 7.5, stating that sufficiently accurate approximations of the Chow parameters approximately characterize the function. Such a result can indeed be established under appropriate anti-concentration assumptions for the distribution D, and in particular under the Gaussian distribution (the focus of this section).

Given the above, the idea of our robust learning algorithm for linear threshold functions will be as follows: First, we will give an efficient routine to robustly estimate the Chow parameters of the target LTF. It turns out that this problem can be viewed as a robust mean estimation problem. As usual in robust mean estimation, in the presence of clean data one can use the empirical estimate. In fact, it can be shown that the empirical estimator provides good guarantees even in the presence of adversarial *label noise*. However, in the presence of arbitrary outliers (in both the labels and the points), this naive estimate incurs error scaling polynomially with the dimension. By leveraging techniques developed in Chapter 2, we give an efficient algorithm for robustly estimating the Chow parameters of *any* Boolean function within near-optimal error.

As we already showed, the exact values of the Chow parameters uniquely determine the threshold function. When the underlying distribution on the examples is sufficiently well-behaved (e.g., Gaussian), a robust version of this statement holds: Sufficiently accurate approximations of the Chow parameters approximately determines the function. The second step of our algorithm is an efficient routine that makes this statement algorithmic: Given approximations to the Chow parameters, it efficiently recovers an approximation to the function. Specifically, this algorithm is proper, that is, it outputs a linear threshold function as its hypothesis.

Our first main algorithmic ingredient is captured in the following theorem.

Theorem 7.6 (Robust Estimation of Chow Parameters) *Let $f: \mathbf{R}^d \to \{\pm 1\}$. There is an algorithm which, given $\epsilon > 0$ sufficiently small and a set S of n ϵ-corrupted labeled samples (for n a sufficiently large polynomial in d/ϵ) from a distribution $(X, f(X))$, where $X \sim \mathcal{N}(0, I_d)$, runs in $\text{poly}(d, 1/\epsilon)$ time and with high probability outputs a vector $\vec{a} \in \mathbf{R}^d$ such that $\|\vec{a} - \vec{\chi}_f\|_2 = O(\epsilon \cdot \sqrt{\log(1/\epsilon)})$.*

Proof The main idea of the proof is to view the underlying estimation task as a high-dimensional robust mean estimation problem. Specifically, we are given a set of n ϵ-corrupted samples from the distribution $(X, f(X))$, where $X \sim D = \mathcal{N}(0, I)$ and our goal is to estimate the vector $\vec{\chi}_f = \mathbf{E}_{X \sim D}[f(X)X]$ in ℓ_2-norm. That is, the problem is tantamount to robust mean estimation for the distribution of $f(X)X$, where $f: \mathbf{R}^d \to \{\pm 1\}$ is our unknown target function and $X \sim \mathcal{N}(0, I)$ is a Gaussian vector. This is a distribution on $\mathbf{R}^d$, that we will call D_f, and our goal is to robustly estimate its mean vector $\vec{\chi}_f$, given access to ϵ-corrupted samples from D_f.

To see how accurately we can efficiently approximate the mean $\vec{\chi}_f$ of D_f in the outlier-robust setting, we will as usual try to understand the concentration and moments of D_f. Let $Z = f(X)X$, where $X \sim \mathcal{N}(0, I)$. We note that

$$\mathbf{Cov}[Z] = \mathbf{E}[ZZ^{\top}] - \mathbf{E}[Z]\mathbf{E}[Z^{\top}] = \mathbf{E}[f^2(X)XX^{\top}] - \vec{\chi}_f \cdot \vec{\chi}_f^{\top} = I - \vec{\chi}_f \cdot \vec{\chi}_f^{\top},$$

where we used the fact that f is Boolean-valued and that $\mathbf{Cov}[X] = I$.

Note that the covariance matrix of the clean distribution D_f is a function of the target mean, and therefore a priori unknown. Moreover, it is easy to see that Z has sub-Gaussian concentration in every direction.

A first observation is that the covariance matrix of Z is bounded above by I in Loewner ordering. Therefore, we can use as a black box a robust mean estimator for bounded covariance distributions to approximate $\vec{\chi}_f$ within ℓ_2-error $O(\epsilon^{1/2})$. This approximation gives us a better approximation to the covariance matrix, which can then be used to approximate the mean within error $O(\epsilon^{3/4})$. Applying this idea iteratively, given a δ-approximation to the mean, we obtain a δ-approximation to the covariance, which then leads to an $O(\sqrt{\epsilon\delta} + \epsilon\sqrt{\log(1/\epsilon)})$ approximation to the mean. After $O(\log\log(1/\epsilon))$ iterations, this leads to the desired error guarantee. □

Note that Theorem 7.6 does not use the assumption that the underlying function f is an LTF, and in fact it holds for any Boolean function.

The next step is to leverage the fact that f is of the form $f(x) = \text{sign}(w \cdot x)$ to approximate the function itself in L_1-norm. Given an accurate ℓ_2-approximation $\vec{\alpha}$ to the target Chow vector $\vec{\chi}_f$, we will compute a hypothesis LTF $h(x) = \text{sign}(v \cdot x)$ such that $\|h - f\|_1$ is small.

For the case of the Gaussian distribution, this can be done with a straightforward algorithm: We set v to be equal to our approximation $\vec{\alpha}$ of $\vec{\chi}_f$. The reason that this algorithm works is that the Chow vector $\vec{\chi}_f$ corresponding to the target LTF $f(x) = \text{sign}(w \cdot x)$ can be shown to be *parallel* to the defining normal vector w. Moreover, the L_1-distance between two homogeneous LTFs is proportional to the ℓ_2-norm between the corresponding normal vectors (assuming they are normalized).

Specifically, we have the following lemmas, which complete the analysis.

Lemma 7.7 *The Chow vector of the LTF $f(x) = \text{sign}(v \cdot x)$ with $\|v\|_2 = 1$ is $\vec{\chi}_f = 2\phi(0) v$, where $\phi(0) = 1/\sqrt{2\pi}$ is the Gaussian probability density at 0.*

Proof It is clear that $\mathbf{E}_{X \sim \mathcal{N}(0,I)}[f(X)(w \cdot X)] = 0$ for all $w \perp v$. Thus, we only need to evaluate $\mathbf{E}_{X \sim \mathcal{N}(0,I)}[f(X)(v \cdot X)]$. It is easy to see that this is

$$\int_{-\infty}^{\infty} \text{sign}(t) t \phi(t) dt = \int_{0}^{\infty} 2t\phi(t) dt = 2\phi(0).$$

This completes our proof. □

Lemma 7.7 says that given good approximations to the Chow parameters of $f(x) = \text{sign}(v \cdot x)$, we can find a good approximation w to v. The final step is to show that the LTF derived from w yields a good approximation to f.

Lemma 7.8 *Given two homogeneous LTFs, $f(x) = \text{sign}(v \cdot x)$ and $g(x) = \text{sign}(w \cdot x)$, for unit vectors v and w, we have*

$$\|f - g\|_1 = O(\|v - w\|_2).$$

See Figure 7.1 for an illustration of this situation.

Proof Let θ be the angle between v and w. We note that in the plane spanned by v and w, the lines $v \cdot x = 0$ and $w \cdot x = 0$ have an angle of θ between them, and the region where $f(x) \neq g(x)$ consists of the points whose projection lies in one of the two arcs of angle θ.

Since the projection of x onto this plane is Gaussian, which is rotationally invariant, the probability that $f(x) \neq g(x)$ is θ/π. Combining this with the fact that $\theta = \Theta(\|v - w\|_2)$ completes our proof. □

Thus, for learning homogenous LTFs over the Gaussian distribution, one can first use the algorithm of Theorem 7.6 to learn an $O(\epsilon \sqrt{\log(1/\epsilon)})$-approximation

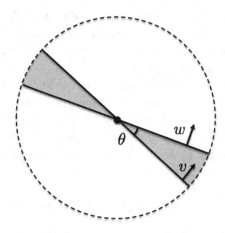

Figure 7.1 Illustration of Lemma 7.8 projected onto the plane spanned by v and w. Notice that the threshold functions f and g disagree only on the gray region, which consists of two origin-centered arcs of angle θ.

$\widehat{\chi}$ to the Chow parameters $\vec{\chi}_f$. One then produces the hypothesis $\widehat{f}(x) = \text{sign}$ $(v \cdot x)$, where v is the normalization of $\widehat{\chi}$. By Lemma 7.7, if $f(x) = \text{sign}(w \cdot x)$, since $\widehat{\chi}$ is an $O(\epsilon \sqrt{\log(1/\epsilon)})$-approximation to $2\phi(0)w$, v is an $O(\epsilon \sqrt{\log(1/\epsilon)})$-approximation to w. By Lemma 7.8, this implies that $\|\widehat{f}-f\|_1 = O(\epsilon \sqrt{\log(1/\epsilon)})$. This completes the proof of Theorem 7.3.

7.3.2 Achieving Optimal Error via Localization

The algorithm of the previous section achieves 0–1 error $O(\epsilon \sqrt{\log(1/\epsilon)})$. It is natural to ask if an efficient algorithm with the information-theoretically optimal bound of $O(\epsilon)$ is possible. In this section, we will show that this is indeed possible. Specifically, we prove the following theorem.

Theorem 7.9 (Robustly Learning LTFs via Localization) *There exists an algorithm with the following behavior: Let $0 < \epsilon < \epsilon_0$, for some sufficiently small constant ϵ_0, and n is a sufficiently large polynomial in d/ϵ. Then, given a set of n ϵ-corrupted labeled samples from the distribution $(X, f(X)) \in \mathbf{R}^d \times \{\pm 1\}$, where $X \sim \mathcal{N}(0, I)$ and f is an unknown homogeneous LTF, the algorithm runs in $\text{poly}(n)$ time and with high probability output a hypothesis LTF $h\colon \mathbf{R}^d \to \{\pm 1\}$ such that $\text{Pr}_{X \sim D}[h(X) \neq f(X)] = O(\epsilon)$.*

It is worth noting that the above guarantee cannot be obtained in a black box manner via a reduction to robust mean estimation for the following reason:

There is evidence that obtaining error $o(\epsilon \sqrt{\log(1/\epsilon)})$ for robustly estimating the mean of a spherical Gaussian in the strong contamination model requires super-polynomial time (see Chapter 8). As a result, a different algorithmic approach is required.

The high-level intuition is as follows: Suppose that the true target LTF is of the form $f(x) = \text{sign}(w \cdot x)$, for some unknown unit vector $w \in \mathbf{R}^d$, and that we start with an approximation $v \approx w$. The approximation means that with high probability over $x \sim \mathcal{N}(0, I)$ we will have $w \cdot x \approx v \cdot x$. In particular, this implies that if $|v \cdot x|$ is large, it is likely the case that $\text{sign}(v \cdot x) = \text{sign}(w \cdot x)$. This suggests that the points far from the critical hyperplane are not very useful for our approximation. Motivated by this observation, our algorithm should instead focus on points x with $|v \cdot x|$ smaller. For example, if we could somehow sample points for which $v \cdot x = 0$, we would find for such points that $f(x) = \text{sign}((w - v) \cdot x)$, which gives us information directly about the error $w - v$ to our current approximation. While we may not be able to find samples for which this holds exactly, focusing our attention on samples where $|v \cdot x|$ is small will have much the same effect. This is the idea of *localization* and it will give us another iterative algorithm that ends up with a substantially better approximation to f.

The main technical obstacle to this strategy is to find a way to "focus our attention" to points where $|v \cdot x|$ is small in such a way that it reduces to a problem that we already understand. A convenient way to achieve this is via rejection sampling. When we are given a sample (x, y), we ignore it except with some probability $p(x)$, where $p(x)$ is large when $|v \cdot x|$ is small. The resulting conditional distribution on nonrejected samples will then give some distribution over (x, y), where the x's concentrate near the hyperplane $v \cdot x = 0$.

A particularly convenient choice for p is the following.

Definition 7.10 (Rejection Sampling) For a unit vector $v \in \mathbf{R}^d$ and a real number $\sigma \in (0, 1)$, we define the (v, σ)-rejection sampling procedure to be the one that given a point $x \in \mathbf{R}^d$ accepts it with probability

$$p(x) = \exp(-(1/\sigma^2 - 1)(v \cdot x)^2/2)$$

and rejects it otherwise.

A simple corollary of this definition is the following property.

Lemma 7.11 *If a point x drawn from $\mathcal{N}(0, I)$ is given as input to the (v, σ)-rejection sampling procedure, it is accepted with probability σ. Moreover, the distribution on x conditional on acceptance is $\mathcal{N}(0, A_v)$, where*

$$A_{v,\sigma} = I + (\sigma^2 - 1)vv^\top.$$

Proof Note that the distribution of x in directions orthogonal to v is Gaussian and independent of both the v-component and the rejection probability. So it suffices to consider the univariate problem of a Gaussian in the v-direction. The probability that the point $x \cdot v = t$ and x is accepted by the (v, σ)-rejection filter is

$$(1/\sqrt{2\pi}) \exp(-t^2/2) \exp(-(1/\sigma^2 - 1)t^2/2)dt = (1/\sqrt{2\pi}) \exp(-t^2/(2\sigma^2))dt.$$

Since this is the probability density function of $\mathcal{N}(0, \sigma^2)$ (up to a multiple of σ), this means that the conditional distribution on the uncorrupted samples that pass the test is $(x, f(x))$, where $x \sim \mathcal{N}(0, I + (\sigma^2 - 1)vv^\top)$. In other words the x-marginal for the uncorrupted samples is another Gaussian whose standard deviation in the v-direction is σ instead of 1. By integrating over t, we obtain the first statement of the lemma. This completes the proof. □

Note that the matrix $A_{v,\sigma}$ has eigenvalue σ^2 in the v-direction and eigenvalue one in all orthogonal directions.

The next step is to understand what happens if this rejection filter is applied instead to the corrupted samples that our algorithm has access to.

By Lemma 7.11, the fraction of inliers that pass our test is proportional to σ. This means that as long as $\sigma \gg \epsilon$, even after adding corruptions, a $\Theta(\sigma)$-fraction of our original samples will pass. Unfortunately, an adversary may introduce errors for which $|v \cdot x|$ is small, and these errors will have a high probability of passing our test. In particular, of the $\Theta(\sigma)$-fraction of our original samples that pass the rejection filter, this may contain up to an $O(\epsilon)$-fraction of our original samples that were errors. Fortunately, it can be no worse than this. This means that the collection of samples that pass our rejection sampling have at most an $O(\epsilon/\sigma)$-fraction of errors.

To summarize, the samples that survive our rejection sampling consist of samples of the form $(x, f(x))$ for $x \sim \mathcal{N}(0, A_{v,\sigma})$ along with an $O(\epsilon/\sigma)$-fraction of adversarial errors. In other words, we have access to corrupted samples of an LTF with Gaussian marginals (with covariance $A_{v,\sigma}$). We can now use our existing algorithms to learn the LTF over this new distribution. The goal will then be to relate this back to the LTF over our original Gaussian.

In order to relate this new problem to something we understand, we make a change of variables in order to make the marginal into a standard Gaussian. Let $M = I + (\sigma - 1)vv^\top$. Notice that $MM^\top = I + (\sigma^2 - 1)vv^\top = A_{v,\sigma}$ is the covariance of our new Gaussian. In particular, this means that $x \sim Mz$, where $z \sim \mathcal{N}(0, I)$. Therefore, the inliers $(x, f(x))$ that we are observing are distributed as $(Mz, f(Mz))$. Applying M^{-1} to the first coordinate, we obtain samples distributed as $(z, f(Mz))$. Notice that

$$f(Mz) = \text{sign}(w \cdot Mz) = \text{sign}((Mw) \cdot z) = \text{sign}((Mw)/\|Mw\|_2 \cdot z).$$

This is now a linear threshold function whose marginals are a standard Gaussian.

Therefore, we have obtained a set of $O(\epsilon/\sigma)$-corrupted samples from an LTF with defining vector $Mw/\|Mw\|_2$ and standard Gaussian marginals. Using Theorem 7.6 and Lemma 7.7, we can learn a vector $\widehat{w}$ with

$$\left\|\widehat{w} - Mw/\|Mw\|_2\right\|_2 = O(\epsilon/\sigma \sqrt{\log(\sigma/\epsilon)}).$$

Our goal is to use this to obtain a better approximation of w.

Suppose that we already know a v such that $\|v - w\|_2 \leq \delta$, for some $\delta \gg \epsilon$. Using this v, and letting $\sigma = \delta$ in the above construction, we learn a $\widehat{w}$ such that $\left\|\widehat{w} - Mw/\|Mw\|_2\right\|_2 = O(\epsilon/\delta \sqrt{\log(\delta/\epsilon)})$. A natural candidate for w would now be $M^{-1}\widehat{w}/\|M^{-1}\widehat{w}\|_2$. To analyze this, let w be proportional to $v + v'$, where v' is some vector perpendicular to v, of norm at most δ. We have that Mw is proportional to $\delta v + v'$, which has norm $\kappa = \Theta(\delta)$. This means that $\widehat{w}$ is an $O(\epsilon/\delta \sqrt{\log(\delta/\epsilon)})$-approximation to Mw/κ. Thus, it is proportional to an $O(\epsilon \sqrt{\log(\delta/\epsilon)})$-approximation to Mw. This means that $M^{-1}\widehat{w}$ is proportional to a vector of the form:

$$(1 + O(\epsilon/\delta \sqrt{\log(\delta/\epsilon)}))v + (v' + O(\epsilon \sqrt{\log(\delta/\epsilon)})).$$

Rescaling so that the v-coefficient is 1, we find that $M^{-1}\widehat{w}$ is proportional to a vector of the form

$$v + (v' + O(\epsilon \sqrt{\log(\delta/\epsilon)})) = w + O(\epsilon \sqrt{\log(\delta/\epsilon)}).$$

Thus,

$$\left\|M^{-1}\widehat{w}/\|M^{-1}\widehat{w}\|_2 - w\right\|_2 = O(\epsilon \sqrt{\log(\delta/\epsilon)}).$$

In other words, if we start with a δ-approximation to w and are given polynomially many ϵ-corrupted samples from $(x, f(x))$, we can efficiently compute an $O(\epsilon \sqrt{\log(\delta/\epsilon)})$-approximation of w. Using the algorithm from the last section to obtain an initial approximation within error $\delta = O(\epsilon \sqrt{\log(1/\epsilon)})$, iterating this technique a small number of times, eventually yields an $O(\epsilon)$-approximation. This completes the proof of Theorem 7.9.

7.4 Robust Stochastic Optimization

The applications in the previous section can be viewed as very special cases of the general task of robust stochastic optimization. In a stochastic optimization problem, one has sample access to a distribution G over *functions* $f : \mathbf{R}^d \to \mathbf{R}$, and the goal is to find a point x (approximately) minimizing the function $F(x) = \mathbf{E}_{f \sim G}[f(x)]$.

This framework encapsulates a number of well-studied machine learning problems. First, we note that the problem of mean estimation can be expressed in this form, by observing that the mean of a distribution D is the value $\mu = \arg\min_{w \in \mathbf{R}^d} \mathbf{E}_{x \sim D}[\|w - x\|_2^2]$. That is, given a sample $x \sim D$, the distribution $\mathcal{F}$ over functions $f_x(w) = \|w - x\|_2^2$ turns the task of mean estimation into a stochastic optimization problem. A more interesting example is the problem of least-squares linear regression: Given a distribution D over $(x, y) \in \mathbf{R}^{d+1}$, where $x \in \mathbf{R}^d$ and $y \in \mathbf{R}$, we want to find a vector $w \in \mathbf{R}^d$ minimizing $\mathbf{E}_{(x,y) \sim D}[(w \cdot x - y)^2]$. This fits in the stochastic optimization framework by defining the distribution G over functions $f_{(x,y)}(w) = (w \cdot x - y^2)$, where $(x, y) \sim D$. Note that finding a minimizing vector for this problem also solves the linear regression problem from Section 7.2. One can also phrase the problem of learning an LTF in this way, for example by finding a vector v minimizing the expected hinge loss $\ell_{x,y}(v) := \max(0, -y(v \cdot x))$. Similar formulations exist for numerous other machine learning problems, including L_1-regression, logistic regression, support vector machines, and generalized linear models.

Stochastic optimization problems are somewhat more general than this. For example, in machine learning it is common to have some class of hypothesis functions $f_\theta(x)$ specified by some parameter vector θ. Given sample data (x, y) and a loss function ℓ, one will often want to find a value of θ minimizing the expectation of $\ell(f_\theta(x), y)$. Thinking of $\ell(f_\theta(x), y)$ as some function $F_{x,y}(\theta)$, this can again be thought of in terms of a stochastic optimization problem.

Finally, we note that the stochastic optimization framework encompasses nonconvex problems as well. For example, the general and challenging problem of training a neural net can be expressed in this framework, where w represents some high-dimensional vector of parameters classifying the net and each function $f(x)$ quantifies how well that particular net classifies a given datapoint.

Before we discuss *robust* stochastic optimization, we make a few basic remarks regarding the nonrobust setting. We start by noting that, without any assumptions, the problem of optimizing the function $F(x) = \mathbf{E}_{f \sim G}[f(x)]$, even approximately, is NP-hard. On the other hand, in many situations, it suffices to find an approximate critical point of F, that is, a point w such that $\|\nabla F(x)\|_2$ is small. For example, if F is convex (which holds if each $f \sim G$ is convex almost surely), an approximate critical point is also an approximate global minimum. For several structured nonconvex problems, an approximate critical point is also considered a satisfactory solution. Given an i.i.d. set of functions $f_1, \ldots, f_n \sim G$, we can efficiently find an approximate critical point of F using (projected) gradient descent. For more structured problems, for example, linear regression, faster and more direct methods may be available.

While there is a lot of work on the best way to perform gradient descent in various situations, the following simple result will suffice for our purposes.

Proposition 7.12 *Let $f : \mathbf{R}^d \to \mathbf{R}$ be a function such that:*

- *For some $R > 0$, we have $f(0) < f(x)$ for all $x \in \mathbf{R}^d$ with $\|x\|_2 \geq R$.*
- *For some $B > 0$, any $x \in \mathbf{R}^d$ with $\|x\|_2 \leq R + 1$ and any vector $v \in \mathbf{R}^d$ we have $\left| \frac{\partial^2 f(x+tv)}{\partial t^2} \right|_{t=0} \Big| < B\|v\|_2^2$.*
- *For all $x \in \mathbf{R}^d$ with $\|x\|_2 \leq R$, $\|\nabla f(x)\|_2 \leq \sigma$.*

Let O be an oracle that given an $x \in \mathbf{R}^d$ with $\|x\|_2 \leq R$ returns a vector that is within ϵ of $\nabla f(x)$. Then there exists an algorithm that given access to O runs in time $O(RB\sigma/\epsilon^2)$ and returns an x with $\|x\|_2 \leq R$ such that $\|\nabla f(x)\|_2 < 3\epsilon$.

Proposition 7.12 says that if we have a well-behaved function f that is large outside of a ball of radius R (meaning that we do not have to search outside this ball for a minimum), We can effectively find an approximate critical point of f. The proof is quite simple: We use gradient descent on f. If $\|\nabla f(x)\|_2$ is large, then by moving x a small amount in the direction of $-\nabla f(x)$, we can reduce the value of f by some bounded amount. Repeating this process, we must eventually find this approximate critical point.

Proof Our algorithm is as follows:

Algorithm `Gradient-Descent`
Input: An oracle O that can approximate $\nabla f(x)$ for f satisfying the hypotheses of Proposition 7.12:

1. Let $x = 0$.
2. While $\|v\| > 2\epsilon$ for $v := O(x)$
   - Let $x \leftarrow x - v/(2B)$.
3. Return x.

The key point in the analysis is the following: Letting $x' = x - v/(2B)$, $f(x')$ is substantially smaller than $f(x)$. To show this, consider the one variable function $g(t) = f(x - tv)$. In particular, by Taylor's theorem we have

$$f(x') = g(1/(2B)) = g(0) + (1/(2B))g'(0) + (1/(2B))^2 g''(z)/2,$$

for some real number z between 0 and $1/(2B)$. It is clear that $g(0) = f(x)$. By the chain rule, we have $g'(0) = -v \cdot (\nabla f(x))$. Note that by the defining property of our oracle, we have $\|\nabla f(x) - v\|_2 \leq \epsilon$, and therefore $g'(0) \leq -\|v\|_2^2 + \epsilon\|v\|_2$. Finally, the last term is at most $(1/(2B))^2 B\|v\|_2^2/2$.

Hence, we have

$$f(x) - f(x') \geq \left(\frac{1}{2B}\right)\|v\|_2^2 - \epsilon\left(\frac{1}{2B}\right)\|v\|_2 - \left(\frac{1}{2B}\right)^2 B\|v\|_2^2/2$$

$$\geq \|v\|_2^2\left[\left(\frac{1}{2B}\right) - \left(\frac{1}{2B}\right)^2 B\right]/2$$

$$\geq (2\epsilon)^2\left(\frac{1}{2B}\right)/4 = \epsilon^2/(2B).$$

Thus, in each iteration of our algorithm, the value of f decreases by at least $\epsilon^2/(2B)$. Moreover, we note that $|f(x) - f(0)| < R\sigma$ for all $\|x\|_2 \leq R$ by the derivative bound, and $f(x) \geq f(0)$ for all other x. Thus, $f(x) \geq f(0) - R\sigma$ for all x. This implies that our algorithm will never need more than $2RB\sigma/\epsilon^2$ iterations.

After the last iteration, we have a point x such that $\|O(x)\|_2 \leq 2\epsilon$, which implies that $\|\nabla f(x)\|_2 \leq 3\epsilon$. This completes the proof. $\qquad\square$

Proposition 7.12 is particularly useful when the function f is convex. In such a case, the only critical point will be the global minimum of f. If we furthermore assume some lower bound on the size of the second derivatives, we can show that any approximate critical point is actually close to a global minimum.

Lemma 7.13 *Let $f : \mathbf{R}^d \to \mathbf{R}$ be a function such that for some $b > 0$, and every $v, x \in \mathbf{R}^d$, $\left|\frac{\partial^2 f(x+tv)}{\partial t^2}\big|_{t=0}\right| \geq b\|v\|_2^2$. Then, if x is a point with $\|\nabla f(x)\|_2 \leq \epsilon$, we have $f(x) \leq \inf_y f(y) + \epsilon^2/(2b)$.*

Proof For $y \in \mathbf{R}^d$, we let $v = y - x$ and define the function $g(t) = f(x + tv)$. By Taylor's theorem we have

$$f(y) = g(1) = f(x) + g'(0) + g''(z)/2$$

for some z. By the chain rule, we have $g'(0) = v \cdot (\nabla f(x)) \geq -\epsilon\|v\|_2$. On the other hand, we have $g''(z) \geq b\|v\|_2^2$. Therefore, we obtain

$$f(y) - f(x) \geq -\epsilon\|v\|_2 + b\|v\|_2^2/2 = (\sqrt{b}\|v\|_2 - \epsilon/\sqrt{b})^2/2 - \epsilon^2/(2b) \geq -\epsilon^2/(2b).$$

This completes the proof. $\qquad\square$

Proposition 7.12 handles the case where we want to find an approximate critical point of a single function f. If we instead want to look at the noise-less version of stochastic optimization (i.e., trying to minimize $\mathbf{E}[f(x)]$ for some distribution over functions f), this essentially boils down to the same problem applied to the function $F(x) := \mathbf{E}[f(x)]$. So long as we know that the distribution over f is reasonably well-behaved, and so long as we can approximate $\nabla F(x)$ pointwise (which can usually be done by taking many sample functions f and taking the empirical average of their gradients), we can apply the algorithm from Proposition 7.12 to find an approximate critical point of F.

In the robust version of this problem, we have sample access to a distribution G over functions f; however, these functions may come with ϵ-contamination. As is usually the case, we will need to make some niceness assumptions on the uncorrupted functions in order for a solution to be possible, even information-theoretically. Proposition 7.12 suggests a basic algorithmic strategy. In particular, it is sufficient for us to be able to approximate $\nabla F(x) = \mathbf{E}[\nabla f(x)]$ pointwise. We can do this if, for example, the distribution of $\nabla f(x)$ satisfies an appropriate stability condition pointwise. A convenient set of assumptions is the following.

Condition 7.14 Let f be a distribution over twice differentiable functions from $\mathbf{R}^d \to \mathbf{R}$ so that for some parameters $R, B, \sigma > 0$ we have:

- For $\|x\|_2 \geq R$, we have $\mathbf{E}[f(x)] \geq \mathbf{E}[f(0)]$ almost surely.
- For any $x \in \mathbf{R}^d$ with $\|x\|_2 \leq R + 1$ and any vector $v \in \mathbf{R}^d$, we have $\left|\frac{\partial^2 f(x+tv)}{\partial t^2}\big|_{t=0}\right| < B\|v\|_2^2$ almost surely.
- For all $x \in \mathbf{R}^d$ with $\|x\|_2 \leq R$, $\mathbf{E}[(\nabla f(x))(\nabla f(x))^\top] \leq \sigma^2 I$.

Notice that these conditions imply that $F(x) := \mathbf{E}[f(x)]$ satisfies the appropriate conditions of Proposition 7.12. Furthermore, the last condition implies that we are able to robustly estimate $\nabla F(x)$ to error $O(\sigma\sqrt{\epsilon})$ for $\|x\|_2 \leq R$ using robust mean estimation. Combining this with Proposition 7.12 and Lemma 7.13, we get the following.

Theorem 7.15 *Let f be a distribution over functions from $\mathbf{R}^d \to \mathbf{R}$ satisfying Condition 7.14. There exists an algorithm that given sample access to ϵ-corrupted samples from f (in the total variation corruptions model) takes $\tilde{O}(dRB/\epsilon^2)$ samples, runs in polynomial time, and with high probability returns an x with $\|x\|_2 \leq R$ and $\|\nabla\mathbf{E}[f(x)]\|_2 = O(\sigma\sqrt{\epsilon})$. Furthermore, if for some $b > 0$ and all $v, x \in \mathbf{R}^d$ we have $\left|\frac{\partial^2 f(x+tv)}{\partial t^2}\big|_{t=0}\right| \geq b\|v\|_2^2$ almost surely, then $\mathbf{E}[f(x)]$ is within $O(\sigma^2\epsilon/b)$ of its minimum possible value.*

For a simple application of this theorem, we consider the case of robust linear regression as presented in Section 7.2. Here we assume that we have samples from (X, y), where $X \sim \mathcal{N}(0, I_d)$ and $y \sim \beta \cdot X + \mathcal{N}(0, \sigma^2)$ for some unknown vector β with $\|\beta\|_2 \leq R$. For a given pair (X, y), we define $f_{X,y}(v) = |v \cdot X - y|^2$. We note that $F(v) = \mathbf{E}[f_{X,y}(v)] = \sigma^2 + \|v - \beta\|_2^2$ is minimized at $v = \beta$. Furthermore, $F(v)$ is larger at any v with $\|v\|_2 \geq 2R$ than it is at 0.

For a given v, we note that $\nabla f_{X,y}(v) = 2(v \cdot X - y)X$. The expectation of $(\nabla f_{X,y}(v))(\nabla f_{X,y}(v))^\top$ can be seen to be $\sigma^2 I + 3(v - \beta)(v - \beta)^\top$. For $\|v\|_2 \leq R$, this is at most $O(R^2 + \sigma^2)I$ (in Loewner ordering). Thus, applying Theorem 7.15, we can robustly learn a vector β_0 such that $2\|\beta_0 - \beta\|_2 = \|\nabla F(\beta_0)\|_2 = O((R + \sigma)\sqrt{\epsilon})$. Iterating this result as we do in Section 7.2, we can get an $O(\sigma\sqrt{\epsilon})$-approximation to β. This result is weaker than that in Section 7.2, because we are only using a fairly weak level of stability in robustly estimating our gradient vectors. However, the advantage of Theorem 7.15 is that it applies in much greater generality.

7.5 Exercises

7.1 (Analysis of Iterative Improvements) Here we will analyze some of the iterative algorithms covered in this chapter.

(a) Our original algorithm for robust linear regression showed that if we had an estimate of β to error at most B, we could find a new estimate with error at most $O(\sqrt{\epsilon}(\sigma + B))$. Show that iterating this algorithm t times one can obtain an estimate with error $O(\sqrt{\epsilon})^t B + O(\sqrt{\epsilon}\sigma)$. Conclude that if ϵ is less than a sufficiently small constant, then after $\log(B/\sigma)$ iterations, one can obtain an estimate with error $O(\sqrt{\epsilon}\sigma)$.

(b) The improved bound in Section 7.2.3 shows how to go from error B to error $O(\sqrt{\epsilon}B + \epsilon\log(1/\epsilon)\sigma)$. Show by a similar argument to the above that if ϵ is at most a sufficiently small constant mutliple of σ, then after $\log(B/(\epsilon\sigma))$ iterations, one achieves an estimate with error $O(\epsilon\log(1/\epsilon)\sigma)$.

(c) In the proof of Theorem 7.6, we show how given an estimate of the Chow parameters with error at most δ one can obtain an estimate with error $O(\sqrt{\epsilon}\delta + \epsilon\sqrt{\log(1/\epsilon)})$. Show that by applying this t times one can obtain an estimate with error $O(\epsilon^{1-2^{-t}}\delta^{2^{-t}} + \epsilon\sqrt{\log(1/\epsilon)})$. Conclude that one can obtain an error of $O(\epsilon\sqrt{\log(1/\epsilon)})$ after $O(\log\log(\delta/\epsilon))$ iterations.

(d) In the proof of Theorem 7.3, we show how to go from an approximation of the LTF with error $\delta \gg \epsilon$ to an approximation with error $O(\epsilon\log(\delta/\epsilon))$. Show that by iterating this one can obtain an approximation with error $O(\epsilon)$.

(e) More generally, suppose that one has a procedure that given an estimate to some quantity of interest with error δ, one can obtain an approximation with error $f(\delta)$ for some increasing function f. Let δ_0 be the largest (assuming there is a largest) value of x such that $f(x) \geq x$ (note that it will always be a fixed point of f). Show that by iterating the above procedure one can always eventually obtain an approximation to the quantity of interest with error at most $\delta_0 + \eta$, for any $\eta > 0$.

7.2 (Information-Theoretic Bounds for Robust Linear Regression) Here we will study the information-theoretic limits of the robust linear regression problem of Section 7.2.

   (a) Show that it is impossible to learn β to ℓ_2-error $o(\epsilon\sigma)$ in the presence of ϵ-contamination.

   (b) Show that for $\epsilon > 0$ sufficient small, there is an (inefficient) algorithm that given $O(d/\epsilon^2)$ ϵ-corrupted samples from (X, y), it returns with high probability an estimator $\widehat{\beta}$ with $\|\widehat{\beta} - \beta\|_2 = O(\epsilon\sigma)$.

   (Hint: There are many ways to go about this. For example, one can note that β is characterized up to small error by the fact that for any nonzero vector v, $\mathbf{Pr}[\text{sign}(v \cdot X) = \text{sign}(y - \beta \cdot X)] = 1/2 + O(\epsilon)$.)

7.3 (Getting $O(\epsilon\sqrt{\log(1/\epsilon)})$ Error for Robust Linear Regression) Note that the algorithms presented in Section 7.2 only achieve error $O(\epsilon\log(1/\epsilon))\sigma$. However, error of $O(\epsilon\sqrt{\log(1/\epsilon)}\sigma)$ is possible. In particular, suppose that we are in the case where $\|\beta\|_2 = O(\epsilon\log(1/\epsilon))\sigma$ (perhaps having reduced to this case by considering residuals), and that we are given ϵ-corrupted samples from the true distribution (X, y), with $X \sim \mathcal{N}(0, I)$ and $y \sim \beta \cdot X + \mathcal{N}(0, \sigma^2)$.

   (a) Show that after a carefully planned rejection sampling based on y, the resulting distribution on the X samples is an $O(\epsilon)$-corruption of samples from $\mathcal{N}(C\beta/\sigma, I_d)$, for some explicit constant C.

   (b) Use part (a) to show how to estimate β to ℓ_2-error $O(\epsilon\sqrt{\log(1/\epsilon)})\sigma$.

   Note: It is believed to be impossible to learn β to error $o(\epsilon\sqrt{\log(1/\epsilon)})\sigma$ in polynomial time. For details, see Exercise 8.7.

7.4 (Multidimensional Linear Regression) Consider the multidimensional version of linear regression, where $X \in \mathbf{R}^d$ is distributed as $X \sim \mathcal{N}(0, I_d)$ and $Y \in \mathbf{R}^k$ is distributed as $Y \sim MX + \mathcal{N}(0, I_k)$, for some unknown matrix M. Give an algorithm that given ϵ-corrupted samples from the distribution (X, Y) learns M to Frobenius error $O(\epsilon\log(1/\epsilon))$.

7.5 (General Relation Between Distance and Chow Distance) While it is straightforward to generalize Theorem 7.6 to robustly learn the Chow parameters associated with homogeneous halfspaces under non-Gaussian (but still well-behaved) marginals, learning the target halfspace with respect to these marginals requires also having a generalization of Lemma 7.8. For this, we usually need some sort of anti-concentration assumption, along the lines of

$$\Pr[|v \cdot X| \le t] = O(t) \tag{7.1}$$

for any unit vector v and any $t \ge 0$.

Show that if X is a distribution satisfying Condition (7.1) and if f and g are two homogeneous halfspaces with Chow parameters $\vec{\chi}_f$ and $\vec{\chi}_g$, respectively, we have

$$\|f(X) - g(X)\|_1 = O\left(\sqrt{\|\vec{\chi}_f - \vec{\chi}_g\|_2}\right).$$

(Hint: Use an argument along the lines of the proof of Fact 7.5.)

7.6 (Alternative Chow Parameter Estimation Algorithm) In Section 7.3, we estimated the Chow parameters by computing the expectation of $Z = f(X)X$ for a Gaussian random variable X and f some Boolean-valued function. Doing so required some nontrivial iterative techniques, as $\mathbf{Cov}[Z]$ is not known a priori. However, note that the second moment matrix $\mathbf{E}[ZZ^\top]$ is known. It is not hard to show that given a set S of sufficiently many i.i.d. samples from Z, with high probability they satisfy the following modified stability condition:
Given any $S' \subseteq S$ with $|S'| \ge (1 - \epsilon)|S|$, we have:

- $\|\mathbf{E}_{x \sim_u S'}[x] - \mathbf{E}[Z]\|_2 = O(\epsilon \sqrt{\log(1/\epsilon)})$.
- $\|\mathbf{E}_{x \sim_u S'}[xx^\top] - I\|_2 = O(\epsilon \log(1/\epsilon))$.

Show that given this condition, there is an efficient algorithm for robustly estimating the mean of Z to error $O(\epsilon \sqrt{\log(1/\epsilon)})$.

7.7 (Robustly Learning Nonhomogeneous Halfspaces) Here we consider the case of robustly learning nonhomogeneous halfspaces, that is, functions of the form $f(x) = \text{sign}(v \cdot x - t)$, for v a unit vector and t a real number with $|t| = O(1)$. We will show that given ϵ-corrupted samples from $(X, f(X))$, with $X \sim \mathcal{N}(0, I)$, one can learn f to error $O(\epsilon)$.

(a) Show that for another halfspace $h(x) = \text{sgn}(w \cdot x - s)$, where w is a unit vector, and $s = O(1)$, we have

$$\mathbf{Pr}[f(x) \ne h(x)] = \Theta(\|v - w\|_2 + |t - s|).$$

(b) Show that by using Chow parameters one can robustly learn a w and s with $\|v - w\|_2 + |t - s| = O(\epsilon \sqrt{\log(1/\epsilon)})$.

(c) Use part (b) and a suitable localization procedure to learn f to error $O(\epsilon)$.

Note: Error $O(\epsilon)$ can actually be efficiently achieved even without the assumption that $|t| = O(1)$; however, the analysis is somewhat more complicated for two reasons. First, when $|t|$ is large, the error dependence on the angle is different and needs to be taken into account. Second, one can no longer afford to do a deterministic localization procedure, as a clever adversary will be able to put too many errors in the region that we are focusing on. Instead, the algorithm will need to slightly randomize the way in which it is doing localization in order to avoid this. For more details, the reader is referred to [64].

7.8 (Logistic Regression) In logistic regression, X is drawn from a normal distribution $\mathcal{N}(0, I_d)$ and then y is taken to be 1 with probability $\frac{e^{v \cdot X}}{e^{v \cdot X} + e^{-v \cdot X}}$ and -1 otherwise, for some unknown vector $v \in \mathbf{R}^d$. As usual, we are given ϵ-corrupted samples (in the total variation contamination model) from the distribution (X, y) and would like to learn this distribution in total variation distance.

(a) A good approach for this problem is to attempt to minimize the log odds score:

$$F(w) := \mathbf{E}\left[\log\left(\frac{e^{w \cdot X} + e^{-w \cdot X}}{e^{yw \cdot X}}\right)\right].$$

Show that $F(w)$ is convex and is minimized (for the expectation taken over the uncorrupted samples) when $v = w$.

(b) Assume that $\|v\|_2 \leq R$, for some known real number R. Show that robust stochastic optimization gives a poly(Rd/ϵ) time and sample algorithm for finding an $O(\sqrt{\epsilon})$-approximate critical point of F.

(c) Assume that $R = O(1)$. Give a polynomial-time algorithm to compute an $\tilde{O}(\epsilon)$-approximation to v.

(Hint: You will want to improve on the robust stochastic optimization procedure by noting that once we are close to v, we can compute a good approximation to the true covariance of ∇f; this allows to exploit stronger stability criteria.)

(d) For larger values of R, use the fact that y is close to a linear threshold function of X to find an $O(\epsilon + 1/\|v\|_2)$-approximation of $v/\|v\|_2$, along with a similarly rough approximation of $\|v\|_2$.

(e) Use the results from parts (c) and (d) along with a localization procedure to compute a vector w so that the logistic regression corresponding to w produces a distribution (X', y'), which is $\tilde{O}(\epsilon)$-close to (X, y) in total variation distance.

7.6 Discussion and Related Work

The literature on "robust" supervised learning is rather vast, and a comprehensive treatment is beyond the scope of this chapter. In the context of the problems studied in this chapter, a number of corruption/noise models have been studied that allow corruption of the labels and/or the examples. Here we focus on the work that is most closely related to the results presented in this chapter.

Robust Linear Regression Various formalizations of "robust" linear regression have been studied in the statistics and machine learning community for decades. The reader is referred to [134] for an early book on the topic focusing on the breakdown point of various estimators. More recent work in robust statistics [78] (see also [133]) generalized the notion of Tukey's depth for regression problems to obtain sample-efficient (but computationally inefficient) robust estimators in Huber's contamination model. These information-theoretic results can straightforwardly be extended to apply in the strong contamination model (see Exercise 7.2).

On the algorithmic front, [18] gave efficient algorithms for linear regression with adversarial label noise when the covariates are drawn from the Gaussian distribution (and other well-behaved distributions). Importantly, [18] only allows adversarial corruptions to the responses but not the covariates. The work by [17] studied linear regression in a weaker label corruption model, where the label corruptions are oblivious, that is, independent of the covariates. Interestingly, in this weaker model it is possible to tolerate a fraction of corruptions that is close to 1.

Early work [29] studied sparse linear regression in the presence of adversarial contamination, but did not provide efficient algorithms with dimension-independent error guarantees. Closer to the scope of this chapter, the work by [10] studied (sparse) linear regression in Huber's contamination model (their results can be easily extended in the strong contamination model). The work [10] observed that robust linear regression can be reduced to robust mean estimation, leading to an algorithm whose error guarantee scales with $\|\beta\|_2$ (see Section 7.2.1). The iterative algorithm described in Sections 7.2.2 and 7.2.3 for Gaussian covariates was essentially given in [70]. The latter work established a stronger version of Theorem 7.2 with sample complexity of $\tilde{O}(d/\epsilon^2)$ (i.e., independent of $\|\beta\|_2$). A number of contemporaneous works [44, 111, 127] developed robust algorithms for linear regression in the strong contamination model under weaker distributional assumptions. The algorithms in [44, 127] leverage the robust stochastic optimization lens of Section 7.4, while the algorithm in [111] uses the Sum-of-Squares method. More recently, the works by [9, 144] obtained optimal error for robust linear regression under weaker distributional assumptions. These works use the Sum-of-Squares method, building on [111]. Finally, [36] develops near-linear time algorithms by combining the robust stochastic optimization frameworks of [44, 127] with near-linear time algorithms for robust mean estimation [30, 71].

Robust Learning of LTFs A prototypical robustness model in the theory of PAC learning is the *agnostic learning model* [87, 107]. In the agnostic model, the goal is to learn a labeling function whose agreement with some underlying target function is close to the best possible, among all functions in some given class. It should be noted that in the agnostic model, the goal is to fit all the datapoints to the model. In contrast, in the outlier-robust setting, we are only interested in fitting the inliers. This qualitative difference can be quite significant. For example, the "agnostic" version of linear regression is readily solvable via least-squares. On the other hand, the outlier-robust setting turns out to be algorithmically more challenging. A stronger robustness model is the *malicious noise model* [109, 142], where an adversary is allowed to corrupt both the labels and the samples. Effectively the malicious noise model is equivalent to Huber's contamination model in the context of supervised learning. Interestingly, the strong contamination model has been studied in PAC learning as well under the name *nasty noise model* [24].

Agnostic learning with respect to arbitrary distributions on the examples is known to be computationally hard, even in simple settings. Specifically, for the class of linear threshold functions, [40] showed (under a plausible complexity assumption) that no efficient algorithm can achieve error at most $1/2 - 1/d^c$, for some constant $c > 0$, even if the fraction of corruptions ϵ is an arbitrarily small constant (though a random function can achieve error $1/2$). Consequently, research on this front has focused on well-behaved distributions. The work [110] studied the problem of malicious learning homogeneous LTFs, when the distribution on the unlabeled samples is isotropic logconcave, and gave the first polynomial-time algorithm with error guarantee *poly-logarithmic* in the dimension. This bound was subsequently improved by [5], who gave an efficient algorithm with error $O(\epsilon)$ for isotropic log-concave distributions. More recently, [64] extended these results to general LTFs and more general geometric concept classes under the Gaussian and other well-behaved distributions. Section 7.3.1 presents a simple special case of the [64] result.

At the technical level, the algorithm of [110] uses a simple outlier removal method to approximate the degree-1 Chow parameters, and then finds an LTF with approximately these Chow parameters. It is worth noting that the outlier removal procedure of [110] can be viewed as a weaker version of the filtering technique from [45]. The algorithm of [5] uses a soft outlier removal procedure together with localization. The work [64] developed a different localization technique that is presented in Section 7.3.2.

Robust Stochastic Optimization The first algorithms for robust stochastic convex optimization were developed in two contemporaneous works [44, 127]. Both these works observe that one can use a robust mean estimator as a black box to robustly estimate the gradient of the objective. Combined with a first-order method, this leads to a generic algorithm for robust stochastic optimization. The work [44] further proposed a different algorithm that uses standard empirical risk minimization and specific properties of the filtering algorithm to iteratively remove outliers. Both of these approaches are fairly general and can be applied to a range of machine learning tasks. More recently, [102] built on these frameworks to develop sample near-optimal and faster algorithms under stronger assumptions.

8

Information-Computation Trade-offs
in High-Dimensional Robust Statistics

8.1 Introduction

The goal of this chapter is to explore the inherent trade-offs between sample complexity, computational complexity, and robustness in high-dimensional statistical estimation. In the previous chapters, we established the existence of computationally efficient algorithms with dimension-independent error guarantees for a range of high-dimensional robust estimation tasks. In some instances, these algorithms have optimal sample complexity and achieve the information-theoretically optimal error (within constant factors). Alas, in several interesting settings, there is a super-constant gap between the information-theoretic optimum and what known computationally efficient algorithms achieve. This raises the following natural questions:

(1) For a given high-dimensional robust estimation task, can we achieve the information-theoretic optimal error in polynomial time?
(2) For a given high-dimensional robust estimation task, can we design computationally efficient robust estimators with optimal sample complexity?

For a concrete example of (1), we would like to know whether the error upper bound of $O(\epsilon \sqrt{\log(1/\epsilon)})$ for high-dimensional robust mean estimation of an isotropic Gaussian in the strong contamination model (given in Chapter 2) is inherent for polynomial-time algorithms, or whether an efficient algorithm with error $O(\epsilon)$ could be obtained. For a concrete example of (2), we would like to know whether an efficient algorithm for robust k-sparse mean estimation with the optimal sample complexity of $O(k \log(d))$ is possible, or whether the $\Omega(k^2)$ sample size required by known efficient algorithms (given in Chapter 3) is inherent.

Unfortunately, the state of the art in computational complexity theory does not provide tools for proving unconditional lower bounds for such problems.

For example, it is not hard to see that approximations to the Tukey median can be computed within the polynomial hierarchy. Therefore, unless we can prove that P $\neq$ NP (which does not seem likely in the near future), it is impossible to prove unconditionally that, for example, $O(\epsilon)$ error is unachievable for Gaussian robust mean estimation in polynomial time. Even proving such a statement under more standard worst-case hardness assumptions seems somewhat out of reach in most cases, as the inputs to our algorithms are mostly random, rather than fully worst-case, and the theory of average-case complexity in NP is much less well understood than its worst-case counterpart.

In light of this discussion, there are two general techniques in the literature that have been successful in obtaining such hardness results:

(1) Proving unconditional lower bounds for expressive, yet restricted, families of algorithms. One of the most popular such family is that of Statistical Query (SQ) algorithms. Others include lower bounds against convex programming hierarchies.

(2) Proving reduction-based hardness, starting from a conjecturally average-case hard or a worst-case hard problem. A few such reductions have been obtained in the literature, starting from different hardness assumptions.

The structure of this chapter is as follows: In Section 8.2, we define the SQ model and provide a general technique to establish SQ lower bounds for high-dimensional learning problems. Building on this methodology, we deduce information-computation trade-offs for a range of robust learning problems. In Section 8.3, we survey a recent line of work on establishing reduction-based hardness results for robust learning problems. Interestingly, some of these reductions are inspired by the SQ lower bound constructions of Section 8.2.

8.2 Statistical Query Lower Bounds

8.2.1 The SQ Learning Model

To motivate the Statistical Query learning model, it is natural to ask what are the kinds of techniques employed by the robust statistics algorithms we have seen thus far in this book. First, our algorithms approximately compute moments of distributions. Another useful operation is approximating the fraction of points that lie in some region. Perhaps more generally, the algorithms do the above after ignoring the points that satisfy some filter conditions. More broadly, all these algorithmic operations amount to approximating the expectations of $f(X)$, for various functions f, where X is the input distribution over the corrupted points. In fact, a wide range of (but not all) algorithms in the learning theory literature – and particularly those with worst-case performance guarantees in the presence of noisy data – are or can be rephrased as algorithms of this kind.

In particular, we would like to consider a restricted class of algorithms that access their samples only by using them to approximate the expectations of certain carefully chosen functions. We formalize this discussion in terms of the following definition.

Definition 8.1 (STAT Oracle)   Let D be a distribution on $\mathbf{R}^d$. A *Statistical Query* is a bounded function $q : \mathbf{R}^d \to [-1, 1]$. For $\tau > 0$, the STAT(τ) oracle responds to the query q with a value v such that $|v - \mathbf{E}_{X \sim D}[q(X)]| \le \tau$. We call τ the *tolerance* of the Statistical Query.

A *Statistical Query algorithm* is an algorithm whose objective is to learn some information about an unknown distribution D by making adaptive calls to the corresponding STAT(τ) oracle.

The SQ model was introduced in the context of supervised learning as a natural restriction of the PAC model. Subsequently, the SQ model has been extensively studied in a plethora of contexts, and in particular for search problems over distributions. The SQ model will be important to us because of two important properties that it possesses.

The Model Is Expressive   As already discussed, most common statistical algorithms can be rephrased in terms of Statistical Query algorithms. More generally, the class of SQ algorithms is fairly broad: A wide range of known algorithmic techniques in machine learning are known to be implementable in the SQ model. These include spectral techniques, moment and tensor methods, local search (e.g., Expectation Maximization), and many others. In the context of algorithmic robust statistics, essentially all known algorithms with nontrivial performance guarantees are either SQ or are implementable using statistical queries. On the other hand, it is important to note that not all algorithms can be efficiently simulated in the SQ model. A notable exception is Gaussian elimination, which is the natural method to learn parity functions.

The Model Is Analyzable   When analyzing statistical query algorithms, one usually considers only the number of queries and their error tolerance as complexity measures, and not the computational complexity of deciding on what queries to make or how to analyze them. While, on the one hand, this makes the SQ model very powerful (perhaps even able to make use of uncomputable functions in deciding what to do), SQ algorithms remain quite limited because they are allowed to access the distribution D *only* through statistical queries rather than by directly accessing the samples. This means that one can often prove information-theoretic lower bounds against SQ algorithms without having to worry about computational complexity issues.

SQ Algorithms versus Traditional Algorithms Although the SQ model is quite different than that of actual algorithms (both in terms of how they access the distribution D and how computational cost is evaluated), there is a fairly reasonable relation between the complexity of a problem in the SQ model and what one would expect the actual computational complexity to be. In particular, a Statistical Query with accuracy τ can be implemented with error probability δ by taking $O(\log(1/\delta)/\tau^2)$ samples and evaluating the empirical mean of the query function f. Thus, an SQ algorithm that makes n queries of accuracy τ can easily be implemented with constant error probability using $O(n \log(n)/\tau^2)$ samples. Most of the time (though not always), if the SQ algorithm is sufficiently adaptive the algorithm can actually afford to reuse the samples for the statistical queries and use roughly $O(1/\tau^2)$ samples total. While the runtime of simulating such an SQ algorithm may be unbounded (due to the fact that SQ algorithms are allowed to do unlimited computation), in practice the runtime is usually polynomial in the number of statistical queries used. Thus, an SQ algorithm that uses n queries of accuracy τ morally corresponds to an actual algorithm that takes $\text{poly}(n)$ time and uses $\tilde{O}(1/\tau^2)$ samples.

8.2.2 Statistical Query Dimension and SQ Lower Bounds

It is important to note that not only are lower bounds for SQ algorithms theoretically possible due to the limited access to the samples, but also that there are practical techniques for proving them. We begin with a special case for which lower bounds are relatively easy.

Problem: For a nonzero vector $v \in \mathbf{F}_2^n$, let D_v denote the uniform distribution over all points $x \in \mathbf{F}_2^n$ such that $v \cdot x = 0$. Given Statistical Query access to D_v, the goal is to determine v.

We begin by noting that if instead we are given sample access to D_v, it is easy to compute v in roughly n samples by taking the orthogonal complement of their span. This is one of the relatively few examples of a learning algorithm that (as we will soon see) cannot be efficiently simulated in the SQ model. In particular, statistical query algorithms cannot do linear algebra (or linear algebra-like things) without access to the individual samples.

To see why an SQ algorithm will have trouble with this problem, let us consider the outcome of a query. If we make a query corresponding to a bounded function f, we learn an approximation to $\mathbf{E}[f(D_v)]$. Using discrete Fourier analysis, we can write this as

$$\mathbf{E}[f(D_v)] = \hat{f}(1) + \hat{f}(\chi_v),$$

where $\chi_v : \mathbf{F}_2^n \to \{\pm 1\}$ is the character $\chi_v(x) := (-1)^{v \cdot x}$ and

$$\hat{f}(\chi_v) := \mathbf{E}_{x \sim_u \mathbf{F}_2^n}[f(x)\chi_v(x)].$$

We next note that by Plancherel's identity we have

$$\sum_{v \in \mathbf{F}_2^n} \hat{f}(\chi_v)^2 = \mathbf{E}_{x \sim_u \mathbf{F}_2^n}[f^2(x)] \leq 1.$$

In particular, this means that for almost all $v \neq 0$ the magnitude of the corresponding Fourier coefficient, $|\hat{f}(\chi_v)|$, will be exponentially small in n. More specifically, if the error tolerance τ of the statistical queries is not exponentially small in n, this means that an adversarial oracle will simply be able to return $\hat{f}(1) = \mathbf{E}_{x \sim_u \mathbf{F}_2^n}[f(x)]$ to nearly every query. More specifically, if the adversary selects a random $v \neq 0$ then for any query f to the STAT(τ) oracle, with probability $1 - O(2^{-n}/\tau^2)$ over the choice of v an adversarial oracle will be able to reply $\hat{f}(1)$ to the query. If an algorithm makes s queries to the STAT(τ) oracle, then with probability at least $1 - O(s2^{-n}/\tau^2)$ over the choice of v, the oracle will be able to respond with $\hat{f}(1)$ to each query f in the list. Therefore, unless $s/\tau^2 \gg 2^n$, there will be a constant probability that an adversarial oracle can answer every query in this way, and the algorithm will have only learned that v is in the (exponentially large) set of possibilities for which these answers are allowable. This readily gives rise to the following result.

Theorem 8.2 *If an SQ algorithm with access to D_v can learn v with constant probability using s queries to the STAT(τ) oracle, then it must be the case that $s/\tau^2 \gg 2^n$.*

Theorem 8.2 shows that any SQ algorithm that learns parities requires either exponentially many queries or queries of inverse exponential accuracy.

We would like to obtain a generalization of Theorem 8.2 that is applicable to any reasonable search problem over distributions. To devise such a generalization, let us spend a moment to think about how the proof of Theorem 8.2 works. We have a base distribution D (in this case, the uniform distribution over $\mathbf{F}_2^n$) and a large set of hypothesis distributions D_v such that for any test function f it will hold that for almost all v's that $|\mathbf{E}[f(D)] - \mathbf{E}[f(D_v)]|$ is small. This is what allows the adversary to always return the answer $\mathbf{E}[f(D)]$ and prevents an SQ algorithm from learning any useful information.

Why are these values usually small? For the parity learning problem, this follows from Plancherel's identity. This in turn can be shown by noting that the characters χ_v form an orthonormal basis for the class of real-valued functions over $\mathbf{F}_2^n$ combined with the fact that no vector with small ℓ_2-norm can have large inner product with many elements of an orthonormal basis.

For our more general SQ lower bound methodology, we will need to generalize the above technique in two ways. First, we will need to define a more general inner product on probability distributions. Second, we will need to generalize from orthonormal functions to near-orthogonal functions. We address these issues separately below.

For the first of these issues, how do we define an inner product over the space of probability distributions (or more generally measures) over some space S? Given two distributions, p and q, one is tempted to take the product of their probability density functions, $p(x)$ and $q(x)$, at a point x and integrate. Unfortunately, this definition behaves poorly under change of variables. To correct this, one can fix a base distribution D, take the product of $(p/D)(x)$ with $(q/D)(x)$, and integrate with respect to D. That is, we consider the quantity

$$\chi_D(p, q) := \mathbf{E}_{x \sim D}[(p/D)(x)(q/D)(x)],$$

which is invariant under change of variables. Furthermore, this is well-defined for any measures p and q for which the above expectation is absolutely convergent.

We now address the orthogonality issue. Our previous argument (for the case of parities) depended on the fact that a vector cannot have large inner product with many orthonormal vectors. Unfortunately, orthonormality is too stringent a constraint in our general context, so we will need the following generalization.

Lemma 8.3 *Let $v_1, v_2, \cdots, v_n$ be vectors in an inner product space with $\|v_i\|^2 \leq \beta$ for each i, and $|v_i \cdot v_j| \leq \gamma$ for all $i \neq j$. Let w be a vector with $\|w\| \leq 1$. Then it can be the case that $|w \cdot v_i| \geq 2\sqrt{\gamma}$ for at most $O(\beta/\gamma)$ many values of i.*

For this lemma, one should think of the case where β is bigger than 1, but not too large, and γ is quite small. The lemma says that if we have many pairwise near-orthogonal (and not too large) vectors, then no unit vector w can have large inner product with very many of them. The proof follows by assuming that a contradictory vector w exists and finding a linear combination $u = w + \alpha \sum_{i:|w \cdot v_i| > 2\sqrt{\gamma}} \pm v_i$ such that $u \cdot u \leq 0$.

In our context, we will want to pick a base distribution D and many other distributions D_i such that for $i \neq j$, the inner product $\chi_D(D_i - D, D_j - D) = \chi_D(D_i, D_j) - 1$ is small. Note that for any function f and distribution D_i, we have $\mathbf{E}[f(D_i)] = \chi_D(D_i, fD)$. This means that $\mathbf{E}[f(D_i)]$ will be close to $\mathbf{E}[f(D)]$ unless $\chi_D(D - D_i, fD)$ is large. We will use Lemma 8.3 to show that this cannot happen for many different values of i simultaneously.

Before we get into the formal statement of our generic SQ lower bound, we will want to formulate it as a decision problem. In particular, we require the following definition.

Definition 8.4 (Decision/Testing Problem over Distributions) Let D be a distribution and $\mathcal{D}$ be a family of distributions. We denote by $\mathcal{B}(\mathcal{D}, D)$ the decision (or hypothesis testing) problem in which the input distribution D' is promised to satisfy either (a) $D' = D$ or (b) $D' \in \mathcal{D}$, and the goal of the algorithm is to distinguish between these two cases.

We note that the hypothesis testing problem of Definition 8.4 may in general be information-theoretically hard. In particular, if some distribution $D' \in \mathcal{D}$ is very close to the reference distribution D, it will be hard to distinguish between D' and D. However, in the settings we consider in this chapter, this will not be the case. Specifically, the distributions $D' \in \mathcal{D}$ will be far from D in total variation distance. Under this assumption, one can reduce the hypothesis testing problem to the problem of learning an unknown $D' \in \mathcal{D}$ to small error.

In particular, we have the following simple lemma.

Lemma 8.5 *Suppose there exists an SQ algorithm to learn an unknown distribution in $\mathcal{D}$ to total variation distance ϵ using at most n statistical queries of tolerance τ. Suppose furthermore that for each $D' \in \mathcal{D}$ we have*

$$d_{\mathrm{TV}}(D, D') > 2(\tau + \epsilon).$$

Then there exists an SQ algorithm that solves the testing problem $\mathcal{B}(\mathcal{D}, D)$ using at most $n + 1$ queries of tolerance τ.

Proof We begin by running the learning algorithm under the assumption that the distribution in question is $D_0 \in \mathcal{D}$ to get a hypothesis distribution D'. We let S be a set so that $d_{\mathrm{TV}}(D, D') = |D(S) - D'(S)|$, and use our final Statistical Query to approximate the expectation of f_S, the indicator function of S. If our original distribution was D, the answer should be within additive error τ of $D(S)$. If our original distribution was D_0, it should be within additive τ of $D_0(S)$, which in turn must be within $(\tau + \epsilon)$ of $D'(S)$. However, we have

$$|D(S) - D'(S)| = d_{\mathrm{TV}}(D, D') \geq d_{\mathrm{TV}}(D, D_0) - d_{\mathrm{TV}}(D_0, D')$$
$$> 2(\tau + \epsilon) - \epsilon \geq \tau + (\tau + \epsilon).$$

Therefore, if our distribution is D, the expectation of f_S will be within τ of $D(S)$; and if our distribution is in $\mathcal{D}$, the expectation of f_S will be within $(\tau + \epsilon)$

of $D'(S)$. We can determine which of these is the case, and note that by the above, they cannot both happen. Thus, determining which of these cases holds will solve our decision problem.   □

We next need a notation for a collection of distributions that serve the role of our nearly orthogonal vectors.

Definition 8.6   We say that a set of s distributions $\mathcal{D} = \{D_1, \ldots, D_s\}$ over $\mathbf{R}^d$ is (γ, β)-correlated relative to a distribution D if $|\chi_D(D_i, D_j) - 1| \leq \gamma$ for all $i \neq j$, and $|\chi_D(D_i, D_j) - 1| \leq \beta$ for all $i = j$.

We are now ready to define our notion of dimension, which effectively characterizes the difficulty of this decision problem.

Definition 8.7 (Statistical Query Dimension)   Fix $\beta, \gamma > 0$ and a decision problem $\mathcal{B}(\mathcal{D}, D)$, where D is a fixed distribution and $\mathcal{D}$ is a family of distributions over $\mathbf{R}^d$. Let s be the largest integer such that there exists a finite set of distributions $\mathcal{D}_D \subseteq \mathcal{D}$ such that $\mathcal{D}_D$ is (γ, β)-correlated relative to D and $|\mathcal{D}_D| \geq s$. We define the *Statistical Query dimension* with pairwise correlations (γ, β) of $\mathcal{B}$ to be s and denote it by $\mathrm{SD}(\mathcal{B}, \gamma, \beta)$.

Importantly, a class with a large Statistical Query dimension will be hard to distinguish.

Lemma 8.8   *Let $\mathcal{B}(\mathcal{D}, D)$ be a decision problem, where D is the reference distribution and $\mathcal{D}$ is a class of distributions. For $\gamma, \beta > 0$, let $s = \mathrm{SD}(\mathcal{B}, \gamma, \beta)$. Any SQ algorithm that solves $\mathcal{B}$ with constant probability using only t calls to the $\mathrm{STAT}(2\sqrt{\gamma})$ oracle must have $t \gg s \cdot \gamma/\beta$.*

Proof   Let $D_1, D_2, \ldots, D_s$ be a collection of distributions in $\mathcal{D}$ obtaining the bound for SQ dimension. The adversary will either use the base distribution D or a random one of the D_i's. They will also have the oracle return $\mathbf{E}[f(D)]$ to each query f for which this is allowed. By Lemma 8.3, we note that even if the distribution is a random D_i, this will be allowed except with probability at most $O(\beta/(s\gamma))$. Thus, unless $t \gg s \cdot \gamma/\beta$, there will be a constant probability in either case that the oracle always returns $\mathbf{E}[f(D)]$, making it impossible for the algorithm to distinguish.   □

8.2.3 Non-Gaussian Component Analysis and Its SQ Hardness

While Lemma 8.8 provides the fundamental basis for essentially all known SQ lower bounds, this still leaves us with the problem of finding families of distributions with large SQ dimension. In particular, we want a method for generating families with large SQ dimension that is expressive enough that it can be used to prove lower bounds for many problems of interest. As many of the problems we have considered thus far involve Gaussian or Gaussian-like distributions, a family where the base distribution D is the standard Gaussian will be a good starting point. We will also need a convenient way of producing many distributions that look like D. In particular, we will do this by producing distributions that are distributed as a standard Gaussian in all but one direction, and will act like some other specified distribution, A, in the remaining direction v. This means that given a single distribution A, we can define a family of distributions by varying the hidden direction v.

This gives rise to the problem known and Non-Gaussian Component Analysis (NGCA). We define the distributions we are interested in as follows.

Definition 8.9 (High-Dimensional Hidden Direction Distribution)   For a distribution A on the real line with probability density function $A(x)$ and a unit vector $v \in \mathbf{R}^d$, consider the distribution over $\mathbf{R}^d$ with probability density function $\mathbf{P}_v^A(x) = A(v \cdot x) \exp\left(-\|x - (v \cdot x)v\|_2^2/2\right)/(2\pi)^{(d-1)/2}$. That is, $\mathbf{P}_v^A$ is the product distribution whose orthogonal projection onto the direction of v is A, and onto the subspace perpendicular to v is the standard $(d-1)$-dimensional normal distribution.

How hard is it to distinguish the distribution $\mathbf{P}_v^A$ (for a randomly chosen v) from a standard Gaussian? If A has an mth moment that differs from that of a standard Gaussian, then $\mathbf{P}_v^A$ will have an mth moment in the v-direction that differs. We can easily detect this by computing the mth moment tensors and comparing them, which can be done in roughly d^m time and samples (and can be implemented by an SQ algorithm of corresponding complexity). As we will see, this is essentially the only thing that can be done in the SQ model.

Thus, in order for the NGCA problem to be hard, it will need to be the case that A matches many moments with the standard Gaussian. Furthermore, to keep the parameter β small, we will need the χ^2-norm of A with respect to $\mathcal{N}(0, 1)$ to be bounded. This motivates the following definition.

Condition 8.10   Let $m \in \mathbf{Z}_+$. The distribution A on $\mathbf{R}$ is such that (i) the first m moments of A agree with the first m moments of $\mathcal{N}(0, 1)$, and (ii) $\chi_{\mathcal{N}(0,1)}(A, A)$ is finite.

Note that Condition 8.10-(ii) implies that the distribution A has a probability density function, which we will denote by $A(x)$. We will henceforth blur the distinction between a distribution and its density function.

We define the hypothesis testing version of the Non-Gaussian Component Analysis problem.

Definition 8.11 (Hypothesis Testing Version of NGCA) Let A be a one-dimensional distribution and $d \geq 1$ be an integer. One is given access to a distribution D so that either

- H_0: $D = \mathcal{N}(0, I) \in \mathbf{R}^d$ or
- H_1: D is given by $\mathbf{P}_v^A$ for some unit vector $v \in \mathbf{R}^d$, where $\mathbf{P}_v^A$ denotes the hidden-direction distribution corresponding to A.

The goal is to distinguish between these two cases.

Note that this is just the hypothesis testing problem $\mathcal{B}(\mathcal{D}, D)$ with $D = \mathcal{N}(0, I)$ and $\mathcal{D} = \{\mathbf{P}_v^A\}$.

Our goal will be to show that the Non-Gaussian Component Analysis problem has an appropriately large Statistical Query dimension, allowing us to prove strong Statistical Query lower bounds for it. Fundamentally, this depends on showing that for two unit vectors, u and v, that are not too close to each other $|\chi_{\mathcal{N}(0,I)}(\mathbf{P}_u^A, \mathbf{P}_v^A) - 1|$ is small.

Lemma 8.12 (Correlation Lemma) *Let $m \in \mathbf{Z}_+$. If the distribution A agrees with the first m moments of $\mathcal{N}(0, 1)$, then for all unit vectors $u, v \in \mathbf{R}^d$, we have $|\chi_{\mathcal{N}(0,I)}(\mathbf{P}_u^A, \mathbf{P}_v^A) - 1| \leq |u \cdot v|^{m+1} \chi_{\mathcal{N}(0,1)}(A, A)$.*

Proof We bound this inner product as follows. First, by definition we have

$$\chi_{\mathcal{N}(0,I)}(\mathbf{P}_u^A, \mathbf{P}_v^A) = \int_{\mathbf{R}^d} \frac{\mathbf{P}_u^A(x)\mathbf{P}_v^A(x)}{G(x)} dx,$$

where $G(x)$ is the probability density function of the d-dimensional standard Gaussian $\mathcal{N}(0, I)$. If $g(x)$ is the probability density function of the one-dimensional standard Gaussian, then we have $\mathbf{P}_u^A(x)/G(x) = A(u \cdot x)/g(u \cdot x)$. Therefore, letting $y = u \cdot x$, we have

$$\chi_{\mathcal{N}(0,I)}(\mathbf{P}_u^A, \mathbf{P}_v^A) = \int_{\mathbf{R}} \frac{A(y)}{g(y)} \mathbf{P}_{u,v}^A(y) dy, \tag{8.1}$$

where $\mathbf{P}_{u,v}^A(y)$ is the probability density function for the distribution $u \cdot \mathbf{P}_v^A$.

It remains to compute the univariate distribution $\mathbf{P}_{u,v}^A$. Note that if u and v are orthogonal, it is easy to see that $\mathbf{P}_{u,v}^A$ is $\mathcal{N}(0, 1)$, and thus $\chi_{\mathcal{N}(0,I)}(\mathbf{P}_u^A, \mathbf{P}_v^A) = 1$. If u and v are *nearly* orthogonal, one would hope that this is *nearly* true. More specifically, suppose that the angle between u and v is θ, so that we have $u \cdot v = \cos(\theta)$. We then have for some unit vector u' orthogonal to u that $v = \cos(\theta)u + \sin(\theta)u'$. Reparameterizing x as $(x_u, x_u', x^\perp)$, where $x_u = u \cdot x$, $x_u' = u' \cdot x$, and $x^\perp$ is the perpendicular components, we have that the probability density function for $\mathbf{P}_v^A$ is given by

$$\mathbf{P}_v^A(x) = A\left(\cos(\theta)x_u + \sin(\theta)x_u'\right) g\left(\sin(\theta)x_u - \cos(\theta)x_u'\right) G(x^\perp).$$

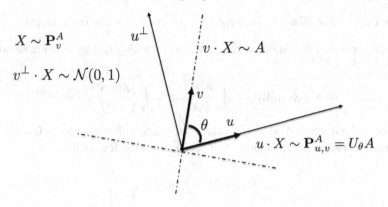

Figure 8.1 Illustration of the integrals in Lemma 8.12.

Therefore, the probability that x_u is equal to y can be obtained by integrating out over the other variables. Noting that the integral over $x^\perp$ separates out and gives 1, we have

$$\mathbf{P}^A_{u,v}(y) = \int_{\mathbf{R}} A\left(\cos(\theta)y + \sin(\theta)z\right) g\left(\sin(\theta)y - \cos(\theta)z\right) \, dz. \qquad (8.2)$$

Thus, we have shown that as a distribution on y, $\mathbf{P}^A_{u,v} = U_{\cos(\theta)}A$, where $U_{\cos(\theta)}$ is the *Ornstein–Uhlenbeck operator* defined by

$$(U_{\cos(\theta)}f)(y) := \int_{\mathbf{R}} f(\cos(\theta)y + \sin(\theta)z)g(\sin(\theta)y - \cos(\theta)z)dz$$

for any function $f \colon \mathbf{R} \to \mathbf{R}$. See Figure 8.1 for an illustration of the relevant variables.

In order to analyze (8.2), it is useful to express the relevant terms with respect to the eigenfunctions of the Ornstein–Uhlenbeck operator, which are well understood in terms of the Hermite polynomials (see Section A.2).

Let $He_n(x)$ denote the nth probabilist's Hermite polynomial, and let $h_n(x) = He_n(x)/\sqrt{n!}$. Then $\{h_n\}_{n\in\mathbb{N}}$ is an orthonormal basis of polynomials with respect to the Gaussian distribution. Namely, $h_n(x)$ is a degree-n polynomial and

$$\int_{\mathbf{R}} h_n(x)h_m(x)g(x)dx = \delta_{n,m}.$$

Furthermore, any function f with $\int_{\mathbf{R}} f^2(x)g(x)dx < \infty$ can be written as a sum $f(x) = \sum_{n=0}^{\infty} a_n h_n(x)$ for some coefficients $a_n \in \mathbf{R}$. Finally, of particular importance to us is the fact that the Hermite polynomials relate to eigenfunctions of the Ornstein–Uhlenbeck operator. Namely, we have the following fact.

Fact 8.13 *For all $n \in \mathbf{N}$, we have $U_{\cos(\theta)}(h_n(x)g(x)) = \cos^n(\theta)h_n(x)g(x)$.*

To apply this fact in our setting, we start by noting that by assumption we have

$$\infty > \chi_{\mathcal{N}(0,1)}(A, A) = \int_{\mathbf{R}} \frac{A^2(x)}{g(x)}dx = \int_{\mathbf{R}} \left(\frac{A(x)}{g(x)}\right)^2 g(x)dx.$$

That is, the function $A(x)/g(x)$ is square integrable with respect to the Gaussian measure. This means that there exist coefficients $a_n \in \mathbf{R}$ such that

$$A(x)/g(x) = \sum_{n=0}^{\infty} a_n h_n(x),$$

or equivalently,

$$A(x) = \sum_{n=0}^{\infty} a_n h_n(x)g(x).$$

Applying Fact 8.13 along with the linearity of $U_{\cos(\theta)}$, (8.2) gives that the distribution $\mathbf{P}_{u,v}^A = U_{\cos(\theta)}A$ has probability density function

$$\mathbf{P}_{u,v}^A(x) = \sum_{n=0}^{\infty} \cos^n(\theta)a_n h_n(x)g(x).$$

Thus, using (8.1), we have

$$\chi_{\mathcal{N}(0,I)}(\mathbf{P}_u^A, \mathbf{P}_v^A) = \int_{\mathbf{R}} \left(\sum_{n=0}^{\infty} a_n \cos^n(\theta)h_n(x)g(x)\right)\left(\sum_{m=0}^{\infty} a_m h_m(x)g(x)\right)/g(x)dx$$

$$= \int_{\mathbf{R}} \sum_{n,m} \cos^n(\theta)a_n a_m h_n(x)h_m(x)g(x)dx$$

$$= \sum_{n=0}^{\infty} \cos^n(\theta)a_n^2.$$

The next step is to gain an understanding of the coefficients a_n. By the orthonormality of the Hermite basis, we have

$$\int_{\mathbf{R}} A(x)h_n(x)dx = \sum_{m=0}^{\infty} a_m \int_{\mathbf{R}} h_m(x)\bar{h}_n(x)g(x)dx = a_n.$$

Noting that $A(x)$ matches its first m moments with the standard Gaussian, we find that for $n \leq m$ the following holds:

$$a_n = \int_{\mathbf{R}} g(x)h_n(x)dx = \int_{\mathbf{R}} h_0(x)h_n(x)g(x)dx = \delta_{0,n}.$$

On the other hand, we have

$$\chi_{\mathcal{N}(0,1)}(A,A) = \sum_{n,m} a_n a_m \int_{\mathbf{R}} h_n(x)h_m(x)g(x)dx = \sum_{n=0}^{\infty} a_n^2. \tag{8.3}$$

Combining the above, we obtain

$$\chi_{\mathcal{N}(0,I)}(\mathbf{P}_u^A, \mathbf{P}_v^A) = 1 + \sum_{n>m} a_n^2 \cos^n(\theta).$$

Thus, we conclude that

$$|\chi_{\mathcal{N}(0,I)}(\mathbf{P}_u^A, \mathbf{P}_v^A) - 1| \leq |\cos^{m+1}(\theta)| \sum_{n=0}^{\infty} a_n^2 = |u \cdot v|^{m+1} \chi_{\mathcal{N}(0,1)}(A,A).$$

This completes our proof. □

We are now prepared to introduce our main technique for proving SQ lower bounds.

Proposition 8.14 (Generic SQ Hardness of NGCA) *Let $0 < c < 1/2$ and $d \geq ((m+1)\log(d))^{(2/c)}$. Any SQ algorithm that solves the testing problem of Definition 8.11 for a function A satisfying Condition 8.10 requires either $2^{\Omega(d^c)}$ many statistical queries or at least one query to STAT with accuracy*

$$\tau \leq 2d^{-(m+1)(1/4-c/2)} \sqrt{\chi^2(A, \mathcal{N}(0,1))}.$$

A heuristic interpretation of this proposition is as follows. If we do not want our SQ algorithm to use a number of queries exponential in $d^{\Omega(1)}$, then we would need $d^{\Omega(m)}$ samples to simulate a single Statistical Query.

The proof of this result relies on three essential components:

1. The theory of SQ dimension to prove lower bounds (Lemma 8.8).
2. Inner product bounds on the $\mathbf{P}_v^A$'s given by Lemma 8.12.
3. A packing result showing that there exist exponentially many nearly orthogonal unit vectors in $\mathbf{R}^d$.

For the last of these we recall the following result (see Theorem A.10).

Fact 8.15 *For any $0 < c < 1/2$, there is a set S of at least $2^{\Omega(d^c)}$ unit vectors in $\mathbf{R}^d$ such that for each pair of distinct $v, v' \in S$, it holds $|v \cdot v'| \leq O(d^{c-1/2})$.*

Proof of Proposition 8.14 By Fact 8.15, we can find $s = 2^{\Omega(d^c)}$ unit vectors with pairwise inner products at most $O(d^{c-1/2})$. By Lemma 8.12, the corresponding distributions $\mathbf{P}_v^A$ satisfy $\chi_{\mathcal{N}(0,I)}(\mathbf{P}_v^A, \mathbf{P}_v^A) = \chi_{\mathcal{N}(0,1)}(A,A)$ and

$$|\chi_{\mathcal{N}(0,I)}(\mathbf{P}_u^A, \mathbf{P}_v^A) - 1| \leq d^{(m+1)(c-1/2)} \chi_{\mathcal{N}(0,1)}(A,A)$$

for $u \neq v$, from this set. This implies that the Statistical Query dimension of this Non-Gaussian Component Analysis testing problem with correlations $(d^{(m+1)(c-1/2)}\chi_{\mathcal{N}(0,1)}(A, A), \chi_{\mathcal{N}(0,1)}(A, A))$ is at least s.

Therefore, by Lemma 8.8, any algorithm that solves the testing problem of Definition 8.11 must either make queries of accuracy better than

$$2d^{(m+1)(c/2-1/4)} \sqrt{\chi_{\mathcal{N}(0,1)}(A, A)}$$

or must make at least $2^{\Omega(d^c)} d^{(m+1)(c-1/2)}$ queries. Note that by assumption $d^{c/2} \geq ((m+1)\log(d))$ and therefore $d^{(m+1)(c-1/2)} \geq 2^{-d^{c/2}}$. Thus, the query lower bound is $2^{\Omega(d^c)}$.   □

8.2.4 Applications to High-Dimensional Robust Statistics

The generic SQ lower bound for non-Gaussian component analysis established in the previous section can be used in a black box manner to obtain optimal SQ lower bounds for a range of high-dimensional robust estimation tasks. Given the results of the previous section, it suffices to find a univariate distribution A satisfying Condition 8.10 such that the distribution $\mathbf{P}_v^A$ belongs in the desired family.

Here we focus on the following estimation tasks: In Section 8.2.4.1, we prove an SQ lower bound for the problem of robustly estimating the mean of an identity covariance Gaussian in the total variation contamination model. Specifically, we show that the $O(\epsilon \sqrt{\log(1/\epsilon)})$ error guarantee of known efficient algorithms is best possible for polynomial query/accuracy SQ algorithms. In Section 8.2.4.2, we move to the problem of list-decodable mean estimation and show a nearly tight trade-off between error guarantee and SQ complexity. Finally, in Section 8.2.4.3, we establish an essentially tight SQ lower bound for robust sparse mean estimation.

8.2.4.1 SQ Hardness of Gaussian Robust Mean Estimation

In this section, we prove an SQ lower bound for robust mean estimation of an identity covariance Gaussian in the total variation contamination model.

Before we state our SQ lower bound, we recall the information-theoretic limits of Gaussian robust mean estimation. As shown in Proposition 1.20, it is information-theoretically possible to robustly estimate the mean of $\mathcal{N}(\mu, I)$ within ℓ_2-error $O(\epsilon)$ in the strong contamination model. On the other hand, no known efficient algorithm achieves this error guarantee. Specifically, both the unknown convex programming method and the filtering technique of Chapter 2 achieve error $\Omega(\epsilon \sqrt{\log(1/\epsilon)})$ in the strong contamination model. The SQ lower bound shown in this section provides evidence that this error gap may be inherent.

To prove our SQ lower bound for Gaussian robust mean estimation, we consider the following hypothesis testing problem. Given access to a distribution D on $\mathbf{R}^d$, we want to distinguish between the following two cases:

- D is the standard multivariate Gaussian, that is, $D = \mathcal{N}(0, I)$.
- D is an ϵ-corruption, in total variation distance, of a distribution $\mathcal{N}(\mu, I)$, where $\|\mu\|_2 \geq c\epsilon\sqrt{\log(1/\epsilon)}$ for some sufficiently small constant $c > 0$, that is, $d_{\mathrm{TV}}(D, \mathcal{N}(\mu, I)) \leq \epsilon$.

We will show that any SQ algorithm that correctly distinguishes between these two cases either requires $2^{d^{\Omega(1)}}$ queries or needs to use queries of accuracy $\tau \leq d^{-\omega_c(1)}$, where $\omega_c(1)$ denotes some quantity that goes to infinity as c goes to 0.

Given the SQ hardness for this hypothesis testing problem, we immediately obtain the same SQ hardness for the robust mean estimation problem. In particular, it follows that any SQ algorithm that robustly estimates the mean within error $\delta \leq (c/2)\epsilon\sqrt{\log(1/\epsilon)}$ has super-polynomial SQ complexity. Formally, we prove the following theorem.

Theorem 8.16 *Let $m \in \mathbf{Z}_+$, $c_m, \epsilon > 0$ be less than a sufficiently small function of m, and d at least a sufficiently large function of m. Any algorithm that given statistical query access to a distribution $\mathbf{P}$ on $\mathbf{R}^d$ such that either (a) $\mathbf{P} = \mathcal{N}(0, I)$ or (b) $\mathbf{P}$ satisfies $d_{\mathrm{TV}}(\mathbf{P}, \mathcal{N}(\mu, I)) \leq \epsilon$ for an unknown $\mu \in \mathbf{R}^d$ with $\|\mu\|_2 = c_m\epsilon\sqrt{\log(1/\epsilon)}$ requires either at least $2^{d^{\Omega(1)}}$ queries or some queries with accuracy smaller than $d^{-\Omega(m)}$.*

Before we proceed, we remark that Theorem 8.16 rules out efficient SQ algorithms (i.e., ones using at most $\mathrm{poly}(d/\epsilon)$ many queries of tolerance at least $\mathrm{poly}(\epsilon/d)$) with error $O(\epsilon)$, but it does not rule out algorithms with *quasi-polynomial* complexity, namely: $d^{\mathrm{polylog}(1/\epsilon)}$. (Note that the parameter m in the theorem statement cannot be larger than $\Omega\left(\sqrt{\log(1/\epsilon)}\right)$). Interestingly, it turns out that there exists an SQ algorithm for the Gaussian robust mean estimation problem (in the strong contamination model) with quasi-polynomial complexity (see Exercise 8.11), and therefore the trade-off established in Theorem 8.16 is essentially tight.

To prove Theorem 8.16, we will combine Proposition 8.14 via the following proposition, which constructs the desired univariate moment-matching distribution.

Proposition 8.17 *For any positive integer m and any $\delta > 0$ less than a sufficiently small function of m, there exists a distribution A on $\mathbf{R}$ satisfying the following conditions:*

(i) A and $\mathcal{N}(0, 1)$ agree on the first m moments.

(ii) $d_{\mathrm{TV}}(A, \mathcal{N}(\delta, 1)) \leq O_m(\delta/\sqrt{\log(1/\delta)})$.

(iii) $\chi_{\mathcal{N}(0,1)}(A, A) = O(1)$.

Proof We note that $\mathcal{N}(\delta, 1)$ satisfies conditions (ii) and (iii). The basic idea of the proof will be to start with the distribution $\mathcal{N}(\delta, 1)$ and modify it so that it matches its low-degree moments with $\mathcal{N}(0, 1)$. We note that in the process of this modification, we can only afford to modify the distribution by $O_m(\delta/\sqrt{\log(1/\delta)})$ in L_1 distance, and we must moreover ensure that the modified "distribution" is still nonnegative. This latter condition is most pronounced in the tails of the distribution, where the probability density function of $\mathcal{N}(\delta, 1)$ was initially quite small. This means that we cannot afford to decrease the density in the tails by much without destroying the positivity condition. In order to avoid this, we will make modifications that do not touch the tails of the distribution.

In particular, let C be a sufficiently small constant multiple of $\sqrt{\log(1/\delta)}$. Choosing the constants appropriately, we can ensure that the probability density of $\mathcal{N}(\delta, 1)$ on $[-C, C]$ is pointwise at least $\delta^{1/10}$. We will then construct a distribution A that agrees with $\mathcal{N}(\delta, 1)$ outside of the interval $[-C, C]$. The fact that the probability density is sufficiently large in the range $[-C, C]$ will ensure that we do not need to worry about nonnegativity. In particular, we will let A have density

$$A(x) = g(x - \delta) + \mathbf{1}_{[-C,C]}(x)p(x),$$

for some function $p\colon [-C, C] \to \mathbf{R}$ satisfying the following:

(i) For each integer $0 \leq t \leq m$: $\int_{-C}^{C} p(x)x^t dx = \mathbf{E}[G^t] - \mathbf{E}[(G + \delta)^t]$, where $G \sim \mathcal{N}(0, 1)$.

(ii) $\int_{-C}^{C} |p(x)|dx = O_m(\delta/\sqrt{\log(1/\delta)})$.

(iii) For each $x \in [-C, C]$, we have $|p(x)| \leq \delta^{1/10}$.

We note that the first condition here implies that $A(x)$ matches its first m moments with $\mathcal{N}(0, 1)$. Moreover, taking $t = 0$ ensures that A is appropriately normalized. This, along with condition (iii), implies that A is actually a probability distribution. Condition (ii) implies the necessary bound on $d_{\mathrm{TV}}(A, \mathcal{N}(\delta, 1))$. Finally, the bound on $\chi_{\mathcal{N}(0,1)}(A, A)$ is easily verified given (iii).

An example of the resulting distribution can be found in Figure 8.2.

It remains to construct the function p. Out of the conditions given, condition (i) is substantially the most restrictive, so we will focus on it. We note that each value of t implies a single linear condition on p. This suggests that as long as we take p from a sufficiently large family, we can simply solve a system

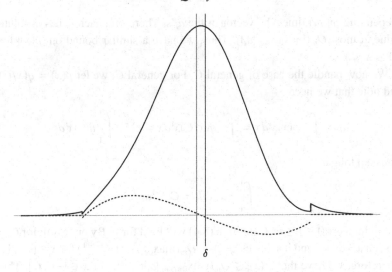

Figure 8.2 Illustration of moment matching distribution A of Proposition 8.17 for $\delta = 0.2$, $C = 2.6$, and $m = 4$. The dotted curve shows the polynomial p.

of linear equations to find it. It is particularly convenient to take p to be a polynomial. To show that this choice works, we present the following lemma.

Lemma 8.18   *Let $C > 0$ and $m \in \mathbf{Z}_+$. For any $a_0, a_1, \cdots, a_m \in \mathbf{R}$, there exists a unique degree at most m polynomial $p : \mathbf{R} \to \mathbf{R}$ such that for each integer $0 \leq t \leq m$, we have*

$$\int_{-C}^{C} p(x)x^t dx = a_t. \tag{8.4}$$

Furthermore, for each $x \in [-C, C]$ we have $|p(x)| \leq O_m(\max_{0 \leq t \leq m} |a_t| C^{-t-1})$.

Proof   We first prove the desired statement for $C = 1$ and then reduce to this case. Let $p(x) = \sum_{i=0}^{m} c_i x^i$ for $c_i \in \mathbf{R}$. We note that Condition (8.4) is a system of $(m + 1)$ linear equations in the $m + 1$ variables c_i. As long as this system is not degenerate, there will necessarily be a unique solution. Therefore, as a first step, we need to show that the system in question is not degenerate. In particular, we need to show that there is no nonzero degree at most m polynomial $p(x)$ such that $\int_{-1}^{1} p(x)x^t dt = 0$ for all integers $0 \leq t \leq m$. To see this, note that since p itself is a linear combination of the x^t for $0 \leq t \leq m$, if this condition was true, it would be the case that $\int_{-1}^{1} p^2(x)dx = 0$, which can hold only if $p \equiv 0$. This establishes that there is a unique solution.

We next need to show that the size of the polynomial is bounded. To prove this, we use the fact that the coefficients of p are some linear transformation (depending on m) times the vector of the a_i's. Therefore, each c_i has absolute value at most $O_m(\max_{0 \le t \le m} |a_t|)$. Thus, we have a similar bound on $|p(x)|$ for $-1 \le x \le 1$.

We now handle the case of general C. For general C, we let $p(x) = q(x/C)$ and note that we need

$$a_t = \int_{-C}^{C} p(x) x^t dx = \int_{-C}^{C} q(x/C) x^t dx = C^{t+1} \int_{-1}^{1} q(x) x^t dt.$$

Thus, so long as

$$\int_{-1}^{1} q(x) x^t dt = C^{-t-1} a_t$$

for all integers $0 \le t \le m$, Condition (8.4) will hold for p. By our result for $C = 1$, such a q exists and it satisfies $|q(x)| \le O_m(\max_{0 \le t \le m} |a_t| C^{-t-1})$ for $x \in [-1, 1]$. Therefore, we have that $|p(x)| \le O_m(\max_{0 \le t \le m} |a_t| C^{-t-1})$ for $x \in [-C, C]$. This completes the proof.   □

To complete the proof of Proposition 8.17, we just need to apply Lemma 8.18 to the sequence $a_t = \mathbf{E}[G^t] - \mathbf{E}[(G + \delta)^t]$. It is easy to see that $a_0 = 0$ and by expanding we can see that $a_t = O_m(\delta)$ for all larger t. Thus, such a polynomial p exists and $|p(x)| \le O_m(\delta/C^2)$ for all $x \in [-C, C]$. From this, conditions (ii) and (iii) follow immediately, and this completes our proof.   □

Remark 8.19   A more careful analysis of this argument can be used to show that the error in condition (ii) can be made to be only $\text{poly}(m)\delta / \sqrt{\log(1/\delta)}$.

Given Proposition 8.17, the proof of Theorem 8.16 is almost immediate. In particular, we can apply Proposition 8.14 to the distribution A from Proposition 8.17 taking $\delta = c_m \epsilon \sqrt{\log(1/\epsilon)}$. The Non-Gaussian Component Analysis hypothesis testing problem is then exactly that of distinguishing between $\mathbf{P} = \mathcal{N}(0, I)$ and $\mathbf{P}$ an $O_m(c_m \delta / \sqrt{\log(1/\delta)})$ corrupted (which is at most ϵ-corrupted for c_m small enough) Gaussian $\mathcal{N}(\mu, I)$ for some μ with $\|\mu\|_2 = \delta$. Proposition 8.17 implies that A satisfies Condition 8.10, and therefore Proposition 8.14 implies the stated lower bound.

8.2.4.2 SQ Hardness of List-Decodable Gaussian Mean Estimation

In this section, we study the problem of list-decodable mean estimation, when an $\alpha < 1/2$ fraction of the points are inliers drawn from an unknown mean and identity covariance Gaussian $\mathcal{N}(\mu, I)$. The goal is to output a list of $O(1/\alpha)$ many hypothesis vectors at least one of which is close to μ in ℓ_2-distance.

In Chapter 5, we showed that the information-theoretically optimal error for this problem is $\Theta(\sqrt{\log(1/\alpha)})$ even with poly(d/α) samples (see Corollary 5.9 and Proposition 5.11). In Chapter 6, we gave an algorithm for this problem achieving ℓ_2-error guarantee $O(\alpha^{-1/k})$ with sample complexity and runtime $(d/\alpha)^{O(k)}$. Interestingly, these algorithms require super-polynomially many samples in order to achieve error that is subpolynomial in $1/\alpha$, despite the fact that this is not information-theoretically necessary. Here we show that the latter sample-time trade-off is qualitatively close to best possible for SQ algorithms. Specifically, we prove the following theorem.

Theorem 8.20 *For each $k \in \mathbf{Z}_+$ and $c \in (0, 1/2)$, there exists $c_k > 0$ such that for any $\alpha > 0$ sufficiently small the following holds. Any SQ algorithm that is given access to a $(1 - \alpha)$-corrupted Gaussian $\mathcal{N}(\mu, I)$ in $d > k^{3/c}$ dimensions and returns a list of hypotheses such that with probability at least $9/10$ one of the hypotheses is within ℓ_2-distance $c_k \alpha^{-1/k}$ of the true mean μ does one of the following:*

- *Uses queries with error tolerance at most $\exp(O(\alpha^{-2/k}))\Omega(d)^{-(k+1)(1/4-c/2)}$.*
- *Uses at least $\exp(\Omega(d^c))$ many queries.*
- *Returns a list of at least $\exp(\Omega(d))$ many hypotheses.*

To prove Theorem 8.20, we will similarly apply the generic construction of Section 8.2.3. The main technical ingredient is the following moment-matching lemma.

Lemma 8.21 *For $k \in \mathbf{Z}_+$, there exists a univariate distribution $A = \alpha \mathcal{N}(\mu, 1) + (1 - \alpha)E$, for some distribution E and $\mu = 10c_k \alpha^{-1/k}$, such that the first k moments of A agree with those of $\mathcal{N}(0, 1)$. Furthermore, the probability density function of E can be taken to be pointwise at most twice the pdf of the standard Gaussian.*

Proof As in the proof of Proposition 8.17, we start with a basic distribution and then modify it in order to correct the appropriate moments. In particular, we will start with a mixture of Gaussians $\alpha \mathcal{N}(\mu, 1) + (1 - \alpha)\mathcal{N}(0, 1)$, and then add to the probability density function a polynomial restricted to the interval $[-1, 1]$ in order to fix the moments. In particular, A will have probability density function

$$A(x) = \alpha g(x - \mu) + (1 - \alpha)g(x) + \mathbf{1}_{[-1,1]}(x)p(x)$$

for some polynomial $p(x)$.

This produces a distribution along the lines of the one in Figure 8.3.

In order to satisfy our requirements, it will suffice to have $|p(x)| \leq 1/10$ for all $x \in [-1, 1]$, and for each integer $0 \leq t \leq k$ it holds that $\int_{\mathbf{R}} A(x)x^t dx = \mathbf{E}[G^t]$. Rewriting the left-hand side of the latter, we have that it is equivalent to

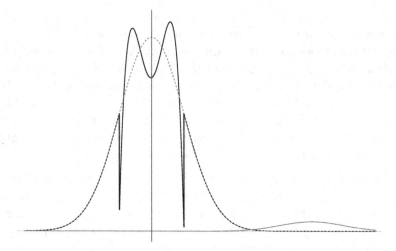

Figure 8.3 Illustration of moment matching distribution A of Lemma 8.21 for $\alpha = 1.5 \times 10^{-5}$, $\mu = 5$, and $k = 4$. The dotted line is the unmodified standard Gaussian $g(x)$. The bump on the right is a significantly exaggerated copy of the $\alpha g(x - \mu)$ component.

$$\alpha \mathbf{E}[(G + \mu)^t] + (1 - \alpha)\mathbf{E}[G^t] + \int_{-1}^{1} p(x)x^t dx = \mathbf{E}[G^t],$$

or equivalently,

$$\int_{-1}^{1} p(x)x^t dx = \alpha(\mathbf{E}[G^t] - \mathbf{E}[(G + \mu)^t]) = O_k(\alpha\mu^t) = O_k(c_k).$$

Invoking Lemma 8.18, we have that there is such a polynomial p of degree at most k with $|p(x)| \le O_k(c_k) < 1/10$ for all $x \in [-1, 1]$. This completes the proof of Lemma 8.21. □

We are now prepared to prove Theorem 8.20. Our starting point is to consider the Non-Gaussian Component Analysis problem stemming from the distribution A given in Lemma 8.21. We note that this distribution clearly satisfies Condition 8.10. We also note that one of the distributions $\mathbf{P}_v^A$ will be a mixture $\mathbf{P}_v^A = \alpha N(\mu v, I) + (1 - \alpha)E$, for some error distribution E. Thus, one should expect that an algorithm for robust list-decoding of Gaussians should reveal some information about this (we will formalize such a reduction later). Finally, in order to apply Proposition 8.14, we will need to bound the quantity $\chi_{N(0,1)}(A, A)$. Since A is a mixture of $N(\mu, 1)$ and some other distribution E, we can write

$$\chi_{\mathcal{N}(0,1)}(A, A) = O(\chi_{\mathcal{N}(0,1)}(\mathcal{N}(\mu, 1), \mathcal{N}(\mu, 1)) + \chi_{\mathcal{N}(0,1)}(E, E)).$$

Since $E \leq 2g$ pointwise, it is easy to see that $\chi_{\mathcal{N}(0,1)}(E, E) \leq 4$. On the other hand, direct computation shows that

$$\chi_{\mathcal{N}(0,1)}(\mathcal{N}(\mu, 1), \mathcal{N}(\mu, 1)) = \frac{1}{\sqrt{2\pi}} \int_{-\infty}^{\infty} \exp(-(x - \mu)^2 + x^2/2)dx$$

$$= \frac{1}{\sqrt{2\pi}} \int_{-\infty}^{\infty} \exp(-x^2/2 + 2x\mu - \mu^2)dx$$

$$= \frac{1}{\sqrt{2\pi}} \int_{-\infty}^{\infty} \exp(-(x^2 - 2\mu)^2/2 + \mu^2)dx = \exp(\mu^2).$$

Thus, $\chi_{\mathcal{N}(0,1)}(A, A) = O(\exp(\mu^2))$. Therefore, by Proposition 8.14, any SQ algorithm that solves the associated Non-Gaussian Component Analysis testing problem must either make queries of accuracy better than

$$O(\exp(\alpha^{-2/k})d^{-(k+1)(1/4-c/2)})$$

or use more than $2^{\Omega(d^c)}$ queries.

This proves the desired SQ lower bound for the NGCA testing problem. Unfortunately, it is not clear if there exists a simple and optimal reduction from the list-decoding problem to the testing problem. We will instead directly prove an SQ lower bound for the list decoding problem.

In particular, using Fact 8.15, we can let S_0 be a set of $2^{\Omega(d^c)}$ unit vectors with pairwise inner products less than $d^{c-1/2}$. We let $S = S_1 \cup S_2 \cup \cdots \cup S_N$, where each S_i is a random rotation of S_0. We note that taking $N = 2^{\Omega(d)}$ we can still make it hold with high probability that for any $v, w \in S$ we have $\|v - w\|_2 > 1/2$.

The adversary will let $X = \mathbf{P}_v^A$ for v a uniform random $v \in S$, and whenever possible will answer a query f with $\mathbf{E}[f(\mathcal{N}(0, I))]$. We note that by Lemma 8.12, the set of $\mathbf{P}_v^A$, for v in some S_i, are $(O(\exp(\mu^2))d^{k(c-1/2)}, O(\exp(\mu^2)))$-correlated. Therefore, by Lemma 8.3, for any query f there will be at most $d^{k(c-1/2)}$ v's in each S_i for which the adversary cannot return $\mathbf{E}[f(\mathcal{N}(0, I))]$. Therefore, if the number of queries is smaller than $2^{O(d^c)}$ with a sufficiently small constant in the big-O, for at least $9/10$ of the v's in S, the adversary will be able to reply this way to all queries.

In such a case, the algorithm will be left with a set of exponentially many possible equally likely answers μv. Since no hypothesis can be close to more than one of these, the only way to have a reasonable probability of success would be to return exponentially many hypotheses. This completes the proof of Theorem 8.20.

8.2.4.3 SQ Hardness of Gaussian Sparse Mean Estimation

In this section, we establish an SQ lower bound for robust sparse mean estimation, as discussed in Chapter 3. Our SQ lower bound gives evidence for the existence of an information-computational gap for this problem. Concretely, given ϵ-corrupted samples from $\mathcal{N}(\mu, I)$, where μ is guaranteed to be a k-sparse vector for some k much smaller than d, we want to efficiently estimate μ in ℓ_2-norm. In Section 3.6, we gave an efficient algorithm for this problem that robustly learns μ to ℓ_2-error $\tilde{O}(\epsilon)$ using $O(k^2 \log(d)/\epsilon^2)$ samples. This sample complexity bound can be much better than the $\Omega(d/\epsilon^2)$ samples required without the sparsity constraint, but it is worse than the information-theoretic optimum of $O(k \log(d)/\epsilon^2)$.

The SQ lower bound of this section provides evidence that the quadratic trade-off is necessary. In particular, we show that any SQ algorithm with queries of accuracy worse than $\tilde{\Omega}(k^{-1})$ (which roughly corresponds to algorithms taking fewer than $\tilde{O}(k^2)$ samples) will require a super-polynomial number of queries. These lower bounds can be made to hold even in the Huber model. It should also be noted that these lower bounds will only hold when d is substantially larger than k^2. This condition can be seen to be necessary, as there are efficient algorithms that succeed with $O(d)$ samples. Formally, we show.

Theorem 8.22   *Fix any $a \in \mathbf{Z}_+$. Let $k, d \in \mathbf{Z}_+$ be sufficiently large, and let $\delta, \epsilon > 0$ be any sufficiently small constants. Let $\mathcal{A}$ be any algorithm which given statistical query access to a distribution $\mathbf{P}$ on $\mathbf{R}^d$ of the form $\mathbf{P} = (1 - \epsilon)\mathcal{N}(\mu, I) + \epsilon E$, for some arbitrary distribution E and μ a k-sparse vector, returns with probability at least $2/3$ a vector $\widehat{\mu}$ with $\|\widehat{\mu} - \mu\|_2 < \delta$. Then $\mathcal{A}$ must either make at least $\Omega(d/k^2)^a/k^2$ queries or make some query with tolerance at most $O_{\epsilon, \delta}(a/k)$.*

Concretely, suppose that $d \gg k^{2+c'}$, for some constant $c' > 0$. Then, by setting a to be slightly super-constant, we have that any SQ algorithm either requires $d^{\Omega(a)}$ queries or at least a query of tolerance $O(a/k)$. Note that the latter corresponds to sample complexity slightly better than $\Omega(k^2)$. Alternatively, if we set a to be k^c for some $c > 0$, and $d \gg k^2$, we get that any SQ algorithm requires either 2^{k^c} queries or a query of accuracy $O(k^{-1+c})$.

To prove Theorem 8.22, we will construct a suitable one-dimensional distribution A and consider an appropriate collection of distributions $\mathbf{P}_v^A$, but this time only for k-sparse unit vectors v on $\mathbf{R}^d$. We start by showing an analogue of Lemma 8.15 for k-sparse vectors, and then use it to prove an analogue of Proposition 8.14. Our analogue of Lemma 8.15 is the following.

Lemma 8.23 *Let $a \in \mathbf{Z}_+$. There exists a set S of $(d/k^2)^a$ k-sparse unit vectors in $\mathbf{R}^d$ such that for any $u, v \in S$ with $u \neq v$ it holds that $|u \cdot v| \leq a/k$.*

Before we proceed with the proof of Theorem 8.22, we make a useful observation. By following the proof of Proposition 8.14 using Lemma 8.23 instead of Lemma 8.15, we obtain.

Proposition 8.24 *Consider a distribution A over $\mathbf{R}$ that satisfies Condition 8.10 for some $m \in \mathbf{Z}_+$, and some $a \in \mathbf{Z}_+$. Then any SQ algorithm that distinguishes between (a) $\mathcal{N}(0, I)$ and (b) $\mathbf{P}_v^A$ for k-sparse unit vector v selected at random from the set S of Lemma 8.23 must either make at least $\Omega(d/k^2)^a(a/k)^{m+1}$ queries or make some query of accuracy less than $O\left((a/k)^{(m+1)/2}\sqrt{\chi_{\mathcal{N}(0,1)}(A, A)}\right)$.*

We note that the proof of Proposition 8.24 is analogous to the proof of Proposition 8.14, except that we will use the set of $\mathbf{P}_v^A$ for v in the set S from Lemma 8.23, instead of the set from Fact 8.15. Theorem 8.22 follows from Proposition 8.24 with $m = 1$ for a specific distribution A.

Proof of Theorem 8.22 We select the one-dimensional distribution A as follows:

$$A = (1 - \epsilon)\mathcal{N}(3\delta, 1) + \epsilon N\left(-3(1 - \epsilon)\delta/\epsilon, 1\right).$$

Note that A has mean 0, that is, matches $m = 1$ moments of $\mathcal{N}(0, 1)$. It is also easy to see that $\chi_{\mathcal{N}(0,1)}(A, A) = O_{\epsilon,\delta}(1)$.

Applying Proposition 8.24 we get that any SQ algorithm that can distinguish between $\mathcal{N}(0, I)$ and $\mathbf{P}_v^A$ for k-sparse v must either make $\Omega(d/k^2)^a(a/k)^2$ queries or make some query of tolerance at most $O_{\epsilon,\delta}(a/k)$. This shows that the hypothesis testing problem is hard. It is relatively simple to show that this hypothesis testing problem reduces to the robust sparse mean estimation problem.

In particular, if our distribution is $\mathcal{N}(0, I)$, it is a (zero error) Gaussian with sparse mean 0, and so our algorithm will return a $\widehat{\mu}$ with $\|\widehat{\mu}\|_2 \leq \delta$. On the other hand, if our distribution is $\mathbf{P}_v^A$ for some k-sparse v, the distribution is an ϵ-noisy version of $\mathcal{N}(3\delta v, I)$, a Gaussian with k-sparse mean. This implies that our algorithm will return a $\widehat{\mu}$ with $\|\widehat{\mu} - 3\delta v\|_2 \leq \delta$, which implies $\|\widehat{\mu}\|_2 \geq 2\delta$. In particular, an algorithm that estimates the mean of an ϵ-noisy k-sparse Gaussian to error δ can solve the hypothesis testing problem by checking whether or not $\|\widehat{\mu}\|_2 > 3\delta/2$. Thus, any such algorithm if implemented with statistical queries must either make $\Omega(d/k^2)^a(a/k)^2$ queries or make some query of accuracy at most $O_{\epsilon,\delta}(a/k)$. This completes our proof. $\qquad\square$

We complete the analysis with a proof of Lemma 8.23.

Proof Our set will consist of vectors v whose coefficients are 0, except for k coordinates where the coefficient is $1/\sqrt{k}$. We note that if v and w are such vectors, their inner product is b/k, where b is the number of coordinates in the intersection of their supports. In particular, for a fixed v, the probability that a randomly selected w has $|v \cdot w| \geq a/k$ is at most the sum over subsets of a coordinates in the support of v times the probability that those coordinates are in the support of w. This probability is

$$\binom{k}{a}\left(\binom{d}{k-a} \Big/ \binom{d}{k}\right) \leq k^a(k/d)^a = (k^2/d)^a.$$

This allows us to construct S via a greedy procedure. If $|S| < (d/k^2)^a$, then the probability that a randomly chosen w will have $|v \cdot w| \geq a/k$, for some $v \in S$, is less than 1, and therefore there exist w such that $|v \cdot w| < a/k$ for all $v \in S$. We can repeatedly add such w to S until $|S| \geq (d/k^2)^a$. This completes our proof. □

8.3 Reduction-Based Computational Hardness

The traditional complexity-theoretic approach of establishing computational hardness involves exhibiting polynomial-time reductions between problems. The golden standard in this setting is to obtain an efficient reduction from an NP-hard problem to our target statistical problem. While the reduction-based approach is very natural, there exist apparent obstacles to basing the hardness of statistical tasks on worst-case assumptions, such as P $\neq$ NP. At a high level, this is due to the fact that statistical problems defined in terms of well-behaved probabilistic models (e.g., the Gaussian distribution) are in some sense average-case problems. Hence, it is natural to seek reductions from computational problems that are believed to be average-case hard.

A very natural starting point for average-case reductions is the planted clique problem, where the goal is to find a hidden clique in a random graph. In Section 8.3.1, we give a reduction from a natural variant of the planted clique problem to the problem of robust sparse mean estimation. This reduction provides additional evidence that there is a quadratic gap between the sample complexity and the computational sample complexity of the latter problem, as indicated by the SQ lower bounds of Section 8.2.4.3.

In Section 8.3.2, we study the robust mean estimation problem under the assumption that the higher moments of the inlier distribution are appropriately bounded. We describe a reduction from a worst-case hard problem showing that a certain natural algorithmic approach for this problem is unlikely to give improved error guarantees.

8.3.1 Reduction-Based Hardness from Variants of Planted Clique

In the classical planted clique problem, the goal is to find a k-clique planted in an Erdos–Renyi random graph. In the hypothesis testing formulation of the problem, we want to distinguish between the case that the input graph G satisfies $G \sim \mathcal{G}(n, 1/2)$ versus $G \sim \mathcal{G}(n, k, 1/2)$, where $\mathcal{G}(n, 1/2)$ is an n-vertex random graph where each edge is present independently with probability $1/2$, and $\mathcal{G}(n, k, 1/2)$ is the graph obtained by planting a k-clique at random in $\mathcal{G}(n, 1/2)$. This problem is known to be information-theoretically solvable as long as $k \geq C \log(n)$, for any constant $C > 2$, and a straightforward quasi-polynomial time algorithm is known to exist. On the other hand, no polynomial-time algorithm is known for $k = o(\sqrt{n})$. Moreover, it is conjectured that this is inherent, that is, that no polynomial-time algorithm exists for the problem for all $k = o(\sqrt{n})$.

For the purpose of establishing reduction-based hardness for robust sparse mean estimation, it appears that the original planted clique conjecture is insufficient. To obtain such a hardness result, we begin by defining an appropriate variant of the planted clique problem.

Definition 8.25 (k-part Bipartite Planted Clique)   Let $n, m, k_n, k_m \in \mathbf{Z}_+$ be such that k_n divides n, and let E be a partition of $[n]$ into k_n sets of equal size. The k-part Bipartite Planted Clique problem, k-BPC$_E(n, m, k_n, k_m)$, is the hypothesis testing problem where one is given a bipartite graph G whose left vertex set is $[m]$ and whose right vertex set is $[n]$ and is asked to distinguish between the following two cases:

- H_0: For each $i \in [m]$ and $j \in [n]$, the edge $(i, j) \in G$ independently with probability $1/2$.
- H_1: One selects a random set $S_m \subseteq [m]$ of size k_m, and then selects a subset $S_n \subseteq [n]$ by picking a random element of each part of the partition E. One then includes all edges in $S_m \times S_n$ in G and adds each other element of $[m] \times [n]$ independently with probability $1/2$.

It is not hard to show that this hypothesis testing problem is information-theoretically solvable, as long as k_m and k_n are at least a sufficiently large constant multiples of $\log(mn)$. Furthermore, although this problem is not quite the same as the vanilla planted clique problem, similar heuristics suggest that this variant may be computationally hard, so long as $k_n = o(\sqrt{n})$ and $k_m = o(\sqrt{m})$.

Our goal in this section will be to reduce the k-BPC problem to the problem of robust k-sparse mean estimation. To that end, we will reduce it to the following decision version of the robust k-sparse mean estimation problem.

Definition 8.26 (Robust Sparse Mean Decision Problem) Given $s, d \in \mathbf{Z}_+$ and $\epsilon, \delta > 0$, we define the problem RSM$(s, d, k, \epsilon, \delta)$ as the decision problem where the algorithm is given s vectors in $\mathbf{R}^d$ such that either:

- H_0: These vectors are drawn independently from $N(0, I)$ or
- H_1: All but ϵs of these vectors are drawn independently from $N(\mu, I)$, for some k-sparse vector μ with $\|\mu\|_2 \geq \delta$.

The goal of the algorithm is to correctly distinguish between these cases.

We note that any algorithm that can estimate a k-sparse mean vector from s ϵ-corrupted samples to ℓ_2-error $\delta/2$ can solve this decision problem simply by checking whether or not the hypothesis mean $\widehat{\mu}$ has ℓ_2-norm more than $\delta/2$.

Our main goal will be to exhibit a polynomial-time reduction from the k-BPC problem to the RSM problem (with appropriate parameters). The basic plan will be to find a randomized function F such that (i) if F is evaluated on the H_0 distribution for k-BPC, we get the H_0 distribution for RSM, and (ii) if F is evaluated on the H_1 distribution for k-BPC, one gets a version of the H_1 distribution for RSM.

To begin with, we think of a bipartite graph coming from an instance of k-BPC as an $m \times n$ array of binary numbers, where we let the (i, j) entry be 1 if there is an edge between i and j and 0 otherwise. Similarly, an instance of RSM is a list of s vectors from $\mathbf{R}^d$, which we think of as a $d \times s$ array of real numbers. To make these instances more comparable, we will take $m = d$. The left vertices of our graph will now correspond to coordinates in $\mathbf{R}^d$ and the vertices on the right side will correspond roughly to samples (or, more precisely, the collections of $n' = n/k_n$ vertices coming from one part of the partition will correspond to collections of about $s' = s/k_n$ samples).

Phrased in this way, an instance of k-BPC drawn from H_0 is an $m \times n$ array of numbers each drawn independently from the Bernoulli distribution B (i.e., the random variable that takes values 0 or 1 each with probability $1/2$). An instance of k-BPC drawn from H_1 has a random $k_m \times k_n$ submatrix of all 1's and the other entries are drawn independently from B. Our first step in order to make this look more like the RSM inputs is to make these entries Gaussian. This is achieved via the following lemma.

Lemma 8.27 *For $\eta > 0$, there exists a randomized function f such that $f(B) \sim N(0, 1)$ and $f(1)$ is $\exp(-\Omega(1/\eta^2))$-close to $N(\eta, 1)$ in total variation distance.*

Proof We let $f(0)$ be distributed according to a distribution D_0 and $f(1)$ distributed according to D_1. If the desired distributions were meant to hold exactly, we would want $D_1 = N(\eta, 1)$ and $(D_0 + D_1)/2 = N(0, 1)$. Solving this system gives us $D_0 = 2\mathcal{N}(0, 1) - \mathcal{N}(\eta, 1)$. Unfortunately, this is not quite possible. The ratio of the densities of $\mathcal{N}(0, 1)$ and $\mathcal{N}(\eta, 1)$ is $\exp(\eta x - \eta^2/2)$. This quantity is bigger than 2 when x is sufficiently large (more than some constant times $1/\eta$), and thus, this difference is not always positive. However, the probability that x is this large (under either $\mathcal{N}(0, 1)$ or $\mathcal{N}(\eta, 1)$) is $\exp(-\Omega(1/\eta^2))$. Let X be some probability distribution with $X \leq 2\mathcal{N}(0, 1)$ pointwise such that X is $\exp(-\Omega(1/\eta^2))$-close to $\mathcal{N}(\eta, 1)$. We then define f so that $f(0) \sim 2\mathcal{N}(0, 1) - X$ and $f(1) \sim X$. It is easy to see that this satisfies our desired properties. $\quad\square$

As a first step, we will start with our k-BPC instance and apply f to every entry. This operation takes an instance of H_0 and turns it into a matrix whose entries are distributed as independent copies of $\mathcal{N}(0, 1)$. Moreover, it takes an instance of H_1 and turns it into something that is $k_n k_m \exp(-\Omega(1/\eta^2))$-close in total variation distance to a matrix whose entries are independent copies of $\mathcal{N}(0, 1)$, except for the $k_m \times k_n$ planted submatrix where the entries are $\mathcal{N}(\eta, 1)$.

This is a good start. The image of an H_0 instance is distributed much like an H_0 instance of RSM. Moreover, the image of an H_1 instance has many of the right properties as well. In particular, for all but $k_m = k$ of the coordinates, the entries in that coordinate are standard normal. Unfortunately, for the remaining coordinates, we get k samples which give $\mathcal{N}(\eta, 1)$, while the rest are $\mathcal{N}(0, 1)$. Instead, what we would like to have is that all but an ϵ-fraction of our samples are $\mathcal{N}(\delta/\sqrt{k}, 1)$ on these coordinates, and the remaining ϵs samples can behave arbitrarily. We will need another procedure to make this happen.

Lemma 8.28 *Suppose that k is at least a sufficiently large constant multiple of $(\log(s')s' + n')\delta^2/(\epsilon\eta^2)$. Then there exists a randomized function $g \colon \mathbf{R}^{n'} \to \mathbf{R}^{s'}$ such that $g(\mathcal{N}(0, I_{n'})) \sim \mathcal{N}(0, I_{s'})$ and $g(\mathcal{N}(\eta e_i, I_{n'})) \sim \mathcal{N}(v_i, I_{s'})$, where for each $1 \leq i \leq n'$, $v_i \in \mathbf{R}^{s'}$ is a vector with $(1 - \epsilon)s'$ of its coordinates equal to $\delta/\sqrt{k}$.*

For each coordinate and each block in our partition, we will apply g to the vector of values in that block. This will map our instance of H_0 of $k - \text{BPM}$ exactly to an instance of H_0 from RSM. Moreover, it will map an instance of H_1 from $k - \text{BPM}$ to something close in total variation distance to an H_1 instance of RSM.

Proof Our function g is actually quite simple. We will let $g(x) = Ax + Y$, where A is some carefully chosen $s' \times n'$ matrix and Y is a random variable distributed as $\mathcal{N}(0, \Sigma)$ for some carefully chosen Σ. It is not hard to see that $g(\mathcal{N}(x, I_{n'})) \sim \mathcal{N}(Ax, AA^\top + \Sigma)$. Therefore, it suffices to find A and Σ such that:

- $AA^\top + \Sigma = I_{s'}$.
- $A(\eta e_i)$ has $(1 - \epsilon)s'$ coordinates equal to $\delta/\sqrt{k}$ for each $1 \leq i \leq n'$.

For the first condition to hold, we note that it is enough to ensure that $AA^\top \preceq I_{s'}$, as we can then set $\Sigma := I_{s'} - AA^\top$. For the second condition, let $w_i = Ae_i$. We need it to be the case that $(1 - \epsilon)s'$ of the coordinates of w_i equal $\delta/(\eta \sqrt{k})$ for each i. We note that $AA^\top = \sum_i w_i w_i^\top$. Thus, it suffices to find w_i satisfying the above condition such that $\sum_i w_i w_i^\top \preceq I$.

This leaves the question of how to construct the w_i. One thing to note is that a set of corrupted samples trying to imitate samples from $\mathcal{N}(0, I)$ ought to have mean close to 0. This translates to saying that the w_i should have the sum of their coordinates roughly 0. This suggests the following construction: For each $1 \leq i \leq n'$ and each $1 \leq j \leq s'$, we let the jth coordinate of w_i be $\delta/(\eta \sqrt{k})$ with probability $(1 - \epsilon/2)$ and $-\big(\delta/(\eta \sqrt{k})\big)((1 - \epsilon/2)/(\epsilon/2))$ otherwise.

We note that this construction does leave open the possibility that we will have more than an ϵ-fraction of coordinates not equal to $\delta/(\eta \sqrt{k})$. However, by Markov's inequality, each w_i has at most a $1/2$ probability of being bad in this way. So, we will instead take w_i generated in this way, conditioned on the number of bad coordinates being at most $\epsilon s'$.

Thus, we need to show that with high probability $\sum_{i=1}^{n'} w_i w_i^\top \preceq I$. For this, we will use the matrix Chernoff bound (see Theorem A.8). We note that before conditioning, the coordinates of each w_i are independent with mean 0 with variance $O(\delta^2/(\epsilon k \eta^2))$. Thus, before conditioning, the expectation of $w_i w_i^\top$ is at most $O(\delta^2/(\epsilon k \eta^2))I$. Since conditioning on an event with probability at least $1/2$ at most doubles this expectation, we have

$$\mathbf{E}\left[\sum_{i=1}^{n'} w_i w_i^\top\right] \preceq O(n'\delta^2/(\epsilon k \eta^2))I.$$

Additionally, it is not hard to see that $\|w_i\|_2^2 \leq (s'\delta^2/(\epsilon k \eta^2))$. Therefore, by the matrix Chernoff bound, the probability that $\sum_{i=1}^{n'} w_i w_i^\top \not\preceq I$ is at most

$$s' \exp(-\Omega((\epsilon k \eta^2)/(n'\delta^2)(n'/s'))) = s' \exp(-\Omega((\epsilon k \eta^2)/(s'\delta^2))).$$

Given that k is at least a sufficiently large constant multiple of $\log(s')s'\delta^2/(\epsilon\eta^2)$, this will hold with high probability.

Thus, picking random w_i will suffice with high probability. One can produce an appropriate function g by finding such w_i, which allows one to define A and Σ satisfying the necessary properties. $\qquad\square$

This completes our reduction. Putting everything together, we obtain the following theorem.

Theorem 8.29 *Let* $m, n, k_n, k_m, k, s, d \in \mathbf{Z}_+$ *and* $\epsilon, \delta > 0$ *be such that:*

- $d = m$ *and* $k = k_m$
- k_n *divides both* n *and* s
- k *is at least a sufficiently large multiple of* $(\log(s/k_n)s+n) \log(k_n k_m)/(k_n)(\delta^2/\epsilon)$.

Then, if there is an algorithm that solves the $\mathrm{RSM}(s, d, k, \epsilon, \delta)$ *decision problem in time T with probability of success* $2/3$, *there is an algorithm that solves the* k-$\mathrm{BPC}(n, m, k_n, k_m)$ *problem in time* $T + \mathrm{poly}(nmsd)$ *with probability of success* $3/5$.

Proof Let η be a sufficiently large constant multiple of $\sqrt{\log(k_n k_m)}$. We consider the graph G given by the k-BPC instance in question and interpret it as an $m \times n$ matrix. We then apply the mapping f from Lemma 8.27 to each entry and then apply g from Lemma 8.28 to each block $\{i\} \times S$, where S is one of the parts of the partition E.

We treat the resulting matrix as an instance of $\mathrm{RSM}(s, d, k, \epsilon, \delta)$ and run the appropriate algorithm. Note that the conditions above are sufficient to imply that the conditions of Lemma 8.28 hold. Also, by the discussion above, it is not hard to see that this transformation maps the distribution over H_0 instances of k-BPC to the distribution of H_0 instances of RSM and maps the distribution of H_1 instances of k-BPC to some distribution close in total variation distance to a distribution over H_1 instances of RSM. This completes the proof. □

In applications of Theorem 8.29, we will usually want to take $n = s$. In order for the k-BPC problem to be conjecturally hard, we will want $k_n = o(\sqrt{n}) = o(\sqrt{s})$ and $k = k_m = o(\sqrt{m}) = o(\sqrt{d})$ (note that the latter condition is necessary to get a $\Omega(k^2)$ sample lower bound for robust mean estimation). Finally, if we allow ourselves to take k_n to be any function that is $o(\sqrt{s})$, we can make the last condition hold so long as

$$\sqrt{s} \log(s) \log(ds)/(\delta^2/\epsilon) = o(k).$$

In summary, subject to the hardness k-BPC, we have shown evidence that robust sparse mean estimation is computationally hard if one is only allowed to take $o(k^2(\epsilon^2/\delta^4)/\log^4(ds))$ samples.

8.3.2 Toward Worst-Case Hardness of Robust Mean Estimation

In the previous sections, we gave SQ lower bounds for a range of robust statistical tasks. We also showed that for some of these tasks, specifically robust sparse mean estimation, one can establish reduction-based hardness from a variant of the planted clique problem.

In this section, we will describe some progress toward establishing computational hardness for robust mean estimation under higher moment assumptions. An interesting distinction from the reduction-based result of Section 8.3.1 is that the reduction to be presented in this section is from a worst-case rather than average-case problem.

To set the context, we recall that if D is a distribution on $\mathbf{R}^d$ with bounded covariance, we can robustly estimate the mean of D to error $O(\sqrt{\epsilon})$ in polynomial time. Moreover, as we showed in Chapter 1, this error is information-theoretically optimal in this general context. In order to do better, one needs to assume some kind of stronger concentration bounds. A natural assumption is that of bounded central moments. In particular, if we assume that the inlier distribution D satisfies the following property: for every unit vector v, it holds that

$$\mathbf{E}_{x \sim_u D}[|v \cdot x - v \cdot \mathbf{E}[D]|^k] < 1, \tag{8.5}$$

then it is information-theoretically possible to achieve error $O_k(\epsilon^{1-1/k})$ using the inefficient higher moments filter from Chapter 6. We remind the reader the straightforward method to achieve this. One merely needs to compute the empirical kth moment matrix, look for directions v for which Condition (8.5) is violated, and filter in those directions. Unfortunately, the problem of determining whether or not such a direction v exists is nontrivial when $k > 2$ (as opposed to the case where $k = 2$, in which case it amounts to finding an eigenvalue of the moment matrix). This is why existing algorithms that take advantage of these higher moments have traditionally needed some additional assumptions beyond bounded central moments, for example, the condition that $\mathbf{Cov}[D] = I$ (which allows one to use stability, as in Chapter 2), or SoS-certifiable bounded central moments (as we used in Chapter 6).

This leads us to the natural question: Is it computationally feasible to robustly learn a distribution under *just* the assumption of bounded kth central moments to error $o(\sqrt{\epsilon})$? Although the answer to this question is widely believed to be negative, one cannot hope to demonstrate this with an SQ lower bound. In particular, the algorithm sketched in the previous paragraph *is* efficiently implementable in the Statistical Query model (assuming k is not large)! Indeed, the kth order moment tensor of D can be approximated using statistical queries, and at that point finding a direction v to filter in becomes merely a computational problem. This leads to an SQ algorithm with complexity roughly $d^{O(k)}$. (See Exercise 8.8 for a matching SQ lower bound.)

What we can consider instead is the computational hardness of this problem. Recent work showed that one can reduce the small-set expansion (SSE) problem to certain variants of this problem. The SSE problem roughly asks, given a graph G, whether or not there is a relatively small subset S of vertices so that $|\partial S|/|S|$ is small. In more detail, given a graph G on n nodes, in the SSE problem the goal is to find a small subset of the nodes (say, a small constant fraction) which is nonexpanding, that is, which has relatively few edges connecting to the rest of the graph. The SSE problem is a well-studied and conjecturally hard problem related to the Unique Games Conjecture. In terms of reductions, one can show the following.

Theorem 8.30 *Suppose that there exists an algorithm that for some $k \geq 4$ and some points $a_i \in \mathbf{R}^d$ can distinguish between the cases where the kth central moment of the a_i's is large in some direction and the case where all of the first k central moments of the a_i are small. Then there exists a polynomial-time algorithm for the SSE problem.*

The proof of Theorem 8.30 is somewhat involved and beyond the scope of this book. The high-level idea is that one could search for a nonexpanding set by searching for its indicator function using techniques from spectral graph theory. Specifically, given a graph on n nodes, one can efficiently find vectors $a_1, \ldots, a_n$ such that for any subset of vertices T, the distance of $1/|T| \sum_{i \in T} a_i$ to the origin depends on the expansion of the set T, with this distance being small for expanding sets and large for nonexpanding ones. Roughly speaking, the search boils down to finding a vector with large higher moments, and this search problem can be made equivalent to the search problem of determining if a point set has bounded central moments.

8.4 Exercises

8.1 (Statistical Query Algorithms and Random Classification Noise) One of the initial motivations for studying the Statistical Query model is a type of resiliency it has against what is known as *random classification noise*. In particular, when trying to learn properties of a Boolean-valued function f, one says that one has random classification noise at rate $\eta < 1/2$ if instead of seeing samples of the form $(X, f(X))$, the algorithm observes $(X, -f(X))$ with probability η. To be slightly more precise, first X is sampled from a marginal distribution, and then Y is set to be $f(X)$ with probability $1 - \eta$ and $-f(X)$ otherwise. The algorithm is then given samples from the joint distribution on (X, Y).

Suppose that one wants an algorithm to compute some properties of f given samples with random classification noise. Show that if there is a Statistical Query algorithm that given access to the *noiseless* distribution $(X, f(X))$ learns these properties using n queries of tolerance τ, then there is a noise-tolerant algorithm that, given access to the distribution with η random classification noise, uses n queries of tolerance $\tau/|1 - 2\eta|$.

8.2 (Statistical Query Algorithms for Robust Estimation) Show that the following algorithms can be simulated using Statistical Query algorithms. For all of these you may assume that all points of the distribution in question are contained in a ball about the origin of radius R (if this is not the case, certain technical issues arise).

(a) The filtering algorithm for robust mean estimation. In particular, if X is an (ϵ, δ)-stable distribution on $\mathbf{R}^d$ and Y another distribution with $d_{\mathrm{TV}}(X, Y) \leq \epsilon$, give an algorithm that given Statistical Query access to Y uses $\mathrm{poly}(d/\epsilon)$ queries of tolerance $\mathrm{poly}(\epsilon/(dR))$ and returns a $\hat{\mu}$ with $\|\hat{\mu} - \mathbf{E}[X]\|_2 = O(\delta)$.

(b) The multifiltering algorithm for distributions of bounded covariance. In particular, suppose X is a distribution on $\mathbf{R}^d$ with $\mathbf{Cov}[X] \preceq I$ and $Y = \alpha X + (1 - \alpha)E$, for some distribution E. Give an algorithm that given Statistical Query access to Y uses $\mathrm{poly}(d/\alpha)$ queries of tolerance $\mathrm{poly}(\alpha/(dR))$ and returns a list of $\mathrm{poly}(1/\alpha)$ hypotheses at least one of which is within distance $\tilde{O}(\alpha^{-1/2})$ of the mean of X.

8.3 (Degree Dependence for Moment Matching) Prove that the bound in Lemma 8.18 can be taken to be $\mathrm{poly}(m) \max_{0 \leq t \leq m} |a_t| \Omega(C)^{-t-1}$. A useful fact to that end is that the *Legendre Polynomials* (which are the orthogonal polynomials in the sense of Section A.2 for X under the uniform distribution over $[-1, 1]$) have the explicit formula

$$P_n(x) = \sqrt{\frac{2n + 1}{2}} 2^{-n} \sum_{k=0}^{\lfloor n/2 \rfloor} (-1)^k \binom{n}{k} \binom{2n - 2k}{n} x^{n-2k}.$$

Use this fact to prove Remark 8.19.

8.4 (Nearly Matching Moments) Lemma 8.12 holds when the first m moments of A *exactly* match those of a standard Gaussian. Unfortunately, sometimes this requirement is too much to ask for. Show that if instead we have $|\mathbf{E}[A^t] - \mathbf{E}[G^t]| < \nu$, for all integers $1 \leq t \leq m$, for some $\nu > 0$, then so long as $|u \cdot v|$ is less than a sufficiently small absolute constant, the following holds:

$$|\chi_{N(0,I)}(\mathbf{P}_v^A, \mathbf{P}_u^A) - 1| \leq |u \cdot v|^{m+1} \chi_{N(0,1)}(A, A) + \nu^2.$$

(Hint: You might need to use the fact that the sum of the absolute values of the coefficients of $h_n(x)$ is $2^{O(n)}$.)

8.5 (Optimality of SQ Lower Bounds for Non-Gaussian Component Analysis) Suppose that A is a distribution on $\mathbf{R}$ supported on $[-R, R]$ and suppose that for some positive integer m we have $|\mathbf{E}[A^m] - \mathbf{E}[G^m]| > \epsilon$. Show that there is a Statistical Query algorithm that given query access to $\mathbf{P}_v^A$

learns a vector u with $\|u - v\|_2 < 1/2$ using $O(d^m)$ queries of accuracy $\Omega(\epsilon/(dR)^m)$.

8.6 (Sparse SQ Lower Bounds) Prove Proposition 8.24.

8.7 (SQ Lower Bound for Robust Linear Regression) Let X be the standard Gaussian in $\mathbf{R}^d$ and let $Y = \beta \cdot X + \mathcal{N}(0, \sigma^2)$ for some vector $\beta \in \mathbf{R}^d$ with $\|\beta\|_2 \leq 1$. Let Z be a random variable in $\mathbf{R}^{d+1}$ such that $d_{\mathrm{TV}}(Z, (X, Y)) \leq \epsilon$. The robust linear regression problem asks one to approximate β given access to Z. It was shown in Exercise 7.3 how to achieve error $O(\sigma\epsilon \sqrt{\log(1/\epsilon)})$ in polynomial time. These algorithms can in fact be implemented in the Statistical Query model. In this exercise we will that this error is in fact optimal in the Statistical Query model.

In particular, show that no algorithm with Statistical Query access to Z can learn β to error $o(\sigma\epsilon \sqrt{\log(1/\epsilon)})$ with polynomially many queries of inverse polynomial tolerance. Note that this lower bound will be somewhat different than our other SQ lower bounds, because it will be hard to make Z imitate a standard Gaussian in the Y direction. Instead, we will want to produce a distribution such that conditioned on the value of Y, one will have an appropriate moment-matching distribution.

(a) Given any unit vector v, positive integer m, and $\epsilon > 0$ sufficiently small, produce a distribution Z_v such that:

   – Z_v is ϵ-close in total variation distance to the distribution (X, Y) when $\beta = v$.
   – For any value $y \in \mathbf{R}$, the conditional distribution $Z \mid Y = y$ is $\mathbf{P}_v^{A_y}$, for some distribution A_y that matches its first m moments with the standard Gaussian.

(b) Prove a correlation lemma showing that

$$\chi_{(\mathcal{N}(0,I),\mathcal{N}(0,1+\sigma^2))}(Z_u, Z_v) \leq |u \cdot v|^{m+1} \mathbf{E}_{y \sim \mathcal{N}(0,1+\sigma^2)}[\chi_{\mathcal{N}(0,1)}(A_y, A_y)].$$

(c) Use this to prove the final SQ lower bound.

8.8 (Lower Bound for Robust Mean Estimation of Sub-Gaussians) Consider the following robust estimation problem. Let X be a distribution in $\mathbf{R}^d$ with sub-Gaussian tails and mean μ with $\|\mu\|_2 \leq 1$. Show that for any positive integer $k > 2$, there is a $c_k > 0$ such that any SQ algorithm that, given access to an ϵ-corrupted version of X, learns μ within ℓ_2-error at most $c_k \epsilon^{1-1/k}$ must either use $2^{d^{\Omega(1)}}$ queries or some query of accuracy $d^{-\Omega(k)}$.

Note: There is a nearly matching SQ algorithm that uses $d^{O(k)}$ queries of accuracy $d^{-\Omega(k)}$ in order to learn the kth moment matrix, and then (using an inefficient algorithm requiring no queries) determines if there is a direction with large kth central moment and uses this to filter. Furthermore, this lower bound can be extended to encompass the assumption that X has a sum-of-squares proof of bounded kth moments, in which case this algorithm can be made to be computationally efficient.

8.9 (Lower Bound for Learning Mixtures of Gaussians) A classical unsupervised learning problem is that of learning mixtures of Gaussians. In particular, given sample access to a distribution $X \sim \sum_{i=1}^{k} w_i \mathcal{N}(\mu_i, \Sigma_i)$ in $\mathbf{R}^d$, the goal is to learn a distribution close to X in total variation distance. Prove that any SQ algorithm that achieves this for $k < d$ must either use exponential in d many queries or use some queries of tolerance $O_k(d^{-\Omega(k)})$. Show that this is the case even if $\|\mu_i\|_2 < \text{poly}(dk)$, and $(1/\text{poly}(d))I \le \Sigma_i \le \text{poly}(d)I$ for all i, and each component $\mathcal{N}(\mu_i, \Sigma_i)$ is far from each other component in total variation distance. What SQ lower bound can you prove for the special case of uniform weights, that is, when $w_i = 1/k$, for all i?

(Hint: You might want to consider the example of "parallel pancakes," where the Σ_i's are all the same but very thin in some hidden direction.)

8.10 (Information-Theoretic Bounds on NGCA Testing) In this exercise, you are asked to show information-theoretic lower bounds for the hypothesis testing version of NGCA (as in Definition 8.11), assuming that the distribution A satisfies Condition 8.10 with $m \ge 1$.

(a) Let d and N be positive integers and let D^N denote the distribution over $\mathbf{R}^{d \times N}$ given by taking N i.i.d. samples from the standard Gaussian $D = \mathcal{N}(0, I_d)$ on $\mathbf{R}^d$. Let D_0^N denote the distribution over $\mathbf{R}^{d \times N}$ obtained by picking a uniform random unit vector v and then taking N i.i.d. samples from $\mathbf{P}_v^A$. Show that

$$\chi_{D^N}(D_0^N, D_0^N)$$

$$\le \mathbf{E}_{u,v \sim_u \mathbb{S}^{d-1}} \left[\left(\chi_D(\mathbf{P}_u^A, \mathbf{P}_v^A) \right)^N \right]$$

$$\le 1 + O_m(Nd^{-(m+1)/2}\chi_G(A,A)) + O(\chi_A(G,G))^N(2^{-d} + d^{-mN/2}).$$

(b) Conclude that if $\chi_G(A, A) = O(1)$ and if N is less than a sufficiently small constant multiple of d, then $d_{\text{TV}}(D^N, D_0^N) < 1/10$, and thus the NGCA testing problem cannot be solved with $2/3$ success probability given only N samples. Note that this is an unconditional lower bound, even for non-SQ algorithms.

(c) Show that distinguishing between samples from $\mathcal{N}(0, I_d)$ and ϵ-corrupted samples from $\mathcal{N}(\mu, I_d)$ with $\|\mu\|_2 > 10\epsilon$ requires $\Omega(d)$ samples, even for constant ϵ. Show that this testing task is information-theoretically possible with $O(d/\epsilon^2)$ samples.

(d) Show that distinguishing between the standard Gaussian $\mathcal{N}(0, I_d)$ and the single spike Gaussian $\mathcal{N}(0, I_d + vv^\top/2)$ for an unknown unit vector v requires $\Omega(d)$ samples.

8.11 (Quasi-Polynomial Robust Gaussian Mean Testing) Theorem 8.16 shows that any SQ algorithm that distinguishes the mean of an ϵ-corrupted Gaussian being 0 versus 100ϵ-far from 0 requires super-polynomial resources. It turns out that the required resources do not need to be substantially super-polynomial. Show that, for some $k = O(\sqrt{\log(1/\epsilon)})$, if $X = \mathcal{N}(0, I_d)$ and X' is a distribution satisfying $d_{\mathrm{TV}}(X', \mathcal{N}(\mu, I_d)) \le \epsilon$ and $\|\mu\|_2 \ge 100\epsilon$, for some $t \le k$ the tth moment tensors of X and X' differ by $\Omega(\epsilon)$. Using this structural result, design an SQ algorithm using $\mathrm{poly}(d^k)$ queries of accuracy $\mathrm{poly}(\epsilon/d^k)$ to distinguish between these cases.

(Hint: Let $f(x)$ be a low-degree polynomial approximation to the function $\sin(c\mu \cdot x)$ for a carefully chosen constant c. Show that if the low-degree moments of X and X' agree, one can reach a contradiction by comparing the expectations of $f(X)$ and $f(X')$.)

8.12 (SQ Lower Bound for Robust Covariance Estimation in Spectral Norm) Consider the problem of robustly estimating the covariance matrix of a Gaussian $X \sim \mathcal{N}(0, \Sigma)$ on $\mathbf{R}^d$ in spectral norm. Specifically, assuming that $\|\Sigma\|_2 \le \mathrm{poly}(d/\epsilon)$, the goal is to output a hypothesis matrix $\tilde{\Sigma}$ such that $(1/2)\tilde{\Sigma} \le \Sigma \le 2\tilde{\Sigma}$, given access to an ϵ-corruption of X. Show that, for any sufficiently small constant $c > 0$, any SQ algorithm for this task requires either $2^{O(1/\epsilon)}\Omega(d^{c/2})$ queries or at least one query with tolerance $2^{O(1/\epsilon)}\Omega(d)^{-(1-2c)}$.

(Hint: Use the generic NGCA construction, where A is a carefully selected mixture of three Gaussians.)

Remark 8.31 An intuitive interpretation of this SQ lower bound is that any efficient SQ algorithm for this robust estimation task, for constant ϵ, requires $\Omega_c(d^{2-c})$ samples, for any constant $c > 0$. This is particularly interesting in light of the fact that information-theoretically $O(d)$ samples are sufficient (see Exercise 4.3).

8.5 Discussion and Related Work

The study of information-computation trade-offs in high-dimensional robust statistics was initiated in [63], which established the first such lower bounds in the Statistical Query model.

The SQ model was originally defined by [108] in the context of PAC learning of Boolean functions. The model was generalized for learning problems over distributions in [75]. The latter work also defined the notion of SQ dimension used in Section 8.2.2. For a discussion on the generality of the SQ model, the reader is referred to [74, 75, 76].

The Non-Gaussian Component Analysis problem was originally proposed in [20] and has since been studied in a range of works from an algorithmic standpoint, see [81, 138] and the references therein. The methodology of establishing SQ hardness for high-dimensional statistical tasks via non-Gaussian component analysis presented in Section 8.2.3 is due to [63]. The applications to robust mean estimation (Section 8.2.4.1) and robust sparse mean estimation (Section 8.2.4.3) appeared in the same work. The SQ lower bound on list-decodable mean estimation (Section 8.2.4.2) was obtained by [65]. It is worth noting that the NGCA-based framework has been leveraged to obtain SQ lower bounds in several subsequent works [48, 56, 57, 61, 62, 67, 68, 70, 79, 80]. Interestingly, for some of these problems, the SQ-hard instances have formed the basis for computational hardness reductions from cryptographically hard problems [23, 58, 82].

The reduction from the variant of the planted clique problem to robust sparse mean estimation presented in Section 8.3.1 is due to [21], and is an instance of a sequence of reductions obtained in that work. The reduction-based hardness for robust mean estimation presented in Section 8.3.2 is due to [93], building on ideas from [12].

The study of information-computation trade-offs in high-dimensional statistical estimation has been a growing field at the interface of Computer Science and Statistics during the past decade. A notable early result in this area is a computational-statistical trade-off established for the task of sparse PCA, under a plausible assumption on the average-case hardness of the planted clique problem [16]. More recently, a line of work has obtained lower bounds against the Sum-of-Squares hierarchy for certain statistical tasks, including tensor PCA and sparse PCA [91].

Appendix
Mathematical Background

Here we review some basic mathematical results that are required to understand some of the arguments in this book. These tools are not entirely standard and would disrupt the flow of the text if inserted directly into the relevant chapters. It is suggested that the reader skim the results in this section before reading and acquaint themselves with any topic with which they are not already familiar.

A.1 Martingales

At a casino you know that every game in the house is stacked against you. But despite this fact, you wonder if maybe some clever strategy of sequential bets would allow you to make money. For example, you could start with a small bet, and if you lose, make a larger bet to recoup your losses. If you lose again, you make an even larger bet, and so on. If you win any of these bets, you will make money and you will only come out behind if you lose enough times in a row that you can no longer continue this sequence of increasingly larger bets. This type of situation can be difficult to analyze directly if your strategy of what bet to place next depends in a complicated way on the outcomes of previous bets. However, the fact that each bet is individually losing suffices to show that even complicated combinations of bets cannot earn money.

A (discrete-time) martingale is a mathematical abstraction of the above notion of making a potentially complicated sequence of fair bets. There are also the related concepts of a submartingale and supermartingale, if the bets are always advantageous or disadvantageous, respectively. To formalize this, suppose that you make a sequence of bets and that X_n is a random variable specifying the amount of money you have after the nth bet. The fact that the $(n+1)$st

265

bet is fair means that even if we know the history H_n of the first n bets, it should hold that $\mathbf{E}[X_{n+1} \mid H_n] = X_n$. Relaxing this expectation somewhat, we find that $\mathbf{E}[X_{n+1} \mid X_1, X_2, \cdots, X_n] = X_n$. Formally, this is the property that defines a martingale.

Definition A.1 A (discrete-time) *martingale* (resp. submartingale, supermartingale) is a sequence of random variables $X_1, X_2, X_3, \ldots$ such that the expectation $\mathbf{E}[X_{n+1} \mid X_1, X_2, \ldots, X_n]$ equals X_n (resp. $\geq X_n$, $\leq X_n$).

The most basic result in the theory of martingales is that any sequence of fair bets is a fair bet; or equivalently all X_n in a martingale have the same expectation. The following lemma is easily proved by induction on n.

Lemma A.2 *Let $X_1, X_2, \ldots$ be a martingale (resp. a sub/super-martingale). Then for any n, $\mathbf{E}[X_n]$ equals $\mathbf{E}[X_1]$ (resp. is at least/most $\mathbf{E}[X_1]$).*

Suppose that you want to stop your sequence of betting early. To do this, you want some rule that, given the outcome of your first n bets, lets you decide whether to take the $(n + 1)$st. This leads to a notion known as a stopping time.

Definition A.3 Given a sequence of random variables $X_1, X_2, \ldots$, a *stopping time* τ is nonnegative integer-valued random variable such that whether or not $\tau = n$ can be determined from $X_1, X_2, \ldots, X_n$.

Unfortunately, using a stopping time cannot allow you to beat the casino either. This is formalized in the following classical result.

Theorem A.4 (Optional Stopping Theorem) *Let $X_1, X_2, \ldots$ be a martingale (resp. sub/super-martingale) and let τ be a stopping time, where $\tau \leq N$ almost surely for some integer N. Then, we have $\mathbf{E}[X_\tau]$ equals (resp. is at least/most) $\mathbf{E}[X_1]$.*

Proof The proof follows from noting that $\{X_{\min(n,\tau)}\}_{n \geq 1}$ is itself a martingale (or sub/super-martingale) and applying Lemma A.2.   □

Note that the assumption that τ is bounded here is critical. The gambler's ruin theorem says that if a gambler makes a sequence of fair \$1 bets until they run out of money, they will do so eventually with probability 1.

The main application of this theory we will need comes from combining Theorem A.4 with Markov's inequality.

Proposition A.5 *Let $X_1, X_2, \ldots, X_n$ be a supermartingale with $X_i \geq 0$ almost surely for each i. Let $x = \mathbf{E}[X_1]$. Then for any $t > 1$, we have*

$$\mathbf{Pr}\left[\max_{1\le i\le n} X_i \ge tx\right] < \frac{1}{t}.$$

Proof Let τ be either the minimum $i \le n$ such that $X_i \ge tx$, or n if no such i exists. Since τ is a stopping time, by Theorem A.4 we have $\mathbf{E}[X_\tau] \le x$. The result then follows from Markov's Inequality. $\qquad\qquad\square$

A.2 Hermite Polynomials

Let X be a real-valued random variable with infinite support such that $\mathbf{E}[|X|^n] < \infty$ for all n. It is not hard to see by induction on n that there is a unique set of polynomials $p_1, p_2, \ldots$ such that:

1. p_n is a polynomial of degree n with nonnegative leading coefficient.
2. $\mathbf{E}[p_n(X)p_m(X)] = \delta_{n,m}$.

This is proved essentially by applying the Gram-Schmidt process to the sequence $1, X, X^2, X^3, \ldots$. These polynomials are known as the *orthogonal polynomials* with respect to X.

When $X \sim \mathcal{N}(0, 1)$ is the Gaussian distribution, these polynomials are (up to normalization) the *Hermite polynomials*. The nth probabilist's Hermite polynomial is a polynomial, typically denoted as $He_n(x)$, that satisfies the desired properties up to normalization. In particular, if we define $h_n(x) = He_n(x)/\sqrt{n!}$, these are the correct orthonormal polynomials for the Gaussian distribution.

There are a few additional facts about Hermite polynomials that is critically leveraged in this text. The first is that they are a basis for the Hilbert space of L^2 functions over the Gaussian distribution. In particular, this means that if f is any measurable function with $\mathbf{E}[|f(X)|^2] < \infty$, there exist real numbers $a_0, a_1, a_2, \ldots$ such that $f(x) = \sum_{n=0}^\infty a_n h_n(x)$ almost everywhere. Furthermore, one can compute these a_n as $a_n = \mathbf{E}[f(X)h_n(X)]$.

Next, it is useful to note that there is an explicit formula for the Hermite polynomials. In particular, we have

$$h_n(x) = \sqrt{n!} \sum_{m=0}^{\lfloor n/2 \rfloor} \frac{(-1)^m x^{n-2m}}{2^m m!(n-2m)!}.$$

Finally, the *Ornstein–Uhlenbeck operators* are a series of operators mapping functions on $\mathbf{R}$ to functions on $\mathbf{R}$, defined by

$$(U_t f)(y) := \int_{\mathbf{R}} f(ty + \sqrt{1-t^2}z)g(\sqrt{1-t^2}y - tz)dz,$$

where g is the Gaussian probability density function. The eigenvalues of these operators can be expressed in terms of the Hermite polynomials. In particular, we have

$$U_t(h_n(x)g(x)) = t^n h_n(x)g(x),$$

where $g(x)$ is the probability density of the standard Gaussian.

A.3 Probabilistic Inequalities

The following basic probabilistic inequalities are used in various places within this book.

We start with Jensen's inequality for convex functions.

Theorem A.6 (Jensen's Inequality) *If $f: \mathbf{R} \to \mathbf{R}$ is a convex function and X a real-valued random variable, then we have*

$$\mathbf{E}[f(X)] \geq f(\mathbf{E}[X]),$$

assuming that both expectations are well-defined.

We will make essential use of the following version of Bernstein's inequality for sums of independent and bounded random variables.

Theorem A.7 (Bernstein's Inequality) *Let $X_1, \dots, X_n$ be independent, zero mean random variables with $|X_i| \leq M$ almost surely. Then, for any $t \geq 0$, we have*

$$\mathbf{Pr}\left[\left|\sum_{i=1}^{n} X_i\right| \geq t\right] \leq 2\exp\left(-\frac{t^2/2}{\sum_{i=1}^{n}\mathbf{E}[X_i^2] + Mt/3}\right).$$

We will also require the following concentration inequality for sums of independent matrix-valued random variables.

Theorem A.8 (Matrix Chernoff Bound) *Let X_n be a sequence of independent random variables valued in symmetric $d \times d$ matrices. Furthermore, assume that for each n, $0 \leq X_n \leq R\,I_d$ almost surely. Let $\mu_{\min}$ be the smallest eigenvalue of $\sum_{n=1}^{N}\mathbf{E}[X_n]$ and $\mu_{\max}$ the largest eigenvalue. Then, for any $0 \leq \delta < 1$, we have*

$$\mathbf{Pr}\left[\lambda_{\min}\left(\sum_{n=1}^{N} X_n\right) \leq (1-\delta)\mu_{\min}\right] \leq d\left[\frac{e^{-\delta}}{(1-\delta)^{1-\delta}}\right]^{\mu_{\min}/R},$$

$$\mathbf{Pr}\left[\lambda_{\max}\left(\sum_{n=1}^{N} X_n\right) \geq (1+\delta)\mu_{\max}\right] \leq d\left[\frac{e^{\delta}}{(1+\delta)^{1+\delta}}\right]^{\mu_{\max}/R}.$$

The following concentration inequality for low-degree polynomials over Gaussian inputs follows as a corollary of hypercontractivity.

Theorem A.9 (Hypercontractive Inequality for Gaussian Polynomials) *Let* $X \sim \mathcal{N}(0, I)$ *be a multidimensional Gaussian and let* p *be a degree-k polynomial. Then, for any* $t > 0$*, we have*

$$\mathbf{Pr}\left[|p(X)| > t\sqrt{\mathbf{E}[p(x)^2]}\right] \leq O\left(\exp\left(-(t/3)^{2/k}\right)\right).$$

The following result can be used to derive packing bounds of the unit sphere.

Theorem A.10 (Packing and Covering Bounds) *Let* x *and* y *be random unit vectors in* $\mathbf{R}^d$*. Then, for* $t \geq 0$*, we have*

$$\mathbf{Pr}[|x \cdot y| > t] < O(1)\exp(-\Omega(t^2 d)).$$

In particular, if $N = ce^{cd/t^2}$*, for some sufficiently small constant* $c > 0$*, then with constant probability* N *random unit vectors* $x_1, x_2, \ldots, x_N$ *satisfy*

$$\max_{1 \leq i < j \leq N} |x_i \cdot x_j| < t.$$

Conversely, for $0 < c < 1$*, we have*

$$\mathbf{Pr}[|x \cdot y| > c] = 2^{-\Theta_c(d)}.$$

This means that a maximal set of points $C \subset \mathbb{S}^{d-1}$ *such that for no* $x, y \in C$ *and* $z \in \mathbb{S}^{d-1}$ $|x \cdot z|, |y \cdot z| > c$ *will have size* $2^{O_c(d)}$*. For such a set* C *and any* $y \in \mathbb{S}^{d-1}$*, there will exist* $x \in C$ *and* $z \in \mathbb{S}^{d-1}$ *with* $|x \cdot z|, |y \cdot z| > c$*, which implies that* $|x \cdot y| > 2c - 1$*.*

We will require an additional powerful result from empirical process theory, known as VC inequality. To formally state it, we recall the definition of the VC-dimension.

Definition A.11 (VC-Dimension) For a class C of Boolean functions on a set $\mathcal{X}$, the *VC-dimension* of C is the largest d such that there exist d points $x_1, x_2, \ldots, x_d \in \mathcal{X}$ so that for any Boolean function $g: \{x_1, x_2, \ldots, x_d\} \to \{\pm 1\}$, there exists an $f \in C$ satisfying $f(x_i) = g(x_i)$ for all $1 \leq i \leq d$.

Equivalently, if C is a collection of subsets of $\mathcal{X}$, we define its VC-dimension to be the VC-dimension of the set of indicator functions of sets in C.

Given this definition, the VC inequality is the following.

Theorem A.12 (VC Inequality) *Let* C *be a class of Boolean functions on* $\mathcal{X}$ *with VC-dimension* d*, and let* X *be a distribution on* $\mathcal{X}$*. Let* $\epsilon > 0$ *and let* n

be an integer at least a sufficiently large constant multiple of d/ϵ^2. Then, if $x_1, x_2, \ldots, x_n$ are i.i.d. samples from X, then we have

$$\mathbf{Pr}\left[\sup_{f \in C}\left|\frac{\sum_{j=1}^n f(x_j)}{n} - \mathbf{E}[f(X)]\right| > \epsilon\right] = \exp(-\Omega(n\epsilon^2)).$$

Theorem A.12 essentially says that with a relatively small number of samples the empirical mean of f is close to the true mean of f for all $f \in C$ simultaneously.

A particularly useful application of this result comes from the following class of functions.

Lemma A.13 *Let C_d denote the class of degree-d polynomial threshold functions (PTFs) on $\mathbf{R}^n$, namely the collection of functions of the form $f(x) = \text{sign}(p(x))$ for some degree at most d real polynomial p. (Note that if $d = 1$, this is just the set of linear threshold functions (LTFs).) Then, the VC dimension of C_d equals $\binom{n+d}{d}$.*

References

[1] D. Achlioptas and F. McSherry. On spectral learning of mixtures of distributions. In *Proceedings of the 18th Annual Conference on Learning Theory, COLT 2005*, pages 458–469, 2005.

[2] Z. Allen-Zhu, Y. Lee, and L. Orecchia. Using optimization to obtain a width-independent, parallel, simpler, and faster positive SDP solver. In *Proceedings of the 27th Annual ACM-SIAM Symposium on Discrete Algorithms, SODA 2016*, pages 1824–1831, 2016.

[3] F. J. Anscombe. Rejection of outliers. *Technometrics*, 2(2):123–147, 1960.

[4] S. Arora and R. Kannan. Learning mixtures of arbitrary Gaussians. In *Proceedings of the 33rd Annual ACM Symposium on Theory of Computing, STOC 2001*, pages 247–257, 2001.

[5] P. Awasthi, M. F. Balcan, and P. M. Long. The power of localization for efficiently learning linear separators with noise. *Journal of the ACM*, 63(6):50:1–50:27, 2017.

[6] A. Bakshi, I. Diakonikolas, S. B. Hopkins, D. Kane, S. Karmalkar, and P. K. Kothari. Outlier-robust clustering of Gaussians and other non-spherical mixtures. In *61st Annual IEEE Symposium on Foundations of Computer Science, FOCS 2020*, pages 149–159, 2020.

[7] A. Bakshi, I. Diakonikolas, H. Jia, D.M. Kane, P. Kothari, and S. Vempala. Robustly learning mixtures of k arbitrary Gaussians. In *Proceedings of the 54th Annual ACM SIGACT Symposium on Theory of Computing, STOC 2022*, pages 1234–1247, 2022. https://arxiv.org/abs/2012.02119.

[8] A. Bakshi and P. Kothari. Outlier-robust clustering of non-spherical mixtures. *Computing Research Repository*, abs/2005.02970, 2020.

[9] A. Bakshi and A. Prasad. Robust linear regression: Optimal rates in polynomial time. In *Proceedings of the 53rd Annual ACM SIGACT Symposium on Theory of Computing, STOC 2021*, pages 102–115, 2021.

[10] S. Balakrishnan, S. S. Du, J. Li, and A. Singh. Computationally efficient robust sparse estimation in high dimensions. In *Proceedings of the 30th Annual Conference on Learning Theory, COLT 2017*, pages 169–212, 2017.

[11] M.-F. Balcan, A. Blum, and S. Vempala. A discriminative framework for clustering via similarity functions. In *Proceedings of the 40th Annual ACM Symposium on Theory of Computing, STOC 2008*, pages 671–680, 2008.

[12] B. Barak, F. G. S. L. Brandão, A. W. Harrow, J. A. Kelner, D. Steurer, and Y. Zhou. Hypercontractivity, sum-of-squares proofs, and their applications. In *Proceedings of the 44th Annual ACM Symposium on Theory of Computing, STOC 2012*, pages 307–326, 2012.

[13] B. Barak and D. Steurer. Proofs, beliefs, and algorithms through the lens of sum-of-squares, 2016. Lecture notes available on http://sumofsquares.org.

[14] M. Barreno, B. Nelson, A. D. Joseph, and J. D. Tygar. The security of machine learning. *Machine Learning*, 81(2):121–148, 2010.

[15] T. Bernholt. Robust estimators are hard to compute. Technical report, University of Dortmund, Germany, 2006.

[16] Q. Berthet and P. Rigollet. Complexity theoretic lower bounds for sparse principal component detection. In *Proceedings of the 26th Annual Conference on Learning Theory, COLT 2013*, pages 1046–1066, 2013.

[17] K. Bhatia, P. Jain, P. Kamalaruban, and P. Kar. Consistent robust regression. In *Advances in Neural Information Processing Systems 30: Annual Conference on Neural Information Processing Systems 2017, NeurIPS 2017*, pages 2110–2119, 2017.

[18] K. Bhatia, P. Jain, and P. Kar. Robust regression via hard thresholding. In *Advances in Neural Information Processing Systems 28: Annual Conference on Neural Information Processing Systems 2015, NeurIPS 2015*, pages 721–729, 2015.

[19] B. Biggio, B. Nelson, and P. Laskov. Poisoning attacks against support vector machines. In *Proceedings of the 29th International Conference on Machine Learning, ICML 2012*, pages 1467–1474, 2012.

[20] G. Blanchard, M. Kawanabe, M. Sugiyama, V. Spokoiny, and K.-R. Müller. In search of non-Gaussian components of a high-dimensional distribution. *Journal of Machine Learning Research*, 7(9):247–282, 2006.

[21] M. S. Brennan and G. Bresler. Reducibility and statistical-computational gaps from secret leakage. In *Conference on Learning Theory, COLT 2020*, volume 125 of *Proceedings of Machine Learning Research*, pages 648–847. PMLR, 2020.

[22] S. C. Brubaker and S. Vempala. Isotropic PCA and affine-invariant clustering. In *49th Annual IEEE Symposium on Foundations of Computer Science, FOCS 2008*, pages 551–560, 2008.

[23] J. Bruna, O. Regev, M. J. Song, and Y. Tang. Continuous LWE. In *Proceedings of the 53rd Annual ACM SIGACT Symposium on Theory of Computing, STOC 2021*, pages 694–707, 2021.

[24] N. Bshouty, N. Eiron, and E. Kushilevitz. PAC learning with nasty noise. *Theoretical Computer Science*, 288(2):255–275, 2002.

[25] M. Charikar, J. Steinhardt, and G. Valiant. Learning from untrusted data. In *Proceedings of the 49th Annual ACM SIGACT Symposium on Theory of Computing, STOC 2017*, pages 47–60, 2017.

[26] M. Chen, C. Gao, and Z. Ren. Robust covariance and scatter matrix estimation under Huber's contamination model. *The Annals of Statistics*, 46(5):1932–1960, 2018.

[27] S. Chen, J. Li, and A. Moitra. Efficiently learning structured distributions from untrusted batches. In *Proceedings of the 52nd Annual ACM SIGACT Symposium on Theory of Computing, STOC 2020*, pages 960–973, 2020.

[28] S. Chen, J. Li, and A. Moitra. Learning structured distributions from untrusted batches: Faster and simpler. In *Advances in Neural Information Processing Systems 33: Annual Conference on Neural Information Processing Systems 2020, NeurIPS 2020*, pages 4512–4523, 2020.

[29] Y. Chen, C. Caramanis, and S. Mannor. Robust sparse regression under adversarial corruption. In *Proceedings of the 30th International Conference on Machine Learning, ICML 2013*, volume 28 of *JMLR Workshop and Conference Proceedings*, pages 774–782. JMLR, 2013.

[30] Y. Cheng, I. Diakonikolas, and R. Ge. High-dimensional robust mean estimation in nearly-linear time. In *Proceedings of the 30th Annual ACM-SIAM Symposium on Discrete Algorithms, SODA 2019*, pages 2755–2771, 2019.

[31] Y. Cheng, I. Diakonikolas, R. Ge, S. Gupta, D. M. Kane, and M. Soltanolkotabi. Outlier-robust sparse estimation via non-convex optimization. *Computing Research Repository*, abs/2109.11515, 2021. Conference version in NeurIPS'22.

[32] Y. Cheng, I. Diakonikolas, R. Ge, and M. Soltanolkotabi. High-dimensional robust mean estimation via gradient descent. In *Proceedings of the 37th International Conference on Machine Learning, ICML 2020*, volume 119 of *Proceedings of Machine Learning Research*, pages 1768–1778. PMLR, 2020.

[33] Y. Cheng, I. Diakonikolas, R. Ge, and D. P. Woodruff. Faster algorithms for high-dimensional robust covariance estimation. In *Proceedings of the 32nd Annual Conference on Learning Theory, COLT 2019*, pages 727–757, 2019.

[34] Y. Cheng, I. Diakonikolas, D. Kane, and A. Stewart. Robust learning of fixed-structure Bayesian networks. In *Advances in Neural Information Processing Systems 31: Annual Conference on Neural Information Processing Systems 2018, NeurIPS 2018*, pages 10304–10316, 2018.

[35] Y. Cheng and H. Lin. Robust learning of fixed-structure Bayesian networks in nearly-linear time. In *9th International Conference on Learning Representations, ICLR 2021*, 2021.

[36] Y. Cherapanamjeri, E. Aras, N. Tripuraneni, M. I. Jordan, N.Flammarion, and P. L. Bartlett. Optimal robust linear regression in nearly linear time. *Computing Research Repository*, abs/2007.08137, 2020.

[37] Y. Cherapanamjeri, N. Flammarion, and P. L. Bartlett. Fast mean estimation with sub-Gaussian rates. In *Proceedings of the 32nd Conference on Learning Theory, COLT 2019*, pages 786–806, 2019.

[38] Y. Cherapanamjeri, S. Mohanty, and M. Yau. List decodable mean estimation in nearly linear time. In *2020 IEEE 61st Annual Symposium on Foundations of Computer Science, FOCS 2020*, pages 141–148, 2020.

[39] A. S. Dalalyan and A. Minasyan. All-in-one robust estimator of the Gaussian mean. *The Annals of Statistics*, 50(2):1193–1219, 2022.

[40] A. Daniely. Complexity theoretic limitations on learning halfspaces. In *Proceedings of the 48th Annual ACM Symposium on Theory of Computing, STOC 2016*, pages 105–117, 2016.

[41] S. Dasgupta. Learning mixtures of Gaussians. In *Proceedings of the 40th Annual Symposium on Foundations of Computer Science, FOCS 1999*, pages 634–644, 1999.

[42] J. Depersin and G. Lecue. Robust sub-Gaussian estimation of a mean vector in nearly linear time. *The Annals of Statistics*, 50(1):511–536, 2022. https://arxiv.org/abs/1906.03058.

[43] I. Diakonikolas, S. B. Hopkins, D. Kane, and S. Karmalkar. Robustly learning any clusterable mixture of Gaussians. *Computing Research Repository*, abs/2005.06417, 2020.

[44] I. Diakonikolas, G. Kamath, D. Kane, J. Li, J. Steinhardt, and A. Stewart. Sever: A robust meta-algorithm for stochastic optimization. In *Proceedings of the 36th International Conference on Machine Learning, ICML 2019*, pages 1596–1606, 2019.

[45] I. Diakonikolas, G. Kamath, D. M. Kane, J. Li, A. Moitra, and A. Stewart. Robust estimators in high dimensions without the computational intractability. In *2016 IEEE 57th Annual Symposium on Foundations of Computer Science, FOCS 2016*, pages 655–664, 2016. Journal version in *SIAM Journal on Computing*, 48(2): 742–864, 2019.

[46] I. Diakonikolas, G. Kamath, D. M. Kane, J. Li, A. Moitra, and A. Stewart. Being robust (in high dimensions) can be practical. In *Proceedings of the 34th International Conference on Machine Learning, ICML 2017*, pages 999–1008, 2017.

[47] I. Diakonikolas, G. Kamath, D. M. Kane, J. Li, A. Moitra, and A. Stewart. Robustly learning a Gaussian: Getting optimal error, efficiently. In *Proceedings of the 29th Annual ACM-SIAM Symposium on Discrete Algorithms, SODA 2018*, pages 2683–2702, 2018. Full version available at https://arxiv.org/abs/1704.03866.

[48] I. Diakonikolas and D. Kane. Near-optimal statistical query hardness of learning halfspaces with Massart noise. In *Conference on Learning Theory, COLT 2022*, volume 178 of *Proceedings of Machine Learning Research*, pages 4258–4282. PMLR, 2022. Full version available at https://arxiv.org/abs/2012.09720.

[49] I. Diakonikolas and D. M. Kane. Small covers for near-zero sets of polynomials and learning latent variable models. In *61st IEEE Annual Symposium on Foundations of Computer Science, FOCS 2020*, pages 184–195, 2020. Full version https://arxiv.org/abs/2012.07774.

[50] I. Diakonikolas and D. M. Kane. Robust high-dimensional statistics. In T. Roughgarden, ed., *Beyond the Worst-Case Analysis of Algorithms*, pages 382–402. Cambridge University Press, 2021. An extended version appeared at http://arxiv.org/abs/1911.05911 under the title "Recent advances in algorithmic high-dimensional robust statistics."

[51] I. Diakonikolas, D. M. Kane, S. Karmalkar, A. Pensia, and T. Pittas. List-decodable sparse mean estimation via difference-of-pairs filtering. *Computing Research Repository*, abs/2206.05245, 2022. Conference version in NeurIPS'22.

[52] I. Diakonikolas, D. M. Kane, S. Karmalkar, A. Pensia, and T. Pittas. Robust sparse mean estimation via sum of squares. In *Conference on Learning Theory, COLT 2022*, volume 178 of *Proceedings of Machine Learning Research*, pages 4703–4763. PMLR, 2022.

[53] I. Diakonikolas, D. M. Kane, and D. Kongsgaard. List-decodable mean estimation via iterative multi-filtering. *Advances in Neural Information Processing Systems*, 33, pages 9312–9323, 2020.

[54] I. Diakonikolas, D. M. Kane, D. Kongsgaard, J. Li, and K. Tian. List-decodable mean estimation in nearly-PCA time. In *Advances in Neural Information Processing Systems 34: Annual Conference on Neural Information Processing Systems 2021, NeurIPS 2021*, pages 10195–10208, 2021. Full version available at https://arxiv.org/abs/2011.09973.

[55] I. Diakonikolas, D. M. Kane, D. Kongsgaard, J. Li, and K. Tian. Clustering mixture models in almost-linear time via list-decodable mean estimation. In *Proceedings of the 54th Annual ACM SIGACT Symposium on Theory of Computing, STOC 2022*, pages 1262–1275, 2022. Full version available at https://arxiv.org/abs/2106.08537.

[56] I. Diakonikolas, D. M. Kane, V. Kontonis, C. Tzamos, and N. Zarifis. Learning general halfspaces with general Massart noise under the Gaussian distribution. In *Proceedings of the 54th Annual ACM SIGACT Symposium on Theory of Computing, STOC 2022*, pages 874–885, 2022. Full version available at https://arxiv.org/abs/2108.08767.

[57] I. Diakonikolas, D. M. Kane, V. Kontonis, and N. Zarifis. Algorithms and SQ lower bounds for PAC learning one-hidden-layer ReLU networks. In *Conference on Learning Theory, COLT 2020*, volume 125 of *Proceedings of Machine Learning Research*, pages 1514–1539. PMLR, 2020.

[58] I. Diakonikolas, D. M. Kane, P. Manurangsi, and L. Ren. Cryptographic hardness of learning halfspaces with Massart noise. *Computing Research Repository*, abs/2207.14266, 2022.

[59] I. Diakonikolas, D. M. Kane, and A. Pensia. Outlier robust mean estimation with subgaussian rates via stability. In *Advances in Neural Information Processing Systems 33: Annual Conference on Neural Information Processing Systems 2020, NeurIPS 2020*, pages 1830–1840, 2020.

[60] I. Diakonikolas, D. M. Kane, A. Pensia, and T. Pittas. Streaming algorithms for high-dimensional robust statistics. In *International Conference on Machine Learning, ICML 2022*, volume 162 of *Proceedings of Machine Learning Research*, pages 5061–5117. PMLR, 2022.

[61] I. Diakonikolas, D. M. Kane, A. Pensia, T. Pittas, and A. Stewart. Statistical query lower bounds for list-decodable linear regression. In *Advances in Neural Information Processing Systems 34: Annual Conference on Neural Information Processing Systems 2021, NeurIPS 2021*, pages 3191–3204, 2021.

[62] I. Diakonikolas, D. M. Kane, T. Pittas, and N. Zarifis. The optimality of polynomial regression for agnostic learning under Gaussian marginals in the SQ model. In *Conference on Learning Theory, COLT 2021*, volume 134 of *Proceedings of Machine Learning Research*, pages 1552–1584. PMLR, 2021.

[63] I. Diakonikolas, D. M. Kane, and A. Stewart. Statistical query lower bounds for robust estimation of high-dimensional Gaussians and Gaussian mixtures. In *58th IEEE Annual Symposium on Foundations of Computer Science, FOCS 2017*, pages 73–84, 2017. Full version at http://arxiv.org/abs/1611.03473.

[64] I. Diakonikolas, D. M. Kane, and A. Stewart. Learning geometric concepts with nasty noise. In *Proceedings of the 50th Annual ACM SIGACT Symposium on Theory of Computing, STOC 2018*, pages 1061–1073, 2018.

[65] I. Diakonikolas, D. M. Kane, and A. Stewart. List-decodable robust mean estimation and learning mixtures of spherical Gaussians. In *Proceedings of the 50th*

Annual ACM SIGACT Symposium on Theory of Computing, STOC 2018, pages 1047–1060, 2018. Full version available at https://arxiv.org/abs/1711.07211.

[66] I. Diakonikolas, D. M. Kane, A. Stewart, and Y. Sun. Outlier-robust learning of Ising models under Dobrushin's condition. In *Conference on Learning Theory, COLT 2021*, volume 134 of *Proceedings of Machine Learning Research*, pages 1645–1682. PMLR, 2021.

[67] I. Diakonikolas, D. M. Kane, and Y. Sun. Optimal SQ lower bounds for robustly learning discrete product distributions and Ising models. In *Conference on Learning Theory, COLT 2022*, volume 178 of *Proceedings of Machine Learning Research*, pages 3936–3978. PMLR, 2022.

[68] I. Diakonikolas, D. M. Kane, and N. Zarifis. Near-optimal SQ lower bounds for agnostically learning halfspaces and ReLUs under Gaussian marginals. In *Advances in Neural Information Processing Systems 33: Annual Conference on Neural Information Processing Systems 2020, NeurIPS 2020*, pages 13586–13596, 2020.

[69] I. Diakonikolas, S. Karmalkar, D. Kane, E. Price, and A. Stewart. Outlier-robust high-dimensional sparse estimation via iterative filtering. In *Advances in Neural Information Processing Systems 32: Annual Conference on Neural Information Processing Systems 2019, NeurIPS 2019*, pages 10689–10700, 2019.

[70] I. Diakonikolas, W. Kong, and A. Stewart. Efficient algorithms and lower bounds for robust linear regression. In *Proceedings of the 30th Annual ACM-SIAM Symposium on Discrete Algorithms, SODA 2019*, pages 2745–2754, 2019.

[71] Y. Dong, S. B. Hopkins, and J. Li. Quantum entropy scoring for fast robust mean estimation and improved outlier detection. In *Advances in Neural Information Processing Systems 32: Annual Conference on Neural Information Processing Systems 2019, NeurIPS 2019*, pages 6065–6075, 2019.

[72] D. Donoho. *Breakdown Properties of Multivariate Location Estimators*. PhD thesis, Harvard University, 1982.

[73] D. L. Donoho and M. Gasko. Breakdown properties of location estimates based on halfspace depth and projected outlyingness. *The Annals of Statistics*, 20(4):1803–1827, 1992.

[74] V. Feldman. Statistical query learning. In Ming-Yang Kao, ed., *Encyclopedia of Algorithms*, pages 2090–2095. Springer, 2016.

[75] V. Feldman, E. Grigorescu, L. Reyzin, S. Vempala, and Y. Xiao. Statistical algorithms and a lower bound for detecting planted cliques. *Journal of the ACM*, 64(2):8:1–8:37, 2017.

[76] V. Feldman, C. Guzman, and S. S. Vempala. Statistical query algorithms for mean vector estimation and stochastic convex optimization. In *Proceedings of the 28th Annual ACM-SIAM Symposium on Discrete Algorithms, SODA 2017*, pages 1265–1277, 2017.

[77] N. Fleming, P. Kothari, and T. Pitassi. Semialgebraic proofs and efficient algorithm design. *Foundations and Trends in Theoretical Computer Science*, 14(1–2):1–221, 2019.

[78] C. Gao. Robust regression via mutivariate regression depth. *Bernoulli*, 26(2):1139–1170, 2020.

[79] S. Goel, A. Gollakota, Z. Jin, S. Karmalkar, and A. R. Klivans. Superpolynomial lower bounds for learning one-layer neural networks using gradient descent. In

Proceedings of the 37th International Conference on Machine Learning, ICML 2020, volume 119 of *Proceedings of Machine Learning Research*, pages 3587–3596. PMLR, 2020.

[80] S. Goel, A. Gollakota, and A. R. Klivans. Statistical-query lower bounds via functional gradients. In *Advances in Neural Information Processing Systems 33: Annual Conference on Neural Information Processing Systems 2020, NeurIPS 2020*, pages 2147–2158, 2020.

[81] N. Goyal and A. Shetty. Non-Gaussian component analysis using entropy methods. In *Proceedings of the 51st Annual ACM SIGACT Symposium on Theory of Computing, STOC 2019*, pages 840–851, 2019.

[82] A. Gupte, N. Vafa, and V. Vaikuntanathan. Continuous LWE is as hard as LWE & applications to learning Gaussian mixtures. In *2022 IEEE 63rd Annual Symposium on Foundations of Computer Science, FOCS 2022*, pages 1162–1173, 2022.

[83] F. R. Hampel. *Contributions to the Theory of Robust Estimation*. PhD thesis, University of California, Berkeley, 1968.

[84] F. R. Hampel. A general qualitative definition of robustness. *The Annals of Mathematical Statistics*, 42(6):1887–1896, 1971.

[85] F. R. Hampel, E. M. Ronchetti, P. J. Rousseeuw, and W. A. Stahel. *Robust Statistics: The Approach Based on Influence Functions*. Wiley, 1986.

[86] M. Hardt and A. Moitra. Algorithms and hardness for robust subspace recovery. In *Proceedings of the 26th Annual Conference on Learning Theory, COLT 2013*, pages 354–375, 2013.

[87] D. Haussler. Decision theoretic generalizations of the PAC model for neural net and other learning applications. *Information and Computation*, 100:78–150, 1992.

[88] J. Hayase, W. Kong, R. Somani, and S. Oh. Defense against backdoor attacks via robust covariance estimation. In *Proceedings of the 38th International Conference on Machine Learning, ICML 2021*, volume 139 of *Proceedings of Machine Learning Research*, pages 4129–4139. PMLR, 2021.

[89] S. B. Hopkins. *Statistical Inference and the Sum of Squares Method*. PhD thesis, Cornell University, 2018.

[90] S. B. Hopkins. Mean estimation with sub-Gaussian rates in polynomial time. *The Annals of Statistics*, 48(2):1193–1213, 2020.

[91] S. B. Hopkins, P. K. Kothari, A. Potechin, P. Raghavendra, T. Schramm, and D. Steurer. The power of sum-of-squares for detecting hidden structures. In *58th IEEE Annual Symposium on Foundations of Computer Science, FOCS 2017*, pages 720–731, 2017.

[92] S. B. Hopkins and J. Li. Mixture models, robustness, and sum of squares proofs. In *Proceedings of the 50th Annual ACM SIGACT Symposium on Theory of Computing, STOC 2018*, pages 1021–1034, 2018.

[93] S. B. Hopkins and J. Li. How hard is robust mean estimation? In *Conference on Learning Theory, COLT 2019*, volume 99 of *Proceedings of Machine Learning Research*, pages 1649–1682. PMLR, 2019.

[94] S. B. Hopkins, J. Li, and F. Zhang. Robust and heavy-tailed mean estimation made simple, via regret minimization. In *Advances in Neural Information Processing Systems 33: Annual Conference on Neural Information Processing Systems 2020, NeurIPS 2020*, pages 11902–11912, 2020.

[95] P. J. Huber. Robust estimation of a location parameter. *The Annals of Mathematical Statistics*, 35(1):73–101, 1964.

[96] P. J. Huber. *Robust Statistical Procedures*. SIAM, 1996.

[97] P. J. Huber and E. M. Ronchetti. *Robust Statistics*. Wiley, 2009.

[98] M. Ivkov and P. K. Kothari. List-decodable covariance estimation. In *Proceedings of the 54th Annual ACM SIGACT Symposium on Theory of Computing*, STOC 2022, pages 1276–1283, 2022.

[99] A. Jain and A. Orlitsky. A general method for robust learning from batches. In *Advances in Neural Information Processing Systems 33: Annual Conference on Neural Information Processing Systems 2020, NeurIPS 2020*, pages 21775–21785, 2020.

[100] A. Jain and A. Orlitsky. Optimal robust learning of discrete distributions from batches. In *Proceedings of the 37th International Conference on Machine Learning, ICML 2020*, volume 119 of *Proceedings of Machine Learning Research*, pages 4651–4660. PMLR, 2020.

[101] A. Jain and A. Orlitsky. Robust density estimation from batches: The best things in life are (nearly) free. In *Proceedings of the 38th International Conference on Machine Learning, ICML 2021*, volume 139 of *Proceedings of Machine Learning Research*, pages 4698–4708. PMLR, 2021.

[102] A. Jambulapati, J. Li, T. Schramm, and K. Tian. Robust regression revisited: Acceleration and improved estimation rates. In *Advances in Neural Information Processing Systems 34: Annual Conference on Neural Information Processing Systems 2021, NeurIPS 2021*, pages 4475–4488, 2021.

[103] D. S. Johnson and F. P. Preparata. The densest hemisphere problem. *Theoretical Computer Science*, 6:93–107, 1978.

[104] D. M. Kane. Robust learning of mixtures of Gaussians. In *Proceedings of the 32nd Annual ACM-SIAM Symposium on Discrete Algorithms, SODA 2021*, pages 1246–1258, 2021. https://arxiv.org/abs/2007.05912.

[105] R. Kannan, H. Salmasian, and S. Vempala. The spectral method for general mixture models. In *Proceedings of the 18th Annual Conference on Learning Theory, COLT 2005*, pages 444–457, 2005.

[106] S. Karmalkar, A. R. Klivans, and P. Kothari. List-decodable linear regression. In *Advances in Neural Information Processing Systems 32: Annual Conference on Neural Information Processing Systems 2019, NeurIPS 2019*, pages 7423–7432, 2019.

[107] M. Kearns, R. Schapire, and L. Sellie. Toward efficient agnostic learning. *Machine Learning*, 17(2/3):115–141, 1994.

[108] M. J. Kearns. Efficient noise-tolerant learning from statistical queries. *Journal of the ACM*, 45(6):983–1006, 1998.

[109] M. J. Kearns and M. Li. Learning in the presence of malicious errors. *SIAM Journal on Computing*, 22(4):807–837, 1993.

[110] A. Klivans, P. Long, and R. Servedio. Learning halfspaces with malicious noise. *Journal of Machine Learning Research*, 10:2715–2740, 2009.

[111] A. R. Klivans, P. K. Kothari, and R. Meka. Efficient algorithms for outlier-robust regression. In *Conference on Learning Theory, COLT 2018*, volume 75 of *Proceedings of Machine Learning Research*, pages 1420–1430. PMLR, 2018.

[112] P. K. Kothari, J. Steinhardt, and D. Steurer. Robust moment estimation and improved clustering via sum of squares. In *Proceedings of the 50th Annual ACM SIGACT Symposium on Theory of Computing, STOC 2018*, pages 1035–1046, 2018.

[113] J. Kwon and C. Caramanis. The EM algorithm gives sample-optimality for learning mixtures of well-separated Gaussians. In *Conference on Learning Theory, COLT 2020*, volume 125 of *Proceedings of Machine Learning Research*, pages 2425–2487. PMLR, 2020.

[114] K. A. Lai, A. B. Rao, and S. Vempala. Agnostic estimation of mean and covariance. In *2016 IEEE 57th Annual Symposium on Foundations of Computer Science, FOCS 2016*, pages 665–674, 2016.

[115] J. Li and G. Ye. Robust Gaussian covariance estimation in nearly-matrix multiplication time. In *Advances in Neural Information Processing Systems 33: Annual Conference on Neural Information Processing Systems 2020, NeurIPS 2020*, pages 12649–12659, 2020.

[116] J. Z. Li, D. M. Absher, H. Tang, A. M. Southwick, A. M. Casto, S. Ramachandran, H. M. Cann, G. S. Barsh, M. Feldman, L. L. Cavalli-Sforza, and R. M. Myers. Worldwide human relationships inferred from genome-wide patterns of variation. *Science*, 319:1100–1104, 2008.

[117] A. Liu and J. Li. Clustering mixtures with almost optimal separation in polynomial time. In *Proceedings of the 54th Annual ACM SIGACT Symposium on Theory of Computing, STOC 2022*, pages 1248–1261, 2022. Full version available at https://arxiv.org/abs/2112.00706.

[118] A. Liu and A. Moitra. Settling the robust learnability of mixtures of Gaussians. In *Proceedings of the 53rd Annual ACM SIGACT Symposium on Theory of Computing, STOC 2021*, pages 518–531, 2021. Full version available at https://arxiv.org/abs/2011.03622.

[119] G. Lugosi and S. Mendelson. Mean estimation and regression under heavy-tailed distributions: A survey. *Foundations of Computational Mathematics*, 19(5):1145–1190, 2019.

[120] G. Lugosi and S. Mendelson. Sub-Gaussian estimators of the mean of a random vector. *The Annals of Statistics*, 47(2):783–794, 2019.

[121] G. Lugosi and S. Mendelson. Robust multivariate mean estimation: The optimality of trimmed mean. *The Annals of Statistics*, 49(1):393–410, 2021. http://arxiv.org/abs/1907.11391.

[122] M. Meister and G. Valiant. A data prism: Semi-verified learning in the small-alpha regime. In *Conference on Learning Theory, COLT 2018*, volume 75 of *Proceedings of Machine Learning Research*, pages 1530–1546. PMLR, 2018.

[123] Y. Nesterov. Semidefinite relaxation and nonconvex quadratic optimization. *Optimization Methods and Software*, 9(1–3):141–160, 1998.

[124] P. Paschou, J. Lewis, A. Javed, and P. Drineas. Ancestry informative markers for fine-scale individual assignment to worldwide populations. *Journal of Medical Genetics*, 47:835–847, 2010.

[125] R. Peng, K. Tangwongsan, and P. Zhang. Faster and simpler width-independent parallel algorithms for positive semidefinite programming. *arXiv preprint arXiv:1201.5135v3*, 2016.

[126] A. Prasad, S. Balakrishnan, and P. Ravikumar. A unified approach to robust mean estimation. *Computing Research Repository*, abs/1907.00927, 2019.

[127] A. Prasad, A. S. Suggala, S. Balakrishnan, and P. Ravikumar. Robust estimation via robust gradient estimation. *Journal of the Royal Statistical Society: Series B (Statistical Methodology)*, 82(3):601–627, 2020. http://arxiv.org/abs/1802.06485.

[128] M. Qiao and G. Valiant. Learning discrete distributions from untrusted batches. In *9th Innovations in Theoretical Computer Science Conference, ITCS 2018*, volume 94 of *Leibniz International Proceedings in Informatics (LIPIcs)*, pages 47:1–47:20. Schloss Dagstuhl - Leibniz-Zentrum für Informatik, 2018.

[129] P. Raghavendra, T. Schramm, and D. Steurer. High-dimensional estimation via sum-of-squares proofs. In *Proceedings of the International Congress of Mathematicians, ICM 2018*, pages 3389–3423, 2019. http://arxiv.org/abs/1807.11419.

[130] P. Raghavendra and M. Yau. List decodable learning via sum of squares. In *Proceedings of the 31st Annual ACM-SIAM Symposium on Discrete Algorithms, SODA 2020*, pages 161–180, 2020.

[131] O. Regev and A. Vijayaraghavan. On learning mixtures of well-separated Gaussians. In *58th IEEE Annual Symposium on Foundations of Computer Science, FOCS 2017*, pages 85–96, 2017.

[132] N. Rosenberg, J. Pritchard, J. Weber, H. Cann, K. Kidd, L. A. Zhivotovsky, and M. W. Feldman. Genetic structure of human populations. *Science*, 298:2381–2385, 2002.

[133] P. J. Rousseeuw and M. Hubert. Regression depth. *Journal of the American Statistical Association*, 94(446):388–402, 1999.

[134] P. J. Rousseeuw and A. M. Leroy. *Robust Regression and Outlier Detection*. John Wiley, 1987.

[135] R. Serfling and Y. Zuo. General notions of statistical depth function. *The Annals of Statistics*, 28(2):461–482, 2000.

[136] J. Steinhardt, M. Charikar, and G. Valiant. Resilience: A criterion for learning in the presence of arbitrary outliers. In *9th Innovations in Theoretical Computer Science Conference, ITCS 2018*, pages 45:1–45:21, 2018.

[137] J. Steinhardt, P. W. Koh, and P. S. Liang. Certified defenses for data poisoning attacks. In *Advances in Neural Information Processing Systems 30: Annual Conference on Neural Information Processing Systems 2017, NeurIPS 2017*, pages 3520–3532, 2017.

[138] Y. S. Tan and R. Vershynin. Polynomial time and sample complexity for non-Gaussian component analysis: Spectral methods. In *Conference on Learning Theory, COLT 2018*, volume 75 of *Proceedings of Machine Learning Research*, pages 498–534. PMLR, 2018.

[139] B. Tran, J. Li, and A. Madry. Spectral signatures in backdoor attacks. In *Advances in Neural Information Processing Systems 31: Annual Conference on Neural Information Processing Systems 2018, NeurIPS 2018*, pages 8011–8021, 2018.

[140] J. W. Tukey. A survey of sampling from contaminated distributions. In Ingram Olkin, ed., *Contributions to Probability and Statistics: Essays in Honor of Harold Hotelling*, pages 448–485. Stanford University Press, 1960.

[141] J. W. Tukey. Mathematics and picturing of data. In *Proceedings of the International Congress of Mathematicians, ICM 1974*, volume 6, pages 523–531, 1975.

[142] L. Valiant. Learning disjunctions of conjunctions. In *Proceedings of the 9th International Joint Conference on Artificial Intelligence, IJCAI 1985*, pages 560–566, 1985.

[143] S. Vempala and G. Wang. A spectral algorithm for learning mixtures of distributions. In *Proceedings of the 43rd Annual IEEE Symposium on Foundations of Computer Science, FOCS 2002*, pages 113–122, 2002.

[144] B. Zhu, J. Jiao, and J. Steinhardt. Robust estimation via generalized quasi-gradients. *Information and Inference: A Journal of the IMA*, 11(2):581–636, 2021. https://arxiv.org/abs/2005.14073.

[145] B. Zhu, J. Jiao, and J. Steinhardt. Generalized resilience and robust statistics. *The Annals of Statistics*, 50(4):2256–2283, 2022. http://arxiv.org/abs/1909.08755.

Index